# SURVIVOR MOMS
Women's Stories of Birthing, Mothering and Healing after Sexual Abuse

**Motherbaby Press**
PO Box 2672
Eugene, OR 97402-0223
USA
(541) 344 7438
Fax (541) 344 1422

Editor: Cheryl K. Smith
Proofreaders: Jessica Cagle and Wanda Walker
Cover design: Cathy Guy
Cover production: Cathy Guy
Interior design and production: Minhoon Kim and Cathy Guy
Cover art image: Boulder, Colorado, artist Sandra Bierman, www.sandrabierman.com,
e-mail: artbier@comcast.net

Copyright © 2008 Motherbaby Press

Monica A. Coleman, *The Dinah Project: A Handbook for Congregational Response to Sexual Violence,* (Cleveland: The Pilgrim Press, 2004), p. 4–5.
Copyright © 2004 by Monica Coleman. All rights reserved. Used by permission.

Copyright © 2004 from *Getting Free: You Can End Abuse and Take Back Your Life* by Ginny NiCarthy, Reprinted by permission of Seal Press.

Pages 206 and 288–89 from *Allies in Healing: When the Person You Love Was Sexually Abused as a Child* by Laura Davis.
Copyright © 1991 by Laura Davis.
Reprinted by permission of HarperCollins Publishers.

Selections from pp. 92, 154, 233, 255–56, 202, 280, 203–04,174, 214, 283, 273 from *The Courage to Heal,* Third Edition, Revised and Updated by Ellen Bass and Laura Davis.
Copyright © 1994 by Ellen Bass and Laura S. Davis Trust.
Reprinted by permission of HarperCollins Publishers.

Excerpts of Claire and Gwen's narratives previously were published in *The Hidden Feelings of Motherhood: Coping with Stress, Depression, and Burnout,* by Kathleen Kendall-Tackett. Reprinted with permission by New Harbinger Publications, Inc., Oakland, California.

**Notice of Rights**
All rights reserved. No part of this book may be reproduced or transmitted in any form or by any means, electronic or mechanical, including photocopying, recording, or any information storage or retrieval system, without written permission from the publisher.

ISBN: 978-1-89-044641-3
Printed and bound in the United States of America

For more information:
**www.survivormoms.com**

All women who have experienced trauma and
are seeking support to be loving mothers.

And to my husband, Scott, and children, Lyssa and Cade,
whose love has helped me take comfort in my own mothering….
~Mickey

To Josiah, my reason why.
And to Alice, who mothered the mother.
~ JSS

# TABLE OF CONTENTS

## Chapter 1
**Life before Motherhood** .................................1
    Kay's Story .................................................1
    History: What Happened ......................................7
    History: Disclosure .........................................13
    The Range of Effects after Abuse ............................17
    Effects: Posttraumatic Stress Disorder ......................19
        Intrusive Re-experiencing ...............................19
        Avoidance and Emotional Numbing .........................21
        Arousal .................................................21
    Effects: Other Trauma-related Problems ......................22
        Dissociation ............................................22
        Somatization ............................................23
        Interpersonal Problems ..................................24
        Substance Abuse and Disordered Eating ...................25
        Poor Self-care: High Risk Sexual Behavior,
        Revictimization and Self-harm ...........................27
    Effects: Depression .........................................29
    Effects: Altered Memory .....................................30
    Outlook for Help and Recovery ...............................31
    Relationships ...............................................33
    Sexual Intimacy .............................................35
    Pregnancy as an Impetus for Change ..........................38
    Breaking the Chain ..........................................39
    Where in the Process ........................................39

## Chapter 2
**Pregnancy** .................................................43
    Elaine's Story ..............................................43
    Pregnancy as a Trigger ......................................45
    Needing Help and Getting It .................................48
    Family Relations ............................................56
    Bodily Experience of Pregnancy ..............................60
    Relationships with Care Providers ...........................63
    Issues for Providers:
    Gaining Skill in the Therapeutic Relationship ...............67
    Three Key Relationship Issues ...............................68
        Trust ...................................................68
        Boundaries ..............................................70
        Transference and Countertransference ....................71
    Conclusion ..................................................72

## Chapter 3
**Labor and Birth . . . . . . . . . . . . . . . . . . . . . . . . . . . . . . . . . . . . . . . . 75**
    Katherine's Story . . . . . . . . . . . . . . . . . . . . . . . . . . . . . . . . . . . . . . . . . 75
    Lynelle's Story . . . . . . . . . . . . . . . . . . . . . . . . . . . . . . . . . . . . . . . . . . . 76
    Overview . . . . . . . . . . . . . . . . . . . . . . . . . . . . . . . . . . . . . . . . . . . . . . 80
    What Is Left Out . . . . . . . . . . . . . . . . . . . . . . . . . . . . . . . . . . . . . . . . 82
    Reading this Chapter . . . . . . . . . . . . . . . . . . . . . . . . . . . . . . . . . . . . 82
    Issues of Care, Control and Coping Strategies . . . . . . . . . . . . . . . . . 83
    Finding Your "Match" . . . . . . . . . . . . . . . . . . . . . . . . . . . . . . . . . . . . 85
    Relationships with Caregivers . . . . . . . . . . . . . . . . . . . . . . . . . . . . . . 87
    Childbirth Classes . . . . . . . . . . . . . . . . . . . . . . . . . . . . . . . . . . . . . . . 92
    Birth Plans . . . . . . . . . . . . . . . . . . . . . . . . . . . . . . . . . . . . . . . . . . . . . 93
    Labor and Birth as Triggers . . . . . . . . . . . . . . . . . . . . . . . . . . . . . . . 95
    Dealing with Pain . . . . . . . . . . . . . . . . . . . . . . . . . . . . . . . . . . . . . . . 96
    Doulas . . . . . . . . . . . . . . . . . . . . . . . . . . . . . . . . . . . . . . . . . . . . . . . 97
    Birth, Paradigms, Traumatic Stress and Empathy . . . . . . . . . . . . . . . 97
    The Art of Attending and Facilitating Birth . . . . . . . . . . . . . . . . . . . 99
    Honoring Complexity and the Efforts of Individuals . . . . . . . . . . . . 105
    A Physician's Perspective . . . . . . . . . . . . . . . . . . . . . . . . . . . . . . . . 106
    A Midwife's Perspective . . . . . . . . . . . . . . . . . . . . . . . . . . . . . . . . . 107
    A Survivor Mom's Perspective . . . . . . . . . . . . . . . . . . . . . . . . . . . . 110
    The Healing Power of Birth . . . . . . . . . . . . . . . . . . . . . . . . . . . . . . 110

## Chapter 4
**Postpartum and Breastfeeding . . . . . . . . . . . . . . . . . . . . . . . . 117**
    Claire's Story . . . . . . . . . . . . . . . . . . . . . . . . . . . . . . . . . . . . . . . . . 117
    Postpartum Depression, Anxiety and PTSD . . . . . . . . . . . . . . . . . . 121
    Processing Birth . . . . . . . . . . . . . . . . . . . . . . . . . . . . . . . . . . . . . . . 121
    Postpartum Mood Disorder . . . . . . . . . . . . . . . . . . . . . . . . . . . . . . 123
    Practical Help and Peer Support . . . . . . . . . . . . . . . . . . . . . . . . . . 128
    Therapy . . . . . . . . . . . . . . . . . . . . . . . . . . . . . . . . . . . . . . . . . . . . . 129
    Medications . . . . . . . . . . . . . . . . . . . . . . . . . . . . . . . . . . . . . . . . . . 130
    Parenting Classes . . . . . . . . . . . . . . . . . . . . . . . . . . . . . . . . . . . . . . 130
    Sharing the Burden with Trustworthy People . . . . . . . . . . . . . . . . . 132
    Breastfeeding . . . . . . . . . . . . . . . . . . . . . . . . . . . . . . . . . . . . . . . . . 133
    Making the Decision Whether or Not to Breastfeed . . . . . . . . . . . . 133
    Breastfeeding and Posttraumatic Stress . . . . . . . . . . . . . . . . . . . . . 135
    Getting Help . . . . . . . . . . . . . . . . . . . . . . . . . . . . . . . . . . . . . . . . . 136
    Breastfeeding and Bonding . . . . . . . . . . . . . . . . . . . . . . . . . . . . . . 137
    Making Adaptations . . . . . . . . . . . . . . . . . . . . . . . . . . . . . . . . . . . . 138
    Breastfeeding as Healing . . . . . . . . . . . . . . . . . . . . . . . . . . . . . . . . 141
    Professional Advice for Lactation Consultants
        and Postpartum Caregivers . . . . . . . . . . . . . . . . . . . . . . . . . . . . 142
    What You Can Do . . . . . . . . . . . . . . . . . . . . . . . . . . . . . . . . . . . . . 142
    Conclusion . . . . . . . . . . . . . . . . . . . . . . . . . . . . . . . . . . . . . . . . . . 144

## Chapter 5
### Mothering and Attachment . . . . . . . . . . . . . . . . . . . . . . . . . . . 147
Sadie's Story . . . . . . . . . . . . . . . . . . . . . . . . . . . . . . . . . . . . . . . . . 147
Kim's Story . . . . . . . . . . . . . . . . . . . . . . . . . . . . . . . . . . . . . . . . . . 150
Will I Abuse My Child? . . . . . . . . . . . . . . . . . . . . . . . . . . . . . . . . 154
Attachment . . . . . . . . . . . . . . . . . . . . . . . . . . . . . . . . . . . . . . . . . . 156
Mental Health . . . . . . . . . . . . . . . . . . . . . . . . . . . . . . . . . . . . . . . 158
Relationship with the Child's Body . . . . . . . . . . . . . . . . . . . . . . . 159
Gender . . . . . . . . . . . . . . . . . . . . . . . . . . . . . . . . . . . . . . . . . . . . . 161
Boundaries and Discipline . . . . . . . . . . . . . . . . . . . . . . . . . . . . . 164
Keeping Kids Safe . . . . . . . . . . . . . . . . . . . . . . . . . . . . . . . . . . . . 166
Telling Children . . . . . . . . . . . . . . . . . . . . . . . . . . . . . . . . . . . . . 174
My Child Was Abused . . . . . . . . . . . . . . . . . . . . . . . . . . . . . . . . 175
Survivors' Other Parenting Thoughts . . . . . . . . . . . . . . . . . . . . 177
Good Enough Moms . . . . . . . . . . . . . . . . . . . . . . . . . . . . . . . . . 179
Breaking the Chain . . . . . . . . . . . . . . . . . . . . . . . . . . . . . . . . . . 180
Healing through Mothering . . . . . . . . . . . . . . . . . . . . . . . . . . . 181

## Chapter 6
### Healing and Survivorship . . . . . . . . . . . . . . . . . . . . . . . . . . . . 185
Deborah's Story . . . . . . . . . . . . . . . . . . . . . . . . . . . . . . . . . . . . . 185
Relationships . . . . . . . . . . . . . . . . . . . . . . . . . . . . . . . . . . . . . . . 189
Family . . . . . . . . . . . . . . . . . . . . . . . . . . . . . . . . . . . . . . . . . . . . . 190
Friends . . . . . . . . . . . . . . . . . . . . . . . . . . . . . . . . . . . . . . . . . . . . 192
Intimate Partner Relationships . . . . . . . . . . . . . . . . . . . . . . . . . 193
Therapy . . . . . . . . . . . . . . . . . . . . . . . . . . . . . . . . . . . . . . . . . . . 197
Getting into Therapy . . . . . . . . . . . . . . . . . . . . . . . . . . . . . . . . 198
Troubles with Therapy . . . . . . . . . . . . . . . . . . . . . . . . . . . . . . . 200
Being in Therapy . . . . . . . . . . . . . . . . . . . . . . . . . . . . . . . . . . . 202
Group Work . . . . . . . . . . . . . . . . . . . . . . . . . . . . . . . . . . . . . . . 203
Confronting the Abuser . . . . . . . . . . . . . . . . . . . . . . . . . . . . . . 206
Recovery as a Lifelong Process . . . . . . . . . . . . . . . . . . . . . . . . . 208
Faith-based Healing . . . . . . . . . . . . . . . . . . . . . . . . . . . . . . . . . 209
Abuse by Clergy . . . . . . . . . . . . . . . . . . . . . . . . . . . . . . . . . . . . 212
On Forgiveness . . . . . . . . . . . . . . . . . . . . . . . . . . . . . . . . . . . . . 214
Alternative Healing Modalities . . . . . . . . . . . . . . . . . . . . . . . . 217
    Massage Therapy . . . . . . . . . . . . . . . . . . . . . . . . . . . . . . . 218
    EMDR . . . . . . . . . . . . . . . . . . . . . . . . . . . . . . . . . . . . . . . 219
    Music Therapy . . . . . . . . . . . . . . . . . . . . . . . . . . . . . . . . . 221
    Art Therapy . . . . . . . . . . . . . . . . . . . . . . . . . . . . . . . . . . . 222
About Being a Survivor: Terminology . . . . . . . . . . . . . . . . . . 224
Activism . . . . . . . . . . . . . . . . . . . . . . . . . . . . . . . . . . . . . . . . . . 225
Conclusion . . . . . . . . . . . . . . . . . . . . . . . . . . . . . . . . . . . . . . . . 227

**Afterword** . . . . . . . . . . . . . . . . . . . . . . . . . . . . . . . . . . . . . . . . . . . . . . . 231
**Resources** . . . . . . . . . . . . . . . . . . . . . . . . . . . . . . . . . . . . . . . . . . . . . . 233
**References** . . . . . . . . . . . . . . . . . . . . . . . . . . . . . . . . . . . . . . . . . . . . . 237

# A Resource for Women and their Care Providers

The narratives in this book, both those that are presented in their entirety and those excerpted throughout the chapters, were written by volunteer participants in an independent research project in the spirit of helping other survivors and health professionals better understand the impact of sexual abuse and traumatic stress on childbearing and mothering. The project was conducted with the approval of the University of Michigan Institutional Review Board. The volunteers gave informed consent to participate. They also gave written approval of the final, edited form of their narratives and consent to include them in this book.

Our purpose in writing this book is to make available writing about individuals' experiences and their opinions, reference to scientific literature, and practical information gleaned from clinical literature of the psychological and health care disciplines, which we expect to be generally useful to readers who are women abuse survivors, health care providers, mental health care providers and others who want to better understand the experiences of a wide range of abuse survivors in relation to childbearing and mothering.

We hope that this information contributes to informed discussion between individual women and their care providers. This book is intended to serve as an information resource. It is not intended to substitute for relationships with care providers or for treatment tailored to individuals' needs. The research on the effects of abuse trauma and posttraumatic stress on childbirth, women's health and parenting is in its early stages. As new information becomes available, information in this book may become out of date. Thus, readers should consult qualified professionals for recommendations specific to their situation.

x

# Acknowledgements

I wish to acknowledge the many individuals who have contributed to this project.

We were blessed with lots of help along the way!

Thank you to all who helped with survey development and contributed to the text. Many thanks to Merilynne Rush, Peggy Holtzman, Kathleen Ilaro, Kris Holloway-Bidwell and Aviva Jill Romm for helping to develop the survey and providing initial encouragement. Thank you to Sandra Bierman for use of your beautiful image for the cover. Thank you to Elizabeth Shadigian for your physician perspective on working with survivor moms in labor and birth, and to therapist Melisa Schuster for your contributions to both the postpartum and the mothering chapters and your expertise on postpartum depression. Thank you to Kathleen Kendall-Tackett for your advice on breastfeeding consulting for survivor moms. Thank you to Marilyn Jeffs for your thoughts on parenting support groups, and to Anita Rubin-Meiller for sharing your experience of doing group therapy for survivors. Thank you to Tiffany Mazurek and Cynthia Price for your perspectives on the role of massage to promote healing. Thank you to Peggy Holtzman for the information on EMDR and trauma recovery, to Kathleen Moore for sharing about your role as a music therapist, and to Sue McDonald for sharing about art therapy. Thank you to Kate Rosenblum, Anita Rubin-Meiller, Merilynne Rush, Melisa Schuster, Amanda Smith, Scott Sperlich and Rob Coury for your valuable critiques and encouragement, and to Sheri Alms, Laurel Sprague and Kim McGinnis for well-timed moral support. We also acknowledge gratefully the academics and writers whose research reports, articles and books we have learned from and cited. It was a companionship of sorts to know you are out there working on this topic, too. We especially thank Ellen Bass, Laura Davis, Penny Simkin and Phyllis Klaus, whose work has been so encouraging.

I am grateful to the staff at the University of Michigan Institutional Review Board for being so helpful to an independent researcher. We are grateful to the nurses, midwives, obstetricians and family practice doctors who allowed us to distribute surveys to their practices. Many thanks go out to Gretchen and Brad Humphries for all your work on database development. Thank you to Sierra Hillebrand for help finding resources and to Sarah Nuxoll for all your efforts in preparing submission documents and helping us keep the faith. Thank you to Holly Baier, for your work on lit searches and referencing, and to Caroline Reed, for your help with formatting. Thanks to Scott Sperlich and Mary Anne Perrone for the inspirational quotes. Thank you to Harriette Hartigan for helping to guide the vision and for being such a loving mentor to me. Thanks to Aimee Centivany for the global perspective on trauma. Thank you to the Black Madonnas for your prayers and therapeutic guidance. Thank you to all my friends and family for your emotional support during the past 11 years; each of you helped in some special way. Thank you to Sidran Press for feedback on structural changes. Thank you to my children Lyssa and Cade for your patience with your mother's long absences. Thank you to my mother Margaret for typing (bet you regret letting me get away with not learning to type properly!) and encouraging so much. Thank you to dearly departed Audrey Simon for sparking my interest in these issues long ago. Thank you to Ann Sterling for always being so supportive of the project, and to Patty Brennan and the Center for the Childbearing Year for helping to get the word out. Thank you to the Midwives Alliance of North American for space on the Web site to publicize the project, and to the Michigan Midwives Association for helping to increase awareness of survivor issues. Thank you to the women at the Center for Cooperative Action in Ohio, whose handbook *We Can Break the Cycle: A Mother's Handbook for Sexual Abuse Survivors* was the only writing resource available on this subject when I started out, and lent needed inspiration.

Thank you to my midwifery partners through the years, who deeply encouraged and supported this process: Carolyn Hejkal, Janet Christman, Merilynne Rush and Amanda Smith. Thank you to our apprentices through the years who were so supportive as well. Thank you to the many clients of New Moon Midwifery whom I have been honored to serve: You shared your lives and taught me so much about survivor issues, and healing of all kinds.

Thank you to all the good people at Midwifery Today and Motherbaby Press, without whose support this book would be a "love's labour lost": especially Jan Tritten, Cheryl Smith and Minhoon Kim. We appreciate all the work you do on behalf of moms, babies and families.

I am deeply grateful to Julia Seng for her co-authorship on this labor of love. Thank you for the "above and beyond" support of this effort. Thank you for your friendship; your wisdom; your writing; the use of your home office at all hours; the wonderful meals; the laughter and tears shared; the writing retreats away; and the day-to-day collaborations. Your dedication to survivor healing is truly inspiring.

I could not have done this work without the abiding support of my husband, Scott Sperlich. His considerable contributions of love, patience, financial resources, typing and cleaning up the messes I left behind were essential to this project.

We are forever grateful to all the "survivor moms" participants of the "Survivor Moms Speak Out" project who shared their experiences and life stories, thereby forming the very basis for this undertaking. Their courage, honesty, struggle and wisdom are evident in these pages and we believe that their words will help facilitate healing for other survivor moms.

~Mickey Sperlich

## An Introduction by Julia Seng, PhD, CNM
## Lake Michigan shore, north of Union Pier, 2006

In the landmark book *Trauma and Recovery,* Judith Herman made the point that certain atrocities, like incest, are socially "unspeakable." This taboo against speaking out seems to be particularly strong during the childbearing year. Since the dawn of time sexually abused girls have grown to womanhood and embarked on the journey through pregnancy to motherhood without any stories from their sisters to guide them through the extra layer of challenge their trauma history contributes or to let them know that they were not alone. The narrative authors gave their stories to this book project to break the silence and to provide this companionship.

In the 1980s we learned from research how common childhood abuse, including sexual abuse, is. In the 1990s we are learning how many intrafamilial and sexual trauma survivors suffer long-term physical and mental health consequences. In 1993 the results of the National Women's Study were published showing that 12% of US women had suffered posttraumatic stress disorder (PTSD) at some point in life, and that, at any given time, about 5% have enough symptoms to meet the diagnostic criteria. Traumatic events of an interpersonal or sexual nature—childhood maltreatment, sexual assault and intimate partner violence—are the most frequent causes of long-lasting emotional, physical and interpersonal loss of well-being for women. Posttraumatic stress from these types of traumatic events also seems most likely to become symptomatic during the childbearing year, since pregnancy is such a psychosexual and familial experience. Among refugee and new immigrant women in the US, experiences of war crimes and deaths of their children may be additional types of trauma that can affect childbearing and mothering. Life-threatening illness, painful medical procedures, a traumatic experience of female circumcision and prior traumatic pregnancy loss are other types of experience that may be associated with more traumatic stress and more challenges during pregnancy. This book is based on stories from childhood sexual abuse survivors. Women with other types of trauma histories, who find themselves wondering how they might be affected in childbearing, also may be able to make use of commonalities. Much of the information about the mental health consequences of trauma will apply in general, even if the details are different.

As a women's health researcher, my work has focused on the health and childbearing of women trauma survivors with PTSD. Since 2000, research on how posttraumatic stress might adversely affect childbearing has gotten off the ground. Research about how abuse-survivor mothers burdened with posttraumatic stress manage the crucial task of interacting with their baby also is proceeding. Soon we will know much more than we know now.

Likely what the research will find and depict in statistical form in health science journals will resemble what the narrators experienced and described in stories for this book: Some women will struggle and sink. Others will triumph to the level of their fondest hopes. Some will go it alone. Others will gather help around them. Some of their children will end up the first generation in the family to be protected and raised by a well-recovered mother. Others will have a mother who goes between days of managing her demons well enough and days when depression or long-swallowed anger swamp her efforts. None of this will be new. Children have been abused, and the adults they become have suffered in mind, body and spirit in the wake of abuse forever. Something is changing, though—slowly. Survivors are speaking out. Professionals who help them are training the next generation of clinicians. Scientific research—from the level of genetic molecules to populations—is finding that stopping the cycle of violence is essential to the mental, physical and social health of all.

My role with this project has been to make some linkages between what the narrators describe as their personal experience and echoes of this information found in results of research studies. By definition, research contributes knowledge that is "generalizable," meaning that it applies to groups of people. Often, what a survivor mom experienced as though it were happening only to her, really happens to many. In order for systems to change—health care delivery, education of health professionals, norms about proper care of children, policy decisions about use of health and child welfare resources—we need both kinds of knowledge: We need to understand the impact of childhood abuse on birthing and mothering deeply, from hearing women's stories. We also need to understand it broadly—from looking at the impact on samples and populations, on the body and on the culture.

This book is a contribution to that first way of knowing. The stories included likely are not representative of all survivors. Probably only those who had the most wonderful or the most challenging childbearing and mothering experiences felt moved to give time and effort to write for this project. Most likely, those survivors who are striving for the most wonderful experiences or fearing overwhelming challenges will seek out this resource. Hopefully they will feel helpful commonality with the narrators and use the "lessons learned" or "pearls of wisdom" to meet their needs.

Although health care and mental health professionals usually rely on scientifically derived knowledge as a basis for clinical decision-making when it exists, some areas of practice depend on experience, philosophy, use of self and "art." While waiting for more research to illuminate this phenomenon, these 81 women's narratives can provide "case" histories, serving as step in advancing clinical knowledge about the effects of childhood abuse and sexual trauma on perinatal outcomes and parenting. The recurring theme in the narratives about the importance—for better or for worse—of relationships with perinatal professionals may also support efforts to spend more time with women in prenatal care.

More research is needed. The information in these stories emphasizes the woman's experiences. Trauma inflicts physiological changes on the vulnerable human who survives it. Posttraumatic stress, pregnancy and early infant development also are biological processes. The intersections of traumatic stress and childbearing likely occur from cellular to social levels and may require understanding and interventions at multiple levels as well. Perhaps themes and incidents reported in the words of these narrators will spark the design of clinical research.

The childbearing year—the time of pregnancy and earliest parenting—is the temporal and physical passage from being one woman to being a motherbaby dyad. The symbiotic relationship the two share during this time is critical to the long-term wellness of both. I hope this book is a source of strength and voice for survivor mothers and that it deepens caregivers' wisdom about the importance of nurture and the therapeutic relationship in maternity care.

~Julia Seng, PhD, CNM

## An Introduction by Mickey Sperlich, MA, CPM
### Lake Michigan shore, 2006

This book was born out of a project begun many years ago and known as "Survivor Moms Speak Out." It was conceived as a means by which to learn more about the issues facing women survivors of sexual abuse who take the journey of motherhood.

While practicing full-time as a community-based midwife, I had the opportunity to work with many women who were survivors, either of childhood sexual trauma, rape, or both. The experience of being their midwife, and witnessing their challenges and triumphs, provided the fuel for this project. Pivotal moments among my interactions with my clients revealed to me the need to learn more about how a history of abuse can have an impact on childbearing and mothering.

I will never forget early in my practice being with a young woman who was fearfully facing her first pelvic exam. She took an hour to be ready to undergo the exam. I remember the long waiting for her to be ready, with each passing moment feeling another measure of her entrenched terror, and at the same time her courage and determined spirit coming to the fore. I learned a lot from her about the importance of being patient and respectful of a woman's boundaries.

I also distinctly remember another client in advanced labor who, upon becoming fully dilated, expressed fear about pushing her baby out. She stated that she couldn't push her baby out because her baby could also be abused. Try as I did to reassure her that they would be okay, it was her truth of that moment and she ultimately elected to have a cesarean. I was not aware of her history as a survivor of sexual abuse, as the birth occurred before we began asking clients about this, so I had missed the opportunity to work with her on this level before she was at the point of giving birth. I came away from this birth realizing my ignorance of abuse issues and resolving to learn more. I also began asking clients, in a sensitive way, about their history of violence, and soon realized that we were seeing a sizeable number of women with some history of various types of abuse.

Another client facilitated my learning about how memory is submerged and retrieved, while I was examining her cervix in labor I was humbled by seeing my client momentarily panicking, believing that I was no longer her trusted midwife but rather the mother who had abused her as a child. She taught me the importance of being "in the moment" with a survivor; of thinking on one's feet about how best to comfort and reassure her that the past is in the past and that we are in the present, that nothing untoward will be done to her and that she is in control of her own body. We worked through this delicate situation together, and she went on to have a positive birth experience. This experience highlighted for me the importance of examining dynamics of the care provider/client relationship. I came away knowing that I needed to further educate myself about the effects of sexual abuse on the childbearing experience, and determined right away that I needed to "do something," although I didn't know what that something would be. So I began studying the broader picture of sexual abuse, writing articles for midwifery publications and talking to lots of women. I spoke at a few conferences and learned much from the participation of the women at these meetings. I puzzled over this problem with my midwifery colleagues.

While good written resources for survivors in general were available at that time, the experience of childbearing and mothering was scarcely mentioned. I recommended or gave away many copies of the women survivor's "bible," *The Courage to Heal* by Ellen Bass and Laura Davis, and many of the narrative authors in our project have credited this book with helping them immensely on their healing journey. (New books have been published, since this project began, that hold promise for survivors. These will be referenced throughout the book.)

Realizing the lack of specific resources for survivor moms about childbearing, I felt "called' to help create such a resource, just as I had been "called" to midwifery. But where would I start? The scientific literature was largely silent on the issue and guidance from obstetric and midwifery clinical texts was absent. Since my greatest teachers have always been the women I serve, I found the most sensible course was to start with the survivor moms themselves—to learn through their lives' stories and wisdom.

In 1998, together with a team of survivors, therapists and midwives, I developed a survey that asked basic questions about the ways in which survivors felt that their pregnancies, births, postpartum and mothering had been influenced by their history as survivors. The survey was put before an Institutional Review Board at the University of Michigan, to ensure that ethical standards were being met for research to be conducted with human subjects. The surveys were distributed at midwifery and birth-related conferences across the country, at doctors' and midwives' offices, and via a contact address on the Web. The total number of surveys circulated over a two year period was 1136. Two hundred and seven surveys were returned, and from this number 81 women completed a narrative or contributed a poem for this book. I have been told that this is a very good rate of return for a research survey with no way to follow-up or remind volunteers to return it. I am amazed at the willingness of these women to share their stories—good and bad—to help other women.

In order to solicit the narrative accounts, I corresponded personally with each of the survey respondents who gave a return address (all but 10!). I received narratives of varying length and content from these women, and edited their stories in correspondence with them.

During the survey and narrative collection phase of the project, I was very fortunate to meet my friend and collaborator, Julia Seng, PhD, CNM. Julia also was interested in how childhood sexual abuse affected women's childbearing, and was focusing her research on the subgroup of abused women who develop Posttraumatic Stress Disorder (PTSD). She had just finished a study of the correlations between women with a diagnosis of PTSD and pregnancy complications as her doctoral thesis. We met the day I attended her formal defense of this study, and she signed on as a collaborator to this project. She is continuing her research into PTSD and childbearing outcomes at the University of Michigan. Her scientific expertise and co-authorship has been essential to the completion of this project.

Having cared for survivors as midwives, we expected the narratives to focus on pregnancy and birth. Indeed, many accounts address how pregnancy and birth were affected, but overall, the message of these stories is that abuse, and the reactions women have to abuse, affect the whole life of the mother, from thinking about having children all the way to being a grandmother, and that the effects are far-reaching and deeply felt.

The women in these stories are each at a different place on their healing journeys. Some of the narrators are just beginning to examine the impacts of abuse on their lives; some are deep in the struggle of recovery. Others have been in recovery for a long while, and feel largely healed from the effects of abuse. They share their experiences across the lifespan; from before motherhood, to pregnancy and birth, postpartum, mothering and the ongoing journey of healing and surviving.

We were unable to print each of the narratives in their entirety. Instead, we excerpted the narratives and arranged them into chapters that follow the childbearing process and lifespan of a mother. We have included one or more narratives in its entirety at the start of each chapter, so that the reader can get a sense of the wholeness of the woman's experience and voice, and to allow us to have a "springboard" for discussing the issues raised within each chapter.

Interwoven with the narrative excerpts are our clinical perspectives as midwives, and contributions from other health care professionals. When we knew of scientific data relevant to an aspect of pregnancy, birth or postpartum that could augment the narratives, we have provided a very brief summary and a reference. We include chapters on mothering and on healing in general because these were so integral to the narrators' accounts. As midwives, our scope of practice and expertise does not extend so deeply to these areas, so we leave the focus more on what the women themselves have to say. It is noteworthy that they do not draw any line separating pregnancy from postpartum from the rest of mothering and recovering. This has implications for the kind of research and clinical care that may be useful in the future.

About reading this book: We strove to make this book relevant to survivors and their caregivers alike. Because of the intensity of the issues and events, reading all of the narrative material presented may be difficult. We have therefore italicized all of the narrative passages, so that the reader can pick and choose how much of this material to read at a time. By separating out literature findings and helpful resources alongside the text, we hoped to make such information easy to access for both caregivers seeking to enrich their knowledge of survivor issues and survivors seeking validation of the impact of abuse on women's lives.

If you are a survivor reading this book, we encourage you to check in with yourself on a regular basis, and limit your exposure if you become triggered by any aspect of the stories or text. This is probably not a book to read through in one sitting! If you are a health care provider or support person, you will benefit from hearing first-hand from survivors about the far-reaching impacts of abuse, looking to the state of the science and reading clinical perspectives.

This project has not been easy to "midwife." The subject matter is hard, and working on it has taken a toll. Whenever the going got rough, though, a divine providence and grace has seemed help my efforts along—whether through a kind, encouraging word, the information I need appearing at just the right moment, or even the cleansing tears that come when they are needed. A large part of my duty as "midwife" to this project has been keeping myself open to that grace. This has not been easy, for in keeping myself open, I am subject to the horror as well as the beauty, and I have come to understand that the abuser is not "out there" somewhere: He or she is living among us, indeed at times may be us, and our survivorship depends not on healing and moving on, but rather on opening our eyes and becoming aware. One of the unexpected gifts of this book is that women were able to share how their experiences as survivors affected the next generation. Some women share how lack of such awareness made them more inclined to enter intimate relationships that were abusive to their children; kept them unaware of the abuse being done to their children; and, in some cases, led them to be abusive in one form or another. These are women daring themselves to open their eyes: to be present to their pain; to admit their own failings but not let these transgressions paralyze their forward motion; to educate themselves; to foster courage to heal and to love; to let that love bring forth children; and to see that those children are raised with their eyes opened and awakened. When we are awake to our humanity, we are better positioned to protect ourselves and our loved ones. We are better equipped to continue our healing. We are able to look around and see that we are not alone. We are better able to initiate lasting change and, ultimately, we open ourselves more to the possibility of love and forgiveness for ourselves and others.

I am deeply grateful to the women represented here on these pages, and I hope you the reader will be as deeply touched and inspired as I have been by their lives. May all of our eyes be opened.

~Mickey Sperlich, MA, CPM

For more information or resources, please check our Web site, whether you are a survivor yourself or are helping survivors. **www.survivormoms.com**

# LIFE BEFORE MOTHERHOOD

***Kay's Story***
*So here I am. Pregnant with another boy. This will be our third. I never thought that I would be the mother to little boys. When I was younger, whenever I pictured myself with kids, I always pictured girls. Perhaps it was because it was familiar to me because, being a girl myself, I could relate and understand what it was like to be a female. Well, at least that's what I tell myself.*

*From infancy to my early teenage years I was sexually abused by a man. Namely, my father. I can remember being terrified by any male, very early on, because I knew what they were capable of doing to me. When my best friend's brother came to pick her up from our house I used to shriek and run in terror. I could never concentrate enough in school in a class with a male teacher because I never knew what intentions they had or what they were thinking. I have a hard time giving hugs to my own grandfather, father-in-law or my brother, even though they are good, gentle men in their own rights. Every time I try, my body betrays me. I stiffen, my stomach tightens up and I panic.*

*I tried on and off to tell people about the abuse as I was growing up. Well, as soon as I realized what was happening to me was not right. As a small child, I thought that it happened to everyone and it wasn't until one night when I was staying over at a friend's house and I was talking about things that had happened to me that I realized that something was very wrong. I couldn't bear to tell my mother, not only because of the threats my father made on her life if I told, but I think I was also scared because I was not sure she would believe me. A mother is the center of a child's life, and I couldn't live with myself if she turned away or told me it was my fault.*

*My mother worked different hours from my father while I was growing up and he was never caught abusing me at that time. Sometimes he would make me stay home from school so we would have the day together. I remember once calling my mother at work after he left for work himself and I almost told her but something stopped me. She asked me why I was home and I told her I was sick. I was eight years old.*

*I tried to tell one of my teachers what was going on at home and she told me to quit making up stories.*

*When I was nine my parents got divorced. I was sent to live with my grandparents while my mom got her life together. I thought that the abuse had ended, because I thought that I never had to see my father again. I didn't tell anyone at that time either. I was too ashamed. I just wanted to bury it deep inside me and make it go away. After a few months, I went back to live with my mother again. At this time my father demanded visitation. No one could understand why I didn't want to stay overnight with him. I was sent to various counselors, some court-ordered, some by my father because he told everyone that my mother was crazy and had poisoned me against him. How was I supposed to tell them what was going on when my father sat next to me every visit with his hand on my* leg? I told the counselors that I didn't have a reason, and soon I was sent to mandatory overnight visitation with him.

The abuse continued.

A year or so after my parents' divorce, my father got remarried. I didn't like his wife very much but I thought that he would be so busy with her that he wouldn't have time for me. I was wrong. I tried everything I could think of to get out of going to see my father. I would play sick, I would hide, I would pick fights with his wife so she would tell him that she didn't want me over there. When that didn't work, I would try to get my friends to go with me on the overnight visitation, because he would leave me alone when there were other people there. I was still seeing counselors. Now, my father didn't go with me so much, because I think that he was content that I wouldn't let out our little secret. One of the counselors asked me if I was scared of my father. I nodded yes. She then asked me if he ever made me do things that I didn't want to do or touched me where I didn't want to be touched. I told her no. She let it drop after that. Fear is a great motivator.

It all came to a head one night when I was staying overnight at my dad's house. I took an overdose of medication because I couldn't take it anymore.

After I got out of the hospital, I received a phone call from my father. I was hoping that he would understand how much he was hurting me, but all he said was that he was not paying any of my hospital bills. He got my mom on the phone and told her that I was crazy and she shouldn't believe anything I told her. He also told her that he never wanted to see me again. That was the last time I ever spoke to him. I was almost 14 years old.

I kept my secret for a few more years. These years were very difficult. I tried to bury what had happened to me and forget. I was acting out quite a lot. I shaved my head. I cut my arms and legs. I failed school, and finally ended up being home-schooled. I got into fights with everyone. I got involved in some things that I'm not proud of. No one could understand why.

When I was seventeen, I told my mother. I don't know why I told her then, but I think I needed to tell someone before I really did something to hurt myself. She just looked at me and said, "I knew it." My mother then told me that I had had a lot of unexplained vaginal and urinary infections as a child. I could remember some things vaguely about how it always hurt when I went to the bathroom, but that was normal for me. We talked for a bit, but I didn't tell her everything because she seemed really uncomfortable. She's still not very comfortable talking about it with me, and I can understand that. You don't want to think that someone you loved and trusted could hurt your child.

I was in and out of counseling for the next few years. My therapist tried to get me to press charges against my father, but I couldn't. I didn't think that I was strong enough.

During these years I got married. My husband kind of knew about my past history of abuse, but I didn't go into much detail at first, because he comes from a very healthy, loving family where he had almost no exposure to abuse of any kind. I was not only afraid that he wouldn't understand, I was also afraid that he would look at me in a different light if I went into detail about things that happened to me. Damaged goods. I closed myself off from him, which was not only difficult for me because I felt very alone, but also difficult for him because he didn't understand what was happening to me or why I was acting the way I did. How could I explain to him why I would cry when we were being intimate? How could I explain to him why I would jump up, lock myself in the bathroom and take long, hot showers when he tried to initiate sex? How could I explain why I went into unexplained rages when he touched me in a certain way? Also, when you keep a secret for so many years it's really difficult to talk about it. After so many years of abuse, I felt like I had a billion layers of memories and emotions hidden inside of me and I didn't want to

# Chapter 1—Life before Motherhood

face them. I was finally in a safe place and I didn't want anything to mess that up.

During my first pregnancy, I was relieved to be having a boy. I was scared to death that I may have a girl. I was afraid that I wouldn't know how to protect her. I didn't realize that I would have the same issues raising a son too. From the time I found out that I was pregnant, I was a whirlwind of emotion. I wanted to love and cherish my baby. To protect him from what I knew could happen. But at the same time I was afraid of becoming too close. I was afraid that I wouldn't know right from wrong. During this pregnancy, I blocked out a lot of emotion and proceeded through it almost numb.

Needless to say that I set myself up for a medically managed birth from the start, because I had convinced myself that it was better not to deal with my own pain now that I was going to become someone's mother. I went to a high intervention OB and when I went into labor I had the works. Morphine, epidural, episiotomy.... This did block out the pain— mental and physical. Looking back now, I regret a lot of things, but it's what I thought was best at the time. The pinnacle came when it was time to push out my son. The doctor breezed in, sliced me open and yanked out my baby. I didn't feel the physical pain, but inside I was screaming "Please! NO!" My husband sensed what I was thinking and turned to me in alarm. This didn't last long because our baby was born dark blue and not breathing. From all the drugs that were pumped into my body to mask the pain, I assume. A team of doctors worked on him for what seemed like forever. They were about to rule him a stillbirth when he let out a feeble little cry. At that moment, I knew there had to be another way. The pain that my child was going through wasn't worth masking my own.

Breastfeeding and bonding were another story. My son was a champion nurser. He latched on quickly and knew exactly what he needed to do. I never experienced any nipple soreness or anything like that. However, I was so mentally uncomfortable I only breastfed him for six months. I had a lot of issues surrounding breastfeeding. It made me feel violated all over again. I felt like I had no control over my body. I felt my stomach drop out when I heard that familiar "I'm hungry!" cry. I used to try to get it done as quickly as possible, which resulted in a fussy baby and a resentful mom. After awhile I just let my milk dry up and started feeding him out of a can.

I was also afraid to become too close to him. I wanted to hold him all of the time, but I was afraid to. I didn't know what was right and wrong. I didn't know that moms are supposed to want to hold, hug and cuddle their babies all of the time. I also felt panic at the feeling of loving someone with my whole being and wild abandon. I felt like I was giving part of myself away.

My second pregnancy was extremely complicated and opened up a lot of issues for me. This pregnancy was like opening up Pandora's box. I had switched to a midwife for this pregnancy and she asked me right away if I had any history of abuse. I took a deep breath and told her yes. She told me that she would help any way she could to make my pregnancy and birth more comfortable and to refer me to a counselor if I needed to go to one.

At this point I was through with counseling. I didn't think that I needed any more.

When I was eight weeks along with my second baby I started spotting. I had a hard time trusting my body anyway, but this felt like the ultimate betrayal. I just knew I was going to lose him. The spotting continued for a couple of weeks, and my midwife put me on bed rest. Around this time I started getting really sick. I would vomit up everything I put in my body. I eventually was put on medication because I was dehydrated and losing a lot of weight. I didn't really want to go on medication, but I had exhausted all other avenues and nothing was working. Miraculously, my little one hung in there and I didn't miscarry.

Up until week 27 of my pregnancy I was having problems putting on weight and I would spot on and off. I started to get panic attacks and have vivid dreams about being abused. I felt like someone else had control of my body and I hated it.

When I was twenty-seven weeks along I started bleeding. I was rushed in for an emergency ultrasound and they said that my placenta had detached a bit from my uterus. My baby was not in any distress, so I got to go home on the condition I went on total bed and pelvic rest.

This put a major strain on me. Not only the usual strain of a mother having to put her life on hold, but this brought back a lot of abuse issues for me. The panic attacks and dreams got worse. I was in a major depression as well. I felt like I was trapped because of my body once again. My relationship with my husband suffered, not only because he was afraid for the baby and me, but also because he felt powerless to help me. He started sleeping on the couch because I couldn't stand to have anyone in bed with me when I was sleeping. We couldn't connect and we fought a lot.

When I was 30 weeks and five days along my waters broke. I was put in the hospital, and transferred over to a doctor's care. I was told to expect my baby to be born any time and that he would have major difficulties. I didn't go into labor. He hung in there, so I was sent to the maternity ward to wait out the rest of my pregnancy. I hated the hospital. I couldn't get any sleep because I had people coming into my room all night to take my temperature, put some more antibiotics in my IV and adjust my fetal monitor. I cannot stand people coming into my room at night. The nurses on the floor thought I was insane because I threw a fit until I got a private room and I wouldn't let anyone in from 10 pm until 7 am. They also couldn't understand why I wouldn't take a shower with someone standing right outside the door.

I also had a lot of issues with my doctor. He treated me like I was an imbecile and wouldn't explain anything to me. He told me that he was going to induce me at 36 weeks and that was that. I didn't want to be induced because I felt that it was better for my baby to be inside me as long as I could keep him in. I mentioned this to my midwife and she said that she would talk to the doctor. The next day the doctor stormed into my room, screaming at me that I was the patient and he was the doctor and how dare I go behind his back. He dropped me from his care then. I was thrilled. I was transferred over to the care of another doctor who let me go home from the hospital, provided that I took my temperature every four hours, was on total bed and pelvic rest with no baths and would come back to the hospital twice a week for non-stress tests and amniotic fluid index tests. So I got to go home.

When I got home I felt like I was going further and further into a downward spiral. I tried to pretend that everything was okay, but inside it was like I was thrown back in time. I turned into a scared little girl again. There was nothing I could do about what was happening to me. At the same time I was also angry and I wanted to take that little girl, shake her and tell her to snap out of it. I felt like my father still had control over my life and I couldn't understand why I couldn't get over it.

To make a long story short, I carried my son to term and he was born on his due date. My labor was very long and difficult. I cannot explain exactly what happened, but I started to get vivid flashbacks of the abuse when in labor. I felt absolutely violated. I freaked out when my midwife gave me an exam to see how dilated I was. I remember holding onto my husband and pleading with him to help me. It wasn't so much the physical pain as it was the mental. I felt like I was a small child. Finally, I got an epidural because I had made myself hysterical and I needed something to bring me back down to earth.

I felt really disconnected from my baby when we brought him home. I held him, fed *him, and took care of him, but I felt like I was just going through the motions. I know now that I was extremely depressed. Breastfeeding was difficult as well. I had a lot more trouble breastfeeding this time than the first. I think it's because I was having trouble bonding with my baby. Again, I didn't want to get too close and breastfeeding still felt like a violation. When my son went on a nursing strike at four months, it was easy not to continue. I stopped breastfeeding altogether.*

*I am now pregnant again, and I'm trying to sort myself out so I can be healthy throughout this pregnancy and start off on the right foot with this baby. I'm also going to try to breastfeed as long as possible. I'm still not sure I can do it. I have good intentions, but there still is a small child in me who panics when people get too close. I am sad to say that this even includes my children sometimes.*

*On a lighter note, I think I've been more mentally healthy with this pregnancy than my others. I am trying to deal with issues as they come out. Talking to my husband and my midwife helps. They may not always have answers for me, but just knowing I have support and I don't have to be scared anymore helps a lot.*

*My children have been a source of great joy and inspiration for me. Being a mother is very healing, because I know I am stopping the cycle of abuse.*

*My children are now four and one years old, respectively, and as I said previously I am expecting a new little one in about three months. I have learned that it is okay to hug them, hold them and cuddle them. I've learned to trust myself as a mother. I would never do anything to harm them. They have taught me a pure, unconditional love. The kind of love that I should have had from my father.*

### The Stroke of Midnight

*At the stroke of midnight,*
*everything will prevail.*
*The street lights...*
*they dim along the beaten trail.*
*A dog howls, a cat meows;*
*now a human scream, in the distance*
*of the trail.*
*Who is it I called?*
*And all was quiet.*
*A shiver up my spine,*
*all I remember is the human scream,*
*for it was mine—*
*at the stroke of midnight.*

by Amy

The process of becoming a mother occurs in the broader context of the lives we lead. As midwives, we began this exploration into the experiences of survivor moms with a narrow focus on how being a survivor of sexual abuse could affect pregnancy and birth. What we learned from these women's narratives is that being a survivor affects life very broadly, and that many aspects of having been abused as a girl, trying to recover and going on with life as a mother are connected. Past, present and hoped-for futures are interwoven. This is consistent with long-standing views that childbearing is a developmental, identity-transforming step for any woman who undertakes it (Rubin 1984), and that it can be a crisis and opportunity for transformation. Having been abused in childhood adds a layer of extra challenges.

Where a survivor is on the continuum of her recovery process seems to affect her experience of pregnancy, birth, postpartum and mothering. Some will be far along in the recovery process, will be able to imagine what their trauma-related needs are going to be during the childbearing year and will be able to negotiate to get their needs met. Others may only be starting to realize what a toll past abuse is taking and may not know where to begin to help themselves to feel better and to navigate childbearing and mothering (Seng, et al. 2002). Kay shares her journey with us on the road to healing. This story, like the others in this book, reveals to us this continuum of past, present and hoped-for future, and the many ways in which being a survivor can have an impact on the reproductive life of a woman. She also alludes to ways to work things out when trauma and childbearing issues intersect.

We have chosen to highlight Kay's story in this chapter about life before pregnancy because her story speaks about many of the issues that survivors face in the years leading up to pregnancy and birth. Of course, Kay's story is not just about the period before she became a mother: She also shares with us many of her thoughts and feelings about her pregnancies, births and early motherhood issues of breastfeeding and bonding, as well as her feelings about the gender of her children. We will look at these issues in more depth in the chapters to follow.

In this chapter about the context in which pregnancy occurs, we will first look at the *histories* of the women who have contributed to this project, the types of abuses they experienced, the ways in which they initially disclosed such abuses to family members or others and the responses they received.(1.1) We also will examine the long-term *effects* of abuse that are common to survivors of sexual abuse, such as posttraumatic stress symptoms, high risk behaviors and depression.(1.2) These effects may manifest in the years right after the trauma or begin later in life, sometimes in response to a life event like childbearing.(1.3) The family, partner and therapeutic *relationships* are an important context for survivors as they enter childbearing. Finally, we will give some attention to how these stories show recovery to be a long-term *process* that may or may not be complete when childbearing occurs, and what this means for survivors and maternity care providers as they work through the transitional year.

## HISTORY: WHAT HAPPENED

The sexual abuse of female children is widespread. Depending on how the question is worded in the research study, scientists find that as many as one in three women experienced some form of sexual abuse in girlhood—from non-contact sexual behavior to completed rape with injury and threat of death. How a girl survives the immediate situation and whether she will surmount it with little long-term damage or suffer consequences over much of the rest of her life varies. The reasons for the variations are complex but include, broadly, the relative advantage, disadvantage and adversity in the social context in which the survivor grew up, the psychological functioning of the adults who raised her, and the genetic heritage that may make a survivor more or less resilient in the aftermath of trauma, and her ability to recover and heal.

The survivor contributors to this book have diverse backgrounds and experiences, and yet their stories have many similarities. While each person's experience is unique, research shows that these experiences are part of discernable patterns of responses to trauma. Most of the contributors, including Kay, are women with a history of childhood sexual abuse or of sexual assault that happened when they were young women. The majority of the writers' narratives tell at least some of the details of their abuse history. Speaking out about what happened is often an important step

▼ 1.1

One in four women is estimated to have been sexually assaulted at least once in her life. In this nationally representative sample of US adult women, 12.6% disclosed a history of completed rape, and 14.3% had been otherwise sexually assaulted. Applying these prevalence rates to census data, this means that 12 million US women have been victims of completed rape and 13.8 million have suffered other sexual assaults. Another 10.3% (an estimated 10 million) have been physically assaulted.

Among physically assaulted women, 39% had had PTSD in their lifetime and 18% currently met diagnostic criteria for PTSD. Among sexually assaulted women the lifetime prevalence was 32% and the current rate was 12.4–16.5%. In some studies, the lifetime PTSD rate after sexual assault is as high as 80%.

Resnick, et al. 1993

▼ 1.2

In a survey of 4023 adolescents, weighted to reflect the US census estimates in terms of race, age and gender, 13.0% of girls had been sexually assaulted, 18.8% had been physically assaulted and 35.0% had witnessed violence. Ten percent met diagnostic criteria for PTSD at the time of the interview, and 22.2% met diagnostic criteria for depression.

Acierno, et al. 2000

▼ 1.3

At the time of the interview, the "most troubling traumatic event" associated with current PTSD symptoms had occurred more than 10 years in the past for 43.8% of the women.

Stein, et al. 1997

The PTSD rate among adolescent females is twice as high as the 4.6% current rate among adult women in a study by the same team using the same PTSD measure.

Resnick, et al. 1993

toward recovery, and is a right that has been denied to women until modern times. Bass and Davis, in their groundbreaking work for survivors, *The Courage to Heal* (1992), wrote:

> An essential part of healing from sexual abuse is telling the truth about your life. The sexual abuse of children, and the shame that results, thrive in an atmosphere of silence. Breaking that silence is a powerful healing tool. Yet it is something that many survivors find difficult.(p. 92)

The narrative writers for this book felt a need to break the silence about how childhood abuse can affect childbearing and mothering the next generation.

These days we generally understand that sexual abuse is an abuse of power and an act of violence. Women did not begin speaking out about this abuse of power in a public way until the 1970s, and the public has taken time since then to acknowledge the traumatic nature of sexual abuse.

That childhood sexual trauma causes long-lasting and profound mental and physical health problems for some survivors is not a new idea. "Hysteria" is a classic diagnostic term for some of the extreme manifestations of sexually-based traumatic stress reactions in women that were being studied by Freud and others more than 100 years ago (Breuer and Freud, 1895/1955). Judith Herman recounts the story of how this knowledge was pushed aside until political movements arose to support understanding about trauma and its long-term negative effects. As she writes in *Trauma and Recovery* (1992, 1997):

> Only after 1980, when the efforts of combat veterans had legitimated the concept of posttraumatic stress disorder, did it become clear that the psychological syndrome seen in survivors of rape, domestic battery, and incest was essentially the same as the syndrome seen in survivors of war. The implications of this insight are as horrifying in the present as they were a century ago: the subordinate condition of women is maintained and enforced by the hidden violence of men. There is war between the sexes. Rape victims, battered women, and sexually abused children are its casualties. Hysteria is the combat neurosis of the sex war.(p. 32)

Following are passages from the narrators describing the nature of the abuse that they endured. Including this background knowledge here is useful because many of the childbearing and mothering problems the writers focus on later make sense, in light of what actually happened to them. Caregivers and allies who are reading this book to be better able to help survivors may not have heard many women's stories and may need to read these to see how posttraumatic reactions during childbearing and parenting are coherent, given what the women experienced as a girls.

Survivors may not need to read this section. Women who are survivors are encouraged to pause and consider their feelings and limit exposure to the passages if reading them is stressful. While knowing what women have experienced and for women to share this information is important, reading about abuse is potentially emotionally triggering, especially if some of the material reminds a woman of her own history. Throughout the book, excerpts from the narratives illustrate points that are summarized and discussed. The narrative excerpts are in italics and can be skipped or skimmed if reading them is too intense to be helpful.

# Chapter 1—Life before Motherhood

Kay's abuser was her father. Although the majority of women report that they were abused by males, females perpetrate sexual abuse as well (Russell 1986).(1.4) Many other contributors report sexual assault of some type by either their biological father or stepfather. The nature of sexual abuse can range from non-contact voyeurism and inappropriate sexualization to completed rape. Background information about the family and home is often a part of the writers' descriptions because the family environment contributed to the harm:(1.5)

*There was never a time I can remember that I wasn't touched inappropriately. My father always had his hands on me or something. One of my few but very vivid memories is when my father had some back surgery and one of us kids would have to stay home with him every day. To this day I can't even identify what would go on…strong feeling about that…not wanting to be home with Dad, "don't let it be my turn…."*

*from Kathy's story*

*He molested me from before I had memory. I was touched almost everywhere that I could be by his sickness. I thought it was normal, although I struggled with feelings of shame and excitement. I was having a sexual awakening way before my time.*(1.6, 1.7)

*from Kelly's story*

*Warning bells were going off in my head but I didn't know what to do; nothing like this had ever happened to me before. I rolled onto my stomach, hoping that would signal him to leave. He started rubbing my back as if he was giving me a massage, and then he finally left. I was a child, a baby. I felt helpless, what was I supposed to do?*

*from Kim's story*

Although some abusers use force or threat, others use the child's affection for them as a weapon in their assault, endeavoring to make the child somehow complicit in the abuse. Making the child feel responsible

▼ 1.4

Perpetrators of child sexual abuse are far more likely (96%) to be male.

Russell 1986

▼ 1.5

In a qualitative interview study with 20 childhood sexual abuse survivors, characteristics of their home environments were an integral part of their abuse. These characteristics included:
- sexual abuse of children
- sexual chaos
- battering
- unchallenged verbal abuse
- scapegoating
- absence of nurturing
- instability of place
- economic instability
- developmentally inappropriate task expectations
- emotional role reversal
- unpredictable and unexplained events
- disproportionate responses
- extremes in paying attention to the child
- neglect of basic needs
- unmonitored home boundaries
- cultural void
- repudiation of sensory experience
- secrecy
- atmosphere of moral threat
- substance misuse

Hall 1996

▼ 1.6

In a ten-year study of girls with child sexual abuse confirmed by protective service agencies, compared with similar girls who did not experience CSA, the abused girls developed a range of sexual distortions. These distortions include sexual preoccupation, sexual aversion and sexual ambivalence that involves both preoccupation and aversion.

The abused girls also were younger at first consensual intercourse (14 versus 15.5 years old) and were less likely to use birth control. Of those who had given birth by the end of the study, the abused girls were younger at the time of their first birth and were more likely to have given birth while still a teen.

Noll, Trickett and Putnam 2003

▼ 1.7

Child sexual abuse is associated with a range of problems related to adolescent and adult sexual health:
- earlier consensual sexual activity
- less contraceptive use
- less condom use
- more HIV risk behaviors
- more partners
- more STDs (with risk for later infertility)
- more revictimization
- more prostitution
- more aversion to sex
- more perpetration of sexual abuse
- less gynecologic care, especially preventive care
- more somatic problems, including chronic pelvic pain and menstrual pain
- more intrusive thoughts leading to avoidance of sex
- more sexual problems including dysfunctions of desire, arousal, and orgasm
- more vaginismus (vaginal muscle spasm and pain with attempted intercourse)
- less benefit from medications to treat sexual dysfunction
- more problematic pregnancies, including in adolescence, unplanned, with greater risk of depression, substance use, low birth weight and prematurity and less social support during pregnancy

Loeb, et al. 2002

or guilty for the situation isolates the child from others, making the child less likely to disclose the truth. Causing the child to feel pleasure from the abuse confounds the issue further, leading many survivors to the belief that they must not have been abused at all since they experienced a physical response or felt pleasure during the assault. Several of the narrators reported feeling confused by this unusual "attention" they received from their father figure or by the distorting things the abuser said to them.

*I remember feeling so ashamed I just wanted to disappear. I guess I felt like I was the one to blame because at times it was enjoyable.*

from Sarah's story

*I never considered it sexual abuse because, though only a child, I felt I was a willing participant. I never talked about it because of the shame. In fact, my sister had even warned me to stay away from him. I felt weak, confused, stupid and very guilty.*

from Ann's story

Abusers who are not fathers, such as friends of the family and extended family members, also use this dynamic to their advantage:

*I knew it was wrong, I knew I shouldn't talk about it.... I felt ashamed, yet I was drawn back to him again and again, because he made me feel special. I remember the romantic feeling of being in his arms as he taught me how to ice skate. I remember the infatuation feelings, conflicting with the shame and fear I felt.*

from Ann's story

Mothers also sexually abuse their children. Although some studies ask about abuse by "parent" without assuming the abuser is male, reports of sexual abuse by mothers is rarer. This type of abuse has the potential to be particularly damaging to the child's sense of self, since the mother-child bond is so primary (Bowlby 1977), with the female child identifying with the mother and the early infancy boundaries between them being so fluid (Schore 2002).(1.8) Some of our authors reported abuse at the hands of their mothers:

*More commonly, however, she would give me a bath, often getting into the tub with me. Not only did she "wash" me with her hands, she also had me "wash" her— putting my hands on her breasts, using my hands to rub her genitals. As strange and*

## Chapter 1—Life before Motherhood

*upsetting as this was, the most frightening thing was that during these episodes, she would seem to disappear, or dissociate: her eyes glazed over, her breathing changed, she was off in another world somewhere. It really seemed to me that she had fallen into a hole in her world somewhere, and as much as I hated what she made me do during these "baths," I was even more terrified that she would disappear and never return.*

*from Carrie's story*

Other types of sexual assaults also were described by the writers, including sibling abuse, abuse by babysitters and abuse by strangers:

*Both of my parents were consumed with caring for my older sister, who was hospitalized for a large portion of her childhood.... Often they would put my oldest teenage brother in charge of the rest of the children while they went to the hospital. He was resentful and angry about this responsibility and took his anger out on us, first by physically abusing us and later sexually abusing us.*

*from Laura's story*

▼ 1.8
A recent study described characteristics of sexual abuse experienced prior to age 16 in a New England university sample of 974 undergraduate women (mean age 18.6 years). Eighteen percent reported experiencing child sexual abuse. Mean age at onset was 11 years. Mean number of incidents was 4. Mean duration was 3 years. For 38% the abuse involved attempted or completed intercourse. For 16% digital penetration. For 6% oral sex. For 41% fondling. In 13% of the cases the perpetrator was a parent or step-parent, 29% were other relatives, 49% were other known persons (boyfriend/girlfriend of parent, family friend, acquaintance) and 9% were strangers.

Twenty-three percent of those reporting child sexual abuse and 12% of those not abused in childhood reported a sexual assault after they turned 16.

A total of 14% of the college women had been assaulted after age 16. The perpetrators of young adult sexual assault included relatives (6%), boyfriends (28%), dates (16%), non-romantic friends (19%), acquaintances (24%) and strangers (8%).

Jankowski, et al. 2002

Sometimes the writers experienced sexual abuse in the context of a group, such as a street gang or cult, that, like a family, they perceived to be an organization that would be good to or protective of them:

*Perhaps six or seven weeks later, one of the other gang members told me that Ronnie wanted to get back with me. I was told to go down by the river that evening, where he would be waiting for me. Being rather innocent, I went. Ronnie wasn't there, but five of the gang were. They took me to a coal storage warehouse along the East River, and all of them raped me! I still remember bits and pieces of that experience, as if they happened to someone else.*

*from Nan's story*

For some of these writers sexual trauma happened first or happened again in adolescence or young adulthood, including date rape, stranger rape and sexual harassment. This age period is the time in the female lifespan where exposure to trauma peaks (Breslau, et al. 1997).

*I come from a family where my father molested my sisters but not me. Nevertheless I grew up in a household that taught me to undervalue myself. As a teenager I was raped twice; both were stranger rapes. Both were unreported and I never sought help. In fact it was years before I realized what had happened to me "counted" as rape.*

*from Katherine's story*

▼ 1.9

That child sexual abuse does not occur very often in isolation from other adversities is a well-known fact. This relationship has been quantified in a study of more than 17,000 adult HMO members. Twenty-five percent of women and 16% of men reported a history of childhood sexual abuse. Among these 1523 with a history childhood sexual abuse, the overall number of adverse childhood events (ACEs) was higher for those with a history childhood sexual abuse (an average of 2.5 *additional* ACEs, compared with an *overall* average of 1.5 ACEs for those not sexually abused). Also, the more severe* the sexual abuse, the higher the average number of total adverse childhood events.

Dong, et al. 2003

*Severity of abuse takes into account age at onset, number of instances, number of perpetrators, whether the perpetrator was a family caregiver, how long the abuse lasted, whether it involved penetration and what level of manipulation, coercion or threat was used.

▼ 1.10

In a large study of adult HMO members, 35% of women and 25% of men reported some emotional abuse in childhood. An emotionally abusive family environment affected adult scores on mental health measures above and beyond the effect associated with specific acts of maltreatment (sexual or physical abuse or witnessing the mother being battered).

Edwards, et al. 2003

Abuse generally does not occur in a vacuum (Dong, et al. 2003; Edwards, et al. 2003).(1.9) Often some form of neglect precedes it, creating a situation ripe for abuse. Kay does not mention feeling or being neglected, but many other contributors do. Many children grow up in homes with physical violence, neglect, abandonment or emotional abuse, substance abuse, alcoholism, discomforts due to extreme poverty or parents who have no sense of protecting the boundaries of their home and their children's safety. Many children grow up with parents who struggle with mental illness, and are ill-equipped to parent. Here is what some of the narrators had to say about growing up in such environments:(1.10)

*I also had to deal with the neglect that went on when we were living with my mom. We didn't have any clean clothes, very little food, if any, and it was the dead of winter living in this broken down farmhouse. Mom was on heavier drugs and was no help whatsoever to my brother and me.*

*from Kelly's story*

*His attitude of control continued into my adolescence. He wouldn't allow me to lock the door on the bathroom while showering and always seemed to come in to talk to me about something while I showered. I had no privacy and was often told to leave the door of my room open, even while changing clothes. As my body started developing the intrusions became more frequent. He would put a hand up my shirt to check my development, joking all the while. Completely mortified was how I felt during those times. My mom was present and acting as if all was normal. I just thought something was wrong with me. Although he never forced me to have sexual relations with him, my sexuality and esteem were severely damaged by his lack of boundaries. It has taken me over half my life to take back control from him.*

*from Wendi's story*

*My mother had a nervous breakdown approximately nine months after I was born. She was hospitalized for a few weeks. She readily admits that she was not able to care for me as well as she would have liked. I spent a lot of time as a baby propped up on the couch, and when feeding time came, my bottle was propped up with a pillow as well. With the emotional condition she was in, my mom did the best she could, and when my dad was home, he helped out as well. My maternal grandmother also spent some time with us to help out. Regardless, the family situation, and perhaps even my genetics, created a little girl who felt insecure, afraid, alone and unloved. This was the perfect set up for a little girl to be sexually abused, and I was.*(1.11)

*from Ann's story*

*My mother left my father, my little sister and me when I was five years old. It's very hard for me to separate the damage that was caused by sexual abuse from the damage caused by my mother's abandonment (especially when it comes to my mothering journey). Then I have to consider what damage my father's neglect and emotional abuse following the divorce caused. I was a pretty mixed-up kid. However, I don't think very many survivors out there are only dealing with sexual abuse. Life is never that simple.*

*from Hope's story*

▼ 1.11

In the National Comorbidity Survey the odds of a child sexual abuse survivor having a mental health condition was most consistently predicted by the survivor's mother having had mental health problems. In this large epidemiological study, child sexual abuse was associated with adult mental health problems above and beyond the effect of other family adversities. Parental mental illness, especially that of the mother, was the most significant other adversity contributing to the risk of the victim's developing mental health problems as an adult.

Molnar, Buka and Kessler 2001

Children learn behaviors from their abusers. For a variety of possible reasons, a child who is being abused may in turn victimize others:

*For some reason, I don't think I ever realized that what we were doing was not normal, until I started abusing my younger brother. I would feel guilty after it was over and knew it was something I was doing that was bad, but couldn't help myself to stop. Finally, five years later, I managed to stop myself from abusing my brother. I don't think my brother ever thought it wasn't normal because he told everyone he knew. Even with all the people who knew, no one ever intervened and tried to stop it and get us help. One night, my mother even caught us, and she just sent us to bed.*

*from Cassandra's story*

In these accounts, by and large, adults failed to pay attention and failed to protect. Sometimes they even failed to believe when the child found the courage to tell what was happening. Secrecy and threat played a role in preventing the writers from telling. Responses of disbelief and denial also played a role in making disclosure of the abuse to supportive people and caregivers later in life more difficult.

### *HISTORY: DISCLOSURE*
Screening for past abuse by health care providers and disclosure by survivors can be stressful. For the caregiver, knowing how to respond helpfully is sometimes hard. And for the survivor evaluating whether disclosure is safe and worthwhile is a reasonable step. This may be especially true for women who have gotten bad responses in the past.

Kay thought about telling her mother that her father was abusing her, but decided not to for fear her father would make good on his threat to kill her mother if she disclosed. Threats are a way the abuser consigns his victim to secrecy. Kay also feared that her mother would turn away from her, thereby leaving her emotionally parentless. She also feared that her mother would tell her it was her fault. Child victims of abuse regularly assign the blame for their abuse to themselves. Herman explains this self-blame in *Trauma and Recovery* (1997) this way:

> ...When it is impossible to avoid the reality of the abuse, the child must construct some system of meaning that justifies it. Inevitably the child concludes that her innate badness is the cause. The child seizes upon this explanation early and clings to it tenaciously, for it enables her to preserve a sense of meaning, hope and power. If she is bad, then her parents are good. If, somehow, she has brought this fate upon herself, then somehow she has the power to change it. If she has driven her parents to mistreat her, then, if only she tries hard enough, she may someday earn their forgiveness and finally win the protection and care she so desperately needs.... It is congruent with the thought processes of traumatized people of all ages, who search for faults in their own behavior in an effort to make sense out of what has happened to them.(p. 103)

This issue of self-blame, and its attendant feelings of guilt and shame, is an important part of understanding the context of the lives of survivors, as is the need to try to preserve important relationships, however flawed.

Kay did try to disclose her abuse to a teacher, who did not believe her and told her to "quit making up stories." Other writers also describe not being believed by the adults to whom they chose to disclose.(1.12, 1.13)

▼ 1.12

Of the 406 of 4008 women in the National Women's Study who reported childhood completed rape or aggravated assault, 24.9% of the rape survivors sustained additional physical injury (beyond the rape itself), and 66.7% of the aggravated assault survivors sustained physical injury. Despite the severity of these assaults, only 11.9% of the rapes and 26% of the aggravated assaults were reported to authorities.

Hanson, et al. 2001

▼ 1.13

The number of incidents of child sexual abuse that come to the attention of child protection professionals is small compared to the prevalence disclosed by adults. Matching data from two national studies, appeared to show that about 2% of adult women who reported a history of child sexual abuse ever were "cases" receiving the attention of police, teachers or child protection services.

Russell 1985
NCCAN 1981

*When I finally gathered up enough courage to tell someone again I was 11 years old. I received such a long and abusive lecture from my father on how evil I was for spreading those ugly lies that I buried my secrets and went on in silence, again.*
*from Hope's story*

*"Are you sure?" I was more stunned by her question than I had been by my father's inappropriate sexual behavior. "Of course I'm sure," I responded. "Why would I make up something like that?" But the damage had been done. She had managed to wipe out 13 years of mother/daughter trust with three words. Twenty-three years later, I still have not reassigned to her the trust she lost from me that day.*
*from Kristy's story*

Some of the contributors were believed when they disclosed, but the adults they told reacted inadequately or inappropriately, either ignoring them or actually blaming them for the abuse.

*After the whole story came out, my parents were shocked into silence. They didn't speak a word to*

## Chapter 1—Life before Motherhood

*me all the way home and the incident was never referred to again.... It was then that I internalized two very profound teachings. 1) It was okay for people to hurt me, and 2) It was not okay to tell anyone about it.*

*from Hope's story*

*After my mom talked with me, it was never discussed again. I tried to forget about it and go on with life. I remember always feeling like something was wrong with me, like I was damaged somehow and not as good or worth as much as other people.*

*from Sarah's story*

*At an earlier time, when I was nearly raped by a gang of teenage boys, my mother's reaction was "Get used to it. That's what happens to girls."*

*from Elaine's story*

Disclosing to the mother was a particularly distressing issue for many of the contributors to this project. Survivors wonder why their mothers did not protect them in the first place:

*I was changing. I was becoming different. Something dies in you and you become numb, just kind of going through the motions. I was always trying to hide what I was feeling: repulsion, revulsion, shame. I felt like everyone must see what was happening to me, everyone except my MOTHER. How could she not see the signs? How could she not see how I would shrink every time he came into close contact, not wanting him to touch me in any way? Becoming verbally attacking, being sarcastic, saying mean and hurtful things, anything to give me a little power back? How could she not see I was crying out in pain? I lost all respect for her in my childhood. Did she not feel the tension that emanated from me? Maybe she didn't want to see.*

*from Kim's story*

*My parents had seen me come in, with my shirt untucked from my skirt and my nylons with rips in them. They said nothing. The next day, my mom asked me, "Did somebody rape you?" I said, "I don't know," and got teary-eyed and ran off. Nothing else was ever said.*

*from Nina's story*

When a mother failed to protect after disclosure, the girl could feel total devastation, especially when the mother's extreme reactions to such disclosure precipitated a chain of disastrous events:

*Then she sat me down, and broke my heart and my spirit in one fell swoop. She told me that we could tell the police, but that that would mean Mark, my little brother, would be taken from us and we would never see him again. And that we would have no place to live, and would have to live on the street and go on welfare. And who knows, Will and I may be taken away, too. And if the police thought that my mom knew, she would go to jail along with Fred. And then she said it.*

*"He did it to you, you decide. Should I leave him or should we just stay and pretend it never happened?"*

*I was twelve, and my mother forced me to make a decision that no adult should ever have to make. She betrayed me so badly that she might as well have been in the room as he fondled and violated me. I realized then that I was all alone. Totally, completely alone. No one cared enough, I wasn't worth enough, for anyone to bother with me. I was an afterthought that was to be used when needed and then discarded. A part of me died that day, and I'd like to think I have resurrected it, but I just don't know.*

*from Amy's story*

The inability of the mother to protect may have several implications for survivors in terms of their ability to trust in their own mothering abilities, and we will explore this more in the chapter on attachment and mothering. Some survivors, like Melanie, had positive experiences disclosing to their mothers the fact of their abuse, and they write about how this positive mothering response made a lot of difference to them:

*Late one night, after they'd had a big fight and he'd gone back to his other home, my mom asked if he could give me a hug and kiss at my graduation. I said that I didn't want him to, and she asked if he'd ever done anything out of line. I told her he had and gave a few of the details. She was surprised, said that she would end the relationship and asked if she could confront him with this accusation, to which I said yes. When she talked to him a day or two later he denied it and said I'd made it up, but my mom defended me and refused to see him again. I don't think we've talked about the abuse since shortly after she confronted him because it's a difficult subject for both of us. I've often wondered how she could not know that it was happening, but I believe that, at least consciously, she really didn't. I know that it's helped a great deal that my mom believed me without hesitation even when he accused me of lying.*

*from Melanie's story*

*I tried to tell my mother, and she did not listen to me. My father would make me read "Hustler" magazine with him, and my mom found them in my room just before my 11th birthday. She also found a letter I had written to a friend about the abuse. She came and took me out of school and finally listened to me. My father moved out that same day, and the divorce proceedings began shortly thereafter.*

*from Tami's story*

Only after attempting suicide was Kay finally able to disclose the abuse to her mother. Her mother believed her and validated her experience by sharing with Kay the physical symptoms of abuse—unexplained vaginal and urinary infections, which Kay had had when she was younger. Kay shares that, although her mother believed her, still she didn't tell her mother everything because she perceived that her mother was uncomfortable. Kay began counseling after this.

Other narrators chose to disclose the abuse to someone other than their mother, like Ann, who told a friend. These disclosures did not always lead to immediate help, but they were a step toward feeling better.

*…my best friend took me aside and told me that she did not know what was wrong with me, but that it was obviously something quite serious, and advised me to talk to a priest, or someone else, someone whom I could trust. I had told no one what had happened up until that point, and I did not break my silence with her.*

*Her suggestion planted a seed within me, though, a seed of hope that perhaps I was not insane.*

*from Ann's story*

Kay's counselor encouraged her to press charges against her father, but she says that she was not "strong enough" to do so. Doing so, in essence, involves disclosing in a very public way, raising concerns about how others will respond. The decision as to whether a survivor chooses to pursue legal action against a perpetrator is complicated, and each survivor must do what is right for her.

On the other hand, adult professionals who are responsible for children do not have this discretion. They are "mandatory reporters" who have a legal obligation to report suspicion of abuse or neglect to authorities. The authorities then may bring criminal charges against perpetrators on behalf of the child.(1.14)

Professionals who provide maternity care also may help a survivor by asking which adults in her life will and will not be allowed to be involved with her child.

▼ 1.14

Professionals who work with children usually are designated by law to be "mandatory reporters," meaning that they are required to make a report to child protection services if they suspect a child is being abused. Teachers, police, nurses and doctors are examples of people who are mandatory reporters.

Childhelp USA's
National Child Abuse Hotline
1-800-4-A-Child

This telephone number can be used 24-hours a day and also serves Canada, Guam, Puerto Rico and the U.S. Virgin Islands

Individual states have toll-free reporting lines too, which are listed on the Childhelp Web site—along with the main instructions: TRUST YOUR INSTINCTS.
www.childhelpusa.org

## *THE RANGE OF EFFECTS AFTER ABUSE*

The person who has been abused lives within the context of her particular history of abuse and current situation and may feel isolated by the impact it has had on her. Health care providers will be most effective if they can focus on patterns of long-term negative effects. We cannot change the past, but we can address posttraumatic mental and physical health problems. Effective psychotherapies and medications are available for a range of trauma-related conditions and more approaches are being developed all the time (Foa, Keane and Friedman 2000). In this section we present an overview of effects of trauma using mental health diagnostic terms that may facilitate women and their maternity care providers in discussion of how to assess and address the long-term negative effects of abuse.

Not every child who is abused goes on to have long-term negative effects that meet criteria for mental health diagnoses. Some are resilient and are believed and made safe by caring adults. Some get help to recover while they are still children. But others experience lingering reactions that become problematic if they cause distress or impairment in work, school or relationships. These problems often warrant help from health care and mental health professionals and/or support organizations. Childhood sexual abuse takes forms that vary and fall along a broad continuum of severity, sometimes with more than one identifiable problem. The same is true for the long-term negative effects of abuse described in these narratives. Most of the writers describe the problems they have

▼ 1.15

Not all women who experience abuse in childhood go on to develop mental health problems.

Women who reported child sexual abuse in the National Comorbidity Survey were 1.8 times as likely to have ever been depressed (39.3% versus 19.2% of women not reporting child sexual abuse). They were 10.2 times as likely to have PTSD (39.1% versus 5.7%). They also were 1.5 times as likely to have an alcohol problem and 2.3 times as likely to have a drug problem.

Molnar, Buka and Kessler 2001

▼ 1.16

Abuse survivors with substance abuse problems need combined treatment. If long-term negative effects of past abuse are not treated, eventual relapse to substance abuse is more likely. However, treatment of substance abuse must be underway because recalling past trauma in therapy is aversive and disturbing and may lead to increased substance abuse.

Stewart, et al. 1998

without using the vocabulary that mental health professionals use. In the following section we provide some information about mental health conditions that survivors experience as a result of what happened to them, problems that can affect the childbearing year and beyond.(1.15) The overarching way that we organize our thinking about the long-term negative effects of abuse is to use the idea of "posttraumatic stress." Posttraumatic stress disorder (PTSD) is a specific mental health condition. Not everyone who was abused develops PTSD; but many survivors experience some of the symptoms some of the time. Almost any person who has ever been badly traumatized may experience a posttraumatic stress reaction. Using PTSD as an organizing concept can be helpful because it makes sense of a trauma survivor's reactions in light of what happened to her. Other conditions associated with child abuse trauma, such as depression, substance abuse or chronic pain conditions may more successfully be treated if the posttraumatic connection is taken into account.(1.16)

We also focus on PTSD because both survivors and clinicians have told us that talking about "posttraumatic stress" is easier than talking about "sexual abuse." Talking about posttraumatic stress also may be more to the point. Health care providers can't do anything about child abuse that occurred in the past, but they can help the survivor who is trying to manage posttraumatic stress happening now. Also, a growing body of research deals with PTSD, how it affects mental and physical health and how to treat it.

While the PTSD conceptualization is useful, it is not always adequate or satisfying. The core symptoms listed in the diagnostic criteria do not capture everything that survivors might experience. Other conceptualizations of the effects of trauma can enrich understanding of this phenomenon. Jennifer Freyd (1996) has written about sexual abuse as a "betrayal trauma." Finkelhor and Browne (1985) study sexual abuse in terms of four "traumagenic dynamics" of traumatic sexualization, betrayal, stigmatization and powerlessness. Although PTSD is officially classified as an anxiety disorder (APA 2000), it is also seen to be a dissociative disorder (involving alterations of consciousness and disruptions in memory (APA 2000).

Because PTSD affects the brain and the body, some areas of research and evolving treatments try to integrate consideration of neurological and physical effects of traumatic stress (e.g., see *EMDR in the Treatment of Adults Abused as Children* by Laurel Parnell). Perhaps the most broad, integrating conceptualization is that presented by Judith Herman (1997) as "Complex PTSD," also referred to as "disorder of extreme stress not otherwise specified ("DESNOS")." Complex PTSD or DESNOS encompasses effects of trauma exposures that occurred early in development and were prolonged, such that the person's very character and way of being in the world seems to be affected. Herman (1997, p. 121) summarized Complex PTSD as having seven components:

1. a history of subjection to totalitarian control over a prolonged period of time;
2. alterations in regulation of emotions (including depression, self-harm, explosive or inhibited anger, compulsive or inhibited sexuality);

3. alterations in consciousness (including reliving, amnesia and dissociation);
4. alterations in self-perception (including sense of defilement, shame, guilt or aloneness); trator;
6. alterations in relations with others; and
7. alterations in systems of meaning (including loss of sustaining faith, hopelessness, despair).

Complex PTSD is not a diagnosis officially recognized by the American Psychiatric Association or the American Psychological Association. But most of its elements are contained in the description of PTSD, frequently co-morbid conditions and associated features (APA 2000).

## *EFFECTS: POSTTRAUMATIC STRESS DISORDER*

While a woman can't be "a little bit pregnant," she can have "a little bit of a problem" with posttraumatic stress, depression or self-care. In reading these descriptions of posttraumatic problems, remember that they can be more or less severe and that, in reality, they often go together in ways that make separating them neatly into categories difficult.

To be diagnosed with PTSD, a person has to have specific symptoms.(1.17) Recent research has shown that a person can have fewer symptoms but still experience enough distress and difficulties to need or want treatment.(1.18) This is especially true among women, who have twice the risk of PTSD compared with similarly traumatized men and four times the risk of partial PTSD.(1.19) The following passages describe the core symptoms of PTSD.

### *INTRUSIVE RE-EXPERIENCING*

The intrusive re-experiencing symptoms are a hallmark of PTSD. These include unwanted memories, as well as nightmares and flashbacks that intrusively bring the trauma unbidden into the present. Re-experiencing refers to a feeling of reliving the trauma, as though it were happening now, with intense emotional or physical reactions. Flashbacks can be visual (images), auditory

▼ 1.17
PTSD diagnostic criteria:
A. Exposure to a traumatic event
  1. Involving actual or threatened death or serious injury, or a threat to the physical integrity of self or others
  2. Where the person's response involved intense fear, helplessness or horror.
B. The traumatic event is persistently re-experienced (one symptom)
C. Persistent avoidance of stimuli associated with the trauma and numbing of general responsiveness (three symptoms)
D. Persistent symptoms of increased arousal (two symptoms)
E. Symptoms lasting more than a month
F. Causing significant distress and impairment

Can be acute or chronic and can occur with delayed onset (symptoms appear more than six months after trauma).

APA 1994

▼ 1.18
In a Canadian community survey study measuring PTSD in the past one-month period, 2.7% of women met full diagnostic criteria. Another 3.4% had partial PTSD (defined as at least one symptom per each of the three clusters instead of the full criteria of one intrusive, three avoidance, and two arousal symptoms).

Those with partial PTSD had levels of functional impairment (difficulty with job, school, family or social roles) similar to those with full PTSD and significantly greater than traumatized persons without PTSD.

Rates of help-seeking were not significantly different in the full and partial PTSD groups. Sixty percent versus 52.6% had sought help from a physician, counselor or member of the clergy.

These findings suggest that people who do not fully qualify for the PTSD diagnosis should, nevertheless, have access to PTSD treatment.

Stein, et al. 1997

▼ 1.19

When full PTSD is considered by gender, a two-fold risk for women is consistently found. In this Canadian survey where partial PTSD was also considered, the ratio of women to men with either full or partial PTSD increased to 4:1.

In a community sample of Canadians, patterns of gender differences in trauma exposures were consistent with patterns in earlier US studies. 74.2% of women and 81.3% of men reported experiencing a traumatic event. Rape (15.5%) and sexual molestation prior to age 18 (19.2%) were more common among women. Combat (0.7%), witnessing severe injury or death (18.8%), being threatened with a weapon (12.4%) and serious motor vehicle accident (19.5%) were more common for men. The most common trauma exposures were equally common in men and women: physical attack (21.0%) and violent death of a friend or family member (34.7%).

The odds of a woman being raped were 10 times greater compared with a man and the odds of being sexually molested were five times greater.

Stein, et al. 1997

(sounds), olfactory (smells), proprioceptive (spatial) and affective (emotional).

Culturally common notions of flashbacks deal with those that are obvious, unmistakable and relate to combat (images of bomb blasts or sounds of helicopter blades). Intrusive re-experiencing of sexual abuse can actually be more subtle, to the point that the survivor may doubt that it is real (sound of a door or a mattress creaking, smelling body odors, feeling like something bad is going to happen).

*I remember being scared of going to bed. I can still see the shadow in the doorway. Being carried upstairs to my room with my father's family all downstairs. A male carried me upstairs. I remember staring up at the ceiling and becoming part of it. Focusing on a certain dot or counting how many dots in the tile. As I write this I can feel a tightening in my throat and my heart racing. Not to mention the mist in my eyes and the sweaty palms.*

*from Paulette's story*

Re-experiencing often is "triggered" by something that reminds the survivor of the trauma, whether she is completely aware of how the current situation is like the trauma or not. Sometimes the mere context of the trauma, with no sexual or physical contact required to trigger re-experiencing, is enough. But situations where sexual or body contact will occur are frequently described as strong triggers. A survivor once told one of the authors that waiting in a gown on an exam table for the gynecologist to enter the room and do a physical examination triggered her into flashbacks of how she felt waiting on her bed in her nightgown for her abuser to come into her room at night. This caused her to have to fight back panic, tearfulness and dissociation at her annual exam appointments. She had no visual or other obvious cue as to what was happening. Identifying why this common health care routine made her feel so awful took several experiences.(1.20) Desire to avoid being triggered drives many of the maternity care needs of survivors. Case reports and interview research describe aspects of pregnancy itself and the medical procedures that go with maternity care as triggers.

▼ 1.20

In the National Comorbidity Survey, rape and sexual molestation were the traumas most commonly associated with PTSD among women. Of all the women with PTSD, 29.9% reported that rape was their most upsetting trauma and 19.1% reported that molestation was their most upsetting trauma.

Kessler, et al. 1995

*At eighteen, I had my first gynecological exam. It was a nightmare. I was totally unprepared for the experience. I was unbelievably tense, and cried. I didn't understand why it upset me so much. I just knew it hurt and reminded me of the ways Don touched me. Unfeeling. Probing.*

*from Otter's story*

## AVOIDANCE AND EMOTIONAL NUMBING

Numbing symptoms of PTSD include avoiding thoughts and feelings associated with the trauma, avoiding activities, situations, people or places that are reminders, being unable to recall aspects of the trauma, losing interest in activities, feeling detached or cut off from others, having decreased ability to experience emotions and having a foreshortened sense of the future. Some of these are also symptoms of depression. About half of PTSD sufferers also have some depression.

Being triggered by reminders into a re-experience of symptoms can lead to avoiding contact with people and places, panic and phobias. Feelings of detachment or alienation from other people can lead to loss of positive relationships. As we will see in several of these narratives, such triggers can get in the way of bonding with a baby as well.

*I was a master at shutting down, and being "dead" inside. My secret had eaten away at me.*

*from Rebecca's story*

*A therapist once asked me, "Why don't you feel any anger or resentment toward your parents?" I didn't have an answer for her except to say, "I remember so little." What I do remember is shrouded in dreams and impressions. I do recall the self-destructive behavior I had during adolescence. I used drugs and alcohol recklessly from age 17 until I married at age 21. Sometimes I mixed very dangerous combinations. Apparently I never worried about overdosing. I don't think I really cared. I must have been hurting, and using drugs to escape and numb my pain.*

*from Cathleen's story*

## AROUSAL

Difficulty falling or staying asleep, difficulty concentrating, being overly alert to danger, irritability or angry outbursts, and having an exaggerated startle reflex are all features of what is known as "hypervigilance" and "hyperarousal." They are a form of bodily preparedness to react to a danger by fighting or fleeing, and can be quite uncomfortable:

*Then I started getting anxiety attacks. I thought I was going crazy. I didn't know what was happening to me. I was starting to deal with past issues. Sometimes I didn't have alcohol or drugs to escape and I couldn't suppress my emotions any longer.*

*from Sarah's story*

*I grew up in Anchorage, Alaska. I never remembered any childhood. It was always just a blackness in my mind. Yes, there were pieces of here and there but they seemed not to be a part of me. I was very independent. I would let no one in my room or on my bed. They might mess it up and that was awful. I had one brother. We survived the Alaskan earthquake. I was very upset with him. Nothing in his room was messed up because it was already on the floor; whereas my room was perfect and after the quake settled it was a mess. This may seem strange to you that I mention this but within its message is the key to my life. I had to be clean and I had to be in control. Otherwise my whole existence was threatened.*

*from Susan's story*

▼ 1.21
When people with PTSD are exposed to stimuli that resemble the past trauma, multiple stress response systems in the body react in ways that differ from those in people who recovered from trauma and did not develop PTSD. Posttraumatic stress physiological reactions are exaggerated and feel more distressing. They also appear to be dysregulated and not integrated across stress response systems.
Liberzon, et al. 1999

The three symptom clusters of PTSD interact with each other in ways that are hard to turn off. A reminder of the trauma can trigger re-experiencing, which causes arousal, which requires numbing. Chronic arousal lowers the threshold for being reminded and re-experiencing, which leads to more and more avoidance. The patterns of interacting symptoms vary and change, making them hard to manage.(1.21)

### EFFECTS: OTHER TRAUMA-RELATED PROBLEMS
People with PTSD can have a variety of additional problems that are recognized as "associated features" of a PTSD diagnosis. These problems tend to occur more for people who have been victims of severe, prolonged trauma that happens early in development when escape is not possible and coping capacities are limited. These include somatization, dissociation and interpersonal problems, substance abuse, disordered eating, high-risk behaviors and self harm, as well as vulnerability to being re-victimized.

▼ 1.22
In a study of urban young adult HMO members, approximately 25% of those with PTSD reported the psychogenic amnesia symptom (inability to recall an important aspect of the trauma).
Breslau and Davis 1992

### DISSOCIATION
The flashbacks of PTSD can be thought of as dissociation because, whatever form they take, they are distorting the sense of time, place, or circumstances. Dissociation also is a coping mechanism where "a disruption in the usually integrated functions of consciousness, memory, identity, or perception of the environment" exists (APA 2000). The narrators in this book most often refer to dissociation in relation to how they used it for self-protection when abuse was going on. Dissociation can occur suddenly during a traumatic event (often called peritraumatic dissociation). It may be transient, occurring but tapering off in the weeks after a rape, for example. This form of self-anesthesia, useful when fight or flight is not possible, can also become chronic when it becomes generalized and used in situations that are perhaps stressful but not overwhelming. In its most extreme form, identity itself is fragmented. Dissociation during the trauma may account for the fragmented, incomplete memory of the trauma that is the "inability to recall" symptom of PTSD.(1.22)

*If you want my body, take it, but you'll never make me feel. It happened again and again, but in my head I walked away while they did it, and they couldn't make me feel it. I wandered around the basement while they violated my body, and I came back when it was safe. It was never really safe, but it was over—until next time.*

*from Colleen's story*

*Much of my life up to then had been a total blank. I was always spacey (some time later, I found that part of it had to do with having an undetected learning disability). In that year I became more so...to the point of complete dissociation. Most of the time I didn't know what day of the week it was. I failed most of my classes senior year because I honestly couldn't remember what I was taking. I knew that no one would have believed that, so I just let myself gain the reputation of being spacey and unreliable.*

*from Shakta's story*

*Shame. Shame. I swallowed the shame. I told no one the truth. Too afraid, too confused. To preserve my dignity, and myself, I split in two. Liz and the sexual Liz. The sexual Liz became the bad one, so the rest of me could stay intact.*

*from Liz's story*

In the context of the childbearing year, the ability to dissociate has a potential benefit. People who dissociate often are able to use self-hypnosis very well. So women who have the capacity to dissociate because of their trauma history may be good candidates for training in self-hypnosis to manage labor. However, dissociation and detachment present problems for mothering (Schore 2002). If a baby's intense cries of hunger or colic trigger the mother, she may dissociate and have trouble responding with an emotional connection that will help soothe the infant. Learning to manage dissociation deliberately may be very important during pregnancy.

## SOMATIZATION

Women with abuse histories (especially those who develop PTSD) seek health care more often for somatic (physical) complaints that are clinically significant because they cause distress or impair ability to function, but are medically unexplained. These problems include pain, gastrointestinal or sexual problems and the pseudoneurological symptoms associated with "hysteria," such as feeling unable to swallow or losing consciousness. PTSD also is associated with more respiratory, cardiovascular and musculoskeletal symptoms, more chronic conditions like irritable bowel syndrome, chronic fatigue syndrome and premenstrual syndrome, as well as more disease in general (Seng, et al. 2006; Kimerling, et al. 2002).(1.23, 1.24) Although some of these conditions are considered "medically unexplained," they are not necessarily imaginary. Trauma and PTSD affect the body and are associated with alterations in multiple stress response systems that can affect immune function and pain thresholds, taking a toll on health over time by mechanisms that are not yet well understood. In these narratives not much is said about loss of health and physical well-

▼ 1.23
Experience of sexual trauma among women is associated with an increase in physical health symptoms and greater us of medical services. Symptoms may include headache, stomachache, back pain, cardiac arrhythmia and menstrual symptoms, as well as higher rates of chronic disease, including diabetes and arthritis, as well as higher rates of disability from physical illness. It is also related to more severe symptoms of irritable bowel syndrome and PMS. More sexual dysfunction and sexual pain problems are noted.

Becker 1982
Golding 1994
Kimerling and Calhoun 1994
Leserman 1996
Letourneau 1996
Zoellner, Goodwin and Foa 2000

▼ 1.24
In a study of young adult members of an urban HMO, those with PTSD experienced three times as many physical symptoms as those without PTSD. Women with PTSD also experienced twice as many symptoms as men with PTSD. Twenty nine percent of those with PTSD rated their health as only fair or poor, compared with 17.3% of those with other mental health disorders and 6.5% of those with no disorder.

Breslau 2001

being in relation to abuse; the focus is on the abuse itself or the experience of pregnancy. But the women refer to specific injuries and upset at the time of the abuse, of which adult somatic complaints may be an echo.

*Later, in my adult years, I would remember lying down and the men's faces being close to me; the stench of stale beer, and then blanking it all out. That year, my attendance in kindergarten was terrible. I missed two-thirds of the school year. I remember day after day of lying in my parents' bed, with my mother there, trying to calm my upset stomach with glasses of ginger ale....*
*from Kate's story*

Although not much research yet exists regarding somatic problems in pregnancy, other research shows that women with PTSD experience more of the severe nausea and vomiting of pregnancy and more contraction episodes. Various authors of clinical papers suggest that survivors have more difficulty tolerating physical discomforts of pregnancy and worry more (Seng, et al. 2001; Simkin and Klaus 2004).

## *INTERPERSONAL PROBLEMS*

An entire range of problems of perceiving the self and others and managing relationships is a logical consequence of the neglect, manipulations, betrayal or outright threat that happened around the abuse. These can range from feelings of shame and guilt that undermine self-esteem, to conduct and personality disorders, with difficulty trusting, problems with authority figures, self-harm and involvement with harmful people filling the range in between.

*...My troubles only began at 13. As my drinking progressed so did my depression, my isolation and the number of assaults. Needless to say, I blamed myself and because of my shame and guilt continued to act out in ways that put me in increasingly dangerous situations. There were date rapes and physical beatings. There were abusive relationships, two abortions before the age of 21 and countless suicide attempts, one that put me in the hospital after I severed seven tendons and a major nerve in my wrist.*
*from Amanda's story*

*I made a bunch of bad choices when it came to relationships. I picked people who treated me abusively without knowing that's what I was doing.*
*from Valerie's story*

During the childbearing year this may play out very intensely in the relationship with maternity care providers. The vulnerabilities and high emotions during pregnancy and birth may contain elements so similar to the abuse and trauma dynamics that a survivor's reactions may seem out of proportion to the reality of the clinical relationship. But these reactions can make sense in light of her past experience with abusive caregivers. This can happen to anyone. However, for a significant proportion of childhood sexual abuse survivors struggling with posttraumatic stress conditions, interpersonal difficulties reach a level of significant impairment. Keeping a productive alliance for maternity care may be a challenge.

Elements of this sort of interpersonal sensitivity can become evident over the nine

Chapter 1—Life before Motherhood                                             25

months of maternity care: Fear of abandonment, intense and unstable interpersonal reactions, impulsivity, self-harming gestures, reactive moods and intense anger can be provoked by big and small events. Cindy distills a mild-mannered sense of the fear of abandonment when she says:

*In terms of relationships, I have had a hard time. I find it hard to believe that people are sincerely my friends and worry that somehow I'll ruin it and they'll be gone.*
*from Cindy's story*

Tamar gives a sense of the level of intensity and the categorical extremes of her emotional reactions to her caregivers when she says:

*...we had to transport me to the hospital where the nurses were great and the doctors the spawn of demons.*

Clients with these tendencies may be helped by anticipating that no single caregiver can fit their ideal. Providers should be ready to hold steady through conflicts and strong reactions. Lots of information can be found in the professional literature of psychotherapy about how to work with the interpersonal reactions that occur for both client and caregiver. But very few midwives or obstetricians have training about how to evaluate and manage personality disorder relationship problems during the emotionally and interpersonally intense processes of prenatal and labor care. A three-way collaboration among client, maternity care provider and a therapist who can help with these challenging dynamics can be useful. If the client does not want to work with a therapist, a consulting relationship for the provider can be a way to increase skill in this level of interpersonal practice.

Many of the narrators told of how a good relationship with their obstetrician or midwife was therapeutic. But many recount events where they felt re-victimized, and evidence now shows that women's perceptions of birth providers as uncaring or untrustworthy predict post-birth PTSD (Soet, Brack and DiIorio 2003). Birth emergencies are more likely to lead to post-birth PTSD in the context of a negative relationship. From a busy health care provider's perspective, clients who expect too much or are too needy are an added source of role stress and burden. Yet, when a bad outcome occurs, the client's perception that the provider was not caring may be associated with patients suing healthcare providers. Clearly, a good relationship is worthwhile for the well-being of both parties. We will focus on maternity care relationship issues in the chapters on pregnancy and birth.

### *SUBSTANCE ABUSE AND DISORDERED EATING*
The symptoms of PTSD are noxious. Not surprisingly, people do things to try to feel better or at least to feel more in control or loved. Some self-medicate with substances to reduce the feelings of hyperarousal or numbness (Miller and Guidry 2001).(1.25, 1.26)

*My mother had to go into the hospital at one time, and I was in a panic because I had to stay at home with him, by myself. It was a feeling of sheer terror. I will never forget it. He would climb into bed with me, and do things. I used to drink beer before I went to school, and some dope, and did a lot of drugs.*
*from Kathy's story*

▼ 1.25

PTSD was comorbid (co-occurring) with other mental health disorders in 79% of women. The PTSD came first 53–84% of the time when the woman also had a mood, substance use or conduct disorder.

Women with PTSD also had a 71.8% rate of depression compared with 25.6% among women who had not ever had PTSD (a 4.5-fold risk). Risk for alcohol abuse or dependence was 2.5 times as great and for drug abuse or dependence was 4.5 times as great.

Only 21% of those with PTSD had no additional psychiatric diagnosis besides PTSD. Nearly half (43.6%) had three or more other disorders.

Kessler, et al. 1995

▼ 1.26

In a study of 1007 young adult members of an urban HMO, 11.6% had had PTSD in their lifetime and 13.9% had a history of drug abuse or dependence. Risk for drug abuse or dependence was 4.5 times greater among those with PTSD and no greater for those who had been exposed to a traumatic event but did not develop PTSD. Depression (without PTSD) conveyed 2.9 times the risk of a drug problem. PTSD *with* depression conveyed a 7.6-fold risk of drug abuse or dependence.

Chilcoat and Breslau 1998

*Life went on for me. I struggled with anxiety and depression when I went away to college. I started a lifestyle of "partying" which involved drinking, smoking marijuana and being sexually promiscuous. Not surprisingly I fell away from the Catholic church and God. I was desperately seeking love, affirmation, feelings of worthiness and acceptance. And now, I realize, I was also seeking revenge, control and power over the males in my life. I thought sex was the answer to feeling acceptable to a man, but deep down I knew better.*

*from Ann's story*

People can misuse food to soothe their feelings. Their eating habits can become disordered in an attempt to arrive at a body image that feels safer or as a way to exert control (Dansky, et al. 1997).

*I became anorexic. I didn't want to look like a woman; I wanted to be little again.*

*from Nina's story*

*I stop eating to numb myself. I vomit to purge the pain. I don't want to feel.*

*from Colleen's story*

*I protected myself by becoming really shy and fat. I was so pathologically shy that I didn't speak.*

*from Kathy's story*

*I began to stuff my emotions, feelings and thoughts into my body. I would binge, and binge and binge, then purge and purge and purge. Then I would smoke and smoke and smoke cigarettes. The scary thing, especially now that I'm a mother, is that I can't understand how my mother couldn't see the signals of my distress. I would constantly throw fits of rage and madness, and then I would say to my mother, "I'm throwing my guts up." She was in such denial that she did not even ask, "Why are you doing this? What's wrong? Did anyone hurt you? What's bothering you?" As a survivor and a mother today, I see how important it is to talk with your children about issues and be open with partners.*

*from Kim's story*

Not everyone who uses substances or food to self-medicate for the symptoms of PTSD becomes an alcoholic, addict or anorexic. But any substance abuse and abnormal nutrition is a problem in pregnancy. Tobacco, alcohol, drugs and extremes of food intake or exercise all adversely affect the fetus. Some women are able to stop using substances and eat and exercise appropriately during pregnancy, but others are not. Research shows that abused women and adolescents may have more trouble stopping (Grimstad, et al. 1998; Stevens-Simon and McAnarney 1994). Risk of relapse postpartum is high. Getting combined treatment for PTSD and substance use before pregnancy, and building in extra support to prevent relapse if posttraumatic stress is exacerbated by pregnancy, is desirable (Stewart, et al. 1998).

## POOR SELF-CARE: HIGH RISK SEXUAL BEHAVIOR, REVICTIMIZATION AND SELF-HARM

Although the exact reasons are still being studied, undoubtedly some abuse survivors go through a time of reacting to the abuse with very strong negative behaviors, especially during adolescence. Sometimes these resolve in early adulthood, but often some degree of poor self-care persists. Some research shows that those girls who develop PTSD are more at risk for harm and self-harm. Numerous studies confirm that a subset of survivors have unprotected sex with multiple partners, have intimate partners who batter and rape them, and resort to self-harming practices from cutting themselves to suicide. These problems may not stop just because the girl is pregnant.(1.27, 1.28, 1.29)

▼ 1.27

*I started cutting myself. I was so full of rage. I felt so unimportant and so trapped. Where could I go at 12 years old?*

*from Nina's story*

Self harm has been defined as conscious intent to harm oneself by a repetitive pattern of low lethality, socially unacceptable behaviors that result in actual alteration of the body. Although not all women who self-harm have a history of sexual abuse, self-harm co-occurs with dissociation, depression and other bodily problems such as eating disorders, and this pattern of problems is often found among women with a history of severe, early childhood abuse.

*One day, in a state of depression, I took a handful of pills and lay down to go to sleep. Thank the Lord my sister came to my room a little later, and I told her what I did. My dad rushed me to the hospital. That's kind of a blur, but that's when I finally started to get help. I was in the psychiatric ward for a few days, I think, and I had to talk to a therapist. I would cut myself with razors and burn myself. I had slashes on my wrist at the time (not deep). That's also when I started dealing with my dad's drinking. I couldn't tell the counselor about what he did to me.*

*from Sarah's story*

Turell and Armsworth (expanding on the definition by Walsh and Rosen) 2000

▼ 1.28

Among an urban sample of young adult HMO members, 46.2% of those with PTSD reported thinking about suicide, compared with 29.9% of those with other mental health disorders and 8.7% of those with no disorder. 17.2% of those with PTSD had ever attempted suicide, compared with 7.4% who had other psychiatric disorders and 1.2% of those with no disorder.

Some survivors use sex to soothe themselves or to meet unmet needs for intimacy. Bass and Davis put it this way, "It makes sense that survivors who received all their attention and affection sexually as children now sexualize even nonsexual needs."(p. 259)

Breslau 2001

*I knew I was a good girl, and I knew better, but I couldn't say no. So many times I remember not wanting to have sex, but just going along with it.*

*from Sarah's story*

▼ 1.29

In two studies of pregnant adolescents, those maltreated in childhood were seven times more likely to have suicidal ideation (specific thoughts of killing themselves) and to have attempted suicide.

*I would leave him and run to one of the young men I liked, and would fuck all the bad feelings away.*

*from Nan's story*

Bayatpur, Wells and Holford 1992
Koniak-Griffin and Lesser 1996

*I became a model child. I did what I was told, I smiled and laughed at school and at home; I never did anything outstanding, or incredible. I just survived. And I slept with everyone. I had eight partners by the time I was 15 years old. I contracted chlamydia from a one-night stand with a college kid who thought I was 18. I thought that sex was a way to be loved, and if I had sex with them, they must love me, right?*
*from Amy's story*

*Let's see, so—promiscuous, drugs, alcohol, high school dropout, college dropout, abusive relationships, bad temper, you name it. My childhood/adolescence really messed me up.*
*from Tina's story*

For some, drug use and sex become entangled when sex becomes a means to pay for drugs. In a qualitative study of PTSD and pregnancy, addicted women wanted maternity care providers to know that past abuse played a big role in how entangled they became with abusive men, drugs and sexual exploitation (Seng, et al. 2002).

*Now it's a vicious cycle this whole drug world has going. Need money to get drugs. Turn tricks to get money. Take drugs to numb the sense of worthlessness turning tricks gives you. Turn tricks to buy more drugs. Do you see where this is going? But I made a lot of money, which was a good thing, as I ended up with a $200 a day addiction.*
*from Kala's story*

Women abused in childhood, especially those who develop PTSD, are more likely to form intimate partnerships with abusers.

*The only way to get a loan for a house at the time was to get married. Things weren't great, but I wasn't feeling really good about myself either, and Dick had a drinking problem. He was verbally abusing me at that time, but we got our paperwork together to be married anyway. He turned to me right after that, moments after that, and said "I got you now, you're trapped."…And I'm sitting here and thinking, "Oh, my God, what is this?" And thinking that, "oh, well, maybe this is what marriage is about, too."*
*from Kathy's story*

During pregnancy, sexually transmitted infections from trichomonas to chlamydia to herpes can cause complications from preterm labor to pneumonia, blindness and even death in the newborn. Blows to the abdomen can cause bleeding from the placenta and death. Recent research has shown that homicide of pregnant women by their intimate partners is actually the leading cause of maternal death in the United States (Horon and Cheng 2001; Krulewich, et al. 2001). Suicide as a cause of maternal death is not yet well-studied, but narrators for this book disclose that they were at risk for suicide during pregnancy. Again, sometimes pregnancy is protective, for a time, against these severe problems; sometimes it provokes them.

Medical standards of care require testing all women for sexually transmitted infections in pregnancy, and screening for intimate partner violence and assessing danger for those involved with an abuser. Adolescents also need to be screened for abuse by their parents as well as their partner. And, although the thought seems terrible to contemplate, pregnant women who are especially at risk due to the accumulation of PTSD, depression and current negative life events like battering need to be assessed for suicidality. Anyone contemplating suicide can reach out and get help.(1.30, 1.31) Women who have thoughts of suicide that they need to manage alone for a while may be able to also make themselves a list of "things to do when I'm desperate," to help decrease the intensity, as suggested in *The Courage to Heal*. Bass and Davis provide a sample list of things people can do to calm themselves down when they are feeling desperate.(1.32)

***EFFECTS: DEPRESSION***
Some abuse survivors are depressed but do not develop posttraumatic stress disorder *per se* because they do not have the intrusive re-experiencing or hyperarousal symptoms that are critical aspects of PTSD.(1.33) Research shows that PTSD and depression occur together and the two disorders overlap because they share symptoms such as loss of interest or pleasure in activities and insomnia. But depression also occurs in survivors without PTSD, and many of the somatic, interpersonal and high-risk behaviors that occur with PTSD also occur with depression. That having grown up in a difficult family environment and being abused would lead to many of the symptoms of depression is understandable. These symptoms include feeling sad or empty, slowed down or agitated, or worthless or guilty, as well as having difficulty concentrating and thinking about death.

*I was very self-destructive. I really hated myself and the things I did. I would get depressed a lot and just sit in my room and cry, and wonder what was wrong with me. I knew, though, that it was related to what my dad did to me.*
*I remember wanting to talk about it, and I did share it with a close friend for the first time when I was 15, maybe. She cried for me, but I just sat there thinking I should be crying too. But I was too detached from my real feelings.*
*I felt like a split personality—the straight "A," innocent student by day, pleasant and successful in school and the young girl who ruminated every night about suicide and felt unclean, unworthy and hopeless. My nighttime prayer before sleep was that I would survive until I finished high*

▼ 1.30

Many free nation-wide crisis services provide 24-hour help and facilitate finding local services:

National Hopeline Network:
1-800-SUICIDE (784-2433)

National Domestic Violence Hotline:
1-800-799-SAFE (7233)
1-800-787-3224 (TDD)

Rape, Abuse & Incest National Network Hotline routes instantly to the rape crisis center nearest the caller:
1-800-656-HOPE (4673)

▼ 1.31

Therapist Types

Psychiatrist—A psychiatrist is a physician who specializes in the treatment of mental disorders. They have the ability to prescribe medications.

Psychologist (clinical or counseling)—A psychologist has a doctorate in psychology and does testing and/or psychotherapy.

Clinical Social Worker—A clinical social worker has a master's degree in social work and is trained and licensed to do psychotherapy.

Psychiatric Advanced Practice Nurse—A nurse with a master's degree who has certification to provide psychotherapy and/or can prescribe medications (varies state by state).

Pastoral Counselor—A clergy person with experience in counseling. He or she may or may not have formal education in psychology.

Peer Counselor—A layperson who has gone through training in one-to-one peer counseling, usually in relation to specific topics such as substance abuse or sexual assault.

▼ 1.32

There are many possible ways of coping. Here is one sample list from *The Courage to Heal* of ways in which a survivor might soothe herself...

**Things to Do When I'm Desperate**
1. Breathe.
2. Get my teddy bear.
3. Put on a relaxation tape.
4. Get in my rocking chair.
5. Call Natalie. 555-9887.
6. Call Vicki if Natalie's not home. 555-6632. Keep calling down my list of support people. [Put their names and numbers here.]
7. Stroke the cat.
8. Take a hot bath.
9. Write a hundred times: "I'm safe. I love myself. Others love me," or "It's safe for me to relax now."
10. Run around the block three times.
11. Listen to soothing music.
12. Pray.
13. Breathe.
14. Yell into my pillow.
15. Watch an old movie on TV or read a mystery novel.
16. Eat macaroni and cheese.
17. Start again at the top.

Bass and Davis 1992

▼ 1.33

Women with a history of childhood sexual abuse who develop depression are less likely to have recovered from that episode of depression within a year.

Review in Zimmerman and Mattia 1999

*school and go off to college, where I would have the possibility of a real life and happiness.*
*from Elizabeth's story*

Another big difference between PTSD and depression (besides the symptom profiles) is that the PTSD diagnosis can be made only in relation to a known traumatic event. If the survivor does not disclose a trauma, her mental health symptoms will not be seen as posttraumatic, and depression (or depression and anxiety together) is a logical alternative for conceptualizing what is wrong. Sometimes survivors do not disclose that they were abused because they feel too embarrassed or confused about it. Sometimes they minimize it, thinking that it was "no big deal" and they should be able to "just get over it." Sometimes they do not make the connection between the abuse and the psychological distress or behavioral difficulties they are having. And sometimes they do not fully remember the abuse, and so cannot make a clear statement to a therapist or health care provider because they do not have a clear understanding of what happened to them.

### *EFFECTS: ALTERED MEMORY*

The issue of traumatic amnesia and delayed recall of sexual abuse is controversial. From the earliest study of sexual trauma in the time of Freud, Charcot and Janet, a focus of theory has been the disruption traumatic stress causes to explicit, narrative memory of what happened (Herman 1997). The phenomenon of traumatic amnesia is widely accepted and is, in fact, one of the recognized symptoms of PTSD (criterion C3: inability to recall an important aspect of the trauma) (APA 2000). At the base of the controversy is the question of whether recall of aspects of the trauma that occur during psychotherapy are reliable or are the result of suggestion by the therapist, a caregiver who has powerful influence on the client. This matters not only for the safe, ethical conduct of psychotherapy, but also because some survivors confront their abusers, sue them for damages or press criminal charges based on what they remember. Research findings exist that support both the point that people forget things and remember them later, with varying amounts of accuracy or distortion, and the point that false memories can be suggested and yet seem very real (Brown, et al. 1998; McNally 2003). However, not all of the research cited in the debate is specific to the context of trauma. In addition, very little research takes into account the defense mechanism of dissociation, which is understandable since it is hard to measure, and distressing human participants in research to the point of causing them to dissociate is unethical. This limitation leaves a gap in our ability to speak about the issue from a firm scientific base. While waiting for better research that explains traumatic amnesia with delayed recall, expert therapists tread carefully when asking about potential past trauma exposures.

In light of that, some of the narrators in this book include descriptions of delayed recall of sexual abuse. In addition, many more describe a sometimes long process of "connecting the dots" or integrating the who-what-where-when-how of the abuse along with their emotional responses and adult understandings. A few describe how birth or other events triggered recall of past sexual abuse and onset of PTSD using descriptions that are similar to such reports in the clinical literature and in qualitative research (Courtois and Courtois-Riley 1992; Seng, et al. 2002, 2004; Josephs 1996).

*Then, one evening, sitting with my legs drawn up on the floor in a friend's living room with the lamp light behind my left shoulder, I remembered. I remembered episodes of "special games" that a 17-year-old male babysitter would play with six-year-old me. I went home that evening and told everything to my husband, and it felt as though I had never forgotten. I felt relieved, at some level, to understand that I was wounded; I wasn't "normal." Then I slid into deep depression.*

*from Kate's story*

*Although I can remember, it was not something that was always in my mind. I can remember, but I forget too, if that makes sense. God just helps me not to think about it.*

*from Tara's story*

*I felt so jealous of the people who had always clearly remembered their abuse.*

*from Lena's story*

*I became symptomatic when my son was born; I began recovering after my mother died.*

*from Lena's story*

*I remembered my childhood incest the year I graduated from college at 25 years old. The next two years were intense ones, full of fierce cycles of pain, anger, forgiveness efforts, relief at "all the pieces finally coming together" and round again.*

*from Beth's story*

*My father died in early November, and I went to attend a residency in early February. There, probably because of some of the people I met, and because I had so much time to be with my grief, all of these memories began to flood back. I became a friend of a man who shared with me that he had been sexually abused, and somehow that allowed me to open the dam. It didn't stop for months, and it was frightening as hell.*

*from Margaret's story*

### OUTLOOK FOR HELP AND RECOVERY

The severity of the long-term effects of abuse is as varied as the severity of the abuse itself, and levels of resilience, coping and support also vary. Abuse occurs in all socioeconomic circumstances and in all ethnic groups, but having more education and income seems broadly to increase the resources available for treatment and for living in environments with lower risk for trauma exposure in

▼ 1.34

In a study of poor women and their health care, those with PTSD had worse perceptions of health care generally, expressing greater dissatisfaction, more barriers, and more problems with the healthcare provider relationship. They were more likely to be nervous or afraid, to be concerned they would not get good care, to not trust the provider, to find the staff rude and to feel staff did not understand their problems. These negative perceptions appeared to affect care-seeking because, although they reported more pain and had more chronic health conditions, the women with PTSD tended to have equal or fewer outpatient visits and hospitalizations, but more ER visits.

Bassuk, et al. 2001

▼ 1.35

In a study of 131 ethnically diverse abused women in a primary care setting, 36% of whom were African American, 34% Hispanic and 30% Anglo American, the level of PTSD symptoms did not differ by ethnicity.

Silva, et al. 1997

In an analysis of service use data, however, diagnosis and treatment of PTSD and other trauma-related mental health problems occurred at half the rate for African American women compared to European American women.

Seng, Kohn-Wood and Odera 2005

adulthood.(1.34, 1.35) Women living in poverty have a harder time. Being a member of an ethnic minority group also may increase the disparity between need for treatment and treatment received. For example, in a study of young adults in Detroit (Breslau, et al. 1997), African-Americans had the same risk for PTSD when controlling for poverty and urban (higher crime) residence. But because African Americans were more likely to be affected by poverty and neighborhood violence, their actual rate of PTSD was twice as high. Yet in an analysis of the Medicaid claims data for women in Michigan from the same time period, the African American women's rate of diagnosis and treatment for PTSD was half that of Anglo American women (Seng, Kohn-Wood and Odera 2005).

We know from these narrators' accounts that many use recovery efforts that do not involve professional mental health services. We do not know, however, the extent to which foregoing psychotherapy or medication is by choice or due to barriers to seeking care. Disadvantage is compounded: poor and minority women have more trauma exposures but fewer material resources to put toward recovering from posttraumatic problems. Needs for the basic necessities and basic safety likely take priority over the need for mental and physical health. Issues of stigma also affect women from non-dominant cultural groups more, especially during the childbearing year. As an African American participant in a qualitative study put it, "being pregnant...not married and not living up to 'society's norms'" was already enough to have to carry as stigma into medical care encounters (Seng, et al. 2002, p. 366).

Adult women who experience racism, classism or heterosexism in the health care system protect themselves from even more stigmatizing reactions by not disclosing their abuse history and needs for trauma-related care.

Adolescent women who are pregnant also are subjected to ageist reactions. Their concerns about mandatory reporting and what would happen to them if abuse they were experiencing came to the attention of the child welfare system may prevent some of them from disclosing their needs. This speaks to the need for health care providers to routinely ask *everyone* whether they have trauma-related needs in a way that shows real openness to hearing about them. It also speaks to the need to look for signs of posttraumatic stress problems, even if the woman chooses not to disclose past abuse and denies any posttraumatic stress problems. The rates of abuse and posttraumatic mental and physical health problems are so high that acting on a "presumptive diagnosis" if trauma-related problems are seen is reasonable. Responding therapeutically without having your tentative diagnosis confirmed by disclosure is possible.

> ▼ 1.36
> Social support (both emotional and material) decreases maternal stress and is associated with better perinatal outcomes. Yet adolescents and adults abused in childhood are less likely to report adequate social support for a variety of reasons.
> Paarlberg, et al. 1999
> Hall 1999

## *RELATIONSHIPS*

The relationships we have are a significant part of our lives, and we already have looked at how abuse within a caregiving relationship can impact the life of a survivor. Our first relationships can be a template for those to follow, and overcoming unhealthy patterns in relationship can be the hardest part of recovering from the effects of sexual abuse. Even hostages in war may develop an emotional attachment to their captors.

Relationships also can be healing, and establishing positive attachments can make all the difference in recovery. Kay shared that at some point she disclosed the abuse to her mother, which was validating for her. She then alluded to being "in and out" of counseling for several years. For many survivors, this therapeutic relationship is the means of much of their healing. The members of a support group are crucial to the recovery of some women. Kay goes on to speak about her relationship with her husband and the intricacies of being married. Because positive attachments are so integral to healing, we will discuss their power more in the chapters on mothering and healing.

A main reason for including a focus on relationships in this chapter on life before motherhood is that some survivors will have good social support, but others will not.(1.36) Maternity care providers cannot assume that the woman's parents or partner will be helpful. They may even be dangerous. Finding out who in her life will support her during pregnancy and postpartum is important.

The fear of being blamed or losing connection in general may render the survivor unable to seek positive relationships or to begin a serious recovery effort. Wendi shared that her lack of trust in other people hindered her from starting recovery until she was able to read a book that allowed her to see the situation from an objective position:

> *I was having all the symptoms of clinical depression but didn't seek help because of a lack of trust. I didn't think anyone would help me.... Enduring his treatment had given me the belief that something was very wrong with me. I felt that if I were a different person he wouldn't have treated me that way. That was the first belief that I had to change to begin to reclaim myself. I learned that as a child I was vulnerable and in need of care and love. I needed to feel safe in my environment to develop a healthy belief system. Since I never really felt safe I developed a belief system that was flawed at its core. Rebuilding a belief system is not an easy task, especially when you don't trust anyone.*
>
> *from Wendi's story*

Kelly entered her recovery through the support of a roommate and connections she made in church. Her roommate provided her with a safe place to be and work to do; the pastors at the churches she attended provided her with spiritual sustenance. She was able to enter therapy as a result of these interactions:

*When I was 20 I had a huge breakdown. I had many different kinds of flashbacks, panic/anxiety attacks, hysterical crying and moaning. I had voices in my head of abused children and many different people. I wanted to die very much. I thought my life was over. My poor roommate Liz took care of me and I couldn't get off the couch for a long time. She hired me at the farm market next door and let me go home anytime that I had an attack. It got pretty bad. Sometimes I would venture to church where there always seemed to be a message of hope for me.*

*from Kelly's story*

Many accounts tell of how having one supportive adult to turn to while growing up can make all the difference for a survivor. For Tara, the supportive adult was her junior high school teacher:

*I learned ways of not being alone with my dad. Yet at the same time, I desperately needed someone who would take his place. The Lord provided that in my junior high teacher. I never told him what had happened. It never really occurred to me to tell. But he took me under his wing, and he unknowingly became a surrogate father. I would go to him for advice about all kinds of things, and somehow I knew that he would understand.*

*from Tara's story*

Some individuals who have been abused finally feel and act on the need for therapy when they are at a safe distance in time and space and their lives are basically stable. Safety is considered a very desirable prerequisite to therapy that focuses on integrating and processing memory of trauma (Herman 1997). Gwen was in such a situation when she finally disclosed to her roommate Michelle what had happened to her, and was able to begin therapy as a result:

*Finally, I was about to leave home and start a new life. Everything that had happened to me I had buried deeply away forever, or so I thought. So, I started college, no problem, and actually had a boyfriend that treated me pretty nice. Things were for once looking up for me. Then one day, my roommate, Michelle, out of the blue tells me she is an incest survivor and wants to know if I would like to volunteer with her at a place called rape crisis services. At that very moment the wall I had built over the years came crashing down in a matter of seconds. Very nonchalantly, I told her I could not volunteer due to my schedule and I tried to forget what she had told me.*

*But as days passed, I could not study or concentrate on anything except that I too had been sexually abused.... Soon afterwards I started group therapy at the place where she had asked me to volunteer. Thus, began my journey. I began learning about myself, the different pieces of myself and how in crisis one would take over: the child who wanted to be good, the teenager who didn't give a fuck about anybody or the adult me who worked hard not to let anyone see how screwed up I really was. Group therapy made me realize I wasn't alone… that responding physically didn't mean you wanted it, and it is still okay to like sex. I began slowly putting the pieces together, making myself whole.*

*from Gwen's story*

We've already discussed the variety of ways survivors may disclose their abuse history. Some survivors are not able to do so until they are in a therapeutic relationship, often having begun counseling for some other reason. Amy was having a hard time with a class at school and ended up sharing her truth about the abuse with the school counselor:

*My senior year, I finally told someone in authority what had happened. I had been put into a pre-calculus class that was a little too hard for me, and I wasn't doing well. When I learned that I was going to get a D in the class, I went to the counselor in hysterics, and told her everything. When I was done, she brought in the school psychologist to talk to me. I cried so hard as she told me that none of it was my fault, that my mother was an awful person for not helping me, and that Fred was an evil man to have harmed me in such a way. I couldn't believe that they were being so nice to me, and that they knew it wasn't my fault. It was also a great relief to hear that my mother was an awful person, and that I could be angry with her, and hate her as much as I hated Fred. Someone listened, someone believed and someone helped me for the first time in my life. They contacted the police and a child psychologist. The police said that I wasn't in any danger now, so they would not pursue the matter, let alone press charges. That still bothers me to this day. I was well within my rights to press charges, but I was only 18, I didn't know that then. And all they had was my word.*

*from Amy's story*

Kathy began therapy in an effort to deal with the alcoholism in her family, and then began her recovery from sexual abuse:

*I remained in therapy through the breakup of my marriage. Started off dealing with the alcoholism in my family. Then the abuse started slowly coming out. I allowed myself to remember and feel bad, and told myself that it was okay to feel bad, and then to start feeling good.*

*from Kathy's story*

Katherine entered therapy in order to deal with anxiety:

*In my early twenties I began having extreme anxiety attacks and sought therapy. I lucked into an extremely compassionate and helpful therapist. Three years later I was anxiety-free. A meditation practice also helped me to heal. I can't overstress the value of a quiet and calm mind.*

*from Katherine's story*

## SEXUAL INTIMACY

The quality of a survivor's love relationships is affected when she is on her healing journey. Being intimate requires a level of trust that may be difficult to achieve because it means risking hurt or disappointment and becoming vulnerable to another person. For those reasons and others, working through feelings that arise in the context of sexual and emotional intimacy is difficult. We will revisit this topic again in the chapter on healing. Kay shared her fears about disclosing her abuse to her husband:

*…I was not only afraid that he wouldn't understand, I was also afraid that he would look at me in a different light if I went into detail about things that happened to me. Damaged goods. I closed myself off from him, which was not only difficult for me because I felt very alone, but also difficult for him because he didn't understand what was happening to me or why I was acting the way I did….*

*from Kay's story*

Other survivors echoed Kay's fears and hesitations:

*At 16 I went to my first dance in the new school. I was surprised that a boy kept asking me to dance, because I had always been a wallflower at the old school. We became a regular couple, and in 1961 he proposed. I was on top of the world but I couldn't say yes because I would not be a virgin for marriage. I had to tell him my awful secret. He still wanted to marry me but we did not realize the trials I would have to overcome.*

*from Elaine's story*

*I had anxiety attacks for months before my wedding. I got so bad I couldn't drive over bridges. I couldn't get in the fast lane on the highway. I couldn't go in the supermarket without feeling like I'd hyperventilate and pass out waiting in line. I was a mess. I really fell apart. It had to do with not being able to "turn back." That was all I could think of, and obsessed on, not being able to turn back. It was the strangest thing. I hope it never happens again!*

*from Tina's story*

*My road to healing starts with my husband. He was the first man who ever loved me unconditionally. I had many relationships and many more sexual partners. None cared like Chris did. He took a heart that was hardened to men and cracked it open. His love showed me that there were other types of men out there that were not just after sex.*

*from Dawn's story*

*We married and were part of a close-knit home church. I still did not connect with women in a deep way. I was quiet, yet nice. I still felt something was wrong with me, and sometimes felt depressed. I never thought about the abuse. Our sex life was fine. I didn't initiate, but could go along and even receive some pleasure.*

*from Deborah's story*

This idea of being "damaged goods" seriously affected some narrators' self-esteem and ability to form meaningful relationships. Some kept the history of abuse partitioned off from their partners, fearing condemnation or wanting to spare the partners the feelings that would be provoked by knowing this information. This may have meant not telling about the abuse at all, or at least not sharing all the details. In this respect Kay worried that the relative safety she felt in her marriage would be compromised by her disclosure:

*How could I explain to him why I would cry when we were being intimate? How could I explain to him why I would jump up, lock myself in the bathroom and take long, hot showers when he tried to initiate sex? How could I explain why I went into unexplained rages when he touched me in a certain way? Also, when you keep a secret for so many years it's really difficult to talk about it. After so many years of abuse, I felt like I had a billion layers of memories and emotions hidden inside of me and I didn't want to face them. I was finally in a safe place and I didn't want anything to mess that up.*

*from Kay's story*

For other contributors, that sense of safety with their partners provided them with their first opportunity to disclose, like Sarah:

*One night I just broke down with my boyfriend and told him I wanted to die. I knew I needed to get help. I started seeing a counselor, talking about the abuse, and reading everything I could about sexual abuse. Just talking to someone about it helped a lot. I didn't feel like I was hiding such a shameful secret anymore. I started to accept myself, and forgive myself.*

*from Sarah's story*

Cubbi also had a positive experience once she chose to disclose to her husband:

*I knew I needed to tell my husband about the abuse; I knew I needed help. It was the hardest thing I had ever done, but I told him. I cried, he cried, we cried together. Then he said, "He's never going to hurt you again" and he got in his car and he confronted my father. My father told my husband that the sex was consensual. Alan banished him from our lives and told him that he was never to contact us again.*

*from Cubbi's story*

Being in a relationship with a partner who does not abuse can be very healing in and of itself. Our contributors shared with us the importance of such relationships:

*Through thick and thin, as they say, stood my husband. My husband comes from a completely different background, class status, educational status and religion. This meant he truly, no matter what he tried, could not understand, and in some cases barely believed, it was all true. But he was and still is the one of the few people in my life who loves me unconditionally. His real support of me through life is unending.*

*from Margaret's story*

The sexual part of the intimacy within a relationship can be particularly challenging for survivors. The writers told of the extreme difficulty in making oneself sexually vulnerable and dealing with the powerful emotions that can arise. For Beth, such feelings emerged on her wedding night:

*My new husband had just made a vow of monogamy for the first time in his life, and we didn't even have a wedding night. I was suddenly in true survivor mode, angry and weeping and not very articulate, and very celibate. I was frighteningly suicidal off and on for the next year and a half.*

*from Beth's story*

Beth's marriage did not survive, but getting married was for her a catalyst for starting her recovery. Others told of how memories and emotions related to abuse emerged only after they were married, often during sexually or emotionally intimate times with a partner. For Dawn, and Cassandra, this happened a year into marriage:

*I didn't remember the rape until years later, after being married for about a year. The memories came flooding back during an intimate time with my husband. Thankfully he was understanding and compassionate.*

*from Dawn's story*

*Many years later, I met my husband. We were together for one year, when the problems of what happened began to emerge. It was like someone opened an attic door and bats came flying out. One day, after having intercourse, all the emotions just burst out and I began to cry hysterically. At that point, I told him what had happened, but he didn't know what to do or say. After that, I began to have severe mood swings, especially during premenstrual times. That went on for about a year. Finally, I began to have trouble controlling my anger.*

*from Cassandra's story*

Dealing with the intensity of emotion that sex can evoke created for some of the narrators a situation where they did what they likely did to survive the abuse in the first place: they dissociated, or "went away" during sex:

*After a disastrous dating relationship with an abusive guy, I married a wonderful man with whom making love was uncomfortable at best and at worst, I wasn't even there for it. I had this uncanny ability to disappear, leave my body and come back at a later point. Sometimes I went into the wallpaper, sometimes into the rest of my day and sometimes into nowhere. This wasn't normal, was it?*

*from Kate's story*

*For years I disassociated during sex. I can remember it was like being up in the corner of the room floating, watching a porno movie, except I was watching myself and feeling pain.*

*from Amy's story*

The extent of difficulty some survivors have, even years after the abuse has ended, mirrors the extent to which recovery is challenging. A healing relationship is a major component of recovery for many of the narrators and for survivors generally. As Judith Herman (1997, p. 133) succinctly stated, "Recovery can take place only within the context of relationships; it cannot occur in isolation. In her renewed connections with other people, the survivor re-creates the psychological faculties that were damaged or deformed by the traumatic experience." For many survivors this need is met by a therapeutic relationship with a psychotherapist, often supplemented by therapy or support groups, 12-step programs, community women's groups, church groups and women friends. Finding the right therapeutic relationship is very important and worthwhile, and we will discuss this more in the chapter on healing.

For *some* of the narrators, pregnancy and impending motherhood was an impetus to seek therapy in an effort to "heal" the effects of the abuse prior to beginning the relationship with the infant. For others, working on abuse issues was "too much to deal with" during pregnancy. But extra emotional support during the childbearing year may be especially important because a well-cared-for woman whose basic needs are met will be best able to meet the needs of her infant.

### **PREGNANCY AS AN IMPETUS FOR CHANGE**
Pregnancy, especially with the first child, is a time of change and challenge for any woman. The more strengths a woman has when she becomes pregnant, the better: enough resources, enough support, enough mental health, enough physical health, enough willingness to mother. Seemingly the further along in the recovery

process the woman is, the less she has to cope with posttraumatic stress and the more she can focus on posttraumatic growth and developing as a mother (Seng et al. 2002).

## BREAKING THE CHAIN

One of the strongest sentiments voiced over and over by the narrative contributors is the idea of breaking the "chain" or "cycle" of violence. The women expressed the strong will to raise their children differently than they were raised. They may not have known exactly what a good parent looks like, but they sure knew what not to do, and they voiced a fierce determination to stop the cycle of violence. They voiced that they could not change the past, but they could take control over the future. Kay told us that she has learned to trust herself as a mother, and that she is determined to never do anything to harm her children.

Many of the narrators wrote of how recognizing that they had inherited a legacy of abuse that they did not want to pass on was a first step toward recovery. Being able to understand the context of their lives, their relationships to others and to themselves, was invaluable. Both Valerie and Heather add their voices to Kay's when sharing their views on the intergenerational cycle of violence and its impact on their lives:

*My parents came from dysfunctional families where they were abused as well. They chose to continue the cycle of abuse by abusing me. I chose to break that circle and walk through what happened to me and not pass it on to my children. I chose to be kind and better than them, despite the torture I endured growing up. I chose to respect life as something beautiful and spiritual, where they chose to destroy it any way they could. When they get older and look back on their lives they will have guilt and regret. I'll have accomplishment, strength and pride for a job well done. I am a survivor and this is what happened.*

*from Valerie's story*

*I come from a family with a history of sexual and physical abuse. My mother's parents were both abusive, one sexually, the other physically. I can only assume a trail of further abuse, leading back who knows how far. My mother hoped to stop the cycle with herself. Instead it is stopping with me*

*from Heather's story*

## WHERE IN THE PROCESS

The narrators frequently expressed the wish to be good mothers and stop the cycle of vulnerability and violence, but this desire was not easily fulfilled. The survivors who wrote narratives for this book were telling complex trauma recovery stories that unfolded over time and usually were intersected by childbearing before recovery was complete. They use metaphors like "journey" or words like "process" to convey that recovery took a long period in their lives, while maternity care providers often use the common medical term "history." "History of childhood sexual abuse" implies that it is in the past. The work of getting it to be truly/mostly in the past is often long and hard. To illustrate this point, we return to the lines from Kay's story that are interspersed to tell us where she was in the process of recovering from abuse trauma, starting when the abuse ended at age 14:

> *I kept my secret for a few more years. These years were very difficult. I tried to bury what had happened to me and forget. I was acting out quite a lot.*
> *When I was 17, I told my mother.*
> *I was in and out of counseling for the next few years.*
> *During these years I got married. My husband kind of knew about my past history of abuse, but I didn't go into much detail at first....*
> *During my first pregnancy...I blocked out a lot of emotion and proceeded through it almost numb.*
> *My second pregnancy was extremely complicated and opened up a lot of issues for me. This pregnancy was like opening up Pandora's box. I had switched to a midwife for this pregnancy and she asked me right away if I had any history of abuse. I took a deep breath and told her yes. She told me that she would help any way she could to make my pregnancy and birth more comfortable and to refer me to a counselor if I needed to go to one.*
> *At this point I was through with counseling. I didn't think that I needed any more.*
> *When I got home I felt like I was going further and further into a downward spiral. I tried to pretend that everything was okay, but inside it was like I was thrown back in time. I turned into a scared little girl again.*
> *I felt really disconnected from my baby when we brought him home.*
> *I am now pregnant again and I'm trying to sort myself out so I can be healthy throughout this pregnancy and start off on the right foot with this baby.*
> *I have good intentions, but there still is a small child in me who panics when people get too close. I am sad to say that this even includes my children sometimes.*
> *I am trying to deal with issues as they come out. Talking to my husband and my midwife helps. They may not always have answers for me, but just knowing I have support and I don't have to be scared anymore helps a lot.*
> *Being a mother is very healing, because I know I am stopping the cycle of abuse.*

The majority of these narratives elucidate a pattern of surviving the abuse, trying to forget it and go on with life, realizing that it is taking a toll and actively addressing the resultant problems. Some survivors undoubtedly accomplish the goal of forgetting the abuse and going on with life, and their process of recovery is done. They may be particularly resilient, or have more support, or the abuse might have been on the less severe end of the spectrum. These women are not the survivors who were moved to contribute stories to this book. They probably are not the ones moved to read this book either. Although they may have a few trauma-related issues that arise during childbearing, they probably are not the clients whose needs challenge the norms of maternity care.

The rest of this book focuses on the survivors who are still on this journey or working through this process as they bear children and become mothers. Some still may have one foot in the "trying to forget" phase and may be very ambivalent about having to deal with trauma issues in pregnancy. Others will know it is taking a toll and are looking for ideas of how to respond to the issues that come up during pregnancy. Still others will be far along in recovery and will know exactly what they need. A few will be way back in a "surviving" phase, either because they are young and still dependent on abusive parents or because they are with an abusive partner.

This chapter focused on what happened in childhood, how it affected the women

# Chapter 1—Life before Motherhood

and how surmounting such a deep adversity in time to become a healthy mother is a process. Providers need to know that usual maternity care may not suffice. Survivors need to know (or already know all too well) that their experiences of pregnancy may not fit the stereotyped cultural ideals. One midwife or doctor may not be able to meet all of their legitimate needs. Conversations at initial prenatal care visits that focus on where the survivor is in the process of recovery can help build a good working relationship and lead to appropriate and satisfying care.

A survivor could ask herself these questions to prepare to talk about it, or a clinician could have them in mind for first appointments with women who disclose an abuse history:

- In just a few words, what happened?
- How is it affecting you now? Your mental health? Your physical health?
- Where would you say you are in the recovery process?
- How do you think all of this will affect your pregnancy? Birth? Adaptation to mothering?
- Can you think what might be your worst fears and best hopes for your child bearing experience?
- What do you think are the most crucial trauma-related needs for your maternity care provider or additional caregivers to meet?
- Who do you have in your life, or what are you going to need, to help meet your needs over this childbearing year and beyond?

Understanding and honoring where one is in the broader context of the long-term journey of recovery is an important step in preparing for motherhood.

# PREGNANCY

*Elaine's Story*
I always figured I was just one of a countless number of women who was sexually abused as a child and I should just forget about it or "get over it." After a few months of pregnancy, however, I was forced to reckon with the issue. As my body grew and changed, prodded by relentless hormonal surges, I felt like I was being attacked over and over again. Dormant feelings and memories from my abuse not only surfaced, but grabbed me around the neck and threatened to suffocate me. I experienced what I learned were affective memories—emotional and physical flashbacks of the abuse that slightly nauseated me and made me grab whatever was around to shield my swelling body. My husband, an incredibly respectful and gentle man, became menacing in my mind and I loathed being touched. Sex, of course, was out of the question.

Things came to a head during my fifth month while we were on a vacation in Hawaii. My husband wanted to have sex, and I wanted "to want" to have sex and tried, but burst into hysterical sobs and disintegrated; I suddenly had a vision of the female fetus in my body being abused when she was eight years old, just as I was. For the first time I felt sympathy for that little girl more than 20 years ago—me—and rage toward a neglectful mother who put her only child in a dangerous position. (She left me in the charge of an older male family member, an out-of-control convicted criminal, every day for a summer. At an earlier time, when I was nearly raped by a gang of teenage boys, my mother's reaction was "Get used to it. That's what happens to girls.")

As a pregnant mom-to-be, I thought I would kill myself if I let the same things happen to this precious new life growing inside of me. Although my outburst during what was intended to be an intimate moment scared my husband away from me for what would be months to come, something valuable turned over in me. I not only acknowledged my abuse, I grieved for the little girl (me) and her horrible introduction to men and sexuality. I forgave myself for all the abusive relationships I fell into as a teenager and adult, for the years of self-destructive behavior and for the bad decisions I made (my past behavior was especially affirmed in reading The Courage to Heal, where I found myself described over and over). I wasn't a perpetual screw-up; I was a survivor managing the best I could considering that I didn't have much of a foundation to start with. My trust in others, my sense of self, my privacy and my self-respect—all these things had been stolen or betrayed during my youth because of sexual abuse and neglect.

I switched my care from a doctor to a midwife, with whom I found more nurturing through my pregnancy—which felt safer. I also sought low-cost weekly therapy with a graduate student at my local university. She helped me get out of the rut of battling my "flashbacks" and just letting them flow through me and away. I learned to recognize the constant fear and anxiety that accompanied me, especially every night when it was time for bed. I never knew when my husband would want to have sex, and I was always terrified "tonight would be the night." To think I had been letting this fear keep me company all through my life! I learned how much I hate feeling powerless and vulnerable—feelings pregnancy exacerbated—and that it was okay to feel that way and ask for help. It seems we survivors are often intent on doing everything on our own. I also began going to a weekly meditation group where I learned a variety of visualization techniques that helped me feel protected, and how to relax through an affective memory.

Unfortunately the problem didn't go away after I had the baby. In a way, it got worse for a while. My nipples were sore in the beginning and every time my baby latched on to nurse, I would be slammed with a flashback. This was happening constantly throughout the day as my baby nursed as often as every 45 minutes sometimes. There were times I hated breastfeeding in front of my husband, and especially in front of my mom and dad—I felt like I was being forced to strip under the threat of violence or death, one thing my abuser did to me daily. (Oddly, breastfeeding alone in public didn't bother me.) But I was determined to overcome my own problems and give this baby the love and attention she deserves. It's something my mother couldn't do, to the point where it was easier for her to let someone harm me than it was to take care of me. I'm also grateful my first baby is a girl. A boy, even an infant one, might have provoked feelings of fear, anger or resentment. It seems I can't shake the idea that all men, no matter how old, are inherently evil or to be feared.

I find writing this that I obviously have issues with my mother. When she visits, I find myself constantly arguing with her dark and pessimistic "philosophies of life," which include "sexual abuse is part of growing up for girls." I'm scared of her infecting my daughter. She once mentioned moving to my town to help with the baby and I shuddered. Part of me knows she did the best she could raising me despite her own problems. Another part of me feels like I'll never forgive her for her selfishness. Though it's sad, in a way it's a good thing, for I feel determined to not repeat her mistakes in raising my own daughter. I only hope I succeed. And maybe she has a second chance as a grandmother.

I wonder if I'll forgive men in general because I can't imagine what it is that makes sexual abuse so common. I wonder if it's something all men are capable of doing or even want to do, and abstinence is just a matter of strength of will. The scariest thing is that I sometimes fear my husband will abuse our daughter. He's a very decent man who gives no such indications and has no history of abuse, but how can you tell who will abuse and who will not?

I am forever marred by my abuse history; and no doubt this will play out in how I mother my child, but good things are coming from it, too. I'm learning to make friends, step by step, with my body, which I grew up loathing. As a child, I learned to view my body as something that could be taken away from me and hurt, and now I'm finally taking it back. I think I will be a more conscientious parent than I might otherwise have been. And I have discovered hidden joys to parenthood that might otherwise have escaped me. I always thought raising children was all about giving, but already my two-month-old daughter has given me so much. She loves to be touched and cuddled, to the point where she rarely sleeps unless in my company; and by giving her unrestricted affection, I am doing the same to my inner child who was neglected and abused. Physical affection feels safe for the first time in my life since I was abused. It seems all the love I shower on my daughter, she in turn showers on me; and while she grows, I heal.

# Chapter 2—Pregnancy

> *I found out I was pregnant in June of '94 and suddenly everything was different for me. It was as if I had a gun to my head; I had to get better RIGHT NOW. I was convinced that, if I didn't, I was going to be the worst mother on the planet.*
>
> *from Shakta's story*

We chose to begin our discussion of the experience of pregnancy for survivor moms with Elaine's story because some very important issues came up for Elaine during her pregnancy and because she was successful in dealing with these issues. We identified several broad themes that arose in Elaine's story: pregnancy as a triggering event in the life of a survivor (2.1, 2.2), needing help and getting it, family relations and the bodily experience of pregnancy. Although Elaine's story does not include details about her relationship with her maternity care provider, other narrators had much to say about difficulties they encountered and help they received from their doctor or midwife. At the end of this chapter we also distill some considerations for establishing good relationships between maternity care providers and survivor clients.

## *PREGNANCY AS A TRIGGER*

Pregnancy is an awesome time in a woman's life, and for many women it can be quite wonderful. But for some survivors, like Elaine, the bodily experiences of being pregnant can trigger memories of abuse and can complicate things.(2.3, 2.4, 2.5) Some women may feel invaded by their growing baby or by the physical changes of the pregnancy and may relate this loss of control over their body to how they felt when being abused.

Elaine, in her story, provides an example of how past abuse became an overwhelming issue in the present during pregnancy. Elaine's awareness that her history might affect her as a mother is critical because it lets her think explicitly about exactly *how* it might affect her, whether these are good or bad effects and what she wants to do about any potential problem areas.

▼ 2.1

Re-experiencing:
  The characteristic symptoms resulting from the exposure to the extreme trauma include persistent re-experiencing of the traumatic event…in one (or more) of the following ways:
1. recurrent and intrusive disturbing recollections of the event
2. recurrent distressing dreams
3. acting or feeling as if it were recurring
4. intense psychological distress at reminders
5. physiological reactivity at reminders

APA 1994

▼ 2.2

Triggers are [environmental or internal] cues—often harmless—that have become associated with the original trauma. In some way, they remind us of the trauma or recall traumatic memories. The association may be obvious or subtle. They may trigger most of the memory or just certain fragments of it. Recognizing triggers, and realizing that their power to elicit intrusions is understandable are steps toward controlling PTSD symptoms.

Schiraldi 2000

▼ 2.3

Researchers found the prevalence of domestic violence to be more than twice as high for women with low birth weight infants as those with a normal weight infant. When other factors such as food insufficiency, substance abuse, depression and PTSD were taken into consideration, the link between interpersonal violence was most strongly associated with low birth weight among those women also experiencing depression and/or PTSD.

Rosen, et al. 2007

A German study found that every ninth woman presenting for obstetrical care has experienced childhood sexual abuse.

Leeners 2007

▼ 2.4

Pregnancy may awaken or exacerbate PTSD in relation to traumatic experiences.

Josephs 1996

▼ 2.5

Types of triggers:
- Sensory: similar sights, sounds, smells, tastes, touch, position or pain, nausea, rapid heart rate
- Anniversary or significant dates
- Similar, stressful events
- Strong emotions
- Related thoughts
- Related routines or behaviors
- Combinations of the above
- Out-of-the-blue (when relaxed or with defenses against remembering down)

Schiraldi 2000

▼ 2.6

Posttraumatic stress becomes chronic or recurrent for more than half of women, especially those whose trauma was repeated and occurred early in development.

Breslau, et al. 1997
Roth, et al. 1997

▼ 2.7

10–12% of US women have PTSD during their lifetime (an estimated 11.8 million women). About 5% of American women have symptoms that meet diagnostic criteria for PTSD at any given time.

Resnick, et al. 1993
Breslau, et al. 1991

Recent studies show that the rate of pregnant women meeting diagnostic criteria for PTSD is higher than the rate for the US general population of women.
- 8.3% in a UK sample
- 7.7% in a St. Louis sample of women in WIC programs
- 5.8% in a Swedish sample

Ayers and Pickering 2001
Loveland Cook, et al. 2004
Soderquist, et al. 2004

Another survivor, Lanie, who thought she had resolved many of her survivor issues years before becoming pregnant, shares her experience of the intrusive nature of memory during her pregnancy:

*I began having nightmares about the abuse during my pregnancy.... I had worked with a counselor to deal with the abuse about eight years prior to this. It was extremely frustrating to me that I was having to deal with things all over again.*(2.6, 2.7)

from Lanie's story

Not much research yet exists on how such increased symptoms of posttraumatic stress disorder (PTSD) itself affect pregnancy. We do know that pregnancy may be more stressful for the woman though; and severe stress can result in a lower weight and less mature infant at birth.(2.8) Women with PTSD also may have less healthy infants if they use drugs, alcohol or tobacco to cope with stress or posttraumatic stress.(2.9) The symptoms of PTSD may just make pregnancy harder, disrupting sleep with nightmares, for example, when sleeping through the night is already harder due to the discomforts of pregnancy.(2.10) Because women with PTSD tend to have more chronic health conditions and to perceive their health as worse than that of other women, they also may find the bodily experience of pregnancy to be worse.(2.11, 2.12) If symptoms of PTSD become severe, a sense of hopelessness and despair, or even just a sense of emotional numbness, may decrease the woman's ability to feel optimistic; and optimism is associated with better pregnancy outcomes.(2.13)

Initial evidence shows that women with PTSD may have more worrisome pregnancy symptoms, like more severe vomiting and more preterm contraction episodes (Seng et al. 2001 and 2007). This may be a manifestation of PTSD-related changes to the body's stress response systems—dysregulations that may affect hormone and immune functions—but much more research is needed to know for sure.(2.14)

Recent research on small samples of women who were pregnant during the terrorist attacks (Engel, et al. 2005) and during a natural disaster (King, et al.

2005) found that both the stress of the event and the mother's posttraumatic stress may adversely affect some maternal outcomes and some infant outcomes.

An additional stressor in the lives of many women during their pregnancy is recovery from a previous pregnancy loss, especially as it can affect a subsequent pregnancy. While recovery from a previous loss is difficult for any mother, a survivor mom can sometimes have additional issues to deal with regarding such loss during pregnancy.(2.15, 2.16, 2.17)

If a survivor is taken by surprise by such triggers, she may experience strong distress and need reassurance. A useful step is to validate that the survivor feels like the old trauma is recurring—that is what the re-experiencing of PTSD is like. She needs to be reminded that she is not so powerless now, and that help is available to help her feel safer.

*The aftereffects of the miscarriage were gruesome for me, and seemed to bring to life much of the symbology I had lived with. It catapulted me into the same black hole that I had once felt within me from the nighttime abuse. I had often felt that there was a large space of toxic, even poisonous darkness in my belly/uterus from the ejaculate of my abuser, and that if I had a baby all sorts of things could happen. On one hand I felt it was the only way to get " it" out—that by opening up so big that a baby could get out, maybe the baby would "push out the darkness/poison" ahead of itself. But on the other hand, how could I possibly protect the innocent baby from such a toxic environment? This was a tremendous mental burden, since protecting my child from an abuse inheritance was an absolute priority. I have wanted to be a mother more than anything in my life and the idea that from the past He could contaminate even this most important being and present moment infuriated me.*

*from Beth's story*

*We waited six years to start a family. With the baggage that was brought into our marriage, it only seemed fair that we clear our own minds and hearts before having someone join us. We were so young, we had some growing up and growing together to do, also. We had a hard time at first. I miscarried our first pregnancy at 12 weeks, and it scared me very badly. I had a few months of serious doubt whether I could handle being a parent*

▼ 2.8
Stress can adversely affect pregnancy processes and outcomes. This can occur indirectly via unhealthy behaviors that increase risk: smoking, alcohol and drug use, as well as high risk sexual behavior, and also via disordered eating, exercising and sleeping. Stress also can occur directly via stress hormones and immunological processes. Social support and positive coping with stress may diminish its negative impact.
Paarlberg, et al. 1995

▼ 2.9
One of the most obvious ways that PTSD could be related to adverse childbearing outcomes is by its connection with substance use. As one PTSD treatment specialist has noted: PTSD is associated with substance abuse. Pregnancy can increase PTSD symptoms. Increased PTSD symptoms are associated with increased risk of relapse to substance use, onset of depression, dropping out of substance abuse treatment and adverse perinatal outcomes.
Brady 1997

▼ 2.10
PTSD and depression both are long-term consequences of child sexual abuse, and both are associated with sleep disturbance. This can include trouble falling asleep or staying asleep, as well as nightmares, intrusive thoughts and worries or feelings of anxiety.
Clum, Nighith and Resnick 2001

Pregnant women have trouble sleeping through the night due to frequent need to urinate and physical discomfort from the baby's movement, as well as the awkwardness of their large belly. Night is also a time when fear of impending labor looms large. Pregnant women with PTSD or depression may be struggling even more than others with sleep disturbance that can affect health, mood and coping.
Kimerling, et al. 1999

▼ 2.11

Even in a young adult sample, PTSD was associated with more symptoms of somatization across the cardiopulmonary, gastrointestinal, sexual, conversion and reproductive symptom categories. PTSD was not associated with more pain symptoms. PTSD was a stronger predictor of these somatic symptoms than other psychiatric disorders.

Andreski, Chilcoat and Breslau 1998

▼ 2.12

PTSD may be a mediator of chronic health problems and disease in trauma survivors since some studies show its relationship to diagnosed conditions to be stronger than the relationship with trauma history *per se*.

In a study of HIV positive women, those with PTSD had worse cell count profiles and faster progression to AIDS than women exposed to trauma who did not develop PTSD.

Kimerling, et al. 1999

People who develop PTSD exhibit more health problems than those without PTSD, including more cardiovascular symptoms, more neurological concerns such as headaches, respiratory problems, gastrointestinal problems, in some studies more pain, and more behaviors that put health at risk, such as smoking and substance use. Health may be affected either by biological pathways, such as stress effects on immunity, or by behavioral pathways.

Friedman and Schnurr 1995

Recent study of diagnoses in health system data (instead of self-report of symptoms) shows that women with PTSD had more chronic fatigue, irritable bowel, chronic pelvic pain, and menstrual pain. When victimization was taken into account, the relationship with PTSD was stronger for all of these conditions.

Seng, et al. 2006

*after that. Wondering if I was worthy. A lot of my old self-esteem problems came into play. Chris was a rock for me, and helped me realize that we could be good parents, and that we could get through this hurdle. We planted a lilac bush in our front yard as a memorial, and I think of our little angel that helped us realize just how precious the children we do have are whenever I look at her. I talk to her on the occasion while I'm in the yard, and tell her about my day, or my life, or the children. I always felt that that first baby was a little girl, and that she is watching me now, knowing how badly I wanted her, and how badly I missed her once she was gone. I miss you, Amanda.*

*from Amy's story*

Mental health problems like depression (which also affect many abuse survivors) are known to increase the risk of less optimal pregnancy outcomes. Such problems occur most frequently when the depressed woman is also using drugs or alcohol or when many additional stressors are present.(2.18, 2.19, 2.20)

Whether we eventually learn that post-abuse PTSD causes physical problems or bad outcomes in pregnancy or not, clearly some women with abuse-related posttraumatic stress have distressing mental health symptoms that they may need or desire help to manage.

The themes represented in Elaine's story pertaining to abuse survivors' experiences in pregnancy echo these needs and desires. Almost everyone who writes about survivors and childbearing acknowledges that survivors have additional issues to cope with and may want additional support (Simkin and Klaus 2004). Few models exist for how the health system could provide this help, but many caregivers who work with pregnant women and abuse survivors are working to find more helpful structures. For example, Cole and her colleagues (Cole, Scoville and Flynn 1996) describe a practice model where certified nurse-midwives and psychiatric nurse practitioners work together with survivors who are pregnant. Often individuals figure out how to meet their own needs.

## *NEEDING HELP AND GETTING IT*

Survivors feel motivated to seek help during their pregnancies for many reasons, including struggles with intimacy in their partner relationships, fears of being a mom, or coping with flashbacks.

*I struggled greatly with intimacy with my husband....*

*We have a good marriage and he loves me dearly and has been my greatest support, though this time was very hard on him as well. I never mentioned any of this to the midwives; it never even entered my mind that I should. I did discuss it with a close friend, who came to the birth.*

*from Lanie's story*

*During my first pregnancy I had a lot of anxiety about being a mother. I was afraid of being a bad mother....*

*I was afraid to have a girl, worrying about how I would protect her from men like the ones I had known....*

*from Dawn's story*

Pregnancy can be challenging for any woman, especially a woman expecting her first baby. Almost all women express fears about medical procedures, labor and birth and being a good mother. Survivor moms may have additional challenges—even those who have managed the effects of their abuse history well up until pregnancy. Elaine responded to the crisis provoked by her emotional flashbacks by getting professional support. She sought a low-cost therapist, used massage, took a class on meditation and switched from an obstetrician to a midwife to get more nurturing. She gathered a team of people to help her from multiple perspectives. This team approach can work very well, especially since it means that women do not have to trust only one caregiver to be able to help with all of their issues and needs.(2.21, 2.22)

Pregnancy is a process of opening up on many levels (2.23) We have found in our clinical practices that women who feel ready to grapple with their issues can make great strides during the course of their pregnancy. Many women have benefited from therapy prior to becoming pregnant, and evidence shows that psychotherapy during pregnancy can be very successful (Spinelli and Endicott 2003).

Some women determine that pregnancy is not the best time for them to enter psychotherapy for trauma-related needs, even though they may be experiencing a lot of PTSD symptoms. Medications can be very helpful for reducing the symptoms of PTSD. The first-choice medications for PTSD at this time are drugs that have been in use for quite a while (mostly the class of antidepressants that are selective serotonin re-uptake inhibitors, called SSRIs).

▼ 2.13
Optimism may counteract some of the negative impact of stress on pregnancy outcomes. In a study of pregnant women with reason to be worried because they were at high risk of poor birth outcomes (due to chronic illness, past history of pregnancy problems or illness during the pregnancy), optimism was associated with carrying the baby to term and achieving better birth weight. Some of the positive effect of optimism occurred because it was also associated with exercising and eating well.

Lobel, et al. 2000

▼ 2.14
Research is needed to understand whether and how dysregulated stress-response systems of survivors of childhood trauma may cause physiological disruptions to pregnancy processes if the survivor reacts strongly to the biopsychosocial stressor of pregnancy.

Horan, Hill and Schulkin 2000

▼ 2.15
PTSD can occur after pregnancy loss, including abortion, miscarriage and stillbirth. Complicated grieving and depression also can occur. These all can affect the woman's experiences in subsequent pregnancies.

Rue, et al. 2004
Engelhard 2004
Engelhard, et al. 2003
Engelhard and van de Hout 2001
Turton, et al. 2001

▼ 2.16

In a follow-up study of 442 women two years after a first-trimester elective abortion, 1% met diagnostic criteria for PTSD related to their abortion experience.

Major, et al. 2000

▼ 2.17

In a large prospective study of women in the Netherlands who enrolled in prenatal care and then experienced a pregnancy loss, those who dissociated around the time of the pregnancy loss had increased risk of developing PTSD via more fragmented memory of the pregnancy loss and via suppressing thoughts of the pregnancy loss. These relationships are consistent with cognitive models of PTSD and suggest that giving up avoidance strategies and telling the story of the loss to get to a more integrated and coherent memory may reduce posttraumatic stress after pregnancy loss.

Engelhard, et al. 2003

▼ 2.18

In a sample of 357 first-time pregnant women, 37% reported childhood sexual abuse. Sexual abuse was not found to be associated with low birth weight, prematurity or labor and delivery complications. However, a sexual abuse history was associated with other factors occurring during the pregnancy that may affect outcomes: higher levels of depression symptoms, more negative life events and more physical and verbal abuse before and during pregnancy.

Benedict, et al. 1999

▼ 2.19

In a study that compares poor and affluent women, rates of elevated depressive symptoms were highest in the last three months of pregnancy (30.6% on the CES-D, a self-report screening scale). More women from low occupational status households had elevated symptom levels (37.1%) compared with women from high occupational status households (28%). For women from low occupational status households, this level of depressive symptoms was associated with lower average birth weight of their infants after taking into account alternative explanations such as prematurity, smoking, other stressors and social support.

Hoffman and Hatch 2000

Studies of the effects of these drugs on infant outcomes are still being conducted. As of this writing, some evidence shows that the risk of birth defects may be slightly increased in infants whose mothers used these medications (e.g., Emerson and Einarson 2005). Other studies show that newborns exposed to the drug in utero may have some symptoms during their first few days of life that go away as the drug leaves their body (e.g., Gentile 2005).

The importance of medication to depressed women is so high, however, that three things must be kept in mind. First, research will continue on this question, so make sure the latest information is considered as part of the decision-making process regarding starting, stopping or continuing antidepressant use. Second, depression, posttraumatic stress and self-medicating with alcohol or other drugs also may have adverse effects. So, the third and most important point is that decisions about medication use deserve collaborative discussion between maternity care providers and pregnant women regarding the risks and benefits in light of the woman's specific condition. In some instances meeting with a psychiatrist may be worthwhile as well, even if a psychiatrist is not part of the current health care team. Many metropolitan areas or university centers may have a perinatal psychiatrist—one who specializes in working with pregnant and postpartum women—to help make this decision and manage the choice of drug and the dose.

Some women feel very strongly that they do not want to expose the fetus to any drugs at all. However, a fetus is also at risk when its mother experiences severe stress. Benefits and risks can be weighed in consultation with a health care provider who can help take into account individual needs. Use of psychotherapy and medication is not an "either-or" situation. Many people choose to use medication and therapy together. In fact, a combination approach is often recommended because the medication can help with symptoms that may increase with trauma-focused therapy.(Foa, Keane and Friedman 2000) (2.24)

Those women who do want therapy during pregnancy may need help to find a therapist (clinical social worker, psychologist, pastoral counselor, psychiatric nurse practitioner or psychiatrist) who has some experience working with trauma survivors and working with pregnant women. Pregnant women have rates of depression similar to rates in non-pregnant women (O'Hara, et al. 1991). Women with a history of depression appear to be at greater risk for having a relapse during pregnancy, as well (Cohen, et al. 2006).(2.25) If an experienced trauma therapist is not available, a therapist who works with depressed pregnant women can be a good choice, too. An obstetrician, midwife, maternity nurse or childbirth educator may be able to make a referral, as Joanna explained:

*When my son was three weeks old the memories started coming back. They began slowly, but cascaded faster and faster into my life. My wonderful doctor handed me a card at one of our numerous visits, telling me that he thought these people could help me. Apparently, he realized that something was going on that I couldn't talk about with him.... He saw the symptoms, yet I'd never told him a thing about my history or what I was going through. I had no idea what he meant, but decided he might be right. It turned out that "these people" ran an organization for survivors of abuse. With their help, I joined a support group and used the book,* The Courage to Heal *(Bass and Davis 1994).*

*from Joanna's story*

Calling the local rape crisis center or women's health clinic to ask for referrals or asking other survivors may also lead to a few good candidates for therapists. Local and national referral services can be another place to start looking.(2.26, 2.27) A good idea is to call a few therapists and see over the phone who seems warm and inspires confidence in his or her skills. Meeting with more than one person may be worthwhile, and some therapists will arrange an initial meeting at no charge. If financial resources are an issue, maternity care programs sometimes have perinatal social workers who can see pregnant women for brief therapy or parenting support at little or no extra cost. Because uninsured women often qualify for Medicaid during pregnancy, this temporary maternity care coverage may possibly cover some psychotherapy and prescription medication. Most maternity care providers or clinic nurses will be able to help with referrals to providers with

▼ 2.20

In a study of 521,490 California births in 1995, women with a psychiatric diagnosis had a two-fold risk of having a low birth weight infant, 2.9 times the risk of bearing an infant with very low birth weight and 1.6 times the risk of preterm delivery. Women with a substance abuse diagnosis had 3.7 times the risk of low birth weight, 2.8 times the risk of very low birth weight and 2.4 times the risk of preterm delivery.

Kelly, et al. 2002

▼ 2.21

The role an ideal maternity caregiver plays depends on where the woman is in the process of recovery from the long-term negative effects of trauma. In a recent study, women far along in recovery wanted a "collaborative ally." Those who were not safe due to addiction or battering wanted a "compassionate authority figure," and those who were not ready to know about how past abuse was affecting them wanted a "therapeutic mentor."

Seng, et al. 2002

▼ 2.22

Women far along in recovery often can anticipate what aspects of pregnancy will trigger posttraumatic stress reactions. Others can be taken by surprise or may not make connections between problems they are experiencing and past abuse—even when the connections seem evident to caregivers.

Seng, et al. 2002

▼ 2.23

"One of the chief characteristics of this 'liminal' or transitional period of any rite of passage [such as pregnancy] is gradual psychological 'opening' of the initiates to profound interior change."

Davis-Floyd 1992

▼ 2.24

Factors to consider when trying to determine whether a drug taken in pregnancy could cause harm include the drug's potential:
- to cause birth defects
- to affect fetal growth
- to cause effects around the first days of life (potentially from withdrawal), and
- to cause problems with development as the child grows

Resources are available to health care providers to look up this information, and they can learn the results of clinical studies.

▼ 2.25

In an analysis of data from 21 research studies involving a total of 19,284 pregnant women, the pooled results indicate that the rate of depression in pregnancy is near 12%.

Bennett, et al. 2004

▼ 2.26

The International Society for Traumatic Stress Studies and the Sidran Foundation together offer an information and a referral resource online:
www.Sidran.org

Veterans with PTSD can learn about resources available to them via links at the Web site of the National Center for PTSD:
www.ncptsd.va.gov

▼ 2.27

Many free nation-wide crisis services will provide 24-hour help and facilitate finding local services:

National Hopeline Network:
 1-800-SUICIDE (784-2433)
National Domestic Violence Hotline:
 1-800-799-SAFE (7233)
 1-800-787-3224 (TDD)
Rape, Abuse & Incest National Network Hotline routes instantly to the rape crisis center nearest the caller:
 1-800-656-HOPE (4673)

sliding scale fees, to community mental health centers or to clinics that charge less because the therapists are supervised trainees.

*Mercifully, love and support surrounded me. At this point in our lives, my husband was in graduate school and there was a counselor on staff whom I could see free of charge. She was experienced in dealing with abuse survivors and we worked together for two full years on a weekly basis. There is no way that I can ever repay the gift that she gave to me of her time, her energy, her love. She mothered me toward health and healing and was the midwife to my most difficult birth.*

*from Katrina's story*

Sometimes women fall into therapy in a crisis, without going through any process of selecting a therapist. That can work out just fine. But the match you have with a therapist is worth evaluating, like Joanna did:

*I tried therapy, but chose the wrong person. I had always believed in God, and I wanted a therapist who would include those beliefs in my "treatment." I found a counselor who was also a minister. I remember the day I tried to tell him what had happened to me. He asked me, "Is it in the past?" I answered that it was, and he told me, "Then it's over. You have to move on." That was it...the entire amount of help I would receive from him.*

*from Joanna's story*

Some women will prefer to build a support network away from the mental health arena and will seek care from birth professionals, including childbirth educators, midwives, physicians, nurses, outreach workers, doulas and lactation consultants.(2.28) Within any community, at least one birth professional usually may be found who is knowledgeable about abuse issues and will be helpful. These professionals will not be able to offer therapy, but they may be able to provide some education or counseling that is helpful. Several women felt helped by trauma-knowledgeable birth professionals.

One woman was encouraged to seek healing through contact with her nurse practitioner:

*After my exam the nurse practitioner asked to see me in her office and gave me the best advice possible. The nurse wanted to know if I had gotten any help for this. I told her "No." She then asked if I wanted to have children some day, and I said, "Yes." "Well," she said, "you're going to need to get this taken care of then if you are going to...have children."*

*from Otter's story*

Knowledgeable friends who care about you can be critical to any healing journey. Two survivor moms talk about the assistance of their friends in their recovery:

*A year after we moved to New York I finally made a good friend, Maxine, whose husband worked with Ray. We quickly became inseparable, and we began to tell each other everything. She was also abused as a child and teen. She became my angel. I again started to see a psychologist, and even though it didn't last very long, it was a big step. Maxine...has given me her love and support. She showed me that everything I was going through was okay, it would pass.*

*from Amy's story*

Carol was able to make use of support from a knowledgeable friend, another survivor mom. With her friend Sal's presence, she felt able to take part in exercises during a childbirth class. She had her good friend accompany her to the class, because she felt intuitively that this time was going to be important for her. She experienced a strong body memory (a sort of "flashback" that takes the form of remembering a bodily sensation) during this exercise, and her friend bore witness to her experience and provided her with a sense of safety:

▼ 2.28
Primary Maternity Care Providers:
Obstetricians/gynecologists—Graduates of medical or osteopathic schools who have an additional three years of obstetrical training and have obtained board certification through the American College of Obstetricians and Gynecologists (ACOG).
Family Practice Physicians—Graduates of medical or osteopathic schools who have two or more years additional training in family medicine, including maternity care, and who have obtained board certification through the American Academy of Family Physicians (AAFP). Not all family practice physicians offer maternity care.
Certified Nurse Midwives (CNMs)—Registered nurses who have an additional one to two years of college training in midwifery and are certified through the American College of Nurse Midwives (ACNM), and who may attend hospital, birth center or homebirths.
Certified Professional Midwives (CPMs)—Apprentice-trained midwives who are certified through the North American Registry of Midwives (NARM) and who attend homebirth or free-standing birth center births.
Licensed Midwives (LMs)—Apprentice-trained midwives who have passed an exam and/or completed requirements as set forth by a state licensing department, and attend homebirths or free-standing birth center births. Only a small number of states license such midwives.
Lay or Traditional Midwives—Apprentice-trained midwives with a variety of formal training modalities. They attend homebirths and birth center births.

*...all of the sudden I was not there anymore. I was in a hole, black all around me. I was crying...just crying and saying "mommy help," "mommy help," and "no grandpa, no grandpa," over and over. I was squeezing the hands of Sal and the other person next to me. My shoulders were tight...but my hips and pelvis were open. I was shivering and had goose bumps....*

*Then I just sobbed and sobbed and sobbed. The group told me what I said later. I could not hear what they were saying during the memory; I was in total blackness...I was not even there. The only voice I could hear was Sal's. I never lost contact with her voice. She brought me back to the present. That's why she was there.*

*from Carol's story*

▼ 2.29

Evidence shows that professional perinatal support given to women during pregnancy, labor and the postpartum period can reduce maternal stress and improve outcomes. Such support can come from perinatal outreach workers or social workers, from nurses or from doulas (certified lay support providers for labor and postpartum).

In several randomized clinical trials, women who were in the group to receive doula services benefited in the following ways:
- their "working model" of how to take care of their baby was less rejecting and helpless, more secure
- they were nearly twice as likely to fully breastfeed
- their labors were shorter
- their rates of cesarean section, epidural anesthesia, forceps and use of Pitocin were lower

Kennell, et al. 1991<br>
Trotter, et al. 1992<br>
Langer, et al. 1998<br>
Manning-Orenstein 1998<br>
McGrath, et al. 1999

▼ 2.30

A "doula" provides laboring women with continuous emotional support, physical comfort, and encouragement.
Resources to find a doula certified by DONA International:
www.DONA.org

Sometimes birth professionals will be able to provide a little extra emotional support during pregnancy and postpartum. One great resource for the pregnant survivor can be the hiring of a doula (a certified labor support provider). Research supports the idea that constant emotional support in labor from a doula has a benefit in terms of better satisfaction and better outcomes of labor and delivery.(2.29, 2.30) Most doulas will choose to meet with their clients a few times during the pregnancy in order to establish a rapport; such an arrangement can be very beneficial. We will discuss the role of the doula in the next chapter on labor, as well.

A survivor's needs for emotional and practical support may outstrip the capacity of the caregivers who have many clients and limited time and resources, even when such needs could be seen by anyone as legitimate. But since stress can be so detrimental in pregnancy, having one's needs met is important. For survivors to receive the social support that women with high functioning, non-abusive extended families enjoy may require creativity and planning.

Some women don't feel ready to talk about how their abuse history is affecting them, so they may need to sort out for themselves what would be helpful: Confronting their worst fears in a journal? Taking a parenting class? Asking an older, nurturing woman to be present as labor support? Asking a close girlfriend to move in to help with breastfeeding the first few days?

Sometimes more than one source of therapy or support over time—or several types at once—is necessary to get what a woman needs. Even if she is just starting to look for ways to get support, she might want to try more than one approach.

> Since then, I have read many books, been in group therapy and individual therapy, and I am also part of an online support group that is really cool, too.
>
> *from Kelly's story*

Some women will experience severe problems that need to be addressed with extensive health care services. Survivors who abuse drugs or alcohol may not be able to stop when they find out they are pregnant, especially if pregnancy stirs up more intense emotions and distress.(2.31) More substance abuse treatment programs combining attention to both trauma and addiction recovery are beginning to be available. Even though using drugs in pregnancy is stigmatized, arranging substance abuse treatment in pregnancy is critical, and maternity care providers or social workers will be able to help with this. Survivors may have other issues that they need to address urgently. They may have a problem with disordered eating that affects their nutrition, pregnancy weight gain and fetal growth and development. They may be engaging in high-risk sexual behaviors that put them at risk for infections that could spread to the baby. They may be in a situation where they are re-victimized.(2.32)

Since we are midwives, readers won't be surprised to know that we think finding the right maternity care provider and setting is also very important. In general, every woman ideally should have her choice of type of provider (direct entry midwife, nurse-midwife or physician) and her choice of location for birth (home, birth center or hospital). According to one saying, women will give birth best where they feel safest. This is probably even truer for survivors. Although this full array of choices will not be available or affordable for everyone, usually women have at least a few different maternity care providers from whom to choose. Time could be well-spent by having an appointment with more than one provider. If a woman starts with one and feels stressed by this person, then making a change is probably worthwhile.

The professional organizations for midwives and obstetricians have "practice locator" search engines or directories online to help locate maternity care providers.(2.33) Childbirth educators are a good source of information about which maternity care provider might be a good match if the woman can adequately explain her needs and hopes. Sometimes calling practices and asking a nurse how the doctors or midwives work with survivors is a good way to get information ahead of time.

Finding an obstetrical practice may be easier since more of them are available. Still, the process should be started early because some of the practices with reputable and well-liked providers fill up quickly. Changing providers early in pregnancy is easier, so women should not wait too long to make a change.

Women sometimes choose midwifery care based on the idea that the midwife/client relationship will afford them more control over their bodies and their experiences (Kennedy and MacDonald 2002). This may be especially true for women who have disclosed a history of sexual abuse. One study showed that women with an abuse

▼ 2.31

In a Norwegian study, women with a history of childhood sexual abuse were more likely to smoke during pregnancy (56% versus 31%). They also reported more discomfort from heartburn, feeling faint, pelvic joint problems, back pain and uterine contractions; and they had more unscheduled outpatient visits. They did not have more obstetric complications during pregnancy or delivery.

Grimstad and Schei 1999

▼ 2.32

Women survivors of childhood trauma such as childhood sexual abuse are more likely to abuse drugs and alcohol, have disordered eating, have patterns of high-risk sexual behavior, and are more often re-victimized as adults.

Roth, et al. 1997

All of these are health risks that negatively affect fetal development and safety.

▼ 2.33

The Web sites of these national professional organizations have practice locators:
Midwives Alliance of North America:
    www.mana.org
American College of Nurse Midwives:
    www.acnm.org
American College of Obstetricians & Gynecologists:
    www.acog.org

▼ 2.34

In one study comparing midwives and obstetricians, women who disclosed a history of abuse chose midwives 50% more than they chose obstetricians. All of these women were low-risk and could freely select between the two types of providers. Disclosers in this research study were 12.5% of the certified nurse-midwives' clients and 8.5% of the obstetricians' clients.

Sampselle, et al. 1992

▼ 2.35

Although not much research has been done on the subject, abuse survivors seem to have trauma-related needs, desires or coping strategies that drive some of their maternity care choices, including:
- type of provider: midwife, nurse-midwife or physician
- entry to prenatal care: from as early as possible to as late as possible
- gender of provider: preference for male, preference for female or no preference
- provider interaction: from remote and authoritarian to warm and collaborative
- location for birth: home, birth center or hospital
- style of care: from low tech/high touch to high tech/low touch

Sampselle, et al. 1992
Seng, et al. 2002

history chose nurse-midwives more often than physicians for maternity care in a setting where both types of providers were equally available.(2.34, 2.35)

Here's what some of our narrative authors had to say about finding maternity care:

*I liked midwife care in particular because it put me in control.*
from Heather's story

*It's a funny thing, but many people have told me how brave I was to have a homebirth. I actually wanted one out of fear; I was afraid of the loss of control and afraid of dying and afraid of pain and afraid of needles and afraid of a whole litany of other things. I figured that I had more of a chance to deal with my fears in my own environment than anywhere else.*
from Shakta's story

*Our decision to birth at home was very important to me from the perspective of a survivor. I knew from helping other women birth that home is where I would feel most safe, most able to control who was present and how I was handled and most able to let down my guard to be vocal and move around as instinct dictated. It was, for me, the place that would most support trust in my own body and abilities.*
from Beth's story

*I have chosen to have three unmedicated homebirths with midwives present, all close to a hospital in case of emergency. I have chosen them for my sense that they would be best for each baby and for me. This approach has minimized the need for unnecessary intervention, allowed for my control of who would be present and allowed for natural labor, unrestricted immediate breastfeeding and the inclusion of many family members.*
from Elizabeth's story

## *FAMILY RELATIONS*

When family-of-origin members or other relatives have been abusers or have failed to protect a child, the role they should be allowed to play in the life of the new mother and infant is an open question. Considering which family members will or will not be allowed to have a relationship with one's child is not a trivial matter, and the narrators had a lot to say about this question. Some began making such decisions about the potential roles of family members during their pregnancies and shared this with us. Some of the stories included breaking off relations with those who had perpetrated abuse against the mother for the sake of the new child. Others told of doing the work of repairing some salvageable extended family relationships during the childbearing year. Some women had the following to say about the ongoing nature of the relationships with abusers:

*I have told my dad he cannot see his granddaughter. I have told him to get help and he has been given referrals to pursue, but I doubt he is getting any help. He admits what he has done but minimizes it. I think this is the most horrible form of denial. It's like saying, I know what I did and it's not so bad, get over it. He is not allowed to call, e-mail, visit or write unless he is writing about his journey in recovery.*

*from Kelly's story*

*Over the next four years, I was able to rebuild my relationship with my father. I learned he had grown up in a highly dysfunctional environment and that his alcoholic father and one of his brothers had also been sexually inappropriate toward other family members. I would love to be able to say we established the kind of love and trust that usually develops between characters toward the end of Disney films, but that was not the case. I was able to care about and enjoy Dad from the perspective of a competent adult who is no longer vulnerable because she knows her strengths, weaknesses and options. And unlike many women, I did get to hear from him the most highly coveted phrase: "I'm sorry."*

*A longtime smoker, my father died of lung cancer when I was 27 and he 56. I truly miss him and the relationship we had developed. Despite molesting me and my sister, he had lots of admirable qualities. At the time he died, I had not yet had children, so I was spared announcing the decision I had made long ago: Dad would not be allowed access to my children unless under my direct supervision. I might not be able to alter history, but I could prevent it from repeating itself.*

*from Kristy's story*

Some women report being abused by their mothers, but more often the relationship between a survivor and her mother was harmed by the mother's failure to protect her.

*My relationship with my mother hasn't improved much. On the rare occasions when I have brought up her role in my childhood drama, she still defends herself for not protecting us. Her explanations today ring as hollow as they did then. Through my adult eyes, I see her fear, helplessness and ineffectiveness as deeply embedded character flaws that influence her behavior in most areas. As a child I took her reactions and inaction personally. As an adult, I know they say more about her than about me.*

*from Kristy's story*

Having an abusive family of origin or breaking off relations with kin can leave a pregnant survivor with far less social support than her non-abused peers.(2.36) Many women experience pregnancy as a stressful time in their lives, and because of not being able to turn to their family of origin, they may have less

▼ 2.36

In a study comparing abused and non-abused women in terms of their relationships with their mothers, survivors reported less satisfaction, less compatibility, less intimacy, more conflict and less assurance in the continuity of their relationship with their mother. They also spent less time with their mothers and would have preferred even less interaction.

Lubell and Peterson 1998

▼ 2.37

Social support (both emotional and material) decreases maternal stress and is associated with better perinatal outcomes. Yet adolescents and adults abused in childhood are less likely to report adequate social support for a variety of reasons.

Paarlberg, et al. 1995
Hall 1996

▼ 2.38

In two studies of pregnant adolescents, those maltreated in childhood were seven times as likely to have suicidal ideation (specific thoughts of killing themselves) and to have attempted suicide.

Bayatpur, Wells and Holford 1992
Koniak-Griffin and Lesser 1996

support available to them during this time.(2.37) This may be especially true for pregnant adolescents.(2.38)

Some women are able to build new support for themselves during their pregnancies, especially in their primary relationship, or are fortunate in their choice of partners:

> *As a stepparent and mother-to-be, I know the quality of my relationships with the other sex is a reference point for how the children develop their own relationships. While my husband and I definitely have our moments, we demonstrate love, physical affection and respect on a daily basis. This is something I never saw in my family of origin and had to learn largely through trial and error.*
>
> *from Kristy's story*

Other women simply reported getting by without having their needs met. They were reliant on their own inner resources in the face of inadequate support from their partner:

> *Although he loved me, like my father, he too was emotionally unavailable.... When I went into labor my husband dropped me off at the hospital, leaving me there and going off to work. He didn't even wait in the waiting room. Back in 1972, the fathers were not allowed in the labor and delivery rooms. I was very afraid.*
>
> *from Jennie's story*

▼ 2.39

In one study of pregnant women, childhood sexual abuse survivors showed a greater degree of suicidal thoughts than non-abused women and were more likely to have made a suicide attempt at some point in their lives prior to their current pregnancy.

Farber, Erbert and Reviere 1996

Some women can become so depressed during their pregnancies that they become suicidal. Women get depression in pregnancy, just as they do at any other time in life. Posttraumatic stress disorder also is linked with high rates of suicide, so friends and caregivers need to take pregnant women's suicidal thoughts very seriously. While we may have a strong impulse to assume that pregnancy is a wonderful time in a woman's life, concerns about hopelessness and despair should not be dismissed.(2.39)

> *One weekend toward the end of my pregnancy I left the apartment, ran away really. Keith wanted sex and I said no, that I felt too sick, and he got a little pushy; so I got in the car and drove to a park in my area. It was raining. I stood at the railing; face up to the rain, it felt so good. I was very heavy with my child (although I couldn't eat much I still gained forty pounds). I looked down into the St. John's River and wanted so much to fall in and sink to the bottom. It was twilight and very steamy, foggy even, as it was gently raining in the aftermath of a very hot July day. I was asking to die. I have asked for that most of my life because I didn't know what living meant. I wasn't violent or even angry; I was simply asking God to take me and my unborn baby to Himself. I had not officially met God at this time so I didn't even know if he was listening.*
>
> *from tedi's story*

Although pregnancy is a time in a woman's life that is heavily idealized in the popular culture, we know that it can also be a time when women suffer violent assault at the hands of their intimate partners.(2.40, 2.41) Murder of pregnant women by their intimate partners is actually the leading cause of maternal death in the United States (Horon and Cheng 2001). Childhood abuse survivors are statistically more likely to experience intimate partner violence as adults. For this reason, assessment for intimate partner abuse is a standard of care in prenatal services (ACOG 1995, Paluzzi and Houde-Quimby 1996). Women should expect to be asked in a prenatal visit if they are safe at home. Providers and nurses often are prepared to help with safety planning and making referrals to shelters that accept pregnant women.(2.42, 2.43) They also can use guidelines developed by national experts to help a woman evaluate how dangerous her partner may be based on his current behaviors (Campbell 1995). Some of the narrators told of instances of abuse happening during their pregnancy:

*When I was 19, I got married to an abusive man. At 23, I found out I was pregnant, which was all I ever wanted. I had dreams of being a mother to lots of children, breastfeeding and nurturing them closely while they grew into adults. My husband was not kind or helpful, although he took great pride in having "knocked me up." He berated me and made me feel very uncomfortable and hit me as well.*

*from Joanna's story*

*I had met this guy on the bus; he was in college. I started dating him a week later. Things went real good at first, then we moved in together after one month. He became real abusive and possessive…I became pregnant and he literally kicked the baby out of me. He threatened to kill me if I ever left him…I was afraid to tell anyone 'cause I thought I would be blamed*

*from Valerie's story*

▼ 2.40

Sexually abused women report lower satisfaction in their committed partner relationships than non-abused women.

DiLillo and Long 1999

(However, this dissatisfaction may be well-founded because abused women also are more than twice as likely to be re-victimized—battered and/or sexually abused—by their intimate partners.)

In a large sample of women in San Francisco, 38–48% of survivors (depending on the severity of their childhood abuse) had physically abusive husbands compared with 17% of non-abused women.

Russell 1986

Very consistent findings were reported in a second study, where 49% of sexually abused women and 18% of non-abused women reported being battered by their partners.

Briere and Runtz 1987

▼ 2.41

Homicide as a result of intimate partner violence is the leading cause of death of pregnant women in the US. More pregnant women are killed than die from the leading complications of pregnancy.

Horon and Cheng 2001
Krulewich 2001

▼ 2.42

Health care providers, including clinic nurses, can help women who are experiencing intimate partner violence develop a safety plan and can arrange referrals to domestic violence programs and shelters. They can arrange for domestic violence program workers to meet with the woman in the clinic facility, if necessary.

Fishwick 1998

Maternity care providers who inquire about a woman's history of abuse may make the mistake of assuming that any abuse is only in a woman's past and may ignore currently abusive situations. Denise muses about this in her narrative:(2.45)

*About a month later I went to meet my midwife, Donna, and she asked if there was anything coming up for me and I told her about the abuse from my father. It is funny how people assume that abuse from a parent must be something from a long*

▼ 2.43

In a test of intervention to decrease further abuse to pregnant women, those who received three sessions with a specially trained nurse in the prenatal clinic experienced less violence over the next 12 months. The intervention included:
1. Safety planning instructions about
   - Securing and copying important papers
   - Copying house and car keys
   - Establishing a code with family and friends
   - Hiding extra clothes should a quick exit be necessary
   - Identifying abuser behaviors that indicate increased danger
2. Information on the cycle of violence, and
3. Information on applying for protection orders, filing criminal charges, and community resource phone numbers.

Each woman was given a brochure with this information, if she felt doing so was safe. If she said it was unsafe, the nurse helped her conceal the shelter hotline by giving it as the number of a female friend or a local business. The nurse offered also to assist with telephone calls to appropriate agencies and to act as an advocate with other care personnel or with the police.

Parker, et al. 1999

▼ 2.44

In a study of 202 women (68 of whom were battered), domestic violence during pregnancy was associated with more health problems, more premature labor, later entry into prenatal care, lower birth weight, use of more health care resources and more prenatal substance use. Higher income and more social support of the mother decreased the likelihood of these problems.

Huth-Bocks, Levendosky and Bogat 2002

▼ 2.45

Pregnancy is estimated to result from 5% of sexual assaults.

Holmes and Resnick 1999

*distant past. On my file she wrote that I had been abused and was still very angry about it—the implication being that I was harping on about something from the ancient past. She referred me to a clinical psychologist who works with her. The first day I went to see her what came out of that session was that it was imperative for me to have a complete break from my parents. I felt so relieved that I was finally getting support from her and from my gynecologist to protect myself and get away from these destructive people.*

*from Denise's story*

While we were working on this book project, people occasionally asked us if the narrators in our project were pregnant as the result of rape. Most of our authors were not but were instead survivors of childhood sexual abuse that may or may not have included intercourse or occurred after puberty. Yet some women do become pregnant as a result of sexual assault.(2.46) Some of the narrators bore infants whom they gave up for adoption or who were raised by a relative. Some chose to terminate a pregnancy that occurred in an abusive context, and some were forced by the perpetrator to terminate an abuse-related pregnancy. But other women chose to continue their pregnancies.

***BODILY EXPERIENCE OF PREGNANCY***

Pregnancy is an inescapable bodily experience with good and bad aspects, a fact commonly known among mothers. Some women love it. Some women hate it. Like Elaine, many of the narrators had strong reactions to the bodily experience of pregnancy. Some reported feelings of fear or invasion, strong reactions to sex and sleep disruptions.

*The body memories worsened during pregnancy and visited me frequently until I began extensive therapy at the age of 35. I didn't understand them; I just knew that I felt dirty, like I was on fire, and couldn't get away or breathe.*

*from Kate's story*

*All during that pregnancy I was a twitchy mess. I felt colonized and invaded even though the pregnancy was planned. The first time I saw the baby move I felt like "Aliens part VI." And I was horribly, desperately lonely.*

*from Shakta's story*

## Chapter 2—Pregnancy

*Eighteen years later, my husband and I were expecting our first child. I was thrilled, but also secretly terrified. I was losing control over the body that I had spent so many years learning to control. I was terrified of ripping during childbirth. The thought of an episiotomy gave me panic attacks. Please, God, don't let anyone cut me there. The dark places in my head had convinced me that my child would be born "damaged." All my "badness" would finally be shown to the world.*

*from Rebecca's story*

Being able to voice feelings about bodily experience and concerns to a caregiver can help with coping, and allow a survivor mom to put things into perspective:

*It helped a lot to be able to voice the wide range of fears that were occasionally surfacing, such as feeling my body was "taken over" by this other being and the resulting control issues...I was surprised to need so much reassurance! I am a midwife myself and have reassured other mothers, but my professional experience seemed to offer nothing to the beginner mother within me. It was priceless to hear that many of my concerns were common to any new mom, and I was rather surprised to be in the ranks of "normal," although I had trouble believing it deep down.*

*from Beth's story*

Trauma survivors report that they experience the psychological state of dissociation during their lives in general. The narrators talked about dissociation—or splitting off elements of the experience—in relation to their pregnancies, often specifically in relation to bodily sensations and concerns.(2.46, 2.47) Heather shares her perspective on the positive and negative aspects of dissociation:

*I got pregnant easily, but pregnancy wasn't very easy on me. I had morning sickness, a bad case of sciatica, genetic counseling (regarding a disorder that runs in my family) and a strong, extremely active baby who even ruptured the muscles around my navel and left my ribs aching where he pushed off of them on his half-hourly wanderings around his home inside me. I had all manner of ills and aches and pains. For a change, dissociation helped: it kept my physical discomfort from affecting my feelings about being pregnant. I loved pregnancy, and the discomforts were completely irrelevant to how much I loved it...*

*I dissociated my experience of pregnancy from the negatives, and that was great. But I also separated my experience of pregnancy from actually having a child. It seemed so peculiar to me to have people tell me anticipatory things about babyhood and parenthood. I was pregnant, thanks, and the goal was labor and delivery, not a baby. Baby development and even my interaction with my growing child was a different process, happening at the same time, but not on the same track. Baby was one process, pregnancy and birth was another process. The two were related, but only vaguely. During labor, I wanted to grind my teeth every time someone said, "You'll soon have that baby in your arms." They didn't get it at all.*

▼ 2.46

The essential feature of the dissociative disorders is the disruption in the usually integrated functions of consciousness, memory, identity or perception of environment. The disturbance may be sudden or gradual, transient or chronic.

APA 1994

▼ 2.47

In a study of women patients hospitalized with depression, PTSD or a dissociative disorder, those who survived childhood sexual abuse had higher scores on dissociation than those who survived sexual assault in adulthood only.

Zlotnick, et al. 1996

*I didn't want to be distracted from my labor by focusing on something that to my mind was fundamentally unrelated to what I was doing. I'd enjoy the baby totally when it got here, but until then, I was just in labor, thanks!*

*from Heather's story*

Several women reported undue hardship with nausea during their pregnancy, and preliminary scientific evidence supports the idea that severe nausea and the excessive vomiting of pregnancy may be more common for women who have PTSD.(2.49) Some narrative contributors really struggled with nausea:

*My pregnancy was awful. I threw up the whole nine months, couldn't keep anything down. I even quit smoking cigarettes as they made me sick also. I finally just quit eating and drank milk constantly.*

*from tedi's story*

*My other pregnancies were a lot different; they came after I had memories of my childhood and was actually dealing with it. [But this first time] I was depressed most of the time and had no energy. I felt ill when anyone touched me. It was awful; when my husband would touch me I felt like I was going to go puke. It wasn't him; it was my body telling me I really needed to work on putting my past behind me. I tried to push it all away.*

*from Valerie's story*

▼ 2.48
A recent study found that women with the PTSD diagnosis were four times as likely to have the severe nausea and vomiting of pregnancy and 40% more likely to have preterm contraction episodes (but no more likely to have a preterm birth).

Seng, et al. 2001

Evidence is also beginning to accrue that women who have PTSD have a greater chance of preterm labor contractions (Seng, et al. 2001), like the episode Claire shares with us:

*Then I started to contract. Since I was at 34 weeks, a point where the baby would be okay if my contractions became labor, my caregivers did not intervene with medications.... The contractions only made me worried, but they didn't hurt. By this time my baby was dancing around all the time, and I felt reassured by his everyday pattern of activity that he was fine.*

*from Claire's story*

In addition to experiencing pregnancy-specific body sensations like nausea and preterm contractions, some survivor moms also reported emotional problems that can take a very bodily form: anxiety and insomnia. Survivors may resort to self-medicating in an attempt to cope with this strong discomfort. If safe, healthy strategies don't work, professional help can be sought, particularly if feelings of anxiety are overwhelming. Seeking therapy or asking a maternity care provider for a safe prescription medication might be the best thing to do in this case. The narrative authors in our project listed many different things they tried on their own to cope when symptoms were "uncomfortable" but not overwhelming: journaling, reading self-help books, prayer, meditation, exercise, yoga, art and art therapy, music and music therapy, becoming politically active, volunteering, joining a support group or 12-step program, taking a workshop, gardening and talking with other women friends, especially other survivors. Taking a series of childbirth education classes can be very helpful in terms of learning more about the normal progression of pregnancy and preparing for labor and birth (although some women say these classes increase their anxiety).

The good news about survivors and the bodily experience of pregnancy is that many survivors report great well-being and no negative effects of past abuse at all. Some of the women in our project reported feeling very positive about their pregnancies:

> *I was extremely healthy during the pregnancy, had no morning sickness or other problems. My family and now husband were all happy and supportive. In fact, it was the most positive time in my life until then. Even my mother treated me well.*
> *from Stacey's story*

> *I have never had any physical difficulties from my abuse that I know of. I have had no problems with intercourse, pelvic exams performed by men or women or my births, which were all fairly uncomplicated.*
> *from Elizabeth's story*

> *When I became pregnant, I knew that it was built into me to know what to do, as it's built into a river to know where to flow, and that I could trust my body to know what to do. I was never afraid. I had and have a strong and clear belief in my ability to give birth and to be a mother.*
> *from Margaret's story*

## RELATIONSHIPS WITH CARE PROVIDERS

A woman's relationship with her care provider during pregnancy can be very intense, due to the intimate nature of the interactions they will share. For many women, being able to trust in this important relationship is critical to their maternity care. The level of nurturing the pregnant survivor experiences can have a direct effect on her overall perception of herself and her pregnancy:

> *My midwives trusted me, the essential, core me. They trusted me to be able to love and care for this ill-conceived child. They trusted me to make good decisions while I was pregnant and even beyond. While they never let go of their conviction that I could birth my baby, they accepted as real my gut feeling that something was terribly wrong with the pregnancy, even as things went along at a steady, if nauseating clip. There have been times when I have wanted to get pregnant again, just to be taken care of by these women for another nine months. It was the first genuinely nurturing experience of my life, and I think it laid the groundwork for what came after.*
> *from Tamar's story*

Whether or not a woman discloses her history as a survivor to her maternity care provider may also affect the care she receives.(2.49) Many care providers have a respectful and sensitive method for determining whether their client is a survivor. Other care providers will not. However, depending on the care provider's level of awareness, the exchange can either be positive and helpful, or it can have negative consequences. In addition, care providers may be survivors themselves, with varying levels of awareness of their own issues around abuse, and may bring some "baggage" to their interactions with clients.(2.50)

*The birth of my son was similar. This time, I picked a different midwife, and we decided not to do any vaginal exams, but to trust my body. She was so nonchalant about my history; it was refreshing. My first midwife pitied me after I shared my story with her. She adopted the attitude of "You poor little thing, let me take care of you." Our relationship was better before I told her. My second midwife never ceased to see me as a powerful capable woman. My prenatal care was also more empowering....*

*from Sara's story*

Although Elaine's story describes a positive, nurturing experience with her midwife, some women will experience negative emotions and conflict at this time. This is not surprising since aspects of maternity care resemble some abuse situations: women feel vulnerable, needing to trust this person whom they do not know well, over whom they have no control and who is going to touch intimate areas of the body. Sometimes this contact will happen in the context of fear or pain, when a medical concern arises or during labor. Other narrators had a lot to say about these intense realities of the maternity care relationship and experiences:

▼ 2.49

Among the women in the Survivor Moms Speak Out project, 84% of those who disclosed abuse to their provider reported that they felt they were treated with respect and compassion. Only 50% of those who did not disclose their history reported feeling respected and treated compassionately.

Sperlich, unpublished data

▼ 2.50

Although female health care providers are more likely to have a history of abuse themselves, the ability to respond sensitively and knowledgeably depends on many factors. Resources are available for any women's health care provider to learn about the effects of childhood sexual abuse on women's health, including:
American College of Obstetricians & Gynecologists, 2000 Education Bulletin: Manifestations of Child Sexual Abuse

ACOG 2000

*Most of the midwives in the practice dealt with the idea well. They noted that many women come up with abuse memories while in labor, and many have their very first or most intense revelations at that time. Frankly, I'd rather not have that interfere with what I expected to be a wonderful event.*

*Unfortunately, one of the midwives was deeply uncomfortable with my history and did not think I was a good candidate for a birth center birth. Fortunately for me, wiser (and more senior) midwives made the final decision, and that one midwife was overruled. Less fortunate for me, it made that midwife very unhappy about attending me at appointments, and she was sending out very nasty vibes. I decided I really didn't want her to deliver my child, even though I had no idea at the time why she was being so negative.*

*from Heather's story*

*My nerves were expressed in nausea and vomiting as a child. I thought that vomiting during the birth would be traumatic for me. So I prepared a copy of my abuse history and I gave it to my midwife so that she would be aware of things that could trigger a hold-up. She absolutely floored me by saying that other people give birth and don't even mention abuse in their past and they get through it. I know that could be interpreted as a positive affirmation from her but it really sounded to me like she was saying that she wasn't really interested and that I should stop being indulgent and just get on with it....*

*I just felt betrayed by her because from the beginning she said that she was very aware of abuse issues and was into the natural way of birthing and into empowering women, etc., but when "push came to shove" (if you'll pardon the pun) we found her very conditioned by her medical background and not very aware or empowering at all....*

*It seemed to me, for some reason that my birth and me were bringing her "stuff" up rather dramatically. I know that she was very busy and stressed and in the process of moving, etc., but I found her behavior unacceptable. I had to back down and placate her because I knew that I was about to go into labor and I didn't have the confidence to do the birth myself, but I was tempted.*

*from Denise's story*

As Denise put it, the possibility exists that a care provider may have their "stuff" brought up during the course of caring for women and for survivors specifically. Some providers who are also survivors will be able to provide very empathic care. However, just because a care provider is also a survivor does not mean that she will be able to use her personal experience to the client's benefit. If she has not had an opportunity to reflect upon the impact of that experience on her work, she may be ill-equipped to respond therapeutically. Conversely, just because a provider is not a survivor does not mean that he or she cannot give very knowledgeable, comfortable care. Susan speaks to this point well.

*Health care providers can help or hurt depending on their personal backgrounds and the view from which they enter your lives. Only truly compassionate people in whatever field will be able to understand what you are going through. It behooves one to learn how to kindly teach others about abuse and its effects. I had many help me and many hate me. I would ask them to be more open to not following standard, rote procedures and really be there for the individual at hand. Listening with the actual intent to hear can be a great kindness.*

*from Susan's story*

*If I had one message for every pregnant survivor, it would be to choose carefully where you give birth and who will be with you. Birth has the power to heal like nothing else. It also has the potential to deepen the wounds.*

*from Sara's story*

The physical contact required in maternity care procedures can be especially challenging for survivors. Many women express discomfort at the thought of having to undergo an internal examination, regardless of their history. But for survivors, such exams can be evocative of past abuse scenarios and very stressful, and they remembered the helpful or unhelpful actions of the provider very distinctly.

*I was nervous about the internal examination. She reacted as if I was being childish....*

*The internal examinations weren't originally such a big issue—I was just tense because it was the first one I had had, and because I had heard that cervical stimulation could cause soreness. As far as I am concerned, anybody gets tense for an internal examination whether they've been abused or not.*

*from Denise's story*

*When a doctor gave me my first cervical check, during an emergency visit, at five months, for dilation, I was upset, because I wasn't prepared for him to check my cervix with his fingers. Because a dilation check had never been done to me before, and none of the books I'd read to that point described it, I was totally unprepared. He did the whole thing without telling me what he was doing, even though I let him know that I was a rape survivor.*

*from Otter's story*

*Time and time again I would come home in tears because of her abruptness or physical roughness. It was not the relationship I had imagined that I was going to have with a midwife. The debate was constant, "Should I change practitioners?"*

*from Amanda's story*

Sensitivity during the internal exam can make all the difference for the survivor client:

*I decided to work with a midwife who was under a group of doctors to do my prenatal care. I made it through all my pelvic exams during the pregnancy except one without any anxiety. The midwife was always very compassionate during her physical exams and never surprised me with any procedure; she always talked me through everything that she did.*

*from Otter's story*

Sometimes, if an emergency occurs in labor, negotiating whether or not to do an internal exam will not be possible. Getting to the point of trust with your provider and accepting that this could happen is important.

Knowing that midwives and doctors have a lot of feelings about these issues may be helpful, too. A survivor client's experience may be difficult despite the best of intentions on the part of her care provider. Debriefing, just asking to talk about how the exam went after she has her clothes back on, can help the woman and the caregiver improve at working together.

Although some survivors might wish to avoid such intrusive procedures altogether, in almost any woman's case at least one or two examinations in pregnancy and a few more in labor are usually part of clinically excellent care and are done for valid reasons. Conversations between women and their caregivers regarding the reasons for such exams and why a survivor might want them minimized are worthwhile.(2.51)

Many articles for clinicians have dealt with the issue of sensitivity during the internal exam. We summarize these considerations for both the client and maternity care provider to think about and even talk about together if internal examinations are an important issue.(2.52)

▼ 2.51

Past or current sexual victimization and intimate partner violence were associated with two- to three-fold increased risk of having a sexually transmitted infection diagnosed during pregnancy.

Johnson and Hellerstedt 2002

Thus, although many sexual trauma survivors may wish to avoid internal examinations, given the risks of negative perinatal outcomes due to untreated STDs (from preterm labor to neonatal pneumonia to blindness), cultures and microscopic examination for STDs are an important part of prenatal care. Alternatives to cervical culture (e.g., urine testing or prophylactic treatment) may be warranted and acceptable to caregivers and clients alike, but require individualized decision-making that weighs the risks and benefits.

## ISSUES FOR PROVIDERS: GAINING SKILL IN THE THERAPEUTIC RELATIONSHIP

Working with trauma-related issues in the maternity care setting presents many challenges. Some of these arise from logistical constraints, such as not having enough time in appointments or not having enough resources to pay for needed services. Many others arise from lack of experience—on the part of *both* parties—with bringing trauma-related concerns into the maternity care setting. Women who bring trauma-related needs into maternity care do so in a vast array of ways, so no easy formula is available for effective, well-received responses. This means that individual clients and providers will have to talk about this sensitive issue. Even if these conversations go well, at times the stress of the relationship may be increased as a result of conflict, discomfort or misunderstandings.

Health care providers may notice that problem areas in the working relationship with survivors challenge their level of expertise in the interpersonal aspects of practice. Most psychotherapists are more accustomed to analyzing and working through problems in the working alliance with clients. Therapists learn about these skills from coursework and professional reading. Many books dealing with the conduct of psychotherapy are written for beginning practitioners and those wanting to become more sophisticated and include a focus on key issues in managing the relationship (e.g., McWilliams 2004). Others are devoted specifically to work with trauma survivors (e.g., Herman 1992/1997, Pearlman and Saakvitne 1995).

▼ 2.52

Things for both client and provider to consider to make internal exams less stressful:

- Have the provider and client discussed whether her history affects her ability to tolerate being examined—prior to starting the physical exam?
- Do both agree that the exam is useful or necessary, or could the exam be declined or the information be obtained another way?
- Does the client know the details of how the exam will be done?
- Does the provider know what the client wants the examiner to do if the client seems a little stressed (e.g., pause or stop/reassure her/ distract her)?
- Does the client know she can stop the exam by as little as a hand signal? Does the provider know to watch for such a signal?
- Does the provider know to avoid asking sensitive or complex questions while the client is coping with the exam?
- Does the client have control over comfort issues like having a female examiner, if desired, or a chaperone, keeping some clothing on, draping, having a friend present, raising the head of the table, etc.?
- Is the client ready and has enough time been allotted for the visit, or should another time be scheduled so there is no rush?
- Will the client have time to talk to someone if she experiences strong emotions or flashbacks with the exam?

Although reading about interpersonal practice can be helpful for understanding the ideas, other steps are necessary to increase skill and comfort. Therapists usually acquire and improve their skill at therapeutic relationship issues during their training and through supervision. Experienced clinicians hear about the client and how the therapy is going, problem-solve and make suggestions or model approaches so that the newer therapist can achieve an advanced level of skill. After formal training ends many psychotherapists continue to seek supervision, especially for complex or challenging clients. Many informally take part in mutual consulting relationships throughout their careers.

Health care providers working with survivors may benefit greatly from a short-term or ongoing form of supportive consulting relationship with an experienced therapist. Such a consultative relationship seems most likely to make a difference if the therapist is experienced working with trauma survivors. A mutual exchange may develop because therapists of trauma survivors often wish they knew more about the physical health problems that some of their clients experience in relation to their trauma histories and posttraumatic stress. In collaborative practice settings, where health and psychological services are delivered in the same building, mutual referral and case consultations do often occur, but these will not be as rich as they could be if the discussion stops short of addressing interpersonal, working relationship issues.

## THREE KEY RELATIONSHIP ISSUES
Trust, boundaries and transference and countertransference are three particularly important issues that we will describe briefly.

### TRUST
In many societies, including ours, physicians, midwives or other healers with reputations in a community and credentials and privileges to practice are considered to be trustworthy. Thus, providers expect to be trusted, even by clients who are meeting them for the first time. But clients who have been harmed by caregivers and authority figures do not enter a health care relationship assuming that the provider is benign and likely to be benevolent. Some will need evidence of trustworthiness from the provider's actions over time.

Providers also assume that clients' expectations of them will be reasonable or negotiable. Unfortunately, some abuse survivors enter a new caregiver relationship holding—and testing—an unrealistic belief that *this* caregiver will be different and will, somehow, meet their every need. These different presuppositions about the relationship can puzzle and frustrate both parties. Addressing them is problematic because identifying the fact that underlying assumptions are causing a problem is not always easy.

Our experience has been that making assumptions explicit can help. A provider can say some things a survivor client may need to hear. For example, "I know it may take some time to feel that I am trustworthy. So here are some things about me you can count on. I will keep your confidentiality, I'll try to remember to ask permission to touch you and I'll keep you informed about your condition." Asking whether the client has any ideas about what would increase her sense of trust is also useful. Typical things a survivor client might say are, "I've had some bad experiences in the past that make me slow to trust, so I hope you won't take it personally if I ask a lot of questions." Or "I need to know you won't dismiss my concerns as 'normal anxiety' if I tell you I'm having a hard time." Or the client might ask for something she needs, to see if the provider will respond in a way that feels trustworthy, such as, "It will really help me to not have a stress reaction if you wait to examine me until I'm ready unless it's a real emergency. Do you think you can do that?"

Having an "introduction to this practice" document can help foster trust by taking the mystery out of practices providers take for granted, but that may differ from the client's hopes or expectation and lead to disappointment or a sense of being treated badly or betrayed. Helpful information may include explaining how clients can reach the provider for non-emergency and emergency needs, defining an emergency, describing how the call schedule for labor works, informing of the frequency and length of appointments and routine physical procedures during each visit. But this written information cannot substitute for the improvement in the relationship that comes from struggling through that conversation together.

One evident instance in which trust builds over time is delayed disclosure of current abuse. Women in a currently abusive situation may not disclose until they have been asked numerous times (Warshaw and Alpert 1999). This repeated asking seems very awkward to providers. But framing the issue as one of trust can decrease the awkwardness. You can get to the point more easily by saying something like, "I asked you this at your last visit already, but I know it takes time to trust someone and decide to say something, so I usually ask women more than once. Are you safe at home, or are you being hurt by anyone?"

Similarly, the rationale for asking about both past and current abuse is to find out what the client needs. If a client has disclosed an abuse history after a routine screening question, but denies that she has any needs related to it, she may have a trust issue. Responding with a focus on trust can leave the door open, using wording such as, "Well, sometimes needs you have will come to mind as you get to know me and trust me. If you think of anything later, please tell me." Remembering to ask at a later visit demonstrates trustworthiness; you can just say something like, "I wanted to check back and see if anything is coming up that is a concern from the abuse you told me about."

Research participants have indicated that they do not discuss trauma-related issues with caregivers until they can judge that the provider "gets it" and is competent at addressing the issues (Seng, et al. 2002). Non-verbal, environmental indicators of openness to meeting trauma-related needs also help show that the clinic personnel are knowledgeable, which increases the odds that they are trustworthy. A bulletin board with support group fliers, therapists' business cards and rape and domestic violence service telephone numbers is a good way to show that trauma-related needs enter into the practice group's definition of women's health care.

As the maternity care relationship develops, a time may come when a client becomes triggered by some aspect of her pregnancy (as discussed earlier in this chapter) or by some procedure or situation. In such situations the client may be helped by communication from health providers that they are aware and compassionate. Women say they want to be responded to with understanding and some problem-solving, but those reactions that feel like pity or horror are overwhelming and unwanted and make continuing to see that caregiver difficult.

▼ 2.53

The internal examination is a frequent trigger, as we have already discussed.(2.53) Women who disclose a history of sexual trauma prior to the exam may be asked whether internal exams are stressful for them and inquire about what helps make them more comfortable. When the reality of past abuse enters the consultation room unexpectedly, providers can respond therapeutically in simple, undemanding ways. If the client has not yet disclosed abuse, and an

A survey study found that women who were survivors of childhood sexual abuse found gynecological exams to be anxiety-producing more often than their non-abused counterparts, and that they sought care more often for acute gynecological problems. Forty-five-and-a-half percent of these women experienced memories of the abuse during gynecological visits.

Leeners, et al. 2007

exam is in process before the stress response is evident—for example, if a client cries or dissociates during a pelvic examination—you can say, "I can see this is upsetting/stressful for you. I'm going to wait for a minute. Are you okay? Can I continue now?"

After the woman is up and dressed, a useful response is, "I'm sorry being examined was so distressing. How are you doing now?" And go on to ask, "Can we do anything differently next time so my examining you doesn't trigger such a strong stress reaction?" If the client doesn't propose any ideas, the care provider could propose chaperone/support; having the door shut tight versus left open a few inches; wearing a gown versus planning to stay partly dressed in a loose skirt and top next time; leaving the head of the exam table elevated; draping or moving the sheet back so the woman can see the provider's hands; asking her if talking about something else helps to distract her or if she needs to breathe or have quiet; or asking whether using footrests is okay or if another way of arranging her legs would feel less vulnerable. If speculum insertion is the stress point, some women can take a narrow plastic speculum home to practice inserting themselves. This problem-solving conversation takes time up front, but builds trust and alliance and saves time for the next nine months.

**BOUNDARIES**
Clear boundaries are needed in areas where either party's well-being would be decreased or the relationship would be stressed if either one could not protect her/his needs. For example, the survivor who has been raped likely needs to be able to put a stop to an internal exam if she is in pain or is triggered into a flashback or dissociation. Her hand signal to stop or her closing her knees assert that boundary, even if she can't find words. The examiner stopping immediately respects that boundary. One who says, "We're almost done, just one more minute" and continues the exam violates that boundary. Similarly, providers hold office hours and are on call for urgent problems. By this schedule and limited contact, they assert that they have many clients and need to have time away from duty. A client who pages her provider three times in a week for non-urgent concerns may be violating the provider's boundary. A client would be respecting that boundary if she asked to have her needs met in a direct way. For example, she could request more time, saying, "Lots of things come up for me that I need to talk to someone about. Is there a way for me to have an appointment with a nurse between regular visits so I can ask more questions?"

These examples make clear that boundary violations can happen quite easily. The provider may think just hurrying to get the internal exam over is the best thing for the client. The client may not realize that she is calling too often. But the person whose boundaries are crossed is likely to feel angry. If the provider stops returning calls, he or she destroys trust. If the client walks out of an examination planning to find a new provider, she has to start building trust all over again with someone new. Being able to *perceive* when boundaries are being violated and talk about it when either party feels boundaries are not respected would be better. This is very hard to do. But naming the issue and having the conversation can build trust and make the relationship stronger.

An effective way to maintain boundaries in the maternity care relationship is to define the nature of the relationship from the beginning. An information document about the practice that addresses "frequently asked questions" can be a key opportunity for the providers to state any boundary needs they have up front—along with the rationale. Again, such a document does not replace the discussion that should occur around these issues, but is a tangible way to portray to the client the parameters of the relationship.

Providers may also conceptualize the birth plan as a similar expression of the client's needs and boundaries for the time when she is in labor and cannot—and should not have to—protect herself as she works to give birth. Sharing written documents allows each person to assert these important needs in time for discussion to take place, before conflict or violation occurs.

Sometimes the provider's bottom line needs (e.g., to only attend the labor once birth is imminent) and the survivor's needs (e.g., to not be examined by multiple strangers) are incompatible. If neither party wants to adapt to or accommodate the other, this should be communicated in time for the client to seek a model of care (obstetrics, family practice, nurse-midwifery, direct entry midwifery; home, birth center or hospital birth) or a particular provider who is a better match for her needs. In this day of extremely constrained health care resources, time spent with any one health care provider will feel very short. Using a team approach rather than trying to get the provider to extend time that really is not available may be a better solution. Discussing what the constraints are early on is difficult but worthwhile.

## TRANSFERENCE AND COUNTERTRANSFERENCE

Mauger, writing in *Reclaiming the Spirituality of Birth*, says of working with a "wounded" mother:

> ...in the case of the wounded mother, (...) her hopes of a good birth experience lie entirely with the person onto whom she has projected the positive mother. As we have seen, the experience of pregnancy and childbirth can appear overwhelming to some women who are afraid they will not be able to deal with, or contain, all the thoughts and feelings that come up during pregnancy.(p. 89)

One cliché is that women fall in love with their obstetrician—or these days with the anesthesiologist who provides their epidural anesthesia. But clichés usually contain a kernel of truth. The positive feelings that a client projects onto the person who attended her birth (especially if she never met the person until 10 minutes before the baby was born) can be thought of as "transference." Transference is when a client "transfers" emotional responses from one relationship onto another relationship. Fond feelings from other times the client has been helped can transfer onto the obstetrician with a fullness and intensity that usually wouldn't be warranted with such a brief rapport.

Conversely, imagine a situation where the birth was difficult, and the provider used emergency procedures that caused pain. An abuse survivor might also transfer feelings about the perpetrator who abused her onto the birth attendant and may choose not to keep postpartum appointments so she does not have to face a caregiver by whom she feels violated.

Things work the other way too. Caregivers react to clients in ways that are not always straightforward and warranted. Certain client behaviors can provoke responses that can be thought of as "countertransference." We can illustrate the idea of countertransference in an example about a client who is distressed during a pelvic exam. First, we need to acknowledge being the provider in this situation is somewhat stressful because the information from the exam is needed, yet hurting a client is not good. Ideally, if the provider is not too stressed to keep using appropriate empathy and good judgment, the provider responds to his or her client appropriately. But a provider might feel and respond in at least two other ways, reacting to what the client's stress and his or her own stress provokes. One countertransference response might be to have guilty, uncomfortable feelings, as though the provider is actually inflicting harm, abusing or raping, when, in fact, the actions are gentle. Another countertransference response might be to react to the client as though she were annoying and to be rough or punitive, in fact acting out harshness. Conversely, one could have countertransference feelings that are positive, but still be harmful because they are unrealistic or can lead to problems. For example, the provider might feel that she can "rescue" this client from this distress by impulsively promising not to do internal exams. Ultimately this could prove untrustworthy because circumstances later may require an exam, and then the client will feel betrayed.

Health care professionals do not have the same kind of training that psychotherapists often have for reflecting upon the emotions that are provoked between client and caregiver. But when clients with an abuse history have to enter a caregiving relationship where intimate, intrusive contact, pain, fear and vulnerability exist, then stress and emotions can become forces to be considered. Learning about the intricacies of the maternity care relationship is an ongoing process for care providers and clients alike. They will make mistakes along the way. Taking the time to establish trust, define the boundaries of the relationship, anticipate client needs that may take up more time than is available, as well as taking into consideration the phenomena of transference and countertransference, can go a long way in creating a good working relationship between care providers and clients.

Clinicians trying to improve the effectiveness of their work with survivors may benefit from case consultation with peers or with a psychotherapist colleague. Such consultation can be especially helpful during the process of defining practice boundaries in response to a client's pushing against them or if emotional reactions to a client are likely to be overly strong—be they from anger, desire to rescue or need to avoid. This support can also be sustaining if the clinician is strongly emotionally moved by hearing what happened to the woman or bearing witness to traumatic stress reactions.

At times dialogue on these issues with a client is not fruitful, so having some general information about "what survivors want" can be better than nothing. A list of desires about interactions between maternity care providers and survivor clients has been distilled from qualitative research interviews into a list of these clients' "desired care practices."(2.54) These eight actions represent what providers can do and what survivors can ask for. Most do not take too much time. They can be thought of as an aggregated list of trauma survivors' general bottom-line needs.

Above all else, care providers need to communicate a message of hope, not in the trite sense of "everything will be alright, honey," but rather an appreciation of how deeply the client has been hurt and an implicit belief that a good alliance helps to get the best outcomes and the best experience across the childbearing year.

### *CONCLUSION*
Overall, in our research, a few common themes arose about being a survivor during pregnancy:
- The experience of being pregnant was a trigger for posttraumatic reactions and required coping with stirred-up memories and feelings about past abuse.
- Feelings of healing, surmounting, being helped and being blessed were positive aspects of childbearing.
- The inescapable bodily experience of pregnancy was often challenging, created feelings of being out of control or "taken over" by the baby and led to feeling violated by insensitively conducted maternity care procedures and brought

feelings of fear of labor and birth. Physical discomforts, symptoms like nausea and preterm contractions, strong emotions, including depression and anxiety, bad dreams and trouble sleeping took a toll, caused worry and required endurance and a lot of coping.
- Problems in family relationships came to the fore and sometimes led to changes in relationships with abusive people for the future child's sake. Many acutely felt that they had less practical and emotional support in pregnancy than other women.
- Many survivors identified needs for help and assembled a team to help meet these needs: friends, a loving partner, a collaborative midwife or doctor, a therapist, a body-focused professional such as a massage therapist or yoga teacher, a childbirth educator or a doula. Others fell back on creative and sustaining inner resources: journaling, meditating and/or praying, releasing hard emotions with crying, talking to their baby and staying hopeful about being a loving, strong and protective mother.

▼ 2.54

ASK about abuse history, how it is affecting her, what she needs from you and, at each visit thereafter, ask how she is doing with regard to posttraumatic stress concerns.

ACKNOWLEDGE that trauma has long-term effects on some people, that she is not the only one and that you are willing to work with her or can refer her to a more appropriate provider.

ASSESS repeatedly her risk for associated problems: substance use, revictimization (current abuse), high risk sexual practices, disordered eating, self-harm, postpartum mood and attachment disorders and safety for her infant.

ASSUME, in the absence of disclosure but in the presence of posttraumatic stress reactions, that the client could be a survivor and respond to her therapeutically, but without forcing the issue.

AVOID triggering posttraumatic stress reactions by learning individual clients' triggers specifically and by increasing awareness of aspects of maternity care that are generally triggering.

ARRANGE more extensive contact that meets her needs via longer or more frequent visits with the main care provider or appointments with team members, and be ready to arrange connections to domestic violence, substance abuse, or mental health services.

ADVOCATE for appropriate program and financial resources to meet these clients' trauma-related needs, and consider using a secondary diagnosis of PTSD for clients who meet diagnostic criteria.

ASCERTAIN by follow-up of individuals and evaluation of practice over time whether trauma-related outcomes are being met in concert with perinatal goals.

Seng, et al. 2002

# LABOR AND BIRTH

**Katherine's Story**
I come from a family where my father molested my sisters but not me. Nevertheless, I grew up in a household that taught me to undervalue myself. As a teenager I was raped twice; both were stranger rapes. Both were unreported and I never sought help. In fact it was years before I realized what had happened to me "counted" as rape.

In my early twenties I began having extreme anxiety attacks and sought therapy. I lucked into an extremely compassionate and helpful therapist. Three years later I was anxiety-free. A meditation practice also helped me to heal. I can't over-stress the value of a quiet and calm mind.

Along the way I decided to become a midwife and went to a small school in California that teaches the art of assisting with homebirth. I also fell in love with the kindest and gentlest man on earth. We were married three years before we found ourselves expecting our first baby.

From my studies, I knew that rape could interfere with the birth process, but I thought I was so far past the intense pain of it and so far through the healing and so "aware and centered" that rape feelings would not hinder me. WRONG. When my water broke and the contractions began the pain in my womb felt to me like the pain of forced penetration. It felt like rape. I panicked. I was conscious enough to tell the midwife I was having rape flashbacks, but she was young and inexperienced and could not really offer any help. In fact, I picked up intuitively that I had freaked her out. Her freaking vibe definitely undermined any possibility that I could cultivate some feelings of strength. It turned out that I also had a fever and because my water had been broken for over 24 hours we transferred to the hospital. I got a blessed epidural and dilated seven centimeters in two hours. I pushed my son out myself and while I was mostly numb I felt his body arrive in this world in exquisite detail. I could feel the shape of his sweet face and the details of his arms and legs as he emerged from my body. While the delivery was a relief, the experience was painful and somehow made me feel like a part of me was still owned by those rapes. Those two men had reached through a decade and through my body to assert themselves during one of the most holy and sacred and private events of my life. I wanted them out.

Nine months later we found ourselves expecting another sweet angel. I was determined that this time would be different. Truthfully, I was also very worried that it wouldn't be. After several conferences with the midwives about what went wrong last time, some journal writing, some sessions with my old therapist and, most importantly, after reading Birthing from Within *(England & Horowitz)*, I went into labor.

At 4:30 in the afternoon I called the midwives and told them I just needed to know if the crampy feelings I'd been having were or were not labor. They were coming every three to five minutes and I did not want night to fall without knowing if I would really kick into serious contractions that night or not. We live 30 minutes from the birth center so we arrived there for a check at 5:00 pm. The midwife checked my cervix and said I was 7 cm! I was stunned. I got off the table and threw up. The midwife said, "Well now you are probably 8 cm, why don't you go downstairs and get a room." We got a room. I had about six strong contractions that hurt a lot and I had to lean into my husband for support. By grabbing him I felt I could literally siphon some of his physical strength into my body and that helped. Walking the whole time also helped. When a contraction started up I would just pace. On contraction number six or so my water broke and the midwife told me to get on the bed. I said, "I can't" and she was very authoritative when she said, "Oh, yes you can." I sort of beached my body on the edge of the bed (like a whale washed up), grabbed my husband around the neck and pushed for all I was worth. I was holding my beautiful baby girl 10 minutes later!

The labor hurt a lot. While I was pushing I remember yelling out, "I CAN'T DO THIS!" The midwife looked at me and gave a little laugh and said so sweetly, "You are doing it." I was also complaining about those last contractions and mentioned I did not think I could do it. Birth hurts and burns and is intense. But this pain was mine. This pain came from the top of my daughter's head as she moved through my body. I was opening and laboring for her. I was focused inside myself and I felt so very strong and like mother earth, moving, sweaty, heaving, working earth. This was not suffering. This was about no one else. There was only room in my body for my daughter and me. This birth was a triumph and victory.

The most helpful change for this birth came from my work with the book, Birthing from Within. That book gave me images of healthy birth as it is for so many women all over the world. I spent my pregnancy focusing on trust in my body, and letting go of fear. Fear closes you down. Trust opens you up. You can choose to trust yourself or God or both but the trust will heal you. Trusting is a choice you can make.

There is a rather famous midwife named Ina May Gaskin. She suggests that laboring mothers try to think of contractions as expansions. This was an image that helped me open. I sat with the pain of a contraction and imagined all that energy moving out, as I grew bigger. This worked for me.

I want to add one more thing. No one. No man will ever come between me and my children and my love for them. No one. Ever. That is truth for me and my choice.

**Lynelle's Story**
*I had an extremely typical American pregnancy. You know the type: OB care from the start, all the necessary tests and a hospital-based childbirth educator. I had read every mainstream book I could get. After all my preparation, I was delivered of my 9 lb 6 oz son in 1993 via cesarean section. A failed Pitocin induction because I was "big" added to the premature artificial rupture of membranes, leaving me with no other choice than to agree with my doctor that I couldn't deliver vaginally.*

*I remember during the prepping for the c-section I felt very panicked. I had once seen a movie in college about a woman who was undergoing hypnosis and re-living a botched c-section where the sedative had worked so she was asleep but the anesthetic had not worked and so she felt everything. It was horrible; she was screaming and crying as they cut into her flesh, her body memories amazingly strong as she recounted that experience. I was terrified I too was going to be able to feel the surgery, even though I had a very strong epidural in place. The hospital staff seemed more annoyed at my panic and told me to "calm down and quit crying." In an effort to appease me they re-dosed the epidural, which only served to completely over-anesthetize me. I couldn't feel anything,* not my face, arms, legs-nothing. I couldn't even be sure I was still breathing. None of this helped to calm me down and my arms were tied to the table in a crucifixion pose to keep my numb arms from falling off the operating table. As I cried and begged them to wait just a minute before they started so I could calm down, my doctor made the first cut. I have a vague memory of praying to God to keep me safe and get me through this, and thoughts of my baby were nonexistent.

When my son, Ian, was removed the doctor popped him over the sterile drape so I could see him. After he was cleaned up he was given to my husband, Dave, who brought him over to me. Since my arms were tied down I asked my husband to rub my son's cheek against mine. I smelled him, sniffing like some primal animal, it being the only way I could relate to my baby since I couldn't move.

I don't remember much after the surgery; I was very ill from being over-medicated. I do remember a room full of people, family and friends, all cooing over Ian in the corner. I was jealous. I was the one who was just cut open, damn it—why wasn't anyone paying attention to me!

It was a bad start to parenting to be sure. The next few days and weeks were awful. I didn't feel bonded to Ian at all. I didn't know what to do when he cried; I didn't know why he cried so much. I didn't know why I cried so much. Dave took one day off work after the c-section and then left me alone with this infant and postoperative pain. I felt so sorry for myself. I began fantasizing ways to hurt myself. Not kill myself, just wound myself enough so I'd have to be admitted to the hospital and no one would expect me to care for an infant and I could get some sleep. I also envisioned hurting Ian—throwing him against the wall in desperation for peace and quiet. Please God, just five minutes of sleep. Thankfully I did neither of those. My pitiful cries for help went largely unheard. Dave was never home; he worked all the time and when he was home he was mad that the house was a mess, dinner was not cooked and everyone was crying.

Finally, a neighbor who had a c-section 10 weeks earlier called to see how I was. I burst into tears and she promptly came over. She forced me to go to a new moms group at the hospital. It was a good start. A room full of women who were just as screwed up as me. So I'm not the only one who doesn't know the first thing about parenting? The group leader recognized my signs of major postpartum depression and had me stay after class for a one-on-one chat. Knowing that I may have a real illness made me feel better, since I thought I was just an awful person. The next day she called me at home and invited me to meet her at the hospital to meet with a lactation consultant. I wasn't having breastfeeding problems other than normal engorgement, but she saw what I couldn't.

At that meeting the three of us decided that given my mental and physical states, what I really needed was some food and rest. I didn't have the energy (or care to) pump breast milk for Ian so I switched to formula. Dave's mom, sister and aunt came to the rescue after that day. I still wonder if the nurse called one of them and told them how very serious my problems were. We had a schedule where either Dave's mom or sister came over every day at 5:00 pm and took Ian away until 10:00 pm. During those precious five hours I could eat or sleep or do nothing at all. On Friday afternoon, Dave's aunt would come get Ian and take him for the whole weekend, returning late Sunday afternoon. Dave never seemed to care that other people were raising our child. I watched the clock like someone waiting for a fix. I would tell myself, "If I can just keep it together until 5:00 pm…I only have to survive until 5:00 pm…."

I didn't care about who had Ian as long as he was gone so I could be alone. It took about four months for me to be "okay" with Ian. I regularly attended the new moms' group and had private chat sessions with the leader. Things slowly got better. When Ian was six months old I discovered I was pregnant again.

About six months into the new pregnancy I heard about doulas. They sounded interesting so I checked it out. I decided I wanted to be a doula and during my eighth month of pregnancy I enrolled in the Seattle Midwifery School's doula training program. Talk about an eye opener! In a few short classes I had a whole new perspective on childbirth, breastfeeding and parenting. I developed an intense desire for a VBAC and knew I would breastfeed this new babe.

At one point in the class we were to watch a c-section video. I thought it would be interesting to see what had been done to me. Wrong! Within the first minute of the video I began to hyperventilate and cry and had to run out of the room before I threw up publicly. Penny Simkin (an angel from God, for sure) was teaching the class and followed me into the bathroom. I was curled up in the corner, on the floor like a frightened animal. She kneeled down and just smiled at me. I whispered that I didn't want to go through that again, meaning a c-section. She reached out a hand and said, "Then don't."

I finished my training and the next day met with Penny for a private counseling session. One of the first questions she asked was if I had ever been sexually assaulted or abused. A few hazy memories leaped into mind, which I promptly tucked away where they had been for years and told her "no, of course not." We chatted for a while and she gave me the name of an OB who was very pro-VBAC. I met with her and at 37 weeks pregnant switched doctors.

Six days past my due date labor began. This labor was very long and drawn out. I labored hard, all day long with the help of my mother-in-law who was very supportive of VBAC. (Side note: Dave had fought with me about the dangers. He wanted another c-section; he didn't want to see a baby come out of my vagina.) After about 19 hours of hard, long strong contractions I was only at 1 cm. My doulas were with me (I had hired two, against Dave's wishes; I was beginning to find my fire) and after I began begging for pain medication they advocated for me to get an epidural even though I was only 1 cm. About two hours after the epidural I felt the urge to push. Anna was born, vaginally, in September 1994.

I immediately breastfed her and bonded like I had not known with Ian. I felt strong and proud and was ready to parent. I had a support system to help me if I began the downward spiral into postpartum depression again (which I didn't). A few days after Anna's first birthday I told Dave I was leaving him. His response was "no kidding."

I began therapy because of depression around what I thought was the divorce. I saw a craniosacral chiropractor (Peter) and a hypnotherapist (Nancy) simultaneously. We began to explore experiences I had locked tightly away. In their gentle hands I allowed myself to relive a rape I had suffered when I was 15, my first sexual experience. I was at a party, drinking, and woke to find myself in bed, being raped by a young man who was at the party. I remembered that it had felt much like the c-section. I was so drunk it was like my brain was functioning but not my body. I was crying out "STOP, STOP" but no sounds came from my mouth; no one was listening. I tried to move but my limbs didn't work. The realization of the similarity of the two events was a turning point for me. Using hypnotherapy, I relived the rape, stopping it in my mind and reframing it. I fought off the boy and told authorities. The pain and shame and anger were diffused; it didn't hurt so much any more. I used the same technique to re-do (my therapist and I call them "do-overs") Ian's c-section. I replayed the memory but this time the c-section was calm and quiet and lovely. I bonded to him and we were in love. It was a catalyst for change in my parenting and in my outlook.

## Chapter 3—Labor and Birth

*Further down the road, Nancy and I worked on letting go of the shame I held from being molested by an uncle when I was a very small child. I realized I had been mad at my dad for not protecting me. He had known that my uncle was a pervert, yet he allowed me to be alone with him. This was especially difficult for me to let go of because I loved my father dearly and he was killed when I was 15. How could I be mad at my dad? He was dead for God's sake; I had martyred him in my mind and allowed no room for human error. In hypnosis, I spoke with my dad and told him about what had happened and how I was mad at him about it. He apologized and I forgave him. We sat by a stream and talked. I devised little angel/demon people to take care of my uncle. I still saw him at family functions and confrontation was not an option for me. Now when I see him I also see these little angel/demon people sitting on his shoulders and flying around. It reminds me of how he'll get his punishment—someone did see what he did—someone he'll have to answer to someday.*

*The c-section reminded me of that molestation because I held Dave responsible for protecting me and he didn't. Much like I held my dad responsible for protection and he failed me too.*

*All in all I spent about two years in intensive therapy. A lot of it was to resolve and let go of the c-section, the rape and the molestation. But I also learned patience and forgiveness. I became my own best advocate. I became my children's best defender and biggest fan. I became a mother. Now don't get me wrong, those were the hardest, most painful years of my life. I would NOT want to do that over again. I cried so many tears.*

*I created a guardian angel out of those hypnosis sessions. She's still with me today. A big, strong Amazon woman who can beat the crap out of anyone and doesn't take shit. She's kind of like Xena, from the TV show (which I LOVE.) When I feel small or frightened or overwhelmed she pops up, carrying her sword and stomping around the room. I get strength from her; we're good friends.*

*Now I'm a new person. People who knew me years ago are astounded at the person I've become. I work in maternal child health as a birth doula and lactation consultant. I regularly pick fights with the medical establishment to test my resolve. I don't let people push me around and I speak my mind regularly, much to the dismay of a few of my more timid family members and friends. I'm a bit of a bitch!*

*Oh yes, and Anna breastfed until she was five-and-a-half years old and is the feistiest girl-child I know. Ian has the heart of an angel; always concerned for the well-being of others. He tempers Anna and me when we get a bit shortsighted. We're a great family!*

> to be vested
> with the expanse of transformation
> through the giving of birth
> to her child
> is like gazing
> on the ocean's shore
>
> desperately striving
> to comprehend the other side;
> the farthest shore,
> to which she may go
> once the waters take her.
> there is no turning back
> when there is no point to reference—
> only the currents to believe in
> and a steady breath upon the waves
>
> *Mickey*

**Labor: The process by which childbirth occurs, beginning with contractions of the uterus and ending with the expulsion of the fetus or infant and the placenta.**

Katherine's and Lynelle's stories are very important for women and caregivers to read because they echo a theme that runs through a large proportion of the narratives written for this book. If we can be so bold as to simplify it to its common essence, we would summarize the narratives this way: For survivors, birth can be a huge challenge because they want it to be a safe and positive experience for them and a strong start to their mothering. But many aspects of birth itself (e.g., pain, being overwhelmed) and many aspects of birth care (e.g., being touched, losing privacy, not being in control, being overpowered by authority figures) are a reminder or reenactment of abuse. In this chapter we are going to focus on what survivors did to cope with this reality. As in the chapter on pregnancy, the quality of the relationship the woman has with her caregiver and the amount of support she gathers around her during this challenging time are key themes in the narratives.

## *OVERVIEW*

Many of the survivors who wrote narratives for the book told stories of experiencing birth itself, or the way they were treated, as a new trauma laid on top of the old trauma, and they suffered emotionally postpartum and had to make a huge effort to recuperate, which got in the way of their efforts to bond with and care for their infants. Many also wrote narratives that told stories of being deeply healed and strengthened, uplifted and primed to bond with their infants by the experience of being well cared-for or of having simply been graced or triumphant in this challenge. What we noticed that is important for survivors to know is that those who could anticipate what would stir up posttraumatic reactions in them were best able to come through the experience feeling uplifted. Many of the most heartrendingly bad experiences occurred with women who had had little or no healing ahead of time, who could not anticipate their emotional needs and who could not get the help they needed.

Notice, however, that we are not saying that the "prepared" survivors had "good" births and the "unprepared" survivors had "bad" births. What seems true from the stories is that the survivors who had thought about and worked through fears and concerns ahead of time came through the events—however they unfolded—feeling fairly good (or very good). If they felt angered or shaken by how it went, they were able to talk about the experience, vent feelings and feel relief and the ability to focus on the here and now. Survivors who had been caught unaware of how triggering or reenacting birth might be for them seemed to have been more alone with their experience. They seemed less able to get relief from the hard emotional reactions if they ended up with a sense of having been violated again.

Because the narratives are written from the survivors' perspectives, they represent the woman's perspective on events. We cannot know if what happened to them felt like a re-experiencing of abuse or if, in fact, the care providers were being abusive. Both things happen. The odds of finding a provider who is great to work with are better if women can think about what they need and use any help available to find a good match with a provider. The odds of bouncing back emotionally if the experience turns out to be a difficult one are probably better for those who know in advance that birth is not something they can control, and that strong emotions can get stirred up—for any woman—but for survivors in particular.

In this chapter we will highlight parts of the narratives that make transparent what about labor and labor care can challenge a survivor emotionally. We also will include excerpts where providers' actions *were* abusive and/or *were perceived to be* abusive. Including this material is challenging for us because saying that nurses, midwives or doctors could ever be abusive to their patients seems taboo. However, saying that parents could ever hurt their children or that husbands could ever hurt their wives was also once taboo. As with pregnancy, the quality of the client-provider relationship seems critical to the quality of the birth experience. A fragile or untested alliance can come apart in labor where the context—which is stressful for both people—leaves even greater risk for flawed communication, misunderstanding and events that become traumatic. The stress of being responsible for birth outcomes and the feelings that can be provoked when "patients" insist that their needs be met can collide to make *some* caregivers feel threatened. Some may react to this uncomfortable feeling by asserting power inappropriately. When this unmindful assertion occurs in the context of vulnerable sexual parts of a woman's body, the dynamics are similar to rape. At the moment when such aversive contact occurs—during the overwhelming event of labor—a woman can do almost nothing.

The narrators' stories indicate the importance of heeding warning signs before labor that a caregiver may not be an emotionally safe person

▼ 3.1

In a study of 499 mothers in Australia, both the level of obstetric intervention and the perception of inadequate care during childbirth were associated with development of acute posttraumatic symptoms. Low perception of technical skill and low appraisal of professional communication increased risk of posttraumatic stress symptoms. Women who perceived their partner or support person to be disappointed or not wanting to talk about the birth also were more at risk.

Creedy, Shochet and Horsfall 2000

▼ 3.2

In a study of 253 Toronto-area women, those most likely to experience postpartum posttraumatic stress symptoms would be identifiable prior to delivery. They were those who had:
- Two or more traumatic lifetime events, which increased risk three-fold, and
- Those with depression during pregnancy, which increased risk by 19 times.

Cohen, et al. 2004

to receive care from in labor. This realization can lead to the possibility of changing caregivers. If such a change is not possible, another option is asking for help from a supportive person (e.g., your partner, an older woman friend, a doula or a trusted girlfriend) who will increase feelings of safety by chaperoning and advocating at the time. They can also help talk through the experience afterward. The narrators provide examples of this process of actively recuperating.

As we present some of the narrators' experiences in this chapter, we will comment now and then about what may have been happening from the provider's perspective. The woman's experience from her perspective is going to be what shapes her response. Knowing that what was happening can be interpreted in multiple ways may lead to mutual empathy and understanding about the events, decreasing the darkness of the shadow cast by past abuse experiences.

We focus on this potential for birth care to be re-traumatizing for a research-based reason, from data that exist above and beyond what these 80 narratives represent. A number of studies done in several countries have similar findings.(3.1, 3.2) An obstetric emergency contributes to the risk of postpartum post- traumatic stress. But a birth that is entirely normal also can be traumatic from the client's perspective if her perception is that her care providers were incompetent or uncaring. These narratives underscore that the sources of this trauma seem to be the sense of being victimized or betrayed by the caregiver, and that the violations feel sexual and/or relational in nature. We wonder if the fact that such traumas are occurring during one of the most important moments of a woman's life heightens their negative power—and heightens the power the woman can feel if she comes away feeling like she was well cared-for and surmounted a major life challenge?

### *WHAT IS LEFT OUT*
Although as midwives we passionately support the preservation of natural childbirth, this chapter will not focus particularly on choices about technologically or holistically managed birth. Many books and Web sites contain information relevant to individual needs in this regard. We strongly encourage survivors to seek out the services of childbirth professionals, who can enter into a conversation with them so that they can weigh the trade-offs of particular choices. Decisions about the type of provider, the place of birth and the embracing or avoiding of medical intervention are very personal and can be difficult for any woman. For abuse survivors, who may be more fearful or stressed about birth, the most important considerations may be about how to feel as safe as possible: safe with the caregiver, safe in the setting, safe from past abuse overshadowing present experience. We have selected excerpts from the narratives with this focus in mind.

### *READING THIS CHAPTER*
The dictionary definition of labor stands in stark contrast to the complexity of the experience. Giving birth is a very powerful life experience, regardless of the details of its unfolding. In this chapter, in order to be true to the reality of the narrators' experiences and the reality of how births take place, we include both positive and negative stories. The stories of bad experiences serve to make transparent what about labor itself (sometimes) or the care received (most of the time) was so challenging for the survivor. This may be very affirming for survivor readers who have had

trauma-related problems in past births. It is also important reading for providers who are not sure how care practices that seem routine to them provoke strong negative feelings for some survivors. Some pregnant women may not feel that reading every story is useful. For this reason we continue putting the narrative excerpts in italics, and we also use subheadings to make skipping sections easier. Almost no research exists on how sexual abuse or PTSD affects birth, so at this point in history, using the experiences of others to imagine what might be useful is the best we have.

**ISSUES OF CARE, CONTROL AND COPING STRATEGIES**
Katherine chose a midwife at a birth center to assist her with her births. Lynelle chose obstetricians to help her birth her babies. Being able to freely choose a caregiver for birth, to build a relationship with that person and then to be assured that, indeed, he or she will arrive when the time comes—these ideals rarely can be met in this day and age. Insurance and Medicaid systems often limit whose services they will reimburse. Group practices are large and the clinicians usually are on call for births on a set schedule that is not flexible enough to allow one provider to promise to attend one client's birth. In Canada and some European nations the health system will pay for birth services whether the provider attends in home, birth center or hospital. In the US, homebirth is an option that women typically must pay for themselves. In some locations a nurse-midwife may not be available. In some states direct entry midwifery is illegal or outside of the law, making the choice for women who want to birth at home much harder. In addition, some women have health conditions or develop pregnancy complications that make high-risk care in a hospital setting the best avenue for a good, healthy outcome for the mother and the baby.

Another very important factor in efforts to find the right caregiver and cope with concerns about birth is the medical system itself. Compared to a woman in the midst of labor, the professionals and the health system are terribly powerful. For survivors who feel better when they are "in control," anticipating their vulnerability in labor and awareness of the power of the medical setting can be a big cause of anxiety and a reason to try to figure out in advance what might be helpful under the circumstances. The following narrators describe their experiences with strategies they tried and how their efforts were or were not helpful.

Kate shares her thoughts about needing to forego the idea of having a homebirth, even though she thought about it:

*In my sixth month I read a book that said that for survivors of abuse, birth in a hospital into the hands of doctors could entail elements of re-victimization. I toyed with the idea of a homebirth but only knew about lay midwives locally and knew that where I live the practice of lay midwifery is illegal. I did not have the resources to break the law. I was trying to be normal.*

*from Kate's story*

Erica explains how her feelings about her care provider and birth changed when her baby turned to a breech position and she went through a second cesarean birth:

*I thought if I went in to see a doctor and said I wanted natural childbirth, that'd be what I got. I wanted to deliver my own baby more than anything, to finally feel, perhaps, like I was a "real" woman.*

*Four weeks before the end of a healthy pregnancy, my doctor discovered that my baby had turned breech. A c-section was quickly scheduled. My protests were met with assurances that a vaginal birth would leave my baby dead or retarded, and I must stop being so selfish by trying for what was, after all, window dressing. It was implied, and I believed, that to feel bad about this would make my baby feel unloved and was proof of my selfishness. Once again, I dutifully climbed up on a table and let a doctor cut my child out of me. I came home with this baby and a frozen heart. I couldn't sleep, even when he did. I went through the motions, feeling raped, feeling defrauded and feeling like I was not a real woman.*

*from Erica's story*

Erica's statements about this chain of events link having to have surgery with many adverse feelings: feeling raped, feeling defrauded, feeling she was not a real woman. She describes having a "frozen heart" and not being able to sleep when her baby was sleeping, which could be symptoms of postpartum depression. As of this writing, finding a provider who will attend the vaginal birth of a breech baby is very hard. In light of that, this mother could have done very little to change the process she had to undergo. But she certainly could have used some help to take care of her wounded sense of self and her deep disappointment.

Kay shares how she chose a more technologically oriented provider and setting because her assessment was that she needed not to have to deal with "[her] own pain" on top of the effort she was giving to becoming a mother. A careful reading of her words indicates that she thought high levels of physical pain management would prevent emotional reactions. In her experience, that did not work.

*Needless to say, I set myself up for a medically managed birth from the start, because I had convinced myself that it was better not to deal with my own pain now that I was going to become someone's mother. I went to a high intervention OB, and when I went into labor I had the works. Morphine, epidural, episiotomy.... This did block out the pain—mental and physical. Looking back now, I regret a lot of things but it's what I thought was best at the time. The pinnacle came when it was time to push out my son. The doctor breezed in, sliced me open and yanked out my baby. I didn't feel the physical pain, but inside I was screaming, "Please! NO!" My husband sensed what I was thinking and turned to me in alarm. This didn't last long because our baby was born dark blue and not breathing. From all the drugs that were pumped into my body to mask the pain, I assume. A team of doctors worked on him for what seemed like forever. They were about to rule him a stillbirth when he let out a feeble little cry. At that moment, I knew there had to be another way. The pain that my child was going through wasn't worth masking my own.*

*from Kay's story*

Kay concludes that the choice to use such pain medication and anesthesia was not worth the price that her child paid for her attempt to conceal her own pain. Notice four important issues here: distinguishing among physical and psychological pain management strategies, the potential value in debriefing, accepting one's decisions and using a bad experience to take steps to heal.

First, the wisdom Kay shares in this narrative is that the ways to treat physical pain—which can be very worth having in labor—are not the same way to treat emotional pain. Lynelle's story conveys this same point. She felt no physical pain, but she suffered anyway. When planning strategies to cope with labor, an important element is to separate, if possible, how much of the fear of birth is concern about physical pain and how much is fear of other stressors, such as fear of loss of control, fear of not being well cared-for or fear that memories of trauma will come up. This sorting-out is worthwhile because epidurals or narcotics will not directly prevent stress that is not directly physical. If psychological pain is of greater concern, then other approaches are likely to be needed. And a combination of physical and psychological "pain" management may be best of all.

The second important thing to notice from Kay's story is that she says, "... our baby was born dark blue and not breathing. From all the drugs that were pumped into my body to mask the pain, I assume." This is an example of one of those times when debriefing would have been a really good idea. Many things can make a baby's transition to extra-uterine life difficult. Kay's self-blaming assumption keeps her from a better understanding that might be less painful. Even if pain medication contributed, other factors may have contributed to the baby's condition as well. If Kay had been able to discuss what had happened with her doctor, she might have learned that the cause was not directly related to her pain medication. Even if she had learned that it was directly related, she and her doctor might have been able to express mutual regret for the problem the imperfect pain management caused, and she would not have been needlessly taking on so much blame.

The third important point is that Kay tells the story as though the emergency that occurred means her decision was necessarily a bad one. Emergencies can occur during birth no matter what decisions the woman makes ahead of time. If her doctor had been present a little earlier, if no emergency had occurred and if she had felt in control about whether she had an episiotomy or not, her sense might have been that her experience was a positive one, and she would have been satisfied with the decision to use a high level of pain management. A useful step may be to remember that birth is a complex, evolving situation with very few absolutely right or wrong choices, and almost no choices that a woman is required to make without input and support from others.

Finally, the tone of Kay's story indicates that when she realized trying to mask her emotional pain was not worth the price she paid, she was ready to confront it more directly. This theme of using a realization gained across the childbearing year as an impetus for recovery and growth comes up very often.

### *FINDING YOUR "MATCH"*
Stephanie hoped for a natural birth but ultimately felt "belittled by the medical establishment":

*I wanted a natural birth and to breastfeed my child, but the system kicked in and, without even knowing, I quickly became a victim once again....*
*My ability to trust myself and know what was best for my child and me was belittled by the medical establishment.*

*from Stephanie's story*

She doesn't say what form this belittling took. But clearly she felt overpowered by messages she took in from the medical context and/or medical professionals that did not match her view of childbirth. Any woman must truly be prepared to resist these messages if she finds them coming at her. Survivors may be less used to resisting authoritative voices. If a natural birth and breastfeeding are very important desires, then survivors may want to find allies who will advocate for them if their own resisting voice fails them. One could say with fairness that everyone wants a good outcome and a good process; but different people in different roles weigh the value of those two things differently. It is important to be realistic that the natural childbirth process is not likely to be as important to most obstetricians and hospitals as achieving a good outcome. This means they may resort to intervention sooner than the client would like them to. Those who value the natural process should look for a provider with similar values.

Dawn says that she was unaware she had choices related to her birth process, so she did not experience any mismatch with her caregivers:

> *I didn't know I had choices and I basically handed everything over to my OB and midwife. I had no idea how to prepare for birth and did not handle labor well at all! I had Pitocin and several doses of Nubain and an epidural. Despite the interventions I had a beautiful healthy girl.*
>
> *from Dawn's story*

To read this birth story may bring great relief after the previous accounts. Dawn did not seem to have strong needs or opinions ahead of time. She was willing to let her providers manage things. Although she says she did not "handle labor well" and had interventions in the process, she does not connect this way of going through the experience to any bad effect. This "going with the flow" can be a perfectly fine approach. It works best, though, if "going with the flow" is how the woman usually lives. If anxiety or personal needs usually lead to strong efforts to be in charge or control situations, then believing that such ways of coping will be set aside easily during the stress of labor may be unrealistic. Ways of working toward a goal of "going with the flow" may help, though.

Several of the narrative contributors brought up the issue of being "in control" and their perception that choosing a midwife-attended birth might facilitate that. Needing to be in control may indicate that the individual fears what might happen if she is out of control. In a birth setting, one needs to consider as possibilities many procedures and/or interventions. One of these is the issue of other people making decisions about what happens to the woman's body, sometimes without her informed consent. Pain and wondering how one might react to and be affected by the perception and reality of pain is another issue. How women plan to cope with these issues is very individual. In the United States, most women choose to birth at hospitals with doctors in attendance, in keeping with the societal norm. However, several of our narrative contributors chose to seek midwifery care based on the idea that such care would afford them more control:

> *It's a funny thing, but many people have told me how brave I was to have a homebirth. I actually wanted one out of fear; I was afraid of the loss of control and afraid of dying and afraid of pain and afraid of needles and afraid of a whole litany of other things. I figured that I had more of a chance to deal with my fears in my own environment than anywhere else.*
>
> *from Shakta's story*

*I now realize I made that choice to seek safety from the medical world. I also was seeking control.*

*from Amy's story*

*Our decision to birth at home was very important to me from the perspective of a survivor. I knew from helping other women birth that home is where I would feel most safe, most able to control who was present and how I was handled, and most able to let down my guard to be vocal and move around as instinct dictated. It was, for me, the place that would most support trust in my own body and abilities.*

*from Beth's story*

*I thought letting go of myself to give birth would be hard. In general, I think partially because of what I went through, I like to be in control of myself. I was afraid that I would have trouble giving birth because I couldn't let go of myself. I think it helped a lot that I was at home, with a midwife and her apprentice I knew and trusted, and the only man around me was my husband, whom I also trust.*

*from April's story*

Although some women may have a high need to be in control, the truth is that birth cannot be controlled. In many ways, birth in its physiologic form is a surrendering to what is, not what we want it to be. That can be frightening for a survivor, who has had to surrender so much of herself already. So, survivor moms need to consider what conditions are necessary for them to feel safe as they enter into the awesome work of giving birth. For most women, choosing a caregiver is the first task. But having a caregiver is not enough: Survivors must work on building a relationship with that person.

## *RELATIONSHIPS WITH CAREGIVERS*

In the chapter on pregnancy we discussed how women go about finding caregivers, the relationships between caregivers and survivor moms and how survivors sometimes have difficulty establishing trust in a caregiver. Many of these contributors expressed a lack of trust in their birth attendants, which may have had an adverse effect on their experiences. Indeed, separating the effects of the events during birth from the relationships the survivors had with their caregivers in terms of the overall quality of their experience is often impossible.

Unfortunately, some often assume that the patient-provider relationship is somehow, magically endowed with an automatic sort of trust by virtue of the provider's role. Not many "rules of thumb" exist for how to create a strong, trusting alliance with a maternity care provider—or group of providers. But the narrators share some ideas.

Liz's narrative includes two strategies. First, she stays in therapy, despite some misgivings about how re-experiencing the psychological pain might affect her baby *in utero*. This means she has an objective third party—her therapist—to help her evaluate how the relationship with her maternity care provider is going. Therapists are in a good position to do this because they have training in what a good therapeutic relationship is supposed to be like, and they should understand survivors' issues. Second, Liz is ready to disclose her abuse history on the midwives' intake form and make planning for her trauma-related needs part of her work with them.

*I was in the midst of this therapy when I became pregnant with my second child. At first I considered stopping therapy, as I did not want to expose my yet-to-be-born child to the dark places we entered during our sessions. I was afraid of what he would hear and feel in utero. After much internal debate, I realized that the personal growth I was doing, the growth of this child's mother, would more than make up for any damage done. I chose different midwives for this birth. As I was filling out the required forms I checked the box marked "yes" for the question "Have you ever been physically, emotionally or sexually abused?" for the first time in my life.* A warrior wears her battle scars with pride.

*Will's birth was different for many reasons. He was my second child, he was smaller than Eric, he was born into water. He was born to a woman who could make noise! I moaned and groaned and felt so open during the labor and birth. Much of this openness I attribute to therapy and to my midwives who allowed me to create the setting, energy and space I needed to bring my child into the world. And to David who was right there in the pool with me, my quiet pillar of support. I felt again the gratitude that something so precious could come out of a place I had loathed for so long.*

*from Liz's story*

For Liz, and many other survivors, sharing her status as a survivor of sexual abuse with her care provider was an important first step in the development of trust within the relationship. While mothers choose whether or not to disclose a history of trauma, just the fact that a practitioner asks the question may be an indicator that he or she has survivor issues on his or her radar screen, and may be more suited to working with survivors.

Whether or not a caregiver asks about a history of abuse, the survivor should let him or her know as soon as possible about particular issues related to care. Working on these issues may take a lot of time and waiting until the last minute will not leave much time for planning. Also, such disclosure can help to avoid being too late to change providers, if the caregiver is found to not be trustworthy or a good fit.

Survivors may ask for what they need, even if they do not disclose the link between the need and their history, if they have a sense that the provider will not be comfortable talking openly about how the needs are trauma-related. For example, they may say that they get very distressed during vaginal exams and need some help with that, without having to say why. A good caregiver will ask, "What helps you with that?" and offers to try to use the woman's ideas. Survivors can use the caretakers' responses to decide how to proceed. Survivors can also talk over their impressions of a caregiver with a trusted friend or therapist to help test whether the reactions are well-founded.

Women who give birth in a hospital, can expect to be asked by the labor and delivery nurse whether they have a history of current or past abuse. This is a standard of care put into place by the JCAHO (an organization that accredits hospitals). Nurses vary on how well they achieve the spirit of this assessment task. Whether a woman plans to give birth in a hospital or at home, she should be prepared for the question and decide how to answer. No one is compelled to answer affirmatively. If it is beneficial to have the nursing staff know this information, the survivor can say something like, "Yes, and I've talked about my needs around that with my doctor/midwife. Can I tell you what would be helpful to me?" Or, "…so can you talk to the midwife/doctor about the plans we made to handle any stress reactions I might have?" Or, "Yes, but I don't think it'll be an issue. Thanks for asking."

On the other hand, if the person asking the question gives signals that he or she is not comfortable and does not really want to know, the mom can honor her sense of privacy by "just saying no" or evade, with a response like, "That's too personal a question." Another option is to ask a partner, support person or doula to say something to the nurse on the mom's behalf, or ask the primary caregiver to brief the nurse.

Many health care providers feel that routine screening for history of childhood abuse is not an appropriate part of health care. Clinicians commonly object that they cannot do anything about past abuse. The general principle behind screening for any condition is that screening is worthwhile if a treatment is available that is known to be beneficial. While screening for past abuse was implemented before interventions were created and tested, some providers find screening beneficial because they go on to learn how the past abuse is affecting the current health situation. Some go on to ask about PTSD, depression or other trauma-related health problems, which opens a door to discussing needs. In the case of screening related to the very taboo topic of sexual abuse, being ready to contribute to this sometimes-awkward dialogue can be helpful. Some providers will follow up on a woman's disclosure with a question like, "And how is that affecting you now?" or "Have you had a chance to talk to anybody about that?" Survivors may find that being prepared to say something more than just "yes" is helpful. For example: "Yes, I was abused when I was a girl, and I would like a chance to tell you about what is stressful for me."

At the very beginning of the health care relationship, some women may not feel safe to disclose. They may say "no" early on, but change their minds, and can bring it up again. Providers should leave the door open for a response such as, "You know how you asked me before about if I was ever abused, and I said 'no'? Well, I wasn't ready to talk about it then, but I know you better now/have some concerns now. Can we talk about it today?"

Sometimes disclosing a history can have a downside, if the caregiver uses this information inappropriately. Caregivers may make assumptions about survivors or have certain expectations, which may or may not be consistent with what is happening. Holly shared her history as a survivor with her midwife but not with her doula, and was upset when her midwife revealed her abuse history in front of the doula during a stall in her labor:

*My husband and I chose to have a homebirth with a midwife and a doula. The labor was progressing quickly and my midwife explained that I was almost at 10 cm. I was excited that I would begin to push soon but then the contractions changed. The contractions became shorter and fewer. My midwife checked the dilation after about one hour and I had gone from almost 10 cm back to 6 cm. I did not realize this was even possible and I was upset by this. My midwife explained that this was most likely due to some fear I was experiencing and to try to let it go. I did not feel I was consciously aware of any fears I may be experiencing and the labor continued to slow down. My midwife appeared annoyed and she became persistent that the change in dilation was due to some fear inside of me. This was troubling to me because I felt she was blaming me for the change in the dilation, and I felt she was being pushy about her belief that this was due to fears inside me.*

*She seemed to be getting frustrated with me and said, "This most likely is due to the abuse from your past; you need to let it go." This statement was extremely upsetting to me. The abuse I experienced had been told to my midwife in private and she said this comment in front of a doula whom I had chosen not to tell. Breaking this confidentiality made me feel even more vulnerable than I was already feeling. I was also very angry that the abuse*

*I experienced was being discussed during the stress of labor. The reminder of the abuse added stress to an already stressful situation. It also seemed to be taking traumatic events in my life and making it into something casual, that I could just let go of so easily.*

*After the birth I began to notice many symptoms of posttraumatic stress disorder, which I have experienced in the past. I could not eat, I was having nightmares, I was hypervigilant and very irritable. I would think often about my labor experience and would feel angry towards my midwife. I decided I needed to confront her on how I was feeling. I explained to her exactly how I was feeling and how I felt during the labor. She was very apologetic and explained to me why she was frustrated during my labor. Confronting my midwife helped with many of the posttraumatic stress symptoms I was having. I felt that I took control of a situation that was feeling out of control.*

*from Holly's story*

Holly's ability to have this beneficial conversation with her midwife may have been a sign of the strength in the relationship. She may have been able to do so because she felt the midwife was basically trustworthy despite the one lapse that was so painful.

Although Kathy did not disclose her history as a survivor to her doctor, she felt supported and guided by her relationship with him and felt that he always had time for her:

*I can't remember my OB ever asking me about my history. But I just love him. After going though fertility treatments, what could be more degrading? Post-coital tests? He said that this should be the most beautiful time of my life, and that he wouldn't do anything I wasn't ready to do. He told me I deserved respect, and dignity. He didn't know me from Adam at that point. I had gone to him because I was a high-risk pregnancy. But I stayed with him, a male OB/GYN, because this man knew what women were about. He always had time for me. I was impressed with that. I was lucky. There's been some incredible guidance.*

*from Kathy's story*

Olivia also felt positive about her relationship with her midwife:

*My midwife was my friend. My visits with her included nutritional counseling and education about my body, what it was doing and why. My older daughter, all of two years old, was encouraged to come and be a part of prenatal visits. I could call my midwife at any time with questions, and my visits with her lasted a minimum of a half hour. A real contrast from five to 10 minutes per visit with my previous OB.*

*from Olivia's story*

Both Kathy and Olivia expressed appreciation for the amount of time their caregivers were able to spend with them. Feeling heard is critical to establishing trust in a relationship. A maternity caregiver in a busy practice often has difficulty finding time to work on establishing such trust. No matter how much time one spends getting to know one's doctor or midwife, the caregiver seen prenatally is not always likely to be the person who attends the birth. Many practitioners work in large practices and share being on call for births with several other practitioners. This modern reality must be taken into account by all women in preparing for their births, and may present a particular challenge for survivor moms striving to establish trust in their caregiver. Survivor moms can prepare for this likelihood by trying to think of the relationship as one entity: Choosing a group practice that has a good reputation for working with survivors is a good start toward that end. Other ways survivors can prepare for birth with a group practice is by trying to meet all the members of the team at prenatal visits, or at informal "meet the practitioner" gatherings that some practices arrange, sharing with each of the team members any particular needs identified for the birth or asking one provider to brief the others on specific needs at one of the clinical meetings many group practices have regularly. Other actions that may help are touring the facility where one intends to birth, and hiring a doula to provide continuity of care (and meeting the back-up doula as well!). We will discuss the doula relationship in more detail.

Not knowing who will attend their birth is a major reason some women choose to birth with midwives. Typically midwives who provide homebirth care do so in a small practice of one to three midwives. Women have a better chance to get to know the providers and reasonably expect that the relationship developed prenatally will serve well during the birth. Likewise, some smaller hospitals will have doctors or midwives still practicing in smaller groups and can also provide reasonable assurance that they attend the birth.

Caregivers may find that developing a satisfying relationship with survivor clients seems like an unachievable task within the paradigm of the standard medical maternity model of care. The system simply is not set up for optimal relationships. Caregivers who want to work effectively with survivors will need to establish strategies for addressing the additional needs of these clients. Being available to a particular client can be hard in a busy practice. Establishing mechanisms within that practice to make the relationship a more central focus and offering to have one particular, or one of a few specified practitioners, attend the birth may be more feasible.

Adding a diagnosis of actual or potential PTSD to the problem list that is driving care is sensible, if the client's trauma-related needs are considered legitimate risk factors for an exacerbation of PTSD and potentially a risk for adverse outcomes like labor dystocia or postpartum depression If the woman has been diagnosed with gestational diabetes or hypertension is a concern, resources for extra visits and surveillance would be available. In response to a "risk for posttraumatic stress" notation, scheduling a few extra visits to assess anxiety, making specific plans for working together in labor and building alliance is reasonable.

Caregivers who are able and want a close relationship can do this extra care themselves, especially if it is considered helpful. One approach is to take on a few clients as special cases and agree to attend their births even when not on call. For some practitioners, this will mean readjusting expectations of workload and considering taking on fewer clients. It could mean being able to address client concerns over e-mail, as more and more practitioners are doing in this day and age. Alternatively, a team approach could be considered. This extra care may take the form of scheduling supplemental visits with a nurse or nurse-practitioner for clients who would benefit from having more than the time usually allotted. Because survivors may make more unscheduled contacts than other women, this extra time may be cost-effective in the end

▼ 3.3

Bradley Method:
    www.bradleybirth.com
Lamaze International:
    www.lamaze.org
ALACE:
    www.alace.org
Birthing from Within:
    www.birthingfromwithin.com

if it meets needs that otherwise might have to be met in late night phone calls and triage visits. Making appropriate referrals to other perinatal team members can help decrease the intensity of the survivor's dependence on one person. Having a referral list of therapists who are trained in working with survivors also is very worthwhile. For clients who don't want a referral to therapy, having a psychotherapist colleague consultant can be helpful if issues or relationship dynamics come up that are outside a caregiver's usual scope of expertise.

### *CHILDBIRTH CLASSES*
Whether birthing in hospital, home, or birth center settings, many women take childbirth classes during their pregnancies in order to educate themselves and their partners regarding the birth process. Several different methods of childbirth classes are taught.(3.3)

Probably the most well-known method is Lamaze. Lamaze began in 1960 as the American Society for Psychoprophylaxis in Obstetrics. In the 1970s it became more popular and was known as ASPO/Lamaze. It is now called Lamaze International, Inc. Most people know this technique from media portrayals of the breathing techniques. The Lamaze Web site now states that "breathing" is no longer the hallmark of Lamaze, and that their mission is to "promote, support and protect normal birth through education and advocacy." The Lamaze Web site has an online locater service for finding a teacher near you. Lamaze classes are popular and well-attended, and often are offered at local hospitals. Originally, Lamaze technique was designed as an alternative to the use of anesthesia in childbirth; however, some hospital-based classes no longer emphasize this. Therefore, when you arrange to attend a class, make sure to ask the instructor what will actually be taught. Many hospital-based classes focus more on adapting to that hospital's routines. Despite this, many Lamaze instructors, especially community-based ones, are attempting to remain true to the roots of the movement.

The Bradley Method® of Natural Childbirth is a technique taught by the American Academy of Husband-Coached Childbirth. It was founded by Robert A. Bradley, MD, together with Marje and Jay Hathaway, for the purpose of making childbirth education available. The technique has a strong emphasis on the promotion of natural, drug-free childbirth, and encourages the active participation of the husband as coach. It also features relaxation technique and consumer-based approach. Classes are typically 12 weeks long, and one of the classes focuses on developing a birth plan.

Another method that uses relaxation technique and a consumerism approach is ALACE, the Association of Labor Assistants and Childbirth Educators. Now also a doula training organization, ALACE was originally begun as a childbirth method called Informed Homebirth/Informed Birth and Parenting. It was begun by midwife Rahima Baldwin, author of the childbirth preparation book *Special Delivery*, as a method designed to prepare women for birth at home. It has evolved over the years to include preparation for women birthing in hospital, birth center, and homebirth. The ALACE Web site says that ALACE is about "restoring women's confidence, strength and joy in childbearing."

An increasingly popular technique is based on the book *Birthing from Within* by Pam England and Rob Horowitz. The technique is a departure from other classes

## Chapter 3—Labor and Birth

in its insistence on the very personal aspect of childbirth. It uses a lot of creative exercises such as making birth art and encouraging women to make a plaster cast of their growing belly to personalize the journey of pregnancy for the participant. England says of her method:

> The Birthing from Within approach prepares a mother for Birthing from Within. She needs insight about what labor and birth will be like from her perspective, and preparation to be in labor and give birth as a mother, not as a trained paraprofessional. The Birthing from Within classes offer guidance through the emotional, spiritual, psychic and social mists which shroud Birthing from Within.

Katherine took childbirth classes based on the Birthing from Within perspective. She credits the preparation she did for her second pregnancy using this technique with being the most helpful thing she did to prepare.

Many of the techniques listed above have an emphasis on visualizing how you would like things to proceed in labor and birth. Carol shares her experience of visualizing her birth:

> *I did a lot of work visualizing how the birth would be. I visualized labor progressing smoothly, flowing from one stage to the next. I visualized our baby descending, crowning, and being birthed.*
>
> *from Carol's story*

Often the above courses are community-based. Many hospitals also offer childbirth education classes. These vary in the extent to which they are childbirth education as compared to education about how birth is managed in that particular institution. This can be good information for those giving birth there because it prepares clients for what to expect in terms of the hospital's routines; but it may not be all that is needed. Asking an instructor how closely she sticks to the philosophy of natural childbirth as understood by the method she teaches is worthwhile.

### BIRTH PLANS

Development of a birth plan can be a good way for survivors to familiarize themselves with the possibilities of events that may transpire during their births and allow them to make choices where possible about the course of their care. Survivor moms may be helped by working with their therapist and/or partner to help them identify some potential specific triggers or concerns and to develop a birth plan that takes their particular needs into account.

Heather wrote a birth plan that took into account some specifics regarding her potential reactions as a survivor to giving birth:

> *So, what did I plan? I wrote about 12 pages of birth plan, including what I wanted to eat, what procedures I did not want, what drugs were acceptable if I needed any, and what things to bring with me, including clothes, food, pillows, and a comfort item (a small stuffed bunny). I specified that if I needed a c-section, they could not bind my hands down at the wrists, since my reaction would be blind panic. They could, however, bind my arm just below the elbow if they needed to, but I preferred to have at least one hand free. I also included specific responses for emotional reactions. For example, if I appeared*

*to be dissociating, anyone could ask me if I actually was dissociating, because asking me is enough for me to identify it and break away. I figured out all my probable responses to pain, fear, or feeling out of control, and what the best actions to counteract them would be. I wrote all the information down, checked it with my therapist, and then handed out the list to my doulas, my husband (for reference) and my midwives. In the end, I didn't need any of it. But I was still glad I had worked it out so carefully.*

*from Heather's story*

In preparing for birth and deciding on a care provider, using a questionnaire may be helpful, like the one developed by CIMS, the Coalition for Improving Maternity Services (www.motherfriendly.org). Their Web site provides information about how to compare the answers of the providers with evidence-based benchmarks.

Birth plans can be helpful for the woman and her partner in preparing for the birth, especially if the "plan" is thought of as a means of understanding what choices are to be made regarding some of the specifics of birth. Sharing the birth plan with a care provider can produce a variety of responses, depending on the relationship with the care provider and the context in which the birth plan is shared. Some care providers may feel threatened by a birth plan, and be less than receptive. The way in which the birth plan is introduced to the care provider may determine the response. A provider may feel "put off" by birth plans that come off as a list of demands, essentially dictating to the provider what a client will and will not accept, regardless of the situation. Given that things can be unpredictable in a birth situation, care providers are leery of plans that do not seem flexible or realistic. They also may be concerned for the clients themselves, if they are setting up expectations for the birth that may not be met, leaving them potentially feeling disappointed or as though they have "failed." Handing a busy midwife or obstetrician a 12-page plan, as Heather did, might not be useful, because they probably do not have time to read that much. The activity of thinking through and drafting a birth plan is probably useful, but reducing it to a shorter letter or bullet points may increase the odds of the provider taking in the information. Having said all that, if a birth plan that is reasonable and flexible (and fairly brief) is not well received by the care provider, then that particular care provider may not be a good match for the survivor. Wanting some assurance that the care provider will honor safe and reasonable

▼ 3.4

In a Swedish study of 1500 women, 1.7% met PTSD diagnostic criteria one month to one year after the birth. Forty percent of PTSD cases occurred where delivery was by emergency cesarean section or instrument-assisted vaginal delivery (forceps or vacuum). Notably, 60% of PTSD cases occurred among women who delivered by planned cesarean or by normal spontaneous vaginal delivery.

Söderquist, Wijma and Wijma 2002

▼ 3.5

Ten of the 28 women whose symptoms met PTSD diagnostic criteria had a history of previous mental health treatment and so may have had pre-existing anxiety or mood disorders, or pre-existing PTSD that increased their vulnerability to traumatic stress reactions related to their birth experience.

Söderquist, Wijma and Wijma 2002

▼ 3.6

When penetration and life threat occur during sexual abuse and rape, the victim is likely to dissociate. Dissociation is a coping mechanism that can persist beyond the trauma exposure and become automatic in situations of severe stress or those that resemble the trauma.

Johnson, Pike and Chard 2001

desires for care during the birth process is quite reasonable.

## LABOR AND BIRTH AS TRIGGERS

We have touched on the ways in which aspects of labor and birth can "trigger" posttraumatic stress reactions because they contain something that reminds a survivor of past abuse. Such a reminder can be contained in almost any aspect of this experience, perhaps because a woman can not really prepare fully for it and because it can be overwhelming—even if it turns out to be overwhelmingly good.

Triggers can take many forms. What they have in common is that they provoke the survivor to feel as though the trauma is happening again. This is a "re-experiencing" phenomenon that is sometimes called a "flashback." In our culture we have a stereotype of flashbacks as being visual, as though a movie of the past were replaying in the mind's eye. But re-experiencing can be much more subtle, to the point of not being recognized. Here are some examples. Body memories are when a sensation, such as vaginal pain during an internal exam, reminds the woman of pain from a rape. Olfactory memory, such as the smell of sweat, can be a trigger. Certain words like "just relax" or "be quiet" can be triggers if a perpetrator used them during abuse. Proprioceptive memories—memory of how the body was in space—can happen if the recumbent position often used during pushing in labor is similar to the position the survivor was in during an assault. Perhaps the hardest to recognize triggers of all are emotional ones. Affective memories, which are memories of a feeling or emotion, can be hard to recognize as being specific to abuse. But feeling afraid or belittled or out of control are all feelings a sexually abused girl might have experienced. As an adult, a woman might not feel these emotions very often, but these all are feelings narrators have described in relation to their births. Avoiding triggers is an active strategy that survivors report using, and they feel very well-helped when their providers join them in this effort to keep traumatic stress reactions to a minimum.(3.4, 3.5)

▼ 3.7

Qualitative research and clinical case reports indicate that childbirth may trigger dissociation in sexual trauma survivors. Women reported tearfully being "out of it" or unable to ask for help because of "going away" or being ungrounded during labor.

Rhodes and Hutchinson 1994
Kennedy 2002
Seng, et al. 2002

▼ 3.8

Unexpected or undesired dissociation during childbirth may prevent helpful, positive recall of a good birth. In general, dissociation is associated with more mental health problems, so it also could be related to greater mental health problems in the aftermath of a traumatic birth experience.

Seng, et al. 2002

▼ 3.9

Dissociation is related to excellent ability to self-hypnotize. Survivors who dissociate may be able to learn specific self-hypnosis strategies to use during labor. However, there may be a thin line between self-hypnotizing to soothe anxiety and pain and slipping into dissociation because the labor is becoming overwhelming. Ideally a woman and her birth attendant would plan distress signals and grounding techniques. The caregiver would need to assess for signs that the calm, quiet appearance of the woman is not belying a problem. The caregiver will also want to maintain a verbal or touch connection so that the woman does not lose contact with the support and presence that are there for her. Mindful use of her dissociative capacity may be an individualized way to optimize her experience of childbirth.

Schiraldi 2000
Seng, et al. 2002

▼ 3.10

Peritraumatic dissociation involves acute alterations in cognitive and perceptual functioning at the time of a traumatic event. It involves depersonalization, derealization, narrowing of attention, time distortion and confusion.

Marmar, Weiss and Metzler 1997

For a more extensive look at the potential triggers for survivors in labor, we recommend Penny Simkin and Phyllis Klaus's book *When Survivors Give Birth* (2004). Included in their book, is a chart highlighting triggers in labor for survivor moms, and various strategies for dealing with these triggers.(3.6, 3.7, 3.8, 3.9, 3.10)

As Katherine's story showed, the intense feelings of being in labor can trigger memories of abuse, and she could tell what was happening. That awareness did not lead to the wished-for help in the moment. Laura also was triggered by the sense of being out of control. She says she used the birth of her child and the awareness of the emotions that got stirred up in the process, as an impetus to deal with "the emotional scars."

*I panicked. I was conscious enough to tell the midwife I was having rape flashbacks, but she was young and inexperienced and could not really offer any help.*
*from Katherine's story*

*I am not sure I would have ever dealt with the emotional scars of my abuse had I not had children. I never would have expected the changes in me that occurred after the birth of my first child, a boy. His birth was difficult and long and I was extremely tense as soon as we arrived at the hospital. Though I liked the midwives who helped deliver him there, I did not feel as if I had any control over the birth process and it brought a lot of emotions to the surface.*
*from Laura's story*

## DEALING WITH PAIN

Many survivors in the narratives described that pain itself or fear of pain were a major concern for them. In this they are much like women who have never been abused. The way in which they may be different is that pain may have different meanings or fear may be more debilitating for survivors. In the full-length narratives at the start of this chapter, Katherine's first birth was facilitated by relief from an epidural, but she did not need that support for her second birth. Survivors wrote positive narratives about all kinds of strategies to work with concerns about—and the actual experience of—pain.

*I labored and birthed my baby without the aid of any pain relievers. I used my own strength and ability to relax. I allowed my body to work and didn't fight against myself. I felt confident in the thought that millions of women from the beginning of time had gone through the same process.*
*from Wendi's story*

The pain of labor can be dealt with in many ways, such as understanding the mechanism of birth and what the contractions are accomplishing, relaxed breathing, being in water, applied heat, massage, being in a loving and familiar environment, listening to music or getting verbal encouragement from caregivers. In a hospital setting where anesthesia is readily available, care providers will likely make every effort to provide epidural analgesia or anesthesia if that is part of the labor plan, whether as a front-line strategy or the fall-back plan. Women who do *not* want to use medication or an epidural for a hospital birth have to be more proactive to make sure staff and support people really understand the desire to have an unmedicated birth.

### *DOULAS*
Having a partner, friend or family member along during labor and birth can be a wonderful thing: someone who is loving and can be totally supportive. However, considering ahead of time how helpful that person will be is important. Will they still be able to advocate when things get intense in labor? Will they be able to hear moans and crying and interpret them as positive signs of good productive labor, and provide confident encouragement? Or will they be overwhelmed?

Some women do not have a steady enough partner, parent or friend to rely on. Although acknowledging this may feel terribly sad, many survivors come from families or couples where the loved ones cause harm. In a time like labor, some survivors might have greater well-being by honoring their judgment that they need to be alone. Sometimes a stranger—a nurse or a medical student volunteer—may be a better source of help and support than family.

An additional source of expert labor support is becoming more available across the US. Having a doula present in labor is now often possible. A doula is a woman trained to provide continuous emotional and physical support during labor. We've already provided information about doulas in the last chapter but, again, the Web site for DONA International is: www.dona.org

### *BIRTH, PARADIGMS, TRAUMATIC STRESS AND EMPATHY*
Trusting in the body is not easy when the body has been invaded and has been an unsafe territory in the past. However, the process of giving birth is a deep bodily experience that cannot be accomplished by thinking about it. Left undisturbed, giving birth is an intuitive process, orchestrated by our primitive brains. For this reason, a woman and her caregivers can work together to facilitate a non-interventive, non-technological birth in the context of a healthy woman and a healthy pregnancy.

However, while a robust process, birth is not always flawless. In the presence of complications, interventions and technology can be life-saving and provide good outcomes that would not otherwise be possible. Not all 21st century women are comfortable with the idea of giving birth without technological support, either

Between these two scenarios, agreed-upon non-intervention and agreed-upon intervention, is a large territory where birth "world views" or "paradigms" can collide and where many of the conflicts and bad interpersonal experiences these narrators had seemed to occur. Most 21st century health care providers who work in hospitals are comfortable with the technology they use and have less experience with natural birth. Perhaps because of the number of complications that physicians, nurses and nurse-midwives see, especially in tertiary medical centers that admit women with high risk pregnancies and obstetric emergencies, a low-trust, highly technological, emergency-oriented paradigm holds sway.

Although seemingly odd, women and providers who must meet in this uncomfortable territory where they do not agree on the level of intervention and the routines of care, may nevertheless be able to empathize with each other.

Both parties may be able to see that the presence of past trauma is operating in the other—though the trauma that is salient to each may be different. For the survivor client, the fall-out of past sexual trauma is what looms large, and her efforts are geared to avoiding re-experiencing or reenacting that. One might possibly apply a posttraumatic stress lens to the whole obstetric team in a hospital setting too, although the traumatic stress they are trying to avoid is less obvious and may be even less talked about. They may be working together to avoid re-experiencing the trauma of a bad birth outcome or the terrible emotions that surround knowledge that one has made a clinical mistake. Just as a survivor who fears being re-victimized or re-traumatized wants some control over how she will be treated, so does a health care provider who has seen bad outcomes and been strongly adversely affected by them want to have some control over the birth process in an effort to prevent a traumatic shift at work. Having empathy for each other's needs to stave off fear and stress by using power and control might help client and provider negotiate how they will mutually respect each other's "bottom line" needs.

▼ 3.11

In a study of 400 women planning a home or birth center birth, 34% had a history of any child abuse. Those with an abuse history were three times as likely to change attendants in the last three months of pregnancy (11% versus 4%), and were twice as likely to be transported to a hospital in labor (13% versus 6%). Of first-time mothers transported to the hospital in labor, 82% of those who were child abuse survivors had cesarean births compared to 29% of those who had never been abused.

Tallman and Hering 1998

▼ 3.12

In one study comparing midwives and obstetricians, women who disclosed a history of abuse chose midwives 50% more than they chose obstetricians. All of these women were low-risk and could freely select between the two types of providers. Disclosers in this research study were 12.5% of the certified nurse-midwives' clients and 8.5% of the obstetricians' clients.

Sampselle, et al. 1992

Knowing your views about birth and being able to ask about your providers' views may be useful to finding a good match where you reach agreement. We referred above to the idea of a paradigm. Paradigms can be thought of as forming when a group of people see and interpret the facts of a situation by filtering them through a set of beliefs, like looking through a shared lens. The anthropologist Robbie Davis-Floyd has described two paradigms of birth in America, ranging from a holistic to a technocratic model(1992). From one end to the other, providers' and clients' views range from thinking that the safest way to give birth is to facilitate physiology without intervening to thinking that the safest way to give birth is to manage all the potential foreseeable risks by using available technological interventions. Knowing as a client where one's own beliefs about birth fall on the continuum between those views is useful. The next task is finding a provider whose views and ability to practice in accordance with those views matches or falls near those beliefs. From our position on the holistic space on the continuum, we judge that women will give birth best where and with whom they feel safest, since feeling safe should reduce stress that can disrupt normal labor processes. We happen to know a lot of survivors who feel stronger and safer on the holistic end with midwifery care, not surprisingly, because those are the survivors we see. Some evidence shows that survivors may choose midwives somewhat more often than physicians, given a choice.(3.11, 3.12) Others feel safest on the technocratic end with medical care. Survivors who have such fear of labor that

## THE ART OF ATTENDING AND FACILITATING BIRTH

Whatever birth paradigm a survivor holds, and wherever she ends up giving birth, care practices can be carried out with respect for trauma-related needs. Sensitive respectful care, and care that makes her feel safe, will likely facilitate good outcomes because it will decrease anxiety that can get in the way of effective labor. Respect for the privacy and body integrity of any laboring mother is paramount to her well-being, but may be especially so for survivors. Imagining why this would make a beneficial difference to her feeling safe is not difficult.

Denise shares how her homebirth midwife destroyed her privacy and her calm coping with labor by touching her without permission or warning:

▼ 3.13

A variety of coping styles have been observed and described in laboring sexual abuse survivors. These reactions could occur in the stress of labor for any woman, but can be at the extreme in some abuse survivors. These can be seen to reflect different aspects of posttraumatic stress reactions.
- Fighting: Irritability, outbursts of anger, exaggerated startle responses, intense distress at events that resemble the trauma (such as feeling fear or pain)
- Taking control: Hypervigilance and attempts to avoid triggers
- Surrendering: Splitting off awareness of thoughts and feelings about trauma using denial, numbing, emotional constriction, and dissociation so that she seems to be coping with no distress at all
- Retreating: Using dissociation to remove herself emotionally and mentally from the situation, absenting herself as though labor were the abuse recurring

Rhodes and Hutchinson 1994

*I was on my bed leaning forward on pillows, wearing my gown because it was cold and I was having some really big contractions. Next thing Donna whips up the back of my gown, exposing my bare behind and... Waves of anger and resentment and fear filled me, and very little progressed in the labor for a long time. Donna also did an internal examination every hour or so and of course I now felt this was something I was being subjected to against my will or otherwise she would leave...so it was just like an abuse situation. "You'll let me touch you there or else."*

*from Denise's story*

Some have suggested anecdotally that survivor moms have more labor "dystocia," that is that they may have longer labors or periods while in labor when their labor "stalls." Women who are very anxious appear to have longer labors (Lederman 1979). One can reasonably surmise that a sexual abuse survivor could experience a high level of anxiety in labor and might experience slower progress or stalling along the way, but no research has yet determined whether this is true or not. Likely survivors experience as much variety in how labor unfolds and in how effectively they cope as do other women.(3.13) Still, long or stalled labors are those that end with interventions, so considering what techniques or support to use with a survivor (and any other woman) to facilitate the most steady labor progress possible is worthwhile.

Penny Simkin, a midwife and childbirth educator who has been working with and writing about survivors in labor for more than a decade, makes a variety of suggestions about helping a stalled labor and other challenges that women survivors and their caregivers face in her book *When Survivors Give Birth* (2004).

Heather was in labor a long time. She feels that her body needed the time it took, and that by laboring a long time she was able to last through a staffing change and get a midwife to attend her whom she liked better and probably trusted more:

*My mind kindly put me in time-warp mode, and I had no idea how long my whole labor had been. I judged how long I had been in labor by how my body was doing, not by the clock, and if you asked my body, it had been 24 hours. Letting my body tell me was a good idea; time is relative when you are in labor. In part, I suspect that my labor was so long because the midwife I so strongly disliked was the one on call when I started having contractions. So even the length of the labor was a good thing—I got a different midwife!*

*from Heather's story*

Stacey was helped during her birth by her doctor's patience with the process:

*My labor, which started out in the hospital birthing center, ended in the delivery room with a dosage of Pitocin and five to six hours of pushing. My doctor never gave up on me; bless her a thousand times. She knew how much I didn't want a cesarean. She even spent the night at the hospital to be near me. Staff would come into my room and say, "Oh, it's so peaceful in here, and the lady across the hall is screaming and going crazy." I comforted myself with the fact that my son was in such great shape, and had great Apgar scores. They told me the babies like it nice and easy.*

*from Stacey's story*

Midwives are generally considered to be good at encouraging women in labor and giving sensitive care. But as our narratives show, women did not always perceive their midwives to be sensitive or caring during their births, and they associated lack of support with slow progress. Paulette felt unsupported and hurried by her midwives:

*My labor with my daughter was bad. Like I was getting Pitocin the whole time. The same midwife that delivered my sons and trained me delivered my daughter. My apprenticeship went bad and I was not given what was really needed. So, the midwife and her partner (my future partner) were there. My mother was in the other room with the boys asleep. I couldn't sit or relax. I just stood up against the dresser and labored alone. The midwives didn't even give me support. The senior midwife told me I should just relax and get it over with.*

*from Paulette's story*

Stacey felt that her midwife was distant, and not warm, and that she wasn't being taken care of well enough:

*Despite being in a great relationship, and this being my second child, I was not more successful in having a quicker birth. This one, in fact, was longer—three days. I went into labor Friday night, and gave birth Monday morning. I had a midwife this time, and*

## Chapter 3—Labor and Birth

*tried my best to have a homebirth. My main midwife, to be honest, wasn't all that great for me. She was kind of distant, not warm. If it had been my first birth, I would have been really unhappy with her.*

*I felt very alone, not connected to anyone attending this birth, like I was not being taken care of well enough. This is actually the first time I have said this.*

*from Stacey's story*

Internal examinations are high on the list of procedures that are triggering. We already have seen in other narrative passages how women can sometimes feel that their caregiver is acting as a perpetrator. How often that perception is well-founded is hard to tell; but sometimes such instances are witnessed by nurses or others who take no action. Survivors told stories of how they valued being examined sensitively and gently. They also described times when, despite what it cost them, they said "no."

*His exam was a painful one. I know he couldn't have done many, or maybe he liked to hurt women. He put his fingers inside of me and pressed very hard on my fundus. So hard that I remember thinking "If I'm not miscarrying he will force the baby out of my body." I told him he was hurting me. I told him to stop. He said he was almost done. He inserted a finger in my rectum to "check the back of my uterus" and hurt me some more. Then he wanted to do an immediate D&C. He told me my life depended on it. I told him where he could go. I was crying and shaking and he told me that if I left now I would be doing so against medical advice. I told him I was leaving anyway, that he wouldn't touch me again. I had to sign papers just to get out of the door. Before I left, the corpsman that was present in the room during the exam told me that if I had been nicer to the doctor maybe he would've been gentler with me.*

*from Judy's story*

Sadie shares her reaction to an internal exam given by a doctor assigned to her for her birth whom she had not previously met:

*During my son's birth, I had to handle a difficult invasion when the hospital doctor, who had been assigned to me, checked me for dilation. I knew that after he'd gotten the information he needed, he kept moving his finger inside me. It was repulsive. The nurses said later he often did that to women. I, who had been calmly in concentration, suddenly blurted to him—"Get out!" I experienced his treatment as a rape. In hindsight, I see that in my response I voiced what I could never say as a child without risking death. Get out! Go away! No more! Don't mess with me! I know the truth about you! I don't care what your authority is; you get away! In that instant, all of this was being conveyed.*

*from Sadie's story*

Sadie was able to respond to the abuse she felt at the hands of this doctor in the way she wasn't able to as a vulnerable child. Other contributors who previously had issues with internal exams were able to go on to have a better experience with different caregivers:

*My other problem was allowing internal exams. They felt like violations again.*

▼ 3.14

In a study with 53 Swedish women referred to a special midwifery service because of fear of labor, 19% had postpartum PTSD, despite the extra care they received. They nevertheless expressed satisfaction with this antepartum care. Instances of great dissatisfaction occurred, however, when different labor and delivery care providers disregarded the birthplans or agreements about care made with the antepartum team.

Ryding et al. 2003

▼ 3.15

In two studies, pregnant women with a history of sexual trauma (Soet, Brack and DiIorio 2003) and pregnant women seeking help for fear of childbirth (Ryding et al. 2003) had postpartum PTSD symptoms at much higher rates (33% and 19% respectively) than the 1.7–6.9% found in prevalence studies.

Soet, Brack and DiIorio 2003
Ryding et al. 2003

*During my last pregnancy, God did a healing there. I was able to have exams without that "raped" feeling afterward. It also shows how much I grew to trust my midwife.*

from Dawn's story

Although seemingly obvious, having a bad experience at the hands of a care provider can stir a deep well of anger and other emotions that seem so far from the ideal and so far from what the woman expected to feel is problematic. Some women are able to resolve the feelings quickly. Others will greatly benefit from help in working through these hard feelings to make room for bonding and recovering from childbirth.

*I was so full of anger and resentment; I didn't want to hold my son for the first hour of his birth. It wasn't his fault. I knew that even then, but with no one but the two of us, I felt angry with us both. The doctor had left as soon as he stitched me up. Once I held my son and began to bond with him I was angry for him instead of at him.*

from Judy's story

Judy's anger and resentment came from feeling that the management of her delivery was not appropriate. Although her narrative recounts being overpowered and subjected to procedures against her will, what is missing from her narrative is information about why the staff acted as they did. Was the baby okay, or was there an emergency? From Judy's perspective, hospital staff repeatedly violated her autonomy and body integrity, and she was shown no respect. Research shows that not only a traumatic birth leads to postpartum PTSD and depression, but to the sense that caregivers are incompetent and/or uncaring. (3.14, 3.15) If an emergency occurred, better communication during the delivery and debriefing afterward may be very helpful. If no emergency necessitated all the harshness and intervention she experienced, then, indeed, Judy's perceptions are accurate and staff are, in fact, colluding in violent treatment. The harmful effects of such disrespect and violation are evident in Judy's initial rejection of the baby, which she was able to surmount as she placed her anger appropriately with the birth attendant who was in charge of what happened in the delivery room. If a survivor is having trouble getting a satisfying explanation for what happened during a traumatizing birth, then seeking a therapist or a friend to vent anger to may be better than nothing to help decrease the amount of energy that goes into trying to recover from the experience of such powerlessness alone.

Although some women protested when they felt violated or overwhelmed, others resort to the form of coping that worked for them during childhood trauma when resisting was not an option. Lanie shares that she ended up dissociating in order to deal with the intensity:

*My baby had arrived. They placed it on my stomach and I said to give it to Jared, my husband. I asked him to please take the baby. I remember someone said "no, take your baby; here is your beautiful baby." At this point I think I just needed to get away from the whole thing and so I just sort of left, went somewhere safe in my mind. My husband said later it is the same place I go when I am afraid of sex.*

*from Lanie's story*

Others use very creative strategies when they have to do whatever is necessary to get their needs met:

*I don't know why midwives think that it's comfortable to push with someone's face staring up your fanny. They might be midwives, and to them it's just another fanny, and they are used to seeing fecal matter and so on, but let me just say that when it's my birth, it's my fanny and fecal matter and it's all very new to me. Even my non-abused friends agree on this point. I felt very inhibited...I finally gave birth in a squat position of course because that was the only semi-private position available to me. When I give birth again I will definitely make sure I am left alone to get on with it myself.*

*from Denise's story*

Another point in Denise's description is that she would have preferred being "left alone to get on with it" herself. This is in contrast to other narrators who felt too alone and unsupported in labor. No one way to feel, no universal pattern of need exists.

In Holly's narrative, she became angry when her midwife insisted that an abuse-related fear of hers could be keeping her from giving birth. Holly felt that was not true for her. But other narrators recount that this seemed true for them.

*When I went into labor, things moved along very well, right up until my son passed my cervix.... My belief is that my body was afraid to allow my son into the world, fighting to keep him inside, where it was safe. My body knew the world as a very painful and unsafe place. I think that as much as I wanted to hold him, I wanted to keep him away from the things I knew were out here.*

*from Joanna's story*

Other survivors may have similar feelings about the relative safety of life in the womb versus being born into the world. Having such fears is reasonable, and confronting them in labor is probably a powerful experience if one has the needed support. Exploring what fears might block labor ahead of time may also be advantageous. Sometimes this emotional groundwork can be done with a maternity care provider or friend. Sometimes seeking a psychotherapist who is skilled at providing support and safety during the process of such hard emotional effort may be most helpful.

We spoke earlier in this chapter about the need for flexibility in planning for birth. Sometimes plans need to be changed despite the best of intentions of both clients and their caregivers. Stacey planned a birth at home but transported for Pitocin augmentation:

*I got stuck at 9½ cm and stayed stuck, even though some of my contractions were really long, five, six, seven minutes. The world would turn white, with a "tear"*

▼ 3.16

In a study that followed 103 women from childbirth education classes through to 4 weeks postpartum, 1.9% met diagnostic criteria for PTSD (similar to rates from other studies of postpartum PTSD). However, fully 34% said their birth was traumatic, and 30.1% were experiencing posttraumatic stress symptoms. A sense of powerlessness and cesarean delivery more than doubled the likelihood of experiencing the birth as traumatic, but for the small number of participants who had a history of sexual abuse, the risk was 12-fold.

Soet, Brack and DiIorio 2003

▼ 3.17

A 10 year follow-up study of 617 Swedish women found that women with a negative experience of their first birth have fewer subsequent children and a longer interval to a second baby.

Gottvall and Waldenstrom 2002

▼ 3.18

American College of Nurse Midwives is the oldest women's health care organization in the United States and is the professional organization for Certified Nurse-Midwives:
www.acnm.org

Midwife's Alliance of North America is the professional organization for traditional, direct entry and Certified Professional Midwives:
www.mana.org

American College of Obstetricians and Gynecologists, women's health care physicians:
www.acog.org

Coalition for Improving Maternity Services: www.motherfriendly.org

Centers for Disease Control and Prevention: www.cdc.gov

*pattern in the middle, the worse the pain, the bigger the hole. I threw up a few times. I still can't drink lemonade with honey.*

*I hung in there, remaining calm, and for the most part, really positive. We packed up for the hospital on the coldest day of 1997, and during the bumpy ride, the baby was already in the birth canal. A few moments of Pitocin, and five (count them) pushes and she was out!*

*from Stacey's story*

Cesarean section represents another "change in plans" that affects many birthing women. Lynelle describes how, despite knowing it could happen, she still felt overwhelmed. More than one in four women in the United States currently undergoes cesarean section for the birth of her baby (2004 CDC statistic: 29.1%, reported on the ICAN Web site). This is a dramatic rise from 1970, when the rate was 5%; and the rate has risen 40% just since 1996 (www.ican-online.org/).

In addition to medical indicators, more and more women are choosing c-sections for other reasons, perceiving them perhaps to be more convenient because the birth can be "scheduled." Survivors may have other reasons for choosing cesarean section. One study undertaken in Sweden suggests that first time mothers who demand elective cesarean section list their reasons as a profound fear of a vaginal rupture that might never heal, and a history of sexual assault (Ryding 1993). So, as with any birth experience, survivors' reactions can vary widely and what may traumatize one woman will be soothing to another.

Although this book focuses on women who enter the childbearing year with posttraumatic stress affecting childbearing because of childhood sexual abuse, some women (approximately 1–3%) develop PTSD as a result of a traumatic birth experience. They too may have extra needs for support if they face another pregnancy.(3.16) Some respond to this need by seeking a different experience. For some this may mean a different setting, such as homebirth instead of hospital. Some whose post-birth PTSD is due to a traumatic vaginal birth experience may seek elective cesarean delivery. Both maternity care and mental health professionals are becoming more aware of the impact of traumatic birth on subsequent pregnancies (Gottvall and Waldenstrom 2002).(3.17) Help to work through post-birth posttraumatic stress and help to plan how to approach another birth are becoming more available.

> *By the time I became pregnant with my second child, I had pretty much gotten up the courage to attempt a homebirth. Actually, it was more out of fear that the hospital bureaucracy would again supersede my desires, and I'd be treated as an "obstetrical cripple" because of my previous surgery. Twenty hours of active labor and four hours of pushing would have earned me another trip to the surgical suite under an MD's care, but I had wonderful, caring midwives who believed in me, and I gave birth to my child.*
>
> from Erica's story

Cesarean delivery, repeat cesarean, VBAC and elective cesarean are procedures surrounded by evolving controversy. Women who have strong feelings about the issue of surgical delivery may want to inform themselves from a variety of sources including advocacy (e.g., ICAN), professional (e.g., ACOG, ACNM, or MANA) and government (e.g., CDC) sources of information.(3.18)

Lynn Madsen, in her book *Rebounding from Childbirth: Toward Emotional Recovery* (1994), offers one reason a woman may choose cesarean section. She also discusses the possible link between the powerful emotions and experiences of birth and the power to heal from abuse and stop its cycle in her family:

> When abuse has occurred and is unacknowledged, any way to give birth without opening, without giving up the protection and shell the woman desperately needs, will be sought on an unconscious level. A cesarean is a way out in this case—a way for the baby to leave the woman's body without her becoming sexually vulnerable. The woman still faces the healing challenge of finding the inner power that will allow her to be open and be vulnerable. In unlocking her anger, fear, grief and rage, she ultimately leads herself to effective self-protection and joy.
>
> Any birth is powerful. Even with unforeseen medical interventions, planned medical interventions, or unexpected loss, potential for healing is present. Days, months or years after a birth, a woman can tap into this power and weave her own tapestry of healing from abuse. Her personal cycle of repeating the abuse pattern within herself or her family will be transformed.

### *HONORING COMPLEXITY AND THE EFFORTS OF INDIVIDUALS*

Many clinicians practicing today have learned about the issues survivors face and want to be excellent providers of care for survivors. They come to this knowledge by a variety of means. Because so little research has been done to guide practice, they often learn from reading or talking to others, or from influential role models during their training. Quite often, though, they still have to learn from working with clients—that is, by trial and error in the process of gaining experience. Of course, some providers are survivors themselves. But just as a survivor giving birth might not quite know what she needs, sometimes a survivor provider still has to work hard to sort out how best to provide this care. Caregiving is an art. At this point we are taking time out of portraying issues that came up around birth provided by the survivor mom narrators to insert narratives from two caregivers who have given this a lot of thought.

## A PHYSICIAN'S PERSPECTIVE

Elizabeth Shadigian, MD, an obstetrician colleague, shared thoughts, feelings and passion about her practice with survivors. We include her writing not only because it is eloquent but also because it may speak to the caregivers reading this book. Her words may give everyone hope that meeting survivors' needs and providing medical care that can help heal old traumatic wounds is—of course—possible.

> In residency, I just started asking women about their history of violence. So many women I asked said "yes," they had been hit as a child, as a teen and/or as an adult by parents or partners. They said yes when asked about forced sex and inappropriate touching. I just couldn't believe how many women said yes, but part of me knew it wasn't just me who'd been hurt so badly as a child and young adult. I read and read to educate myself, but my patients taught me what the books could not teach.
>
> Many women just wanted to be able to see a doctor and know that they would not be expected to have a pelvic exam. They just wanted to talk—to share their pain and discuss their worries or diagnoses with no other strings attached. They wanted options, not edicts. They wanted a safe place to tell their deepest feelings and share their most painful experiences, thoughts and fears.
>
> I found as a physician that pregnancy and childbirth brought out both self-nurturing in women and a desire to nurture their unborn or newly born baby. At the same time there were always doubts of their own mothering abilities and fears that they would not do well enough in labor or as a mother. Then there was the question of leaving the new baby with others, especially grandparents and strangers who would touch the baby in the hospital. Even after a healthy baby, decisions may be repetitively questioned—did she do enough to avoid a c-section? Did she have to have an epidural? Did she have good enough breast milk?
>
> Women's reactions are so varied about their pregnant bodies, especially those who have a history of being physically and sexually violated. The range is as broad as it is individual. Pelvic exams may be intolerable for any reason, or a woman may dissociate and become limp during a pelvic exam, as if her soul fled her body. This can be true in and out of pregnancy.
>
> A woman may fear a cesarean section as it mimics her being held down, immobilized and undefended. The cesarean section and, in fact, all surgical procedures may bring back a torrent of traumatic body memories, even if her mind is prepared. Sweating, feeling trapped, she may trust those around her intellectually, but her body wants to run and claw and fight.
>
> She may feel dirty being pregnant, a visible manifestation of her sexuality and sexual encounters for all to know and see. She may feel that her old uncleanliness (really from her victimization) could then be transmitted to her baby, especially if she was to have a vaginal birth—the dirtiest part of her contacting a new life and forever spoiling it.
>
> These are only a few ruminations of women I have known—incredibly intelligent, sophisticated and yet devastated women grappling with a past that haunts them wherever they go each day, even into motherhood.
>
> For others birth and mothering are a saving grace, a way of exorcizing the demons of the past. As they trust their bodies to bring forth new life,

they feel their physical and emotional strength returning to them—new life reawakening their own bodies and childhoods—now reborn with innocence and strength.

What do I do as a physician to help? First, I ask. I care enough to ask about physical and sexual assault. Then, I listen. I listen very carefully, very emotionally to each woman's story of her personal hell. Each woman, I tell her that she is not alone. She is not bad. She is loveable and loving and lovely inside and out. I will help her see this by telling her how good she looks, how wonderful it is that her body is growing the baby so well. I will refer her to a therapist who understands violence and mothering and healing. I will be therapeutic to her at each visit and during birth. I will continue to listen for years after, too.

I will acknowledge anxieties and give tours of operating rooms, let her touch speculums and other medical equipment so that she may have power over what is around her and ultimately over herself.

I hug freely and pass out tissues without end. I try to create a safe environment, safe enough to recite scary histories and to share fears and anxieties, triumphs and heartache. I try to live in the present moment, unafraid to bear witness to others' suffering as honor to my own and theirs.

Part of my personal journey is revealing hearts covered in darkness, gently, gradually lifting the silence around violence against women. My clinical work continues to drive my teaching medical students, residents, midwives, physicians and other health care providers about interpersonal violence to empower them to reach out and create a safe environment for women to tell their stories. Telling their stories then allows healing to start or to continue, and through an empowering medical encounter, to incorporate physical and sexual safety for their bodies. Therapy is an integral part of their healing, which I always recommend, but this comes slowly, if ever, to some and easily to others. I am patient. I can wait for her. She will let me know when the next step should come. I still wait…and listen.

## *A MIDWIFE'S PERSPECTIVE*
Midwives have an opportunity and obligation to help survivors of sexual abuse while also setting clear boundaries.

As a midwife I recognize that people who have survived sexual abuse, or any abuse, have had their personal and essential boundaries irrevocably transgressed. The fencing of their innermost being has been torn asunder and they have then had to establish a makeshift patchwork of intricate coping mechanisms and behaviors in order to keep the chaos of the world outside their inner sanctum. Through birth, we as midwives necessarily stand at the gateway; yet we must help our clients keep their fences intact.

The first thing we can do is examine ourselves. Many of us are survivors, with our own patched-up systems of defense. How does this impact our ability to draw clear boundaries around ourselves as we relate to the outside world, and specifically to our clients? Do we avoid interactions with clients whom we consider too "risky" for us, and allow our clients' needs to go unanswered? Or do we consistently over-extend, promising and giving our clients more than we can healthfully provide? We must first be absolutely clear about our own boundaries if we expect to be available to help our clients, some of whom will be survivors like us.

Often when boundaries are violated the victim is denied the right to normal, natural expression of the feelings provoked as a result of the trauma—fear, grief and anger. Because of this initial denial it is imperative that midwives be very clear about providing help where it is presently needed. We must take care of first things first—our clients are seeking our care as midwives, not as therapists or ministers. This is not to suggest that a midwife not be sensitive to her clients' pain, but just that we should give help where help is asked for and not go delving about in matters that are out of the scope of our practice. We need to understand that our clients may need more assistance than we as midwives are equipped to provide. And furthermore, our client must ask for such assistance, and not have it foisted upon them. Letting clients know exactly what can and cannot be done for them is helpful in defining boundaries and establishing a sense of safety and trust. Being clear about boundaries does not mean we can't be flexible, however. We will need to make accommodations for our survivor clients: spending time on the phone processing a difficult prenatal interaction, scheduling a little extra time at our visits and being generally creative about helping clients get their needs met. Being flexible is a key state of being for a midwife to inhabit.

Ina May Gaskin, midwife and author of *Spiritual Midwifery,* writes about flexibility and birthing:

> We have found that there are laws as constant as the laws of physics, electricity or astronomy, whose influence on the progress of birthing cannot be ignored. The midwife attending births must be flexible enough to discover the way these laws work and learn how to work within them. Pregnant and birthing mothers are elemental forces, in the same sense that gravity, thunderstorms, earthquakes and hurricanes are elemental forces. In order to understand the laws of their energy flow, you have to love and respect them for their magnificence at the same time that you study them with the accuracy of a true scientist.(p. 282)

Survivors are in all different places in their healing process, and although they may check the box on our health history form indicating that they are survivors, or even share much more than that, it does not mean that we should ask a client to divulge details of her history or to encourage her to explore the possibility of having been abused based on our suspicions. We need to really listen to our clients in order to respond to their specific needs. Learning about abuse issues and how they can affect childbearing and mothering is a noble pursuit, and certainly can inform discussions with clients who choose to bring it up, however it is important to leave control over such discussions in the client's power.

Following is a list of ways in which midwives can establish a practice wherein survivors can feel safe:

1. When a survivor chooses to divulge her history as a survivor, either as part of a health history screening or on her own initiative, we need to let her know that first off she is not unusual, that there are many survivors, and we have had experience working with them, and that she is not alone. We need to make sure that she understands that we believe her when she speaks her pain, that we are present to that pain just as we will be present to the pain of labor. We do not run from the abuse or attempt to sweep it under the rug. Neither do we recoil in horror in the telling. If a woman has a "body memory" or becomes triggered while under our care we communicate our perception of the seriousness of the situation, accepting that she has been violated in the past and that she is re-experiencing that violation. We show compassion for her in all her emotions. We do not expect her to be "getting over it" already or tell her she needs to forgive or forget. We hope to help her not feel shamed by this reaction by assuring her that it is a normal reaction to trauma, hopefully helping her to avoid feeling guilt or embarrassment.
2. We are informed about professional resources in the community that may be helpful to our clients and we make referrals when appropriate.
3. We encourage our clients to establish a broad base of support, which may include family, friends, women's support groups, church organizations, 12-step programs, etc.
4. We strive to treat our clients with respect and honor. As midwives this means acknowledging the need to ask permission before touching or performing procedures. It means informing the client continually about how our care is structured and what our clients may expect from us in general. To this end, I would recommend that all midwives prepare and use an informed consent agreement with their clients in order to promote the specific delineation of boundaries and expectations.
5. We let our clients know that we are open to input, that we really want to hear how they are feeling and experiencing our care. We accept that we make mistakes, and encourage our clients to help us understand how we can find ways to improve. Likewise, our clients can benefit from a debriefing after any procedures or the birth itself, which may have been intense for them and provoking.
6. We avoid judging our clients, or making evaluative statements about their lives, such as, "you're better off for having come through this," or "this was a lesson you needed to learn, "or "this must be your karma." Such statements ultimately revictimize.
7. Above all, we need to communicate a message of hope, not in the trite sense of "everything will be alright, honey," but rather a perception that we appreciate how deeply she has been hurt, and that we still believe in our hearts that with commitment to the healing process, things can fundamentally change for the better.

As I think about these recommendations, and about the way that midwives and doctors I respect care for survivors I realize that the sensitive care we are recommending for survivors is the way everyone deserves to be treated.

## A SURVIVOR MOM'S PERSPECTIVE

### Key birthing tips for those involved in a labor:
- Being relaxed and being able to maintain relaxation is pivotal.
- Also absolutely essential is for the woman to learn to have self-reliance and empowerment, backed by a strong feeling of inner calm.
- Respect the woman's intuition.
- Respect the wisdom of the woman's body.
- Those present must have a harmonious relationship with the mother. Any disruption of trust or trace of conflict can disrupt the labor badly. Be confident enough and able to have anyone you're uncomfortable with in any way leave immediately (including your midwife, family or doctor).
- The birth experiences of those present have a profound impact on the labor. The mother has to process it.
- The more we encourage a woman to find her voice, tell the truth, let go and be all that she is and feels during pregnancy, the less likely pathology will develop in labor.
- Be patient in all aspects of labor—especially if the woman birthing is calm about the situation.

*from Denise's story*

## THE HEALING POWER OF BIRTH
*The sensation of giving birth to my daughter was amazing. I use words like "indescribable," and I mean it. Physically it felt like rape feels; it hurts so bad that your mind goes away in a shower of sparks. Mentally it was an inversion of that experience. An initiation rather than a violation. When it was all over and the sparks coalesced into thought, I had a baby and the room was awash in sunlight.*

*from Shakta's story*

Shakta's words show us that birth is a full, rich experience. For many of the moms in our project, birth was a healing experience. Some of the contributors had difficult first births but went on to have a positive experience with their second baby's birth, like both Katherine and Lynelle. In processing their first births, they gained a lot of knowledge about their needs, and did a lot of work at establishing good relationships and circumstances related to the second birth. They accessed resources and developed relationships with caregivers who could support them in their choices.

In this last section of this chapter, we say very little. The narrators' voices are strong and clear, and we hope they speak to you directly.

Lynelle calls what happened to her as a result of a powerful birth experience "finding her fire":

*My doulas were with me (I had hired two, against Dave's wishes; I was beginning to find my fire) and after I began begging for pain medication they advocated for me to get an epidural even though I was only 1 cm. About two hours after the epidural I felt the urge to push. Anna was born, vaginally, in September 1994.*

*I immediately breastfed her and bonded with her like I had not known with Ian. I felt strong and proud and was ready to parent. I had a support system to help me if I began the downward spiral into postpartum depression again (which I didn't).*

## Chapter 3—Labor and Birth

*A few days after Anna's first birthday I told Dave I was leaving him. His response was "no kidding." I began therapy because of depression around what I thought was the divorce.*

*from Lynelle's story*

Stephanie had a doula who helped her have a positive birthing experience, but her sense of well-being and humor seemed to carry her a long way in that direction all on her own:

*We spent the next couple of hours blissfully laboring in Kitty's living room. I will always remember the tea, the sandwich she made me, all the great back pressure they applied and the many trips to the bathroom. The funniest part was Kitty noticing that I began to push and saying, "Stephanie, are you pushing?" To which I responded, "No." I knew I was, but I also knew that meant I had to get up and go to the hospital. She said, "I cannot catch this baby, Steph," and insisted we get into the car.*

*The drive to the hospital, though short, was painful because I was ready to push. We got into the hospital bed, and Casey was birthed within 20 minutes of arrival, at 1:10 pm. Not only did I have a beautiful boy, but in spite of what the doctor thought was best, I trusted myself to know my body and to do what was right for me, regardless of others' feelings or beliefs, for the first time in my life.*

*from Stephanie's story*

Katherine attributes her positive second birth to the trust she was able to develop in her body:

*I spent my pregnancy focusing on trust in my body, and letting go of fear. Fear closes you down. Trust opens you up. You can choose to trust yourself or God or both, but the trust will heal you. Trusting is a choice you can make.*

*from Katherine's story*

Heather learned this trust in the body from her mother:

*I looked forward to labor, because of my mother's descriptions of the power, wonder, passion and beauty of birthing a child. I had always loved to listen to my birth story, how she had started labor in the morning, continued cleaning the house, called the babysitter, packed her bags and then called my dad. She was so calm, she trusted her body so completely, and she knew what to do.*

*from Heather's story*

Kate drew on her midwife's trust in the birthing process:

*I look back on Nate's birth as both the result of and a vehicle for healing from the abuse. Choosing to birth at home with a midwife who trusted the process of birth and the ability of my body to birth were crucial. By choosing to be at home I put myself at the center of the birthing process: I took responsibility for the possible risks of being at home and gave myself permission to say and do what I needed and wanted. I gave myself a voice. I also declared myself valuable enough to have friends around me to support me and share in the miracle. In choosing Mary to be my midwife I learned what "normal" pregnancy and birth is all about. I drew on her trust of birth and my body to learn to do the same for myself. I not only stayed in my body during Nate's birth; I also learned to trust.*

*from Kate's story*

For Liz, trusting in her body resulted from the positive connections she made with her body and sexuality through giving birth and the trust she felt communicated by her assistants:

*Giving birth gave me the first positive, blessed connection with my own sexuality. My genitals had held only shame for me before; I never owned them, never loved them. Now look what had come out of them! Sex could not be all bad if this beautiful child was the result. I also experienced the strength and power of my beautiful, female body, because everyone trusted it that day. Everyone trusted me and my body to bring this baby here. With the help of some wise and gentle hands, I too began to trust myself. To trust, and therefore respect, my body.*

*from Liz's story*

Contributors shared about the positive aspects of being able to control the particulars related to their births:

*I searched for months to find a midwife who would let me call the shots. I finally found a wonderful woman who facilitated a great birth. I say facilitated because she was in the background, just allowing things to happen. She always asked permission to touch me or check me. She never ordered me around. My husband caught the baby. I finally had a nice, gentle hospital birth. Now I have a beautiful little boy! God used Bobbie, my midwife, as another agent of healing.*

*from Dawn's story*

*Being totally in control of that birth situation and the two that followed has been essential to my well-being. I do not think I could have a baby in the hospital unless the baby's life was in danger. Being treated with respect and compassion during the births of the first baby and the next two was very important to me. I had to be acknowledged as a person and not merely as a body. I bonded with my baby immediately.*

*from Ann's story*

*The circumstances around her birth were very different, as I chose to have a homebirth with two incredible midwives, whom I spent many hours with in the months leading up to her birth. When I envisioned a water birth as the most soothing and peaceful way for me to give birth, they supported my instincts. Her birth was gentler and easier than my first, and I felt in control and supported during the whole process. Nursing my daughter was again very painful and difficult for me at first, but I had a lot of support this time around to help me stick with it. I ended up nursing her for two years and having no problems with depression after her birth.*

*from Laura's story*

Birth is an awesome process and we have described many of its potential challenges. Yet for some of our survivor moms the birth itself happened with ease:

# Chapter 3—Labor and Birth

*I was scared of my body. I was scared I would hurt the baby. I wasn't quite sure why, because I have never been an abusive person; I just was afraid. I was too small to carry a baby full term but somehow I managed to carry her three weeks overdue. She was born; labor was fine, drug-free and easy. I swore to my baby that I would give her what I didn't have. I would always love and protect her. So far that's all I've done.*

*from Valerie's story*

*Giving birth is something I've always wished I could have done a dozen times! My husband and I had compromised with three children, but two became a great many to afford some days. The experience of giving birth, the feelings, both physical and emotional, I completely enjoyed. And I know it isn't just remembering the good things now—during my labors I knew nothing was more wonderful to be doing than that.*

*from Margaret's story*

Carrie even identified being a survivor as helpful to the birthing process:

*As far as the birth experience goes, ironically, my history as an abuse survivor was helpful. I have a lot of experience "disappearing" into myself, so during contractions I did just that—I went really deep. Of course, two-plus years of Alexander Technique lessons were a big help as well. But I also believe that having worked out a lot of my issues about my mother really prepared me well for the intensity of the birth experience. Compared to the intensity of re-experiencing my forgotten abuse, birthing a baby was easy!*

*from Carrie's story*

Joanna shared that although labor was the worst pain she had ever experienced, still it was an enjoyable experience:

*I had two hours and 20 minutes of labor this time, and although it was the worst pain of my entire life, I was so much more relaxed and in control than the last two times. I actually was able to enjoy this birth, and the videotape shows me smiling and happy throughout. My husband did, in fact, deliver our son, and it was a joyous day for both of us.*

*from Joanna's story*

Many survivors felt a sense of empowerment as a result of giving birth:

*If I could birth my baby boy, I could do anything. I felt beautiful and whole. He breastfed beautifully, and I loved the closeness. The idea that my body could be such a source of creativity and life—it was a whole new discovery. It belonged to me and my baby, and there was a sense of worth that sex and men never could give me.*

*from Amy's story*

*No one in that room was going to be able to rescue me, and I wanted so dearly to "give birth" rather than "be delivered." A half hour later I was holding my sweet son and feeling a surge of something that I'd never felt before: true power. Power that comes from having done something difficult and important, not the false power that is conferred by some man wanting to use my body.*

*While not quite as quick as the previous baby, the breech birth was in some ways less difficult. When it was all over and we weighed my "littlest" baby, she was a full pound heavier than my firstborn breech, the one who doctors said I could never have delivered* myself. I laughed such a laugh of freedom, and of pleasure, and yes, of power. Each birth brought me a piece of myself that had been distorted by fear and shame. Other women are no longer competitors. I learned, in a way much deeper than just head-knowledge, that women are powerful, whether or not someone "wants" them.

*from Erica's story*

The birth experience itself made me feel powerful and womanly, and I was proud of my body.

*from Tara's story*

There comes a point in labor, especially when laboring without labor-enhancing drugs and narcotics, when you just have to let go of control of your body and let things happen. It's a spiritual surrender.
I struggled with that surrender for literally hours. I prayed and cried. I got angry. I remember distinctly when my perception of God changed from a male godfather-type figure to a woman: A woman who had given birth. I couldn't pray to God for relief in my travail unless She really understood where I was coming from. My belief system at the time was that I was being sacrilegious, at least, and perhaps heretical and idolatrous. I let go. My midwife was a religious person…She only accepted, comforted and trusted me to do what I needed to do to get my baby born.
My birth experience was powerful and spiritual. I learned to trust my instincts, myself, my body. I learned that spirituality is not something you can put in a box with a label. Spirituality is a personal and individual thing.

*from Olivia's story*

Filled with courage and power from the birth, I went into psychotherapy. This was a major hurdle as I come from a family of teachers, social workers and psychologists. (We help others; we can't possibly need help ourselves.)
Entering therapy was like entering a new world for me. I realized I wasn't crazy—that the things I felt and did, my "coping techniques" were normal. I began the long process of turning myself from victim into myself as survivor. And being proud of it.

*from Liz's story*

Childbirth took a long time, but it was very empowering.

*from Cassandra's story*

Women shared not only that they felt empowered, but they also identified birth as a healing experience. They felt a renewed appreciation of their sexuality. They felt divine connection, purification and wholeness:

Before his actual birth, I still had the association of sex as violation. After he was born, I was able to see and feel the connection between sex/intercourse and life. I remember thinking to myself, "So this is what sex is meant for." It was as if the violation of rape dissolved once my son emerged from my body. It was so incredible and so freeing. It was amazing how immediate the letting-go process was once I had a different association. I feel so grateful for that experience.

*from Lisa's story*

# Chapter 3—Labor and Birth

*I stood in the shower shaking and crying and with each contraction there was an even greater release. It was as if the earthquake were passing through my entire body. I was not fearful; it was healing. The energy was so strong it was all I could do to hold back…to wait until it was time to push. Finally, I was ready. I found a calm place deep inside and with everyone gathered around I slowly and quietly birthed my sweet baby…life, not death.*

from Karin's story

*My body did me proud, and that was immensely healing on its own. Nobody in the world is as strong as you are when pushing your child into the world. No athlete ever worked so hard. No conquering warrior is as triumphant. Nobody is as divine, as humble or as whole as you are right then. I did it. Me, with this body, this mind, this will. No matter how damaged I was in the moments before labor started, this primal, potent process made me real, and whole and, finally, fully me.*

*I was a mother, and I was just beginning to understand what that meant. I was a Goddess incarnate, the Changing Woman of one thin but beautiful thread of my heritage. I breathed the same air, felt the rhythm of the same beating heart, and held my child to my breast with the same arms as have an eternity of mothers in both directions, before and yet to come.*

from Heather's story

*I truly believe my pregnancies and births of my sons would not have been as wonderful or gone as smoothly had I not done all the healing work I did. I believe it allowed me the strength to deal with whatever (memories, etc.) might arise and still be present (during the pushing). I feel whole, and I feel blessed that my sons chose me to be their mommy, and that I have been able to be present for each of them from the beginning.*

from Carol's story

*I was barely even aware of the sexual/spiritual pain I held, of all the hurt and abuse that I endured, all of the confusion. What I felt was the power in my body. Each contraction, each power rush of energy which began in my womb and then radiated outward, filled my whole being with focus and strength. And then I realized that this flood of strength was being given to me; it was mine. I surrendered to the pain, to the power in my body, to fighting with my fear. Really, I was surrendering to myself. I accepted that I was not really in control, but that I didn't have to be "under control" to be strong.*

*But, it wasn't about being out of control either. It was about accepting what was coming at me, not trying to stop it or control it necessarily, but using it to my advantage. I realized that the pain was there to work through, to come out of on the other side, stronger than ever. The pain of my sexual abuse, the pain of my labor, it was a test, a mission for me to look within and find it in me to overcome.*

*Later, I reflected upon what it was I was releasing in those moments. Obviously, I was releasing the baby that I'd held for nine months, but there was more than that. It was as if all the abuse, all that filth, all the shame and guilt and pain of my molestation at 11 years of age, and the subsequent sexual abuse I'd suffered, all of it was in a big gooey glob beneath my daughter's head. It was as though she wouldn't come out until I'd released it all. I couldn't be a mother until I pushed it all out of me. And as I pushed, it all came pouring out of me. And I felt as though my birth canal, my vagina, was being purified so my baby could pass through it into holy light. It was a cleansing, a reclaiming. And when at last she did emerge from me, she felt so pure and uncontaminated, so perfect, and I felt freed at last, so grateful to her for carrying me through such a challenging phase of my (our) lives.*

from Mary's story

Benig Mauger, in her book *Reclaiming the Spirituality of Birth*, speaks to both the challenges and the healing aspects of birth for trauma survivors:

> Giving birth often opens up new areas of consciousness in women and with it, all forms of earlier conflicts and traumas may resurface. Many women first become aware of past traumas during pregnancy and birth and for some, the experience of childbirth can be the catalyst for healing and change. It can be transformational.
>
> Thinking about this, I believe that the experience of childbirth by its very nature has the effect of dissolving all boundaries, so that what has previously been contained can no longer be so. It is far from uncommon for memories of past sexual and violent physical abuse to resurface during a labor and birth experience. Sometimes, as we have seen, the trigger may be the technicalities of the labor and delivery, but it can often be simply the experience itself. Childbirth is one of those times when it is possible, quite naturally, to enter an altered or non-ordinary state of consciousness and to experience what was previously repressed. (…) It appears that at such times we are in a very transitional state. Or as Jean Shimoda Bolen would say, we are in a state of liminality.(p. 184–85)

We have been speaking of the continuum of recovery for survivors. Where women were on their healing journey affected their birth, but reciprocally, their birth also affected their healing journey. The quality of the birth experience greatly impacts the kind of early parenting experience to follow. We see this in Katherine's triumph and victory at her second birth, and her resolve to protect her bond with her children. We see this relationship between birth and early parenting dramatically in Lynelle's narrative in her struggles with bonding and depression after her first child's birth and her ability to "find her fire" and experience healing with her second birth. From reading the accounts of these two women and the many other contributors, we further our understanding of the potential mutual impacts of survivorship on labor and birth. And now, as must happen after the experience of birth, attention shifts to postpartum recovery, mothering, and the rest of the survivorship journey that lies ahead.

# POSTPARTUM AND BREASTFEEDING

### Claire's Story
*I'll tell you right from the start that this is a story that has a good ending. Well, a good enough ending. "Supermom," I'm not. But my child is eight now, and, by my standards, I'd have to say that he's having a normal childhood. And he seems to think I'm a normal mom. Isn't that great?*

*I'll tell you the story of my childbearing year, but you have to know that understanding about the incest and other abuse and trauma came a few years after the birth. It was mostly my sinking efforts to mother a toddler that eventually made me seek help from a therapist. Only well into the process of coping with the posttraumatic aftereffects of the abuse in therapy did it become clear how me and my pregnant body worked out a way through the minefield of the maternity year.*

*We planned to get pregnant. We'd been married nearly a decade, and it seemed like it was time. The day my period should have come, the nausea started. Except for rare moments of distraction and during my sleep, it didn't leave me until the 22nd week of gestation. It was my 24-hour companion for about four months. It is the main reason I will never be pregnant again. Carsickness or a bout of stomach flu always confirms for me that I could not tolerate another moment of that awful sensation—not by choice. I didn't vomit except twice. I just had the sensation that swallowing my own saliva or food would make me vomit. I could drink. And anytime I got the slightest sense that I might be able to eat, I did. Often I could accept food if I was watching a good movie or eating out in a restaurant.*

*Things got easier in the fifth month, and they stayed that way until the seventh month. Then I started to contract. Since I was at 34 weeks, a point where the baby would be okay if my contractions became labor, my caregivers did not intervene with medications. I just took it very, very easy for a few weeks because it made me feel that I was giving the baby the best chance to be born near term. I was especially motivated to do this because I had planned to give birth with nurse-midwives in a freestanding birth center, and if I went into labor before 37 weeks I would have to deliver in a hospital.*

*The contractions only made me worried, but they didn't hurt. By this time my baby was dancing around all the time, and I felt reassured by his everyday pattern of activity that he was fine. I cried a lot during this time. The Persian Gulf War had just started, and thoughts of suffering and war seemed to fill me with grief, especially because I could not help but wonder if I would someday have to surrender my firstborn son to war. I just cried and cried.*

*The 37th week came and went. I kept contracting. I assumed that my resting was keeping that baby in there, so, wanting to get this labor business over as soon as possible, I got up and got busy. I expected my cervix to open and let him out. So* you can imagine how completely beside myself I was when my due date was 10 days behind me. I'd been contracting for seven weeks. My baby felt huge. I had gotten to the point where I refused to think about labor. All I could let myself think about was holding that baby.

When I'd discussed feeding plans with my nurse-midwife at the beginning, I'd said that I planned to "try" to breastfeed. She said that I shouldn't be tentative about it. Either do it or not do it, but sitting on the fence usually means you're looking for an excuse to stop doing it. That made me mad, and I blurted out to her that I'd been molested and "breast stuff" was complicated for me, so I meant exactly what I said when I'd said I'd try: If it didn't go okay, that's it. End of pressure tactics. She wrote in pencil, discreetly, on the inside cover of my chart "history of sexual abuse."

Oh. Is that what that was?

I'd been molested by an adult at a camp the summer I was 13. I'd remembered this 12 years after it had happened when, in a conversation with my husband, we'd been reminiscing about the awful times in gym class during puberty when we'd felt so very bad about our bodies. Remembered emotional state. Zap. Remembered experience of body and soul shame. As the flashback was happening, my husband saw it for what it was and gently drew the story out of me. So when the midwife asked me about breastfeeding, I knew about that…episode. From this vantage point, I can call it an episode. It was only the tip of the iceberg, it turns out. But knowing about that night of abuse and how it had affected my relationship with my breasts, I was able to tell my midwife to back off and let me cope according to my own needs, taking the baby's needs into account as best I could.

Turns out that breastfeeding was a challenge in the extreme, but he and I managed it for seven months. I consider it to be one of the crowning achievements of my life. A grueling victory snatched from the hands of a child molester. And an act of sweet generosity to my child and myself, full of warmth and comfort (after the sore nipple stage). I would not trade knowing and remembering that I nursed my infant for anything. I had no idea I had that kind of fierce perseverance in me.

But I jump ahead. Had I been the first woman to remain pregnant forever, you'd have heard of me. Of course I did finally begin to labor in earnest. (Just in case any of you are pregnant and experiencing pre-term contractions now and wondering how you'll know if they become real labor—trust me. You'll know.) The deep achy tightening of productive contractions came—welcomed—with a deep rush of adrenaline. My hours in active labor were wonderful. Challenging, but wonderful. I was the center of a small universe: midwife, nurse, husband, sister, bedroom and bathtub. Finally it seemed my cervix was all gone, and they said I could start to push whenever I felt like I needed to. And I lay down on the big double bed on my back, and I drew up my knees to bear down, and…the paperwork about my labor says I pushed for an hour and 15 minutes there. My husband and sister say I pushed for a long time there. I wouldn't know. It's a blank. But eventually they got me up to empty my bladder, and I was present again. The baby was born minutes later as I knelt on the bed. No more of that recumbent position. No. No. And the baby was huge and happy. And I was fine.

Over the next days and weeks, I had several follow-up visits. Some were routine, but a few were because I just had a lot of trouble breastfeeding. Then too, I was glad of the contact with the midwives because I just couldn't stop crying. I felt bursting with pride at this incredible thing I'd done, and yet all I could feel when I looked at that perfect little one was grief, grief, grief. I could not understand it. The emotions were so intense that I could not sort them out or make them calm down. I thought the tears would simply never leave me. I thought I'd float away, and he would miss his mama, but he would not be able to find me because it would all have gone blank as soon as I finally wore out my ability to tolerate the intensity of the grieving pain.

Eventually I wore out. I wouldn't say I felt peaceful. I just felt like a dry autumn leaf. Resigned. Powdery. Lightweight. Just waiting to blow away or disintegrate. And, by turns, I began to feel normal things too. Like fatigue, humor, boredom, longing for grown-ups to talk to, longing to go to work again, longing for a babysitter. Reassuringly normal feelings.

It is true that there was a sort of gap between how I'd envisioned myself mothering and how I was managing in reality. But I think this is normal. I felt normal.

Until my boy started to get on toward a year or more. There came that time when they start to have a will of their own, and they sometimes cry in anger, asserting themselves. And it terrified me. I had to get him to stop. When he out and out cried like that I'd fill with adrenaline as though my life were in danger—as though his life were in danger. It all became very confusing. I was afraid I'd hit him or shake him to get him to stop it, so I'd find myself sitting outside on the front stoop while he wailed in the safety of his crib. I prayed that the social worker who lived across the street wouldn't turn me in for neglecting my baby. But we were safer if I got outside where the piercing cry was muffled for me.

Other things started being obviously "not right" then, too. I sometimes would cry uncontrollably and feel nauseated. I'd spend whole days lying on my bed the whole time he was at daycare instead of working. I felt the gap widening between how I wanted to be with him and how I seemed to be as a mother. And then came some way, way stronger-than-usual reactions to things that were related to memories of being molested. Adrenaline rushes and strange sensations and panic and dread. I started to feel as though I was "losing it." Or worse. Maybe I was becoming mentally ill, like my mother.

No.

No. That would be intolerable for me and for my family, and I would not allow it.

It was time to go back to see that therapist who had helped me process the initial flashbacks of being molested at camp.

I did not know then that that decision was the first step on an odyssey of remembering and adapting and growth that has run right alongside all the other events of my life over the past several years. I understand now that when I was my baby's age, crying like that…well, it was dangerous. Little by little flashbacks and body memories and emotional memories have come up to the surface enough for me to learn about my history what I need to know to heal. And what I need to know to mother my son.

The four months of pregnancy nausea makes perfect sense to me now. So do the endless contractions. I understand them as body memories and expressions of distress and anxiety, which came from a place in my knowledge of my life where there were no words. And "going away" from the labor pain when I found myself in that awful position again—it was a well-practiced form of self-protective dissociating. And the ceaseless feelings of grief during the pregnancy and postpartum? That makes sense to me if I understand it as being "triggered" by the feelings of bonding with my baby. I had long ago turned off all intense emotion because usually it was bad: terror, despair and loss. So when the feelings of maternity started raging around in me, those wonderful feelings that seem to make so many other women "glow"—they made *me wail with grief. It got all mixed up. Who is the baby/who is the mother? Which role am I feeling? I feel motherlove, and it zaps me into feeling baby-need. Round and round. So much loss.*

*But the baby I mothered is a schoolboy now. He still freely expresses his needs for being occasionally babied a bit. Sometimes he curls up next to me on the couch to read. Sometimes he still holds my hand when we cross a street. Sometimes he asks if he ever had a pacifier when he was a baby. He laughs straight-out and simply when I tell him that he was never fooled by any size or shape of rubber nipple, and so, no, he'd had several given to him, but he'd never adopted any of them. This is a kid who flat out relishes having been a baby and having his mother nearby to give him tiny tastes of youngest childhood as needed during these rough-and-tumble days of elementary school where he is having to leave the joys of being mothered for more rare moments.*

*I was lucky. Mine was a wanted pregnancy. My partner was present and unquestioningly willing to carry the weight of caring for baby and mother when I was not capable of carrying my load. Many times he was able to give me the reassurance that meant the most to me, saying, "You feel like you are going crazy, but you are acting okay and our son is fine and loves you just like any kid loves a good-enough mom."*

*Being a "good enough" mom is not how I ever would have described my goal for mothering. My therapist gave me that term; "No need to berate yourself for not being 'supermom.' 'Good enough' parents will do just fine for most kids." I sense this is true. And I know that all of the work that goes with being some ideal of a "supermom" was not humanly possible for me. I had to spend too much time in therapy and learning to take care of myself to be able to achieve any pinnacle of maternal accomplishment. But I have kept my child safe, as far as I know. And he is not afraid of me. He has faith in me and expects that I'll do what he needs me to do for him when it's important. And I am strong and mostly good-humored. And I look forward to the rest of my life as his mom. I look forward.*

# Chapter 4—Postpartum and Breastfeeding

> Is ours not a strange culture that focuses so much attention on childbirth—virtually all of it based on anxiety and fear—and so little on the critical time after birth, when patterns are established that will affect the individual and family for decades?
>
> Suzanne Arms

We have chosen to highlight Claire's narrative at the beginning of this chapter on postpartum and breastfeeding because she speaks about some commonalities among survivor moms, especially for new mothers. Claire struggled with the decision of whether or not to breastfeed. She had a difficult postpartum period, with the normal, expected emotions of early motherhood punctuated by intense feelings of depression and anxiety. She eventually sought help for these feelings and came to understand the linkages between her history as a survivor and her current feelings about raising her baby and how these two were related. She came to a resolution that she was a "good-enough" mom, which enabled her to move forward on her healing journey and in her mothering. In this chapter we will look at the interplay between the immediate postpartum period and survivor issues.

## *POSTPARTUM DEPRESSION, ANXIETY AND PTSD*

Claire's narrative describes a period of depression in the immediate postpartum period, which retreated after a few weeks, only to return with vengeance and with additional intense PTSD reactions when her son turned one year old and began expressing his needs in a more willful manner. Claire did not recognize then that her symptoms were related to early childhood sexual abuse. She did not know about PTSD. But she knew she was overwhelmed by feelings of anxiety during this period and realized eventually that she needed to re-enter therapy in order to deal with the strong, inexplicable moods, reactions and emotions.

Especially in the first days postpartum a new mother may have difficulty knowing what she needs. One place to start is by telling the story of the birth.

## *PROCESSING BIRTH*

Most women need to talk about their birth experience and process what happened to them with other women or caregivers. Hopefully this can start to happen with caregivers in the days after the birth. Those who have had a positive birth experience will want to share that with others and relive the experience. Having a six-week visit with caregivers also may afford the opportunity to process the birth experience and to ask any follow-up questions relating to the birth. It can also provide a time for dialogue with the caregiver on how issues relating to past abuse may have affected the experience and how the new mother is processing that information now. For Lanie, talking about this at her six-week visit enabled her to start making connections between her history and her birth experience:

> *At my six-week check-up Brenda asked if there was something in my past that had made me react the way I did. I was floored; it had not even crossed my mind that this horribly disappointing birth and my abuse were connected. The more I thought about it,*

*the more it made sense. The fear of having a daughter made sense too. I really hate that I did not want her after she was born; I was just too out of it at that moment. My feelings were just too intense.*

*I am very thankful that Brenda brought it up. Now it's no longer such a big secret. The whole thing has always been this big secret I have to live with.*

*from Lanie's story*

▼ 4.1
A randomized controlled trial of a postpartum counseling session with follow-up telephone session demonstrated that this intervention improved the likelihood that women who had traumatic births would recover well psychologically. Women who had the counseling had decreased trauma symptoms, fewer symptoms of depression, and less stress and self-blame. They also felt more confident about future pregnancies.
Gamble, et al. 2005

▼ 4.2
Elements of an effective brief intervention for traumatic birth developed by nurses in Australia included:
- establishing a therapeutic relationship between midwife and woman
- accepting and working with women's perceptions
- supporting expression of feelings
- filling in missing pieces
- connecting event with emotions and behaviors
- reviewing labor management
- enhancing social support
- reinforcing positive approaches to coping
- exploring solutions
Gamble, et al. 2005

▼ 4.3
In preparing to process traumatic birth with a caregiver, a woman could ask herself the following questions:
- How would you tell the story of your birth?
- How do you feel about it?
- What are you unsure about?
- Do you think you are having any difficult feelings related to birth events?
Gamble, et al. 2005

Women who had a negative birth experience may need to talk about the birth and process it with someone. Often this is done with the caregiver.(4.1, 4.2, 4.3) However, when a woman has a lot of anger or grief about the particulars of her birth and how she was treated, she may do better to speak with a therapist, especially someone who specializes in the postpartum period. Talking with other supportive people in life can also be helpful. Certainly many of the birth stories shared by survivor moms in the previous chapter on labor and birth fall into this category. Some of the women had positive, "routine" birth experiences that were difficult for them because of their history and how birth itself was triggering for them. But others had experiences that might be considered traumatic, regardless of the woman's status as a survivor, either because of an emergency or because the provider's behavior was uncaring, incompetent or abusive.(4.4, 4.5)

Most mothers need to talk about their birth experiences, whether they were good or bad. Telling a good story can help a woman take in feelings of pride and strength. Talking about a birth that was hard can decrease its impact by getting out the many emotions and helping her turn it into a narrative instead of a nightmare. Friends and family, a caregiver who was supportive or a therapist can help with talking it through.

Women who feel depressed, anxious or preoccupied with thinking about their birth will find that a therapist is a good choice. This is because a therapist may be better prepared to hear any sexual abuse-related aspects.(4.6)

Recent studies show that women who have had traumatic birth experiences may be more likely to decide to forego or postpone subsequent children (Gottvall and Waldenstrom 2002). These women also may possibly be among those requesting elective cesarean section for their second birth (Reynolds 1997, Ryding 1993). New research also shows that brief counseling in the aftermath of a traumatic birth can improve the woman's well-being, including giving her more confidence about future pregnancies (Gamble, et al. 2005).

## POSTPARTUM MOOD DISORDER

Strong emotions are normal in the postpartum period, but if they become distressing, preventing normal eating and sleeping when the baby is sleeping, and if they persist beyond 10–14 days, they may signal a postpartum mood disorder. Postpartum mood disorders are serious and common, but they can be treated.

Although most people focus on postpartum depression, other mental health problems may occur in the postpartum period. These include postpartum anxiety, panic, psychosis (which is rare) and, as we now know, postpartum PTSD.(4.7) Women who feel overwhelmed by thoughts or feelings or have trouble eating or sleeping normally (under the circumstance of living with a newborn), certainly deserve help.

Evaluations for postpartum mood disorders should include a physical exam, since other conditions like thyroid problems or fever can mimic symptoms. Research is clear that treatment is vital, however: children of mothers who suffer from postpartum mood, anxiety and thought disorders are worse off. Such children are less safe, have poorer health and disadvantages in development and growth, as well as greater vulnerability to later mental health problems accross the rest of their life span (National Institute of Child Health and Human Development 1999). Mothers with untreated mood disorders also unnecessarily miss out on the pleasures of their child's babyhood. None of the narrators in this book told of regretting getting help for postpartum depression. On the contrary, many realized in retrospect that they had been very depressed and wished they had gotten help sooner. Women who have postpartum depression, anxiety, post-tramatic stress, panic, or obsessive or unreasonable thoughts deserve treatment, and their baby deserves for them to have treatment.(4.8, 4.9, 4.10)

Some women dismiss symptoms as normal or hormonal changes.(4.11) Hormones returning to normal after birth can create some mood swings. Sometimes

▼ 4.4
Numerous studies now show that women can develop PTSD after a traumatic birth experience. These studies show that:
1. PTSD can develop after an obstetric emergency, but not all births where there was an emergency lead to PTSD.
2. Births that seem entirely normal to staff can be perceived as traumatic by the woman.
3. PTSD is more likely to develop if the woman perceived her caregivers and staff to be incompetent or uncaring.
4. Women with prior abuse and past history of mental health problems are more at risk of postpartum PTSD.

Creedy, Shochet and Horsfall 2000
Soderquist, Wijma, and Wijma 2002
Soet, Brack, and DiIorio 2003

▼ 4.5
In the course of a study of the onset of PTSD as a result of traumatic childbirth, PTSD was measured during pregnancy as well. Out of 289 women in British prenatal clinics, 8.1% scored in the PTSD range on a self-report measure of PTSD during pregnancy. At six weeks postpartum 6.9% still had PTSD and at six months postpartum 3.5% were still symptomatic. When the women who had PTSD prior to birth were removed from the analysis, at six weeks and six months postpartum there were 3.2% and 2% rates of new cases of PTSD related to traumatic birth. These rates are similar to the 1.7% to 5.6% rates of postpartum PTSD found in other studies.

Ayers and Pickering 2001

▼ 4.6
Postpartum depression affects approximately 13% of women who have recently given birth.

O'Hara and Swain 1996

▼ 4.7

In a community-based study of women at eight weeks postpartum, the rate of generalized anxiety disorder was elevated compared to the rate of women in the general population. Between 10–50% of the 147 women in this study reported anxiety symptoms, suggesting that postpartum anxiety disorders are more common than depression.

Haugen, Jackson and Brendle, Jr. 2005

▼ 4.8

Postpartum Depression is diagnosed using the criteria for Major Depressive Episode:
A. Five or more symptoms present during the same two-week period and representing a change from previous functioning (of which one must be either depressed mood or loss of interest or pleasure)
  1. depressed mood
  2. markedly diminished interest or pleasure in activities
  3. significant weight loss or gain
  4. insomnia or hypersomnia
  5. agitated or slowed movements
  6. fatigue or loss of energy
  7. feelings of worthlessness or guilt
  8. diminished ability to think or concentrate or indecisiveness
  9. recurrent thoughts of death or suicidal ideation, plan or attempt
B. Not mixed with manic symptoms
C. Causing clinically significant distress or impairment in social, occupational or other important areas of functioning
D. Not due to substance use or a medical condition
E. Not due to bereavement

APA 1994

▼ 4.9

Postpartum "blues" are more transient and occur within the first two weeks after birth. They are characterized by low mood and mood swings, crying, anxiety, insomnia, poor appetite and irritability.

Steiner 1998

adjusting hormones or thyroid levels or treating a physical problem like anemia from blood-loss or a low-grade fever from a minor breast or uterine infection can make women feel better. If symptoms of depression or anxiety or unusual thoughts persist, however, getting them evaluated can be helpful.(4.12)

Cathleen experienced the physical effects of postpartum mood disorder:

*This was much more severe than the normal blues moms get. I became physically weak with it to the point that I slept almost constantly and couldn't function well enough to properly care for my children.*

*from Cathleen's story*

After therapy, Laura was able to make some connections between her history and her current postpartum depression:

*I slipped into a deep depression that went undiagnosed for a year and a half, because I was too exhausted and overwhelmed to seek help. I reluctantly began therapy, and through the help of the therapist, was able to finally make some connections between my childhood and what I was experiencing as a young mother.*

*from Laura's story*

Our colleague, Melisa Schuster, a social worker psychotherapist, specializes in treating women who are struggling with issues related to postpartum adjustment. She says that:

Women who have experienced sexual abuse, physical or emotional abuse, or neglect may have a higher risk of experiencing postpartum depression or anxiety. The demands of a newborn can seem absolutely overwhelming for someone who did not experience having [her] own needs met, or who did not experience being nurtured or who never had nurturing role models.

The kinds of postpartum symptoms a woman with an abuse history can experience depend on a wide variety of variables: how severe was her abuse, is

# Chapter 4—Postpartum and Breastfeeding

the abuse ongoing, how much recovery has she accomplished, what kinds of supports does she have in place.

Many women who experience postpartum reactions (depression, anxiety, obsessive-compulsive disorder) describe the symptoms as "coming out of the blue." But many women with postpartum depression that I have worked with report some history of abuse, whether sexual abuse, physical abuse or emotional abuse and neglect. They usually don't associate their symptoms with their abuse history, but as they begin to engage in therapy, they begin to realize that symptoms and history have a lot to do with each other.

Some women going through postpartum depression have disturbing thoughts. Paulette shared that she felt that she was going crazy:

*At 12 weeks postpartum, I went into a deep depression. I thought I was going crazy. I had no support. My mother lived in California and I lived in Texas. I even had a sexually abusive thought, that I instantly dismissed, but thought I was going crazy. I was not treated for the depression or even aware of my own abuse at this time. But I know it really hurt the bonding relationship. I could never relax and just didn't know where to go for help. I was just so depressed. Suicidal even.*

*from Paulette's story*

Talking to a therapist can be very useful for putting thoughts and feelings into context; as Melisa Schuster explains:

The first thing I do for women with postpartum depression is to normalize their feelings. Many women feel terribly guilty about how they feel. We're told that this is supposed to be the happiest time in our lives, and no one talks about how hard mothering really is. So I reassure them that their feelings of disappointment, sadness, confusion and anger…are normal and shared by other mothers, and then I urge them not to add a layer of guilt on top of those other feelings.

▼ 4.10

Elements specific to postpartum depression have been discerned through qualitative interviews with affected new mothers. These elements include:
- sleep and eating disturbance: not being able to sleep when the baby is sleeping despite extreme fatigue, loss of appetite and being unable to eat
- anxiety or insecurity: feeling fragile, inadequate, vulnerable or overwhelmed by the responsibilities of motherhood
- intense, rapidly changing emotions: feeling joyless, angry, and unable to stop crying or control explosive emotions
- mental confusion: loss of control over thought processes, obsessive thinking and inability to concentrate
- loss of self: feeling like not the same person as before, feeling unreal and as though merely acting
- guilt and shame: feeling not good enough as a mother, being ashamed of negative thoughts about the baby
- suicidal thoughts: considering ending life as a way out of a living nightmare, believing the baby to be better off

Beck and Gable 2002

▼ 4.11

There is evidence that postpartum depression improved with:
- antidepressant therapy
- estrogen
- individual psychotherapy
- home visits by a nurse
- and possibly group therapy

Review of case reports and studies of selective serotonin reuptake inhibitor (SSRI) antidepressants paroxetine and sertraline and the older antidepressant nortriptyline found that these drugs have not been found to have adverse effects on breastfeeding infants. The SSRI fluoxetine has been reported to be associated with more problems in the infant, from irritability to poor feeding and sleeping.

Gjerdingen 2003

▼ 4.12

Beck and Gable have produced a Postpartum Depression Screening Scale, to help determine whether or not a new mother meets the threshold for Postpartum Depression. Finding out your score on this scale can help you determine whether or not you have significant symptoms of postpartum depression. Items on the scale include things like having trouble sleeping even when your baby is asleep and getting anxious over even the littlest things that concern your baby. Clinicians can use this tool to assess postpartum depression in just minutes. The scale can be purchased by qualified professionals through Western Psychological Services, at www.wpspublish.com, or by calling toll-free: 800-648-8857.

Beck and Gable 2002

▼ 4.13

Interview study of postpartum depression reveals that depressed mothers contemplate not only harming themselves, but also their infants.

Beck 1992

Emotional numbness associated with PTSD may contribute to delayed bonding or attachment disorder on the part of the mother.

Ballard, Stanley and Brockington 1995

▼ 4.14

In a study of 95 adolescent mothers, a childhood history of sexual or physical abuse in and of itself was not predictive of problems in maternal-child interaction. Childhood abuse was associated with severe depressive symptoms in the early postpartum period, chronic depressive symptoms thereafter, and attempted suicide in the past year. Chronic stress (from poverty, social inequality, sexual exploitation, domestic violence, and lack of resources) also was associated with chronic depressive symptoms. Chronic depressive symptoms increased a young mother's risk for problems interacting with her child and likely represents a persistent risk for maternal-child interaction problems.

Lesser and Koniak-Griffin 2000

We read about Lynelle's struggle with postpartum depression in one of the two narratives that begin the chapter on labor and birth. We are revisiting her words here because her experience of postpartum crisis was so important to her overall story and highlight a crucial point often left out of discussions of motherhood:

*I felt so sorry for myself. I began fantasizing about ways to hurt myself. Not kill myself, just wound myself enough so I'd have to be admitted to the hospital and no one would expect me to care for an infant and I could get some sleep. I also envisioned hurting Ian—throwing him against the wall in desperation for peace and quiet. Please God, just five minutes of sleep. Thankfully I did neither of those. My pitiful cries for help went largely unheard....*

*from Lynelle's story* (4.13, 4.14)

As Lynelle wrote, her "pitiful cries for help went largely unheard." Melisa Schuster recognizes this as a central challenge for women with postpartum depression:(4.15)

Much of my work with women with postpartum depression is helping them to identify their needs and devising strategies for getting those needs met. A survivor mother often has difficulty figuring out what needs she has (like the need for support, expressing feelings, taking care of herself, taking time to be alone or to pursue her own interests). Mothering is an intense job, especially in the early weeks and months; mothers who know how to take care of their own needs and "recharge their batteries" are better able to handle the challenges of caring for a baby who has seemingly unending needs.

Getting your needs met may be difficult in the context of a culture that does not honor the postpartum period or make allowances for women who are healing from their births. Kathleen Kendall-Tackett has written about the postpartum period from a cross-cultural perspective. She points to an anthropological review of literature undertaken by Stern and Kruckman in 1983, which found that postpartum disorders were less prominent in cultures that had in common the following characteristics: they recognized a distinct postpartum period; they had in place several protective measures reflecting the new mother's vulnerability, including social seclusion and mandated rest; they provided functional assistance for the new mother; and the mother's new role and status were recognized socially. (Summarized in Kendall-Tackett 1994)

Kendall-Tackett has written about postpartum adjustment and the changing roles of women as mothers in her book *The Hidden Feelings of Motherhood* (2001).(4.16) In it she explores the issues of stress, burnout, depression, home, work and dealing with the challenging child.

Indeed a woman's role and status in life is greatly changed by becoming a mother. Amanda emphasizes the changed reality of relationships once baby is born:

*Births are so important but like weddings, they are events. Everyone puts so much planning and preparation into the event and barely begins to touch on the changed reality of being in these long-term relationships. For now and forever, I will be a mother. No matter how much time I spend thinking about leaving and just abandoning all the work these children and my husband require, I will always be their mother. Same goes for my husband.*

from Amanda's story

Within the general culture of the United States, most women seem to be expected to "get back on the horse and ride." Women usually are allotted six to 12 weeks maternity leave from paid employment, but they certainly are expected to be highly functioning in society before that. They fly across the country to show new baby off to family, they join a gym to try to drop the baby weight and they resume all the household and child-rearing duties. While support and attention may have been given to the needs of the mother during the pregnancy, often the support dries up after the baby is born. But mothers still have basic needs.(4.17)

The mother can quickly become overwhelmed when her basic needs are far from met. Combined with postpartum depression, the overwhelmed mother risks becoming desperate and having thoughts of harming the infant or harming herself. These feelings do occur, even though mothers often don't talk about them with friends or family. Lynelle shared having had such feelings. One sign of postpartum mood disorder is having thoughts of hurting oneself or one's baby. While minimizing or denying having such thoughts or impulses is only natural, simply talking about them may help to reduce them.

▼ 4.15

Postpartum Resource Organizations:

Depression After Delivery, Inc. (DAD)
www.depressionafterdelivery.com

Postpartum Support International (PSI):
www.postpartum.net
800-944-4PPD

▼ 4.16

Some books on the postpartum period, including mental health and adjustment struggles:
*The Hidden Feelings of Motherhood*
   by Kathleen Kendall-Tackett
*Rebounding from Childhood*
   by Lynn Madsen
*Postpartum Survival Guide*
   by Ann Dunnewold and Diane G. Sanford

▼ 4.17

Supportive people can help any postpartum woman, but especially one with postpartum blues or depression by thinking of these basic needs:

N—Nourishment
U—Understanding
R—Rest and relaxation
S—Spirituality
E—Exercise

Details available at www.ACNM.org
Adapted from Sichel and Driscoll

Hopefully telling someone about feeling overwhelmed and the difficulty of having these thoughts is also a step toward getting help. Women with PTSD, who have higher risk for self-harm already, may react to these strong feelings by dissociating. They also may feel emotionally numb or detached from their infant. Having such thoughts, even if they are able to deny or dissociate in order to distance from them, can be a problem. Remembering that having feelings is not the same thing as acting on them is important—having such feelings does not mean one is a bad mother. It means one is a mother who is having postpartum trouble, and needs support. Although most mothers do not actually hurt their infants, some do. Women who have thoughts of hurting themselves or their babies need to tell somebody what is happening.

Caregivers can help their clients to anticipate the needs of the postpartum period by discussing what support they will need once the baby is born. Survivor moms still will need to know everything that any new mother would need to know about managing the first few weeks, and they may have additional concerns. Caregivers certainly need to make the client aware of the physical needs of recovery after birth—that they will need to rest in order to heal properly. First-time mothers often do not have any idea of the extent of change that is coming in their day-to-day life, and do not recognize that they might need extra help.(4.18)

Also of importance is routine assessment of the survivor mom's risk for postpartum mood disorders and parenting support. Women with very low social support should have planned home visits by a nurse, social worker or doula, or respite care. A follow-up visit sooner than the customary six-week check-up may be wise.

▼ 4.18

Postpartum Planning List:
- Who will come stay with you the first week after birth to help with meals, laundry, household tasks?
- Who will coordinate your "meal fairies?"
- List the telephone numbers of four people you can count on to help after the baby's birth.
- List three things you can find relaxing, rejuvenating or inspiring that you can do after birth to take care of yourself.
- Choose one group you will attend in the first two months after birth to connect with other parents. List it here with the telephone number.

Compiled for clients of Melisa Schuster, LMSW

▼ 4.19

Most doulas are in private practice and charge for their services. Some communities have doula training programs with apprentice doulas who may provide care for a lower fee. Some programs for low-income women also know of volunteer doulas.

Doulas who attend women in labor usually meet with them more than once prior to the due date. Some birth doulas also provide postpartum care.

### *PRACTICAL HELP AND PEER SUPPORT*
Melisa Schuster makes suggestions for postpartum support:

> I always encourage women to plan to have lots of help following the birth of their babies. If you can't have your mother, mother-in-law, sister or best friend come to stay with you after the birth for a week or more, then consider hiring a postpartum doula. A doula is a woman trained to support women during labor and in the postpartum period. Remember that your helper is there to prepare meals, walk the dog and do laundry while you take care of and bond with your newborn.
>
> We already have discussed the role of a doula in helping moms with their births. Many doulas do postpartum work as well, and some even

specialize in helping women and their families in the postpartum period. Especially in cases where families are living apart from their extended family, or as with many survivors, have dysfunctional or severed relationships with their families of origin, hiring a doula to help and support the new mother can be extremely helpful during this time.(4.19) The doula can perform a variety of duties for families, specific to their needs, including household chores, running errands, childcare and emotional and breastfeeding support. In some locations doulas may be available to low-income or adolescent mothers through community programs. Sometimes friends go together to pay for doula services as a gift to the new mother—especially for women who already have a toddler at home and don't need more baby clothes or equipment, but do need some practical help during those first days. Otherwise, if the mother can't afford a doula she could consider asking for help from a retired mother of grown kids at church or in the neighborhood.

Although seemingly obvious, anticipating needs for extra support and making arrangements during pregnancy is a good idea. Being five days postpartum with a crying baby, a sore bottom and sore nipples, older children who need attention, a messy house and a partner who has had to go back to work is not an optimal time to begin accessing resources.

Once a mother has recovered from the birth itself, she can start reaching out to other mothers, and accessing further resources in the community.

## *THERAPY*

Even women who are far along in their recovery from the effects of sexual abuse can benefit from revisiting therapy during the postpartum period:

> I once worked with a woman who had experienced severe sexual abuse but who had also had a lot of therapy and was functioning well in the world. Even she had distorted perceptions of her child, projecting her own symptoms onto her infant. Therapy for her was a "reality check," giving her information about normal child development, reassuring her that her child was not damaged. She also needed help in learning how to develop a healthy relationship with her child, not having experienced a good, protective relationship with her own mother.
>
> The good news is you don't have to repair or heal your relationship with your own mother in order to become a good mother yourself. If we all had to wait for the perpetrators of abuse to come to their senses, admit their wrongs, make amends and change their ways, we'd all be waiting a long time indeed for healing and recovery!
>
> Melisa Schuster, LMSW

We will address therapy and recovery more extensively in the chapters to follow. The postpartum time can be especially challenging, as it was for Claire. But getting into therapy in her son's babyhood, the postpartum period, helped her to develop a positive and realistic attitude about being a "good-enough mom," and set the tone for her mothering to come.

## MEDICATIONS

Postpartum mood disorders often can be helped by medication. Women who already had some depression, anxiety or PTSD during pregnancy may have declined medications then to keep from exposing their fetus. But they might consider using a medication postpartum. Maternity care providers can set aside a time at one prenatal visit to focus specifically on the planning ahead for the postpartum period.

For some mothers, accessing classes and even getting into individual therapy will not be enough to help cope with the effects of postpartum depression. These mothers may benefit from anti-depressant medications:

*On a well baby visit, the doctor checked over my son and then asked how I was doing. I spilled my guts. I told him that I was falling apart at the seams and that nothing seemed to be going right. He gave me a test for depression, where I continued a long tradition of astonishing scores. He gave me a prescription for Paxil and told me to please not kill myself before I saw the psychiatrist.*

*from Tamar's story*

## PARENTING CLASSES

Taking a parenting class or joining a new parent support group can be particularly helpful for parents, especially for those who have not had good role modeling from their own parents. Marilyn Jeffs, BSN, MPH, is a pediatric nurse and parent/child educator who teaches group parenting classes. She also teaches individuals. She has the following to say about how she works with new moms:

*One of the hardest things for new mothers to handle is that babies are demanding and take all of your time. 24/7. Stressed mothers may assign adult reasons to infant needs, e.g., "He's crying again, he's angry at me." Babies cry. Until a child is three or four years old everything has to be immediate. A parent may be distressed at this impatience. They are overwhelmed, they are not getting enough sleep and their babies are all take, take, take. If you are stressed you don't have much to give. Parents wonder why their child is so demanding, why they can't wait to have their needs met. They ask, "How can I teach her to wait?" This is really not possible with an infant; really it is not until a child approaches two-and-a-half or three years old that you can try to teach the concept of waiting to a child. At that time you can play a game with a child where you go to give them something but then delay, saying "Oh, wait just a minute" and then praise them for waiting as you hand the object to them. But you have to work at this. In the meantime, parents need to learn how to take care of themselves in the midst of this overwhelming time. If you have been in therapy in the past, you may need to re-enter therapy, because your child will bring up issues for you.*

*Parenting classes are important because they can give you tools to use. For whatever profession you are in, you went to school or had some other training. But parenting, the most demanding of work, no one teaches this. I tell my students, "You are your baby's first teacher. I am here to guide you with this and make parenting as easy for you as possible." You parent the way you were parented. Some of us have had wonderful parents; some are not so fortunate. But all of us are capable of change; it's lots of work, but it can be done. You need to be honest with yourself and look at the type of parenting you have had. It is a conscious choice. I have found that most of the parents in my groups share that they were spanked as children. A mother who was raised with corporal punishment must make a huge effort not to hit. When a child is old enough, I encourage time-outs for both the parent and child when necessary. But at any age parents can place their child in a safe place, like the crib, and remove themselves and find a place where they can scream and cry and vent, until they can calm down. I teach parents relaxation breathing and other ways to calm themselves.*

*In individual parenting sessions with new moms, I try to identify whether or not the mother could benefit from counseling and make a referral if appropriate. The older the child is once we begin the sessions, the more of a need there is to see the family in their home setting, and so I will make a home visit to see the interactions between parents and child. If the child is two years or older, I request to see the parent alone for part of this time to discuss freely their concerns. If there is a lot going on with the mother/baby dyad I will continue individual sessions before recommending the dyad for a group setting because I do not wish for one parent's issue to dominate the group time.*

*In a group setting, I try to spend time focusing on each mother/baby dyad. Sometimes I will suggest individual sessions for moms whom I am currently seeing only in group. I will always let my group participants know that this is a safe place and that anything that is said in the group stays in the group. I let them know that it's okay to cry, that I have dealt with many women with postpartum depression. Some of the women in the group are referred by therapists, who are treating them for postpartum depression, but many of the women find me on their own. The group sessions complement therapy, helping moms to feel that they are not alone. One parent helps another, and I reinforce that.*

*If I think a mom has had a hard time in a group setting, I will follow up with her with a phone call. Oftentimes moms will compare themselves to other moms or their child with other children and feel embarrassed or shamed by their or their child's behavior. I try to tell them that there is a broad range of normal, and that their child's behavior is in that range. For example, if I have a group with mostly mild-mannered children and only one "spirited" child, I will need to encourage that mother that although her child is different from the other children in group, still her child is a normal, although energetic child. I discuss the idea of "fit," that sometimes our child's personality or temperament may not match ours. If your child is remarkably different from you, you may have a hard time accepting that and learning to work with the differences. Or, your child may be remarkably similar to you and you may see something in your child that reminds you of you, and you may not like it.*

*I discuss and show videos of normal child development. It is important that moms understand that children are not miniature adults. This is a very hard but important thing to grasp. Your expectation of your child's behavior needs to be appropriate to the child's development. I encourage a mother to accept her child the way he or she is.* **Remember that the word discipline comes from the word disciple, which means to teach. So think of what you are teaching your children when you discipline them.**(4.20)

▼ 4.20

Helpful books on parenting:
  Your Child's Self Esteem
    by Dorothy Corkille Briggs
  Your Baby and Child
    by Penelope Leach
  The Happiest Baby on the Block by
    Harvey Karp, MD
  Touchpoints
    by T. Berry Brazelton
  You Are Your Child's First Teacher
    by Rahima Baldwin
  Growing Together
    by William Sears, MD
  Raising Your Spirited Child
    by Mary Sheedy Kurcinka

Local libraries have many to choose from, some of which are bound to fit your general philosophy of parenting.

## SHARING THE BURDEN WITH TRUSTWORTHY PEOPLE

Some respite from childcare is important all along the way. Mothers need to consider early on which adults in their life are safe, trustworthy, nurturing people who can provide babysitting. This needs to be a trusted person or people, so the mom can relax when they are in charge. During the first days and weeks postpartum a mother doesn't even need to leave the house. Just giving care of the baby to someone else for an hour or so in order to nap or take a bath without being "on duty" can be quite helpful. If untrustworthy people or those who are known to be abusive offer to babysit, early planning can ensure that a strategy is in place to prevent this. Keeping a child safe from harm is critical. We will discuss this more in the next chapter on mothering and attachment.

Susan describes a program in her area designed to help single parents, and to help with older children:

*Another thing I would advise is to allow others to help you raise, love, nurture and discipline your children, as long as you can agree with what they say they believe and actually do. A friend of mine taught me in these last two years that raising a child takes a community. This is true. Don't get it confused with "group parenting" or believing that the biological parent is not necessary, as many are promoting around the world. It's just a way to spread yourself a little bit better, as you are only one person.*

*To give you an example so there is no confusion, there is a college program in my town called Project Pals. For single parents, each child of the family, age six years or older, is assigned a college student to take them somewhere once a week for about an hour. ...being single and having five little ones, this program has really helped all of us. It has taught my children much.*

*from Susan's story*

What is likely to work best for the treatment of postpartum depression is some combination of practical help with chores, peer support, therapy, medication and sharing the burden with those you trust.

The good news about postpartum depression is that it is treatable. The vast majority of women make a full recovery. Treatment includes individual therapy, support group attendance and sometimes use of antidepressant medication. While many women are reluctant to take medications, research indicates that some antidepressant medications are safe to take while breastfeeding. My clinical experience is that medications work really well for postpartum depression.

Melisa Schuster, LMSW

In most of this chapter so far, we have talked about postpartum feelings and coping issues that potentially apply to any and all moms, including survivor moms. These next sections pertain to women considering or managing breastfeeding.

▼ 4.21

In a study addressing the question of breastfeeding with a sample of 360 primiparous women, 74% were African American; 77% were low-income and 12% were sexual abuse survivors; a higher percentage of sexual abuse survivors (54%) indicated an intention to breastfeed than did their non-abused counterparts (41%).

Benedict, Paine and Paine 1994

## BREASTFEEDING

Many of the contributors to our project, like Claire, expressed a strong desire to nurse their babies, despite the difficulties. Claire says she considered nursing her son of the crowning achievements of her life, and calls the act a "grueling victory snatched from the hands of a child molester." This resolve may be common to survivor moms in particular. Nearly 90% of women surveyed prior to the narrative collection for this book experienced at least some period of breastfeeding. The literature suggests that this may be the case more generally as well.(4.21, 4.22) Also of note is that only one-third of those surveyed reported that they felt their history of sexual abuse affected their breastfeeding relationship. We will present here what some women had to say about why breastfeeding was difficult for them, what helped them and what accomplishing or relinquishing desired breastfeeding meant to them.

Breastfeeding is a bodily experience, even though it is wrapped with cultural meanings. Hormones involved in breastfeeding, especially, also are involved in feeling bonded, enacting maternal behaviors and getting to feel less stress when nursing.

Experts agree, "breast is best." Certainly plenty of research supports this.(4.23)

Despite all the known advantages, breastfeeding is not always a simple thing for a woman to accomplish. Survivor moms often succeeded, but sometimes did not. They described their issues, how they managed, what things defeated them and the meaning they derived from trying.

▼ 4.22

A more recent study surveyed a nationally representative sample of 1220 mothers with children younger than age three. Seven percent of this sample reported past sexual abuse. Women who were sexually abused were more than twice as likely to initiate breastfeeding (OR=2.58) as the non-abused women. The abuse survivors were also more likely to be divorced, separated, or never married, to have lower incomes, an unwanted pregnancy, and late prenatal care than their non-abused counterparts.

Prentice, et al. 2002

▼ 4.23

Breastfeeding is widely considered the preferred method of feeding babies, providing many benefits to moms and babies.

Benefits to babies include:
- nutrient-rich food/easily digestible
- enhanced protection against sicknesses like respiratory infections, allergies, ear and urinary tract infections, diabetes, juvenile rheumatoid arthritis, many childhood cancers, Sudden Infant Death Syndrome
- enhanced lifetime protection from obesity, some lymphomas, insulin-dependent diabetes, Crohn's disease, ulcerative colitis, and for girls: breast and ovarian cancer

Benefits to moms include:
- helps the uterus to return to its normal size after the birth
- convenience
- helps with birth control and child spacing
- helps with weight loss
- reduced risk of reproductive cancers

Accessed May 13th, 2006 from www.lalecheleague.org/NB/NBbenefits.html

## MAKING THE DECISION WHETHER OR NOT TO BREASTFEED

A mom has every right to make a choice regarding how she will feed her baby. Some survivors of sexual abuse experience discomfort, ambivalence or downright revulsion at the thought of breastfeeding. If breastfeeding feels too uncomfortable for a woman, she can choose to bottle-feed instead. She must weigh the potential benefits of breastfeeding with the potential negative feelings she might have as a result of breastfeeding. Choosing to bottle feed may be an unpopular decision among her friends or caregivers, and she may feel unsupported in this decision. Reaching out to friends or professionals who understand her and can respect her choices and her privacy regarding this issue is important.

During her pregnancy, Claire was already aware of the "episode" of molestation she had been subjected to as an adolescent, and surmised that she might have issues related to breastfeeding as a result. She is not alone as a survivor in having issues related to breastfeeding. Other moms expressed negative feelings related to breastfeeding. Otter also determined that she would wait to see how she felt:

*Breastfeeding was the only thing I wasn't really concerned about doing right. I wanted to breastfeed, but always knew in the back of my head I was bottle-fed and so were millions of other kids, so if this boob thing didn't work there was a backup plan.*

*from Otter's story*

Tedi thought she might want to try breastfeeding, although the idea made her "squeamish":

*My daughter was born at the end of July in St. Vincent's hospital. I had wanted to try to nurse her although it made me feel squeamish, but unbeknownst to me, my mother had told the nurses to give me the shot that makes your milk dry up.*

*from tedi's story*

As we can see from tedi's story, one impediment to breastfeeding is the lack of family support. Another impediment has been the lack of societal support. Conversely, because breastfeeding rates have increased in recent years, survivors may now experience societal pressure to breastfeed, rather than lack of support. Breastfeeding is much more common and culturally supported than it used to be. Oftentimes in the past, choosing not to breastfeed was very easy. Babies went to the nursery after the birth, not many mothers nursed their babies and, for those who did, it was considered a very private act.

*Back then, you gave birth, and the baby was cleaned and you were cleaned. You rested in your room and the baby was put in the nursery so that the mother could get some rest. So, once again the baby was taken away until it was time to feed the child. Other than that, they did the rest. They did ask if you were going to breastfeed or do the bottle. I chose the bottle.*

*from Trixie's story*

Survivors who still are in contact with family members who were also perpetrators might choose not to breastfeed in order to protect themselves from the exposure:

*Back home when we would visit our families, my father seemed turned on by the fact that I was a married woman. As in high school, he continuously told crude, dirty jokes and the content and frequency worsened as I grew older. They were senselessly dirty. He never tried anything but, when I got pregnant, he would look at me in a way that would cause such terror in my body. I made the decision to not nurse my* babies. Even though we lived five hours away, I didn't want him to think of me in that way. I knew that when we visited them, I could never go to another room and nurse my children. I couldn't bear him knowing.

*from Kate's story*

### BREASTFEEDING AND POSTTRAUMATIC STRESS

Kate's need to protect herself from exposure fits our understanding of how posttraumatic symptoms can influence breastfeeding. We have already discussed the common features of PTSD, including intrusive re-experiencing, avoidance and numbing and hyperarousal. A woman can be bothered by some PTSD symptoms without having all of them: You do not have to have a diagnosis of posttraumatic stress disorder to have some of the symptoms of PTSD. When a person is having episodes of intrusive re-experiencing, she is reliving certain aspects of the trauma. Or, a person may have avoidance and numbing behaviors in an effort to avoid reminders of the abuse. This can impact breastfeeding in a number of ways. A survivor mom may feel extremely uncomfortable with nakedness, for instance, and therefore have a hard time exposing her breast in order for the baby to feed. She may have a hard time with the sensations of milk being expressed, or seeing the milk squirt out. She may have shame around the sexual arousal that can happen as a result of suckling. Her feelings of shyness and shame may be present in the close exchange between mother and baby, and she may have a hard time meeting the baby's gaze while nursing. The nipple soreness may remind her of soreness she had after "sexual" contact. She may also be simply overwhelmed by the heavy and insistent demands of her baby's needs, and feel exploited and stuck in circumstances out of her control. The intimacy of breastfeeding may just be too much, as Tina explains:

▼ 4.24
In the survey part of this book project we asked if the women experienced breastfeeding effects related to abuse:
Yes: 154 = 32.77%
No: 278 – 59.15%
Unsure: 33 = 7.02%

*I have a very hard time with breastfeeding. The intimacy and the sexual nature of the contact was more than I could stand. It was so stimulating to me that I had to stop. I feel very afraid of that kind of closeness with my children. Any time I hug them nude or rub their buttocks, something in my head says, "Maybe this is wrong." I'm sure that everyone experiences this to some degree, but I am especially sensitive to it.*

*from Tina's story*

For Kay, breastfeeding felt like a violation, like she had no control over her body. She also struggled with the feelings of closeness she had toward her first baby:

*I was so mentally uncomfortable I only breastfed him for six months. I had a lot of issues surrounding breastfeeding. It made me feel violated all over again. I felt like I had no control over my body. I felt my stomach drop when I heard that familiar "I'm hungry!" cry. I used to try to get it done as quickly as possible, which resulted in a fussy baby and a resentful mom. After a while I just let my milk dry up and started feeding him out of a can.*

*from Kay's story*

April felt that the biggest impact of her history of abuse was related to her breastfeeding struggles. She felt that her breasts made her vulnerable, by marking her as a potential victim:(4.24)

*I breastfed both of my babies for about 13 months, but I wouldn't say I ever really enjoyed it. I think that's the biggest impact on my mothering that my abuse experience had. In my mind, my breasts were advertisement of my sex, marking me as a potential victim. They were mine, and it was very hard to give them for hours every day to my babies. I started going to La Leche League meetings before my first child was born, and that mom-to-mom support helped a lot. I think every woman who wants to breastfeed should go, because breastfeeding is a lot more complex than it seems, looked at superficially.*

*from April's story*

### GETTING HELP

Breastfeeding can indeed be more complex than it seems, and you may need extra help in managing. You can turn to your midwife or pediatrician for help, and other friends or family members who have experience with breastfeeding.

▼ 4.25

If there is no La Leche League group near you in our Group Web listings and you can't find the information locally, dial 1-800-LALECHE (US) or (847) 519-7730.

www.llli.org, or www.lalecheleaguecanada.ca for the Canadian Web site

As April mentioned, another excellent source of support and information can be accessed through the La Leche League International (LLLI). La Leche League formed as a woman-to-woman helping network for breastfeeding moms in the 1950s. Breastfeeding was out of vogue then, and La Leche League helped to increase awareness and support for moms who were going against the grain of the popular culture by choosing to feed their babies in the time-honored way.

La Leche League leaders provide one-on-one support through phone consults and regular meetings for nursing moms. You can find a meeting in your area by accessing the Web site or checking your local phonebook. We recommend that pregnant moms attend a LLLI group during their pregnancy in order to connect with other nursing moms, and to meet leaders to help them with issues with breastfeeding, which may arise later. You will be more likely to call a league leader with a concern about nipple soreness if you have already met that person.(4.25)

Some moms who try nursing find that it can be difficult and doesn't always work out, even for those who are very determined. Many women cease breastfeeding early on when faced with physical discomforts, such as sore nipples due to improper latching, poor positioning or sucking, and engorgement. The overwhelm of being a new parent, especially if there's not enough help and support, can add to these physical discomforts, and make breastfeeding too demanding:

*After he was born I went back to a very depressed state till just three months ago when I decided to get back in therapy. I tried to breastfeed all three of my boys; it didn't work; I felt like a failure, but it just didn't feel right to me. It was awkward and painful, so they all ended up being bottle fed, just like my daughter.*

*from Valerie's story*

*Nursing my son was incredibly difficult and painful for me, and without much support at home, I gave up after a few weeks and began bottle feeding. I still regret this lost opportunity to bond with my son.*

*from Laura's story*

*Once at home I tried to continue breastfeeding, but it just didn't work. I feel that I was just too uninformed, as well as overwhelmed, at age 17. I became engorged and the pain was too much. Parenting was a massive undertaking for both Eric and me. No one helped us with the "parenting" part. Sure, we got money for diapers and donations of clothes, but not one iota of help with what to do when the baby is crying inconsolably. And no one was there to tell me that it was okay to touch the baby's penis while I was changing him. I would be in tears, thinking I had damaged his boundaries if I cleaned him there. And obviously I had to clean him. It was terrible.*

*from Jennifer's story*

Jennifer was also struggling with her baby's inconsolable crying, and trying to figure out how to deal with boundary issues around her baby's nakedness, something other women have written about as well:(4.26)

*I can't believe that with all that happened to me, I chose to breastfeed. And now, I'm allowing him to self-wean. The scariest part of nursing, though, is when he wants to nurse naked. All of me and all of him. I'm not lying when I tell you that nursing can incite some sexual feelings. Then you have this naked little person who also becomes aroused.... This to me was scary. But I was so aware of everything that was happening because of the healing that I knew I wouldn't hurt him. This has enhanced the bond that we share because it allows us to be free with one another. I sure hope this freedom of "communication" continues....*

*from Cassandra's story*

### BREASTFEEDING AND BONDING

If breastfeeding were the only challenge in the postpartum period, it might be easier to achieve. But some mothers develop depression or posttraumatic emotional numbness. Without the feelings of bonding, the emotional impetus to breastfeed may be missing. Bonding and let-down of milk both depend on an important hormone—oxytocin—which is also a "stress management" hormone. All this stress may possibly disrupt how oxytocin is working for some women.

▼ 4.26

For babies who are colicky or crying, Harvey Karp, MD, recommends the "5 S's", which are five steps parents can take to activate a baby's innate "calming reflex":
1. Swaddling
2. Side/Stomach position (stomach position is NOT for sleeping, however)
3. Making Shhhhing sounds
4. Swinging
5. Sucking

Dr. Karp details how to do these five steps in his book *The Happiest Baby on the Block: The New Way to Calm Crying and Help Your Baby Sleep Longer* (Bantam Books, 2002).

▼ 4.27

Oxytocin is the hormone involved in labor contractions and milk ejection. It also is considered a part of our "anti-stress" system. Pleasant touch, warmth, fullness, sexual activity, social interaction and a sense of security all boost oxytocin levels. Holding and nursing a baby seem to bring this benefit too.

Moberg 2003

▼ 4.28

The oxytocin-related anti-stress system gives us a sense of "calm and connection" which may include feeling relaxed, contemplative, happy, companionable, placid, sensitive, emotional and/or dependent. This hormone also fosters growth and healing.

Moberg 2003

Some survivors may be trying to bond and breastfeed without as much of this "love hormone" as other women have.(4.27, 4.28)

Whether or not hormones are affected, dealing with the intense feelings of bonding with a newborn may be hard for survivor moms:

*I was also afraid to become too close to him. I wanted to hold him all of the time, but I was afraid to. I didn't know what was right and wrong. I didn't know that moms are supposed to want to hold, hug and cuddle their babies all of the time. I also felt panic at the feeling of loving someone with my whole being and wild abandon. I felt like I was giving part of myself away....*

*I felt really disconnected from my baby when we brought him home. I held him, fed him and took care of him, but I felt like I was just going through the motions. I know now that I was extremely depressed. Breastfeeding was difficult as well. I had a lot more trouble breastfeeding this time than the first. I think it's because I was having trouble bonding with my baby. Again, I didn't want to get too close and breastfeeding still felt like a violation. When my son went on a nursing strike at four months, it was easy not to continue. I stopped breastfeeding altogether.*

*from Kay's story*

Kathy expresses how her ability to feel the emotion of "overwhelming love" and protectiveness helped her breastfeed despite frustration:

*Breastfeeding was difficult because the baby wanted to be fed every hour, and I didn't have enough milk, so it was frustrating. And then Phil was helpful in some aspects, but in other ways he wasn't. Adam nursed until he was 12 weeks old, with supplementing. It was difficult for me to breastfeed. Everybody wants to watch. I felt very protective, holding this little creature in my arms. Breastfeeding was hard but the overwhelming love overcame that difficulty. "I can tolerate this," I told myself, because I was doing it for the sake of my child, even though it wasn't comfortable to me.*

*from Kathy's story*

Amanda highlights how her own desire to breastfeed and strong determination helped her:

*I love my daughter to the utmost of my ability. She is such a trooper. Three weeks after she was born, I put her back to my breast. We sat on the couch most of that day and 13 hours straight the next, as she worked to re-establish my milk supply. She's never had another bottle and the mere mention of pumping still puts my stomach in knots. I remember praying, "Please let me be able to breastfeed. Nothing else went my way. Please grant me this." But never because I loved the act. I breastfed because it was the right thing to do, it was what I believed was the best, but I've never enjoyed it. I joke that my oxytocin hookup is broken. I've never experienced those "warm, fuzzy mommy feelings" everyone at La Leche League talks about as a major advantage to breastfeeding.*

*from Amanda's story*

## MAKING ADAPTATIONS

Some survivor moms made adaptations to be able to breastfeed in ways that balanced their needs with those of their infants. Ann shared that nursing was difficult due to

## Chapter 4—Postpartum and Breastfeeding

that feeling that her body was not her own, but she was able to continue breastfeeding by having some limits she honored:

*I would like to add here that breastfeeding has been difficult for me at times, due to feeling that my body is not my own. I have had to completely control all nursing situations, and immediately put a stop to any uncomfortable sensations. For example, it is important to me that the baby not touch or twiddle with the other nipple while nursing. I need to be in control of giving of myself to my baby in that way.*

*from Ann's story*

Carrie accepted that she was not getting emotional benefits from breastfeeding, but she drew satisfaction from the nourishment she provided as long as her babies needed it:(4.29)

*I never enjoyed breastfeeding the way other mothers describe it; I never got that nursing "high" I've heard about. I appreciated being able to provide the food my babies needed, but when they weaned themselves I didn't miss it much. I think it must have reminded me too much of the enmeshment my mother forced on me as a toddler.*

*from Carrie's story*

▼ 4.29
Number of women in the survey part of this book project who reported breastfeeding for any length of time:

422 = 89.78% of women reported some breastfeeding
43 = 9.15% of women bottlefed exclusively
Average length of at least 50% breastfeeding: 16 months

Judy says that she was repulsed every time she offered her breast to her son, although she nursed her son for nearly a year, despite severely cracked nipples:

*I had a hard time nursing him and was angry with him for this. Even though I nursed him for almost a year, until he weaned himself, I was repulsed every time I offered him my breast. My breasts have no feeling in them, even now. To touch the skin of my breasts, I can't feel it. I can feel pressure and when my nipples cracked in the beginning I could feel the pain. So, in another way I was robbed. Where so many women have pleasure when their breasts are stimulated I feel abhorrence, I feel dirty. Does this stem from my abuse? I think so. I don't know how to get past that. I have learned to live with it.*

*from Judy's story*

▼ 4.30
International Board of Certified Lactation Consultants Web site:
www.iblce.org

IBCLC consultant registry:
www.iblce.org/us%20registry.htm

Although Judy "learned to live with" abuse-related difficulties during breastfeeding, for some mother-baby pairs, the emotional price the mother would pay might possibly not be worthwhile. If breastfeeding stirs up feelings of repulsion and keeps PTSD reactions triggered or memory of abuse fresh in the mother's mind, bottle feeding could be very beneficial. Being less burdened by these adverse reactions could free up the woman's ability to be present in the current moment and to just enjoy the cuddling contact with her feeding baby.

For dealing with difficult breastfeeding circumstances, contacting a lactation consultant may be helpful. A lactation consultant is a person who has received special training and certification in breastfeeding and is available to help moms with a wide range of breastfeeding problems. Some lactation consultants will have experience working with survivor moms and may be able to help with some of the difficulties related to how breastfeeding and past abuse can be linked. The International Board of Certified Lactation Consultants (IBCLC) has a Web site with a locator to help find such a practitioner.(4.30)

Kim sought the help of a lactation consultant during her third pregnancy. At that time she thought she would be able to work through her feelings with this professional support. But the "emotional struggle" became too intense. Although Kim does not emphasize it, we note that she also was suffering physical pain from nipples that cracked—a setback that could derail any woman's efforts:

*By the time I became pregnant with baby number three, I had started to make a little headway. I was then able to talk about my abuse. Nothing graphic or probing—only feelings and circumstances. I was able to give voice to the child I had been without feeling the shame of being a victim. When baby three was born we visited the lactation consultant. I learned all the interesting facts and benefits, the how to and how often. I tried to discuss my discomfort: she told me to try to not think of my breasts as a sexual vehicle, but as a way to nurture my baby. With that frame of mind I went home and tried my best. Week one we progressed well. Into week two I started to feel uncomfortable again, and by the time week three came I had developed scabs and bleeding, and every time I had to nurse it was such an emotional struggle. I had both physical pain and emotional pain. I stopped nursing. I was in such distress. Why couldn't I nurse? What was wrong with me? Other women seemed to enjoy breastfeeding and had much success: What was I doing wrong?*

*from Kim's story*

Stopping nursing caused Kim as much distress as the emotional struggle and physical injury had. She blamed herself, asking, "What was wrong with me?" Self-blame is an unfortunate reaction to have. Feelings of loss and anger would be reactions that are more accurate than self-blame.

Of note here is that Kim was "starting to make a little headway" in talking about her abuse history. If she was making this progress in a psychotherapy relationship, she might have been able to get additional trauma-focused help. As her narrative makes clear, the time between the onset of emotional and physical discomfort and stopping nursing was short. Discussing the abuse-related problems she had breastfeeding her first two infants before the birth of her third baby might have helped.

Breastfeeding was so important to Kim that she chose to try again with her fourth child despite describing feelings that would make such an effort unworthwhile to most women. She attributes this final success to daily phone contact with support:

*We made a decision that baby number four was going to be our last one. It made breastfeeding more important to me to become a success. I had daily phone contact with support. You would think that taking your child to your breast and gazing into their eyes while they nurse would be the most natural and fulfilling thing in the world to every woman. As my mind is screaming and I'm trying to hold still, I tense and become rigid, and repulsed. All I have is a maddening desire to end the contact. It was too powerful to be ignored any longer. Breastfeeding invoked a roller coaster of emotions in me, none that I could ignore.*

*from Kim's story*

Other abuse-related issues may contribute to making breastfeeding difficult. Candice identified that the reason she wasn't able to nurse her son had to do with his gender. We will discuss issues relating to the gender of your child in the chapter on mothering:

*I do realize a lot of factors contributed to the failure of my breastfeeding, but when it really comes down to it, I didn't want to breastfeed that boy. Breastfeeding lasted less than three weeks.*

*from Candice's story*

### *BREASTFEEDING AS HEALING*
Breastfeeding is not difficult for all survivor moms, certainly. The vast majority of narrators for this book had breastfed for at least a period of time. Breastfeeding has some anti-stress properties. Mary alludes to this by saying she found it soothing.(4.31, 4.32) She says that she loved breastfeeding, and that it was a great source of comfort to her during a difficult time:

*I loved breastfeeding. It gave me a chance to sit down, lie down, rest, love and be loved, provide perfect comfort for all life's ills and spills....*

*from Mary's story*

For Rebecca, breastfeeding and birth were events that were emotionally healing for her:

*My son, and then 15 months later, my daughter, was born perfectly healthy. They were big, beautiful, perfect babies. God didn't hate me. He had blessed me. All my shame, inhibitions, mistrusts, fears—they were gone.*

*I held my newborn son, and put him to my breast. My body, the one that I had always thought so horrible, had given birth. Now it would sustain the life of my child. There are no words to explain the depth of that feeling.*

*Almost five years have passed. I have high self-esteem. I am a confident woman. I love myself. I give all the credit of my emotional healing and well-being to the birth and breastfeeding of my babies. Ten years ago, I would never have believed that I could do these wonderful things. I was so wrong. Peace.*

*from Rebecca's story*

▼ 4.31
Oxytocin is a hormone involved in reproduction, lactation and stress regulation. Higher levels of oxytocin have been associated with lower blood pressure in response to a stressor in a laboratory study. Breastfeeding mothers in that study were the ones with the higher levels of oxytocin. Furthermore, their oxytocin levels were higher when they had been holding their infants than when they had been separated for an hour.

Light, et al. 2000

▼ 4.32
There is some evidence that the hormones associated with breastfeeding may provide some protection against over-reacting to stressors and possibly some protection against postpartum mood disorders. One theory about how this may work is that breastfeeding immediately after birth may keep some of the pregnancy hormones at levels that are similar to pregnant levels, which may prevent an abrupt state of "withdrawal."

Carter, Altemus and Chrousos 2001

Melanie also experienced healing related to her sexual response after having breastfed:

*Having children has been a wonderful experience for me. In unexpected ways, it has helped me overcome some of the effects of abuse. Before my children, I really disliked having my breasts touched, which I attribute to the abuse. Once in a while I didn't mind it, but generally breast touching was not allowed in our relationship. This was frustrating for my husband and disappointing for me. Interestingly, I really wanted to breastfeed our children, and wasn't worried about my experiences interfering with it. When my first child arrived with health problems and was unable to breastfeed, I used a breast pump to express milk for her. This became physically painful for me, but otherwise was not difficult. After I stopped expressing milk and our sex life returned to something more normal, I discovered, much to my surprise, that I was not only no longer turned off when my husband touched my breasts, but that I actually enjoyed it.*

*from Melanie's story*

Heather was able to separate the feelings produced by nursing from other sexual feelings, and for her nursing was a positive experience:

*I generally find that the sensation of nursing is not sexual at all. For me, it is like the feeling you get when someone scratches your back and hits a place that has had an itch for so long that you have started to ignore it. A feeling of relief, and pleasure, but not sexual in nature. My comfort with it has extended as our nursing relationship has continued, and I find myself still nursing him at almost two years old, and still not finding it damaging or sexual.*

*from Heather's story*

## PROFESSIONAL ADVICE FOR LACTATION CONSULTANTS AND POSTPARTUM CAREGIVERS

In the following section we are reprinting (with permission of the author) an excerpt from a study module for La Leche League leaders written by health psychologist, Kathleen Kendall-Tackett, an expert on the effects of childhood sexual abuse on breastfeeding women. This excerpt may be useful for both caregivers and mothers.

### WHAT YOU CAN DO
• **Offer Suggestions That Will Make Breastfeeding More Comfortable**
With any mother who is having trouble, find out which situations make her uncomfortable, physically, psychologically or emotionally. These can vary from woman to woman, but if you can anticipate times and situations where mothers might be particularly vulnerable, you enhance your ability to intervene. Three particularly difficult situations mothers have described to me include early postpartum, nighttime feeding and playful older infants.

Early postpartum can be a difficult time. The sudden life changes, the lack of sleep and the sometimes overwhelming demands of caring for a newborn may be too much. This situation is exacerbated if the mother had a difficult birth, where she either felt psychologically traumatized by the experience or where it reminded her of her abusive past. As described earlier, these mothers may be particularly prone to depression. It is important to know of mental health resources in the community that can help mothers cope during this stressful time.

Nighttime breastfeeding may be difficult for the entire period of lactation, especially if the woman was typically abused at night. The association of nighttime feedings with her earlier abuse may be too strong to allow her to breastfeed comfortably. Some mothers can comfortably breastfeed if they allow someone else to handle night feedings.

Other mothers may find that they are more comfortable with expressing milk and using a bottle all the time. But some may find that using a pump is also uncomfortable in that it involves an outside object manipulating their breasts. Some mothers learn to use distraction (such as watching TV) to help them cope with the uncomfortable feelings they may be having while breastfeeding.

Many survivors are comfortable breastfeeding an infant, but have trouble with older infants who pull back and smile, or who play with the breast while breastfeeding. Some mothers may even feel enraged by this normal infant behavior, or are just too uncomfortable to allow it to continue. One helpful strategy is to help mothers to reinterpret the behavior of playful infants, explaining that this is part of normal social development. If a baby is touching the mother during breastfeeding in a way that she finds annoying, show her how to re-direct the baby's behavior. The fact that she does not have to just "take it" can also be a revelation for mothers who are not used to being able to set boundaries on other people touching their bodies.

Toddlers can trigger "out-of-control" feelings when they are insistent on breastfeeding. They are bigger, and their behavior may seem more "adult" to the mother. Acrobatics while nursing may particularly upset the mother and trigger unpleasant memories of abuse. Remind the mother that she can set appropriate limits gently with her breastfeeding toddler as well, including where and how often she nurses.

### • Be Careful in Your Examinations
In this same regard, be careful in your examination of mothers. Empower her to set limits in terms of how undressed she needs to be when you examine her. Allow her to cover up as soon as possible, rather than leaving her exposed. When possible, examine her sitting up rather than lying supine, as this can be one aspect of medical care that is difficult for trauma survivors (American Medical Association 1995). Always ask permission before you touch a mother.

### • Help Mothers Learn What Is Normal
Mothers who have been sexually abused may have difficulty knowing what is normal within their own bodies. Many mothers derive at least some sensual pleasure from breastfeeding. But mothers who have been sexually abused may be concerned about whether these feelings are appropriate. You can reassure mothers about this or perhaps even bring up some of the pleasurable aspects of breastfeeding. Further, by emphasizing the biological function of breasts, you can de-emphasize the view of breasts as primarily sexual organs.

In addition, help mothers be realistic about what they can expect from breastfeeding. For women with trauma histories, it isn't always a wonderful experience, but can become a tolerable experience. And that may be a more realistic goal for mothers who are struggling.

If a mother reveals that she has been sexually abused, talk with her about the importance of seeing a mental health professional who can help (if she is not already doing so). She may need specific treatment for depression, PTSD or substance abuse. The best situation would be for you to work in conjunction with mental health providers. Ask mothers for permission to contact their mental health providers. And be sure to set some boundaries for yourself. While you want to be sympathetic and supportive, be cautious about becoming the main source of emotional support for issues that are only tangentially related to breastfeeding. For a mother experiencing serious difficulties, or difficulties outside the realm of breastfeeding, you must refer her to a qualified care provider.

• **Educate Care Providers about Normal Course of Breastfeeding, including Breastfeeding on Demand, Co-Sleeping and Late Weaning**
Experts in lactation can make a significant difference in this area. Many in the sexual abuse field feel that attachment-parenting practices, such as those listed above, are negative results of the sexual abuse experience. You can educate mental health providers, either directly or via the mother, about the normality of these practices, especially from a global perspective.

## *CONCLUSION*

Women vary in their reactions to past sexual abuse, and not everyone who has been sexually abused will have all the problems just described. Sexual abuse survivors will also have a wide range of reactions to breastfeeding. Some women who have been sexually abused cannot tolerate even the thought of breastfeeding. Others find that breastfeeding is enormously healing. Still others have mixed feelings or more neutral feelings, and breastfeed because they want the best for their babies. With awareness of possible difficulties, and perhaps in conjunction with a mental health provider, mothers who have survived sexual abuse can have a positive breastfeeding experience.

Kelly shares her journey toward a positive breastfeeding experience:

*With breastfeeding I've had to consider the difference between my sexuality and sex. What I mean is the difference with who I am as a functioning mother and who I am sexually as a wife. The first attempts at breastfeeding were stressful because of my daughter's low birth weight and that was mostly on my mind. Once our breastfeeding relationship was established, I started getting confused and had feelings of shame sometimes. While breastfeeding when she would lick and root around at the beginning of the feeding, I would feel embarrassed. The sensations while nursing can be wonderful and exhilarating. I have a very strong let down reflex that I am even experiencing now as I write about it! These great experiences have been hard for me to put into context because of being sexually abused. I was taught that my body was an object. A sexual tool. My breasts were spoken of in the context of sex.*

*My husband loves my breasts, as much as the next healthy guy does. Then here is this tiny little girl who's gotta eat and I want her to have the best and that comes from a sex organ? No, my breasts were probably foremost made for her survival. That is more important than the sexual enjoyment I have with James. I am realizing more and more that we are eating and, yes, bonding but not in a shameful way. Yes, it may even be sort of sexual but not in the shameful way either. I can't deny that I am a woman who enjoys the wonderful feelings when my baby looks up at me so dependently nursing. I think that is a good thing! So what if it has to do with my breasts. If milk came out of my fingers that would be fine too! I have taken flak for breastfeeding and that has been hard and gets confusing too, but I have been strong and forged ahead with Chloe. We are very close and it does involve our bodies, but in a way that is redeeming. It's like I am being given a chance to use my body for what*

## Chapter 4—Postpartum and Breastfeeding

*it was made for when for so long it was not being used and respected in the way it should have.*

*from Kelly's story*

Whether or not survivor moms choose to breastfeed, or feel confident in their bonding with their newborn, for moms to do all they can to support good mental health as they face the many challenges of parenting is vitally important. **Nothing is more important to the well-being of a child than his or her mother's mental health.**

As Claire shared in her narrative, being a "good enough" mom, one who makes her own mental health a top priority, and makes a conscious effort to healthfully care for her infant is okay. Like Claire, she is able to say:

*And I look forward to the rest of my life as his mom. I look forward.*

# MOTHERING AND ATTACHMENT

*Sadie's Story*
When my son was born, the doctor told me he would die. He was very little and very early. In that moment, I listened to myself and strongly, without hesitation, told the doctor that he was wrong. My son would make it. I didn't know at that time that I had nearly died many times throughout my own childhood and each time, in some hidden part of me, had vowed: I won't be stopped. Let me first tell you about him.

He was in the hospital for three months. I stayed with him for long hours every day in intensive care, with my hands holding his feet and head through the holes of the isolette where he rested. I tried to give him the kind of secure boundary he would have felt if he was still growing inside me. When I would enter the intensive care unit and pause at the sink to scrub up, put on the hospital gown and get ready to see him, I would always pray in my own renegade way—not taught by a particular religion but born of a longing and a knowing to stay connected with spirit.

I felt I was entering a temple when I came into the NICU. Some days he didn't want much touch, just perhaps one finger. Each day I'd say to him, "What will feel like love to you today?" I'd sense what he needed that moment. I felt fiercely protective of him. I was also determined that he'd have my breast milk to support him. I began pumping my breasts diligently the day he was born. The milk was frozen in plastic bags until he was ready to receive it through a tube. When he was three pounds and still in the neonatal intensive care unit, I began nursing him.

I found out later that he carried a memory of nursing as a turning point. When he was two he spontaneously created a NICU with blocks and Fisher Price toys and he replayed that moment. He showed how the baby couldn't come home until the mother doll had nursed the baby doll. This was part of an unwinding process he went through when he was two, three and four years old. He'd play out hospital experiences as part of his own healing.

One day when he was three, very uncharacteristically he curled up and said he didn't want to be touched. I recognized what was happening to him and discovered how to bring him back from that place where the past was upon him, forward gradually into the present. I said, "Yes, when you used to feel like that, here is how I'd hold you." Over many minutes he gradually got his bearings as I followed his play from retreating to crawling to standing and coming out again in a kind of recapitulation. I let him take the lead and set the pace. Other days when he wanted to see pictures of the hospital time, we'd look at the scrapbook. Through these and other experiences, he began to integrate knowledge of what had happened to him with the reality of his safety today.

It wasn't until I filled out a survivor survey for this book that I realized the sorts of resonances, the contrasts and coincidences, between our two stories. He had a life and death struggle and I had a life and death struggle of a very different sort. I watched him struggle against all odds in the NICU—when he was two pounds the hospital mixed his IV wrong and he was given a lethal dose of salt. And when he got a systemic infection, I talked to him through the isolette, begging him to stay here in this body while medicine was being flown to him in an airplane. If someone had told me at the time that there were two miracles going on here, I would have had no comprehension. Now, I glimpse that it must have been healing for me to watch someone completely vulnerable survive all odds, as well as healing to be able to embody the kind of mothering I sorely wanted. Today he is a teenager, strong and smart and funny and utterly loveable. I love being his mother.

It is difficult to make a jump here and express my own experiences, as if even to write on the same page about how my own parents harmed me might somehow reach and hurt my son. A year before I got full memories, I was driving back from seeing a movie, "Like Water for Chocolate," where I got to see on the movie screen a mother like mine who was incredibly emotionally abusive. As I drove, I said a prayer that the abuse in my family would not pass to the next generation. Within seconds a deer sprang onto the highway, hit the windshield and died instantly. Going to a Native American pow wow in our region the next day, people I spoke to suggested that the deer had taken on the impact and was indeed trying to make the prayer come true. They said that the deer is a symbol for incest. It was one of the clues that led to my being ready to receive memories.

I knew I was a motherless child, but I had to hide this from myself. No one knew that my mother was mentally ill, fractured by the abuse by her own parents. At times she would dote on us, and I remember clearly times she baked cookies or cared for me while I was sick, but then she would suddenly flip. The grief I feel from being betrayed by my mother is so deep that it feels impossible to touch. To the world my mother portrayed herself as a proper dignified person with bright red lipstick, a commanding smile and a charismatic manner. But this person of the sunny face could at any moment become replaced by a monster, a criminal the world never saw, a jailor who I totally depended upon for my very survival. This is a story that I wish wasn't true. It has taken painstaking work through flashbacks, old poems, nightmares and excellent therapy, to piece it all together.

The main thing I want to say to other survivor mothers is that we are not doomed or tainted by what happened to us. The strength we used to survive is ours. This strength is real and we bring that to our good mothering. It feels to me that I survived the unsurviveable. I faced death too many times. Gradually I'm learning to appreciate my own struggle. When I look at what happened to me, I have to realize that I have lived like a wildflower with the force of spring rising up against all odds.

I have a good friend who encourages me to brag. My brag is that I'm a great mom. In fact, when my son was younger, people who watched me talk to him or play with him would stop and comment on my thoughtful mothering. It really meant a lot to me. As was not the case with my own mother, the way I treated him both publicly and privately was consistently caring. Being a great mom is my ongoing prayer. I have worried a lot. And at the time I thought my protectiveness was due to his prematurity. Now I see how fervently I didn't want to pass along a drop of the mistreatment I received.

My memories didn't surface until my son was 13. What I have learned is horrific to tell and yet explains the morning terror that has plagued my life. Both my parents sexually abused me for many years. Sometimes my mother would choke me or threaten me with a knife. Repeatedly she told me she hated me and that everything that was happening to me was my own fault. "You make your own problems," she would tell me. Or, "If people knew what you were really like, you'd really be in trouble." The acid of her hate, the entrapment of her blame, and the ever-present fear that I would lose my life made a deadly combination. Sometimes she would force me to say, "I'm sorry." I felt that

# Chapter 5—Mothering and Attachment

*I was holding the whole family together and that everything depended upon my being a good girl and an "A" student. I became a person no one would ever guess was enduring daily torture at home.*

*Throughout my life a creepy sensation has haunted me—a sensation of my bones turning to sand, and I become nothingness. I didn't know what this meant. Now I know it is the memory of being sexually abused by the person who was meant to transmit to me the earth's love through responsible energy. The person meant to model safety and love, totally trampled my boundaries and invaded me, until I turned to sand. I carry hidden terror and rage and grief that are just beginning to unwind.*

*I also felt betrayed by a world that couldn't step in and protect me. I felt confused that there was no one who could stop my parents or see through their disguises. I also felt determined to help make a world that does care and does act responsibly.*

*I decided when I was young that I'd be a teacher. I'd pick out teachers I wanted to emulate, and at the same time I vowed to not repeat the unwanted behavior I saw in others. I must have made the same inner decision as a mother. Even though I had a despicable mother, I could imagine how a good mother would behave and chose this as my model.*

*How I was able to survive the torment of sexual abuse is a mystery. My belief is that I wouldn't have made it without the help of spiritual forces. To me, the invisible force of the divine is as real as gravity. I believe that aligning myself with the divine—which personally for me means reaching to Mother Mary, and Quan Yin each day—is what helps me be able to be a wonderful mother despite the horrors I endured.*

*The birth experience itself was incredibly positive. My son was so early that I hadn't begun classes with my midwife on what birth was like. So I kept praying to place myself in God's hands. I couldn't work with my midwife, but instead with hospital staff I'd never met before. I was in the hospital hooked up to a monitor, in the midst of whirring sounds, bright lights and blaring television. Yet through this all, I could pray and concentrate and do whatever had to be done to give my son a gentle birth so he'd have the best chances of survival.*

*In retrospect, I think these are the skills that we who are sacred survivors have honed. Our story is not only of horror, but ultimately of the sacredness of life. We have learned to be faithful to the light. We have over and over again proved ourselves courageous, persevering and trustworthy.*

*During my son's birth, I had to handle a difficult invasion when the hospital doctor, who had been assigned to me, checked me for dilation. I knew that after he'd gotten the information he needed, he kept moving his finger inside me. It was repulsive. The nurses said later he often did that to women. I, who had been calmly in concentration, suddenly blurted to him—"Get out!" I experienced his treatment as a rape. In hindsight, I see that in my response I voiced what I could never say as a child without risking death. Get out! Go away! No more! Don't mess with me! I know the truth about you! I don't care what your authority is; you get away! In that instant, all of this was being conveyed.*

*I said it was an incredible birth. It might seem impossible in these circumstances, but I felt surrounded by light. The doctor threatened to do a cesarean if the birth didn't happen faster, and I remained unrattled and delivered my son vaginally, which I knew would help him as a preemie. Despite my surroundings, I was in charge, in charge not by being super in control, but by choosing each moment to place myself in the hands of spirit. I was within a river I trusted. Spirit was in charge. Again, birth and life were stronger.*

**Kim's Story**
*I was sexually abused by someone I once knew. A man who eventually married my mother. Someone 12 years younger than her and nine years older than me. Was that a factor in my abuse? I doubt it, but at that time the age was relevant to me. I was 11, starting puberty, already menstruating, aware of the opposite sex. I was caught between adolescence and my own time line.*

*It started innocently enough, hugs that went on a little too long, always trying to pull me into his lap, always seeming to be in the same places I was, asserting himself into a fatherly role. Even then I felt something wasn't right, that there was something odd about him. Something that made me not want to be near him. But my experiences with people at that age were so limited that I wasn't aware that something awful could happen.*

*One night he wanted to "tuck me into bed." He stayed longer than necessary, with the excuse of talking. Some time had passed, and as I grew a little more relaxed, his hand went inside my pajamas. He was rubbing my belly at first. As I look back on it, I think the belly rubbing was a way to see if I would stop him, or yell out to my mom, or something…he was trying to gauge my reaction. I didn't resist, he started rubbing between my breasts and around them, carefully not touching my nipples. Warning bells were going off in my head but I didn't know what to do; nothing like this had ever happened to me before. I rolled onto my stomach, hoping that would signal him to leave. He started rubbing my back as if he was giving me a massage, and then he finally left. I was a child, a baby. I felt helpless. What was I supposed to do?*

*That was the only time this happened for about a year. We had moved and he didn't come to live with us for 12 months. I don't remember the exact moment when it started again. I do remember he had gotten bolder as time went on and that I remained silent. He didn't have to threaten me; I was afraid. Who was I going to tell?*

*I don't remember the frequency of those visits. Only that he would come in the middle of the night when the rest of the house was sleeping. Nothing can describe the dread you feel when you're surface sleeping, always listening for noises that could mean he was coming. Hearing him walk past your room to the bathroom and praying like mad he would just keep going and not visit you that night. Always trying to pretend you were deeply asleep so he couldn't manipulate your body into touching his. Or the guilt you feel when you have your first orgasm and you don't even know what it is. You can't control your body to stop; you wake up and realize that it wasn't some sick twisted dream you were having.*

*I was changing. I was becoming different. Something dies in you and you become numb, just kind of going through the motions. I was always trying to hide what I was feeling: repulsion, revulsion, shame. I felt like everyone must see what was happening to me, everyone except my mother.*

*How could she not see the signs? How could she not see how I would shrink every time he came into close contact, not wanting him to touch me in any way? Becoming verbally attacking, being sarcastic, saying mean and hurtful things, anything to give me a little power back? How could she not see I was crying out in pain? I lost all respect for her in my childhood. Did she not feel the tension that emanated from me? Maybe she didn't want to see.*

*Finally I had to do something. I was 15 and knew he couldn't do this any longer. But who do I tell? At this point no one knew. I didn't tell my mother. I didn't tell a family friend. Nor did I tell a schoolteacher, or even my best friend. I requested counseling, and they agreed to take me.*

*I knew what I was going to say that day. I knew I was going there to tell. Only I didn't know the new "hell" I had unleashed. Testimonies, affidavits, physical*

# Chapter 5—Mothering and Attachment

*exams, individual counseling. Luckily, he confessed, which made the ordeal a little easier. Until my mother decided she could forgive him, and wanted the family to stay together. So we had to endure hours and hours of intolerable family counseling. She wanted to keep the family together, and she had him come home. I had to move in with a family friend because of the ongoing trial; he couldn't be anywhere within a certain amount of feet of me. So here I was, a girl of 15 having been moved out of her home because of her mother's love for her husband. A husband, who did this horrible thing to her child, was more important. From the time he made bond, and all throughout his trial, and finally his sentencing, I had to live away from home. His admission of guilt saved me from having to testify*

*What happens to little girls who were sexually abused? They become mothers. I married a wonderful man, who has been with me from almost the very beginning. We had one child and things were fine. I tried to breastfeed, but had some troubles. I figured it was just inexperience, and a lack of education. During my pregnancy with child number two things started to change. I lost desire for sex. Everyone told me it was hormones. Then it became much more than that. I didn't want to be hugged or kissed or touched and anything beyond that. I couldn't be intimate with my husband without having these thoughts or memories or feelings invade my head. After baby two was born, and postpartum depression set in, impacted by baby's colic, and my sexual dysfunction, these feelings during breastfeeding started to emerge. I became uncomfortable with the sensations. I hated the suckling, the demand of it, and the restraint. It didn't take much to persuade me to quit. By the time I became pregnant with baby number three, I had started to make a little headway. I was then able to talk about my abuse. Nothing graphic or probing; only feelings and circumstances. I was able to give voice to the child I had been without feeling the shame of being a victim. When baby three was born we visited the lactation consultant. I learned all the interesting facts and benefits, the how to and how often. I tried to discuss my discomfort: she told me to try to not think of my breasts as a sexual vehicle, but as a way to nurture my baby. With that frame of mind I went home and tried my best. Week one we progressed well. Into week two I started to feel uncomfortable again, and by the time week three came I had developed scabs and bleeding, and every time I had to nurse it was such an emotional struggle. I had both physical pain and emotional pain. I stopped nursing. I was in such distress. Why couldn't I nurse? What was wrong with me? Other women seemed to enjoy breastfeeding and had much success. What was I doing wrong?*

*In the time after baby three I grew more comfortable talking about my abuse and with much more frequency. I am not ashamed to be a survivor of sexual abuse. I am not defined by what happened to me. I am who I am despite it. We made a decision that baby number four was going to be our last one. It made breastfeeding more important to me to become a success. I had daily phone contact with support. You would think that taking your child to your breast and gazing into their eyes while they nurse would be the most natural and fulfilling thing in the world to every woman. As my mind is screaming and I'm trying to hold still, I tense and become rigid, and repulsed. All I have is a maddening desire to end the contact. It was too powerful to be ignored any longer. Breastfeeding invoked a roller coaster of emotions in me, none that I could ignore.*

*In the time since the last one was born, I have put some work into healing myself. I can't ignore that I am still deeply being affected by my abuse. I've turned to God for comfort and guidance. I've had some mother's studies classes that I attend. I have begun to understand how many things I can link to one event in my life. The rage I have, the inability to make a decision, the breastfeeding, my sexual frigidity, are all linked to unresolved issues of sexual abuse. As I continue to work on this, more things will likely surface. I probably won't ever work through it all. I am not afraid to face it. It is something I will always have to live with and work on.*

*What have I learned so far? I may have been the immediate victim of my perpetrator but it affects everyone that loves me closely. It affects my husband. He has been hurt by my denials and refusals. He has had to live with a picture in his own mind. He has had to learn extra patience and tenderness, and to sometimes just let me have the space. I have needed to deal with how and what I was feeling. It has affected him as a father; he knows how there can be predators out there and has become as protective as I, or even more at times. It affects grandparents, too. My in-laws are really vigilant in making sure that no moves can be misconstrued. They are careful in some topics that are talked about, for fear of bringing up bad memories for me. It still is a constant battle when my children spend time with my mother. All those feelings, resentments and memories I remember as a child makes it difficult for me to allow a normal Grandparent/Grandchild relationship with her. As I deal with my problems right now, the people who are most affected by my abuse are my children. I know how important showing affection in the simplest ways is for a child. And I can't freely show affection. A simple touch of the shoulder or smoothing their hair or a quick squeeze has to be carefully orchestrated and forced. And these are my children. I carried them inside of my body for nine months. Birthed them, nurtured them and raised them, and yet I can't hug them, because I don't want physical contact. How do I deal with the guilt and frustration? It has affected my decisions on how I raise the kids. I am not a normal mother. My security has been shaken. My kids are more sheltered, more protected, more supervised than other kids they know. Every time they go out to play, or have a birthday invitation or play date, or sleep-over, or use a public restroom, I always wonder if there is a perpetrator lurking about. Anytime they leave the house without my husband or me we wonder will their caregiver be as vigilant as we are? Will they remember to hold their hands in public, or never let them walk more than two steps behind them? Not let them talk to strangers?*

*Will these structured and controlled movements be harmful to my kids as they grow and mature? As they grow, I am sure that some changes will have to be made and a certain amount of letting go will have to be done so they can retain their independence. It only takes one time, one minute, to change a person's life forever. I found the strength to survive the abuse; I know I could never survive that sort of thing happening to a child of my own if I could stop it. Who knows more about the abuse and the cries for help, than one who has suffered through it?*

# Chapter 5—Mothering and Attachment

> Civilization will start on the day when the well-being of newborn babies will prevail over any other consideration.
> — Wilhelm Reich

Beginning fresh
every day
to raise them up,

She brushes golden hair
in long strokes through
earthy smelling bristles.
Dips into white water fountains
to smooth their tangles
Breathes in deep,
conjuring
the long-gone smell of
milky flannel.

She weaves her tapestry
with their sun spun hair
inserting beads of her
own soul;

a cloak of green and gold finery
in which to wrap them.

For one day, they will
walk the river's shores alone

panning for her soul

And finding that pebble
of living green,

They will become
one with the river.
— Tina

We chose to highlight both Sadie and Kim's stories because we felt that they represented a range of feelings about mothering. In this chapter we will present what the survivor moms had to say about attachment to their infants and about issues and concerns that have come up about mothering over the years, as the infants grow through childhood and beyond. Many of the concerns are common to most parents, but the experiences of having been abused in their own childhood seem to add a layer of uncertainty or complexity for survivor moms. Many of these areas of concern are about the interpersonal relationship between moms and children, about keeping kids safe and about how healing overlaps with mothering.

These excerpts from the narrators shed light on the issues. Sometimes these mothers share some wisdom from their perspective. This is not the whole story, though. Mothers should consult additional sources that address aspects of mothering in which they are uncertain how to act. The mother-child relationship is very important and mothers who feel hampered by feelings of depression, strong irritability or rage, or other problems that childhood abuse survivors have, should seek support and help from a health or mental health professional.

Without good role models for parenting, women may find that they often do not know how to respond as mothers, and have to "make it up as they go" to a greater extent than women who had adequate, healthy parents. Parenting support is available through classes or one-on-one coaching. A pediatrician, family doctor or nurse-practitioner may be able to make a referral. Child care professionals and teachers may also be good sources of information and referral.

Wendi states very clearly how giving birth was only a beginning, and that, afterwards, she felt unsure of herself and her abilities as a mother:

*Birth was such an empowering event in my life, yet afterwards I felt very alone and unsure of myself. There I was with this newborn baby and no one there to tell me what to do. I constantly struggled with the dysfunctional patterns I had learned in childhood. I knew I didn't want to parent in the way I was parented but was confused as to how to change. I used my daughter as a mirror to show myself how I was feeling. If she was upset it usually stemmed from me. Over time I learned to deal with my emotions better. I learned from my daughter how to love and how to trust. It was a difficult adjustment learning to trust myself.*

*from Wendi's story*

▼ 5.1

Discontinuity of care with one's parents has been described as a traumatic attachment experience. Parents who had erratic and abusive experiences with their own parents may not develop a good 'internal working model' for caregiving.

Bowlby 1977

▼ 5.2

In a population study of California hospital discharge coding for pregnant women in the year 1992, the frequency of having any psychiatric diagnostic code was 1.5%. Seventy-five percent of these were for substance use (which is often discovered via urine screening). Only 1.6% of these diagnoses were for mood disorders and 0.8% were for anxiety disorders. Although these very low rates may only represent underreporting and not underrecognition of maternal mental health conditions, it suggests that new mothers likely are being undertreated.

Kelly, et al. 1999

We will turn to other survivor moms' concerns about attachment and mothering, but first we want to give attention to what was a burning question for some of the narrators, and one that seemed taboo to discuss.

### WILL I ABUSE MY CHILD?

All mothers may wonder or worry what kind of mother they will be. Many of the narrators expressed this one particular form of worry: They worried that they would repeat negative patterns from their own upbringing, including patterns of abuse. In Sadie's story at the beginning, we read how she prayed that she would not pass the cycle of abuse on to the next generation.(5.1, 5.2) Kathy shares that she was afraid to have children because of this:

*It has been difficult for me. I was afraid to have children because I was worried I might abuse them, which has not happened. I am overprotective at times. I watch every man that comes near them.*

*from Kathy's story*

# Chapter 5—Mothering and Attachment

Melanie says that she had read that she was at higher risk of abusing because of her history and this is scary to her:

*I've read statistics about how often those who have been abused, in turn abuse their own children, whether sexually, physically or emotionally. I can't believe that I would or could actually abuse my children, but it scares me to death that I'm at a higher risk to do so because of my past. Every time I get upset with them or yell at them I hate myself for it and wonder why I react the way I do. Is it because of the abuse? Am I headed for something worse? I guess that fear is a good thing and remembering and acknowledging it will hopefully help me to keep from doing anything to hurt my kids. I try very hard to be the best, most understanding mother I can be, but the fear is real and I resent that it's there.*

*from Melanie's story*

Although some mothers go on to sexually abuse their children, this is not as likely as mothers may fear, given that adult survivors have reported that the vast majority (96% in Russell's landmark study) of all perpetrators of sexual abuse are male (Russell 1986). Still, moms may fear that they will abuse, and that others who are aware of their history may also doubt them. Denise says that she felt everyone was watching her to see if she would be an abuser:

*One major issue for me is that I felt really watched. I had just come out about the years of abuse, and now I felt that everyone was watching me to see if I was going to abuse my child. This is because of that popular psychology theory (which is very destructive) that became very popular in the seventies, and which I actually read as a child while I was being abused. It made me even more fearful and scared of telling anyone what was happening because I felt branded or ruined for life.*

*Even as a child I was such a nurturing type of person that the thought that I might one day be a terrible mother was absolutely horrible…my fears regarding that were largely instrumental in my deciding to have an abortion later in life. I have met many other survivors who haven't had children for the same reason. It's ironic that because of 20 years of my father threatening to kill me I opted to end my own child's potential life rather than bring it into this "unsafe" planet.*

*from Denise's story*

Gwen feared abusing her son, and, like other mothers, had thoughts about the possibility of abusing him:

*The first time I had issues with my abuse and raising my son was when he was five. This was the same age when I remembered my abuse beginning. I freaked out the whole entire year. I was afraid to give him a bath or touch him in any way. I would have thoughts about abusing him. At this time, I was in individual therapy, and there I learned that all this was normal as long as I did not act on it. I believe if I ever get to that point I will commit myself somewhere for help.*

*from Gwen's story*

Kelly, too, worries that she might abuse, yet she feels that awareness, support, growth, and healing make this less likely:

> *I have been worried at times that I will someday abuse Chloe, because so many people say that if you were abused you will abuse too. I believe that since I am aware of the damage that sexual abuse causes, and that since I have assertively confronted the abuse, have support and have grown and healed so much, that it is not going to happen. I am not that person.*
>
> from Kelly's story

## ATTACHMENT

Circumstances caused Sadie to form an intense early attachment with her prematurely born son. She strove to *"give him the kind of secure boundary he would have felt if he was still growing inside me."* She came to understand his changing needs, asking, *"What will feel like love to you today?"* She pumped her breasts from the beginning and believed in him when there was little hope. The relationship between mother and child is a primary and fundamental one, which defines the quality of other attachments in our lives.

Some moms never feel a strong attachment for one reason or another. Paulette felt unable to connect with her boys and realized that this was a handicap:

> *I never felt like I was close to the boys. I felt I did the best I could with nothing....*
>
> from Paulette's story

Some survivor moms wrote about the intensity of this attachment. For some, like Sarah, the feeling was strongly positive.

> *Having a healthy baby was definitely the most wonderful experience I've ever had. I felt fulfillment like I never knew. I felt important and needed. I loved her so deeply and strongly it scared me. I loved staying home with her and taking care of her.*
>
> from Sarah's story

Others, like Susan, sensed that the intensity of the bond with their child caused reactions in themselves that were hard to understand at the time. Sometimes the intense feelings led to intense ways of parenting that may have been problematic.

> *I always felt very close to my babies until they could walk. Then inside myself I changed totally towards them and was almost afraid of them. It's a form of dissociation from my own pain. I know that now.*
>
> *I was terrified to leave my babies. I slept with them in my bed. I never let them cry for any reason. I was trying to protect them, not realizing at the time I felt I was protecting my life as well.*
>
> from Susan's story

Ann felt the pressure to be the perfect mother in order to overcome the effects of her childhood upbringing. The intensity of the attachment she felt to her baby was so strong she became physically ill at the idea of leaving her:

> *Because of my dysfunctional childhood, and now seeing all the effects it had on me as an adult, I had decided I wanted (actually needed) to think I was a perfect mother. This meant I put a lot of pressure on myself and my anxieties continued. I hadn't truly turned her over to God. I just wasn't sure I could trust Him. After all, look what He allowed to happen to me.*

*I became a very controlling mom. I became very protective. I was also very affectionate. I held her constantly as an infant (I was not going to repeat a cycle!). I actually spent the night vomiting the first night I tried to leave her. Probably the healthiest choice I made was to go back to work and put her in day care at six months. It helped me to put things into perspective. There was a world outside of my daughter and my husband.*

*from Ann's story*

Hope became, in her words, the "ultimate attachment parent":

*I had no clue what I was doing. I did know one thing, though. I knew that I was going to protect her from sexual abuse. My mother's family has a history of sexual abuse that goes back into obscurity. It had touched every family member I knew, but it was not going to happen to my baby. I became the ultimate "attachment parent." I never left her with anyone I didn't fully trust. I slept with her in my bed for years. I taught her the word "stop" and I made sure everyone respected it when she used it. I taught her that everyone has a right to their own space. I avoided any mention of sexual abuse per se, but made certain she was safe and strong. It was a lot of work. I didn't go out alone much. I couldn't take a job because I was terrified of leaving her in daycare. It ticked off more than a few people who didn't think tickling a child was a big deal, even after she said, "Stop." It wasn't easy for me but I knew what I had to do in order to live with myself. I was obsessed, but happy.*

*from Hope's story*

Cathleen shares her experience with uncertainty about attachment right after the birth of her baby:

▼ 5.3
Studies of the effects of PTSD on parenting are still rare. One study of male Vietnam era war-zone veterans and their adolescent children found that the emotional numbing symptoms of PTSD were associated with lower perceived quality of the father-child relationship.

Ruscio, et al. 2002

*The nurse brought me my breakfast. I ate and began a conversation with the new mom in the bed beside me. At noon I still had not asked to see my baby. Truthfully, I was frightened. I didn't understand at the time that I was emotionally a child myself. The responsibility seemed overwhelming; I had no confidence in my ability to be a good mother. Finally a nurse brought Shaun in. She was very helpful in getting me started on breastfeeding. After getting through the first few days when I was sore, I began to really enjoy the bonding that formed between Shaun and me and the extra closeness I felt while breastfeeding my baby.*

*from Cathleen's story*

Entering into such a profound attachment is not easy. Some women feel strong and immediate bonding with their infant. Others take a while longer, with a delay in starting to experience strong positive feelings for the infant. Emotional numbing, an aspect of posttraumatic stress that many survivors experience (5.3), prevents re-experiencing *bad* feelings but also can prevent *good* feelings—which may get in the way of getting to *feel* bonded to the baby. It is possible to take perfectly good care of a baby without feeling the lovely emotional sense of attachment. But doing all that long, hard mothering work without this felt-sense of a bond is probably more challenging. Hormones—including the hormone involved in breastfeeding, oxytocin—play a role in attachment. Severe stress and posttraumatic stress may possibly disrupt the working of this helpful hormone.

Mothers might be able to express attachment problems by saying that they are feeling "emotionally numb" or feeling that the "love hormone" is just not flowing for them. They may look like they are doing fine, because they are managing well in caring for the baby. If they don't feel fine about their bonding, they will likely find that sharing this with a professional helps.

## *MENTAL HEALTH*

We focused on mental health in the postpartum chapter because depression, anxiety and postpartum stress occur then, and postpartum is such a critical time in the mother-baby relationship. Paying attention to mental health is important for the long-haul, as well.

Denise expresses a particular worry about sometimes feeling "detached" from her son. The experience of not being "in body" is also called "dissociation" or "derealization" and can be a posttraumatic after-effect of childhood abuse. Denise expresses concern about how this coming ungrounded might affect her ability to be present for her parenting role:

*The one thing that I also really struggle with is staying "in body." I often just drift off, and go to that place of "nothingness" that I went to when I was being tortured and abused. So sometimes, although I am totally there for Xavier in a physical sense, mentally and spiritually I am miles away. When I catch myself, I obviously bring myself back quickly. The problem is that I think through all the years of trauma I have developed the kind of detachment that Buddhist monks spend whole lifetimes trying to achieve. I fully realize it can be a very good thing in the larger context of the meaning of life, but sometimes it worries me in terms of parenting.*

*from Denise's story*

Mothering is demanding even with the most accommodating child on the best days. Most kids and most days present challenges. Many survivor moms suffer occasional depression or have some anxiety or irritability from posttraumatic stress. As a result, kids' behavior and moms' limitations can collide.

Catherine suffered depression long after her children were born. She says that, for a time, her kids were basically "on their own." But she also points out that she did not commit suicide because of their presence, not wanting to traumatize them. This situation is bad for both the mother and the children—she cannot meet their needs, and they certainly cannot be expected to meet hers.

*I would spend days just sitting in a chair, unable to move. The kids were basically on their own most of the day. The older two were only four and two years old. The only reason I did not attempt suicide was because of the kids—they were always around, and I would never do it in front of them.*

*from Catherine's story*

Susan tells how she dealt with her stress by yelling. Parents do yell. It's a life-saving action if a child is in danger. But Susan's yelling seemed to be venting her stress. She may have been feeling the hyper-aroused, irritable, angry symptoms of posttraumatic stress. Children's noisy play or bickering may have been an irritant that led to outbursts of anger and yelling. She developed the strategy of giving herself "time-outs," which may have decreased her sense of overload:

> *When I am stressed, watch out. I learned to give myself "time outs" years ago. I never beat my kids but I did yell a lot. As more memories come I am calmer in many ways. I can even envision playing with my children someday.*
>
> from Susan's story

All three of these mothers were experiencing impairment in their mothering role. This is a reason to seek mental health treatment—in and of itself. In addition, the mother will benefit from better well-being.

Susan's "time-out" coping strategy is also worth discussing. She never beat her children, so time-outs may have worked well enough for her. However, uncontrolled anger—especially combined with emotional numbness, detachment or dissociation—may put a mother at risk for shaking her baby or beating her child. Shaken baby syndrome causes life-long disability and death.(5.4) Survivor moms know how devastating abuse feels and what long-term damage it does to the child and the parent-child relationship. Seeking help if "stress" threatens to become "rage" is essential.

▼ 5.4

In a comprehensive study of 364 cases of shaken baby syndrome—an extremely serious form of abusive head trauma—19% of the infants and young children died. Of those who survived, 55% had ongoing neurological injury and 65% had visual impairment. Only 22% of the surviving children showed no sign of health or developmental impairment at the time of discharge from the hospital.

King, et al. 2003

▼ 5.5

Mothers with a history of childhood sexual abuse reported more overall parenting stress and more feelings of anxiety about intimate aspects of parenting (changing diapers, bathing, showing affection) than non-abused mothers.

Douglas 2000

## RELATIONSHIP WITH THE CHILD'S BODY

Survivor mom narrators discussed concerns stemming from when they must deal with their children's bodies and issues surrounding intimate aspects of parenting.(5.5) Some concerns were about mothers not wanting to touch or be touched themselves. Some were about wondering what was appropriate in touching the child.

They worried about touch in general, how much and how often is okay. In Kim's narrative at the beginning of this chapter, she shared how she had a hard time freely showing affection. She shared that:

> *A simple touch of the shoulder or smoothing their hair or a quick squeeze has to be carefully orchestrated and forced. And these are my children. I carried them inside of my body for nine months. Birthed them, nurtured them and raised them, and yet I can't hug them, because I don't want physical contact.*
>
> from Kim's story

For some, having to diaper their child can be sensitive and bring up difficult feelings:

*I feel very weird and afraid to touch my children's genitals. I can wipe them with a wipe, but feel like it's a violation to touch them with my bare hand, even though I'm dying to. It isn't a sexual thing for me to touch them there, it's forbidden (in my head) because I was abused. I try to tell myself to go ahead and touch them if I want to (because I need to be normal), but it always causes me anxiety. I hate that.*

*from Tina's story*

*I find that I touch him a lot less in public. My mother was very touch-phobic and my father was totally touch-invasive, and I lived with the whole secretive touch thing. I have an automatic reflex to give him a lot more space in public and I suppose that it ties in with the whole thing that I am scared that people will think that I am an abuser. Don't you think that it is just totally unfair? I've lived through the whole ordeal myself and now I am permanently scared that people will think that I am the perpetrator.*

*from Denise's story*

*My biggest fear with my first child, who was a boy, was that because I was abused, that I might abuse him, maybe partly because I was so fascinated by his tiny genitals, so different than an adult man's. But I came to realize that abuse is a choice and I would never choose to abuse my adorable little boy. I never want any child anywhere to go through what I went through. That realization made me angry, too, that my father's own brother would choose to do that to me.*

*from April's story*

Dealing with their children's explorations of their bodies can be a challenge for survivor moms:

*A year ago my middle son and a neighbor child, a little girl, came to me and told me that they had been comparing the differences in their bodies. They were completely innocent and did not realize that looking at each other was something that was not okay for them to do. I did not know what sort of punishment, if any, was appropriate. I wondered if this was a sign of things to come. I wondered if I was overreacting to something normal or if this wasn't normal. Did I do something wrong, something to provoke this? How much of my past was ruling my thinking? I run into problems like this almost every day.*

*from Judy's story*

Kathy points out that involving other adults can be helpful. She enlisted her son's father to help when she was uncertain about what was normal and she felt upset:

*My son had an incident with another kid where they were exposing themselves to each other. It was probably a normal kid thing, but I lost it. I told Phil that he would have to deal with that one, that I could not. All I could think was "I've raised an abuser." Talking to other parents really helped....*

*from Kathy's story*

Kathy also makes the point that talking to other parents helped her. This sort of support, sharing ideas and information, is important for any parent trying to do a good job. Knowing that you can get input from others can ease the burden in deciding what seems right to you as the parent.

Amanda shares her feelings about dealing with her daughter's exploration of her body:

*My three-year-old goes naked quite frequently and tends to play with her genitals while watching TV or reading or the like. I try not to freak, I just tell her "that's something to do in the privacy of our own room." I have never understood the whole masturbation thing at all, which makes it harder still for me to understand my daughter. It seems like I spend a lot of my time trying not to pass on my own hang-ups—sexual dysfunction, embarrassment about bodily functions, eating disorders, poor body image, lack of affection and intimacy....*

*from Amanda's story*

Stacey says that she felt triggered by her daughter's relationship to her body:

*I have noticed more "triggering" with my daughter. I was awestruck with the natural purity of her little body and being, how free she is able to be, due to not being abused. It was, in fact, extremely painful, making me feel/see something I lacked, but joyful to see someone else have it, a sublime experience to be sure. That she can move her legs around in that 360 degree curve that babies do is amazing. I can't relax my body like that. She has also taken her time potty training, and I noticed that I didn't mind, that the covering of diapers made me feel safe for her. I suppose there is more of that kind of thing to come, but I will have to deal with it. I hope that my personality does not keep my daughter from anything in the world that she needs to experience. I hope I can manifest some of my dreams in the world that I want to, for her to see. I certainly have learned how a parent should not act, and because of this, the every day act of loving my children is healthy for me.*

*from Stacey's story*

### GENDER

Like Stacey in the section above, many of the narrative contributors expressed feelings related to the particular gender of their child. Some felt that dealing with having sons was easier, like they would be able to protect them better. Yet other moms worried that the sons would potentially become abusers.(5.6, 5.7)

Moms expressed worry at the possibility of being unable to protect their daughters, and others felt triggered by their daughters' gender, identifying with them.

Jennifer thinks that she might have been overly protective, if she had had a daughter:

*I think it is interesting that I have boys. I am somewhat glad that I don't have girls.*

▼ 5.6
Both abusing and being abused are gendered phenomena:

Surveys of child sexual abuse in large clinical populations of adults have been conducted in at least 19 countries in addition to the US and Canada. All studies have found rates in line with comparable North American research, ranging from 7–36% for women, and 3–29% for men. Most studies found females to be abused at 1½ to 3 times the rate for males.

Finkelhor 1994
World Health Organization 2002

▼ 5.7
In the National Comorbidity Survey, 10.5% of females and 2.3% of males reported molestation. Females were most often molested by a relative. Males were most often molested by an acquaintance.

Five percent of females and 0.6% of males reported rape. Acquaintances were more likely to perpetrate rape than relatives.

The prevalence rates of childhood sexual abuse reported in the National Comorbidity Survey applied to the 1990 US Census data would translate to approximately 9.6 million female and 1.8 million males experiencing sexual abuse before the age of 18. These rates only describe people living in households. People in residential treatment, jails, prisons, shelters, or homeless were not included in the survey. These populations are known to have much higher rates of childhood sexual abuse than the US general population.

Molnar, Buka and Kessler 2001

*Not because I wouldn't love to have a daughter, but because I feel I would be an overbearingly protective mother. I think that I would unconsciously damage her sense of safety.*

*from Jennifer's story*

Lanie worries about protecting her daughter as she grows:

*My sweet daughter is almost a year old and I have fallen completely in love with her. She is so full of joy and always happy. I worry about protecting her as she grows. I don't ever want her to be ashamed of being pretty or being a woman, like I was.*

*from Lanie's story*

Amy feels that although she is protective of both her son and her daughter, her daughter "brings out the mother lion" in her:

*I have noticed that since we had Anne, I have had a few issues come up because she's a girl. I look at any man who comes near her with suspicion. Ray insists that I am much more protective of her then I ever was of Jacob. It's because I have so much hope for her, so much joy for her, I want to make sure she never has anything taken from her future, or from her childhood. I want all of this for my son, too. And I do know that boys are molested and preyed upon. But there is something about my daughter that brings out the mother lion in me; I just can't explain it. I will defend both my children to the death, and the person that would ever lay a hand on my children had better be right with God because they won't survive long after I am through with them. But with Anne it goes further. I feel that I am making up for my mother in how I raise my daughter.*

*from Amy's story*

Lisa expressed similar feelings of protectiveness for her daughter:

*The issues and challenges that come up for me with my daughter are totally different than those with my son. I am acutely aware of how people respond to her. I have an overwhelming need to protect her and keep her safe physically. I want to insure that she likes her body, that she not experience shame about her sexuality or femininity. I wish for her to experience herself in a way that I did not experience as a child and that I am still seeking to experience as an adult.*

*from Lisa's story*

Kristy went from not wanting children at all, to hoping for boys, to being able to welcome the possibility of a daughter:

*Parenting is an arena where I can see the progress I have made in processing my childhood sexual abuse experience. There was a time when I vowed never to have children, probably because I feared what might happen to them at the hands of another family member or a perverted stranger. Then I went through a phase where I wanted to become a parent to a son or two, probably because I felt sons were somehow safer than daughters from potential sexual abuse. I'm now seven months pregnant with my first child and welcome the possibility of having a daughter. While*

## Chapter 5—Mothering and Attachment

*I recognize I could not possibly prevent everything bad from happening to her, I feel I would transmit to her the resiliency to handle whatever life might send her way.*
from Kristy's story

Elaine feels grateful to have a girl:

*I'm also grateful my first baby is a girl. A boy, even an infant one, might have provoked feelings of fear, anger or resentment. It seems I can't shake the idea that all men, no matter how old, are inherently evil or to be feared.*
from Elaine's story

Kala shares that she finds it hard to fully trust her husband or sons alone with her daughter:

*I can see a lot of what has negatively affected my role as a parent, like I still don't trust my husband or my sons alone with my daughter. I have been, and I guess always will be, very suspicious of men and I have to make a conscious effort not to "male bash" in front of my children. The last thing I would want is for my daughter to hate men altogether, and for my sons to feel that they deserve to be treated poorly by a woman. But at the same time, I see the positive. Each child knows they are loved dearly and nothing about them should be ignored. They respect me and I respect them. They aren't afraid to say "I love you" and they know how to make good decisions. Sometimes they don't make the best decisions in the world and they fall down. As their mom, though, I help them stand back up and help them to keep going without judging them.*
from Kala's story

Gwen feels that having a girl could prove to be her biggest challenge yet:

*Now, I am pregnant for the third time. This time they tell me it is a girl. And, for the first time my nurse-midwife knows I am an incest survivor. A part of me feels this may be my greatest challenge yet. I believe I am up to the task. I will love her and give of myself. I will try to instill in her independence, self-esteem and the knowledge that she is loved: all the things that had been warped for me. I hope I continue to do that for all my children.*
from Gwen's story

Deborah felt particularly challenged by mothering her girls during their adolescence:

*Mothering adolescent girls was especially hard for me. I read some books to them about the physical and emotional changes of puberty. I did not add personal comments. I'd often think of things to share about love and sex and how wonderful it could be, but could never say them. I knew the right words but I feared my feelings would betray my ambivalence. I relied on church youth group leaders to cover it for me. I very briefly told them of my abuse after I wrote this account.*
from Deborah's story

Some survivors find that they start to have symptoms of depression and/or uncover memories of childhood sexual abuse once their child reaches the age they were when they were abused. This was true for Cathleen:

*A very important insight discovered during counseling was that a picture I had chosen of myself to best represent my "inner child" was of me at age four and 10 months old—the exact age (I was to discover later) that my daughter was when all of my symptoms of depression first surfaced in the fall of 1988. Somehow Leia reaching the age I had been when the abuse began was triggering for me.*

*I began to understand that the inner child, the part of me that was hurting so, was in fact my deepest inner being; the part of me that feels deeply, needs and loves. It is not only my feelings, but in fact the creative part of me, the part where self-expression flows. As a child I had been hurting so much that I effectively cut off that part of my soul; numbing, repressing and burying everything there.*

*from Cathleen's story*

▼ 5.8

There have been few studies specific to PTSD and parenting. In one study of male combat veterans, it was the emotional numbing symptoms of PTSD that were associated with poor scores on the measure of the quality of their relationship with their child.

Ruscio, et al. 2002

This finding is consistent with previous research showing that dissociation and detachment are risk factors for parents abusing a child.

▼ 5.9

Honestly facing your strengths and weaknesses is essential. No one is a perfect parent. The goal isn't perfection. It's a healthy, growing relationship.

Ask yourself:
- What works? How do I feel successful as a parent?
- What am I proud of?
- Do I feel inadequate in any way? How?
- What would I like to change in my relationship with my kids?
- Are there areas where I feel confused? What are they?
- Are there patterns with my kids that remind me of my family of origin? Are there things that push my old buttons?
- Where do I feel stuck?
- When do I feel out of control?
- Am I able to protect my children adequately?
- How do my partner and I work out our differences about parenting?
- Do I have a support system of other parents I can talk to?

Bass and Davis 1992

## BOUNDARIES AND DISCIPLINE

As discussed in the last chapter, good discipline is about good discipleship. Being a good teacher means helping children know where boundaries are, maintaining those boundaries for them when they are young and helping them learn how to maintain their own boundaries as they grow. Survivor mothers raised without the benefit of good discipleship can have difficulty discerning the boundaries.(5.8) For moms who are depressed or under great stress, having a consistent plan for setting boundaries is not easily accomplished. Parents may lose their composure, or check out of the process altogether. They may apply boundaries that constrict, and spend a lot of energy maintaining them. Or they may be afraid to set boundaries at all for fear of conflict or rejection.(5.9, 5.10)

Kathy says she is cautious about dealing with discipline:

*So there are still issues I have to deal with. I'm very cautious about dealing with discipline. I have the idea that because it was done to me, I could do that to my child. I couldn't survive that. I tried so desperately to stop it. He's a good kid. That makes it easier.*

*from Kathy's story*

Cindy felt afraid to discipline for fear that her children would leave her:

*You see, I think that in my insecurity I was afraid to say no because I was reluctant to hurt or discipline them because I was sure they would*

*leave me. Because I wasn't worthy of having them. I never wanted to hurt anyone, and often we all paid for it.*
*I see that now, but I can't change it. They've turned into really remarkable people, considering, but I'm hoping they will raise their kids differently than I did.*

*from Cindy's story*

Lisa says she is aware of the importance of teaching her child about boundaries:

*Now that he is older, six-and-a-half, I am aware of how important it is for me to teach him how to honor someone's boundaries and how to respect the word "NO." I often ask myself how to teach him these important life lessons without tainting it with my own wounds or projecting my perpetrator onto him.*

*from Lisa's story*

Susan shares her struggles with setting and maintaining boundaries:

*I want to mention boundaries. If you are a therapist reading this you will see that I had no boundaries. I was never safe. For a child, as I have learned, boundaries bring security. It's what keeps them calm. I never had any, and the ones I did have were of my own choosing, as I had decided that the pain was too great to continue on in pursuit of that course of action. I learned in every instance that I was able to carry it out, that saying something, doing it, making it stick was the greatest gift I could give to my children. It is my greatest weakness. Every time I try to set a boundary, my past kicks in and fear and death and I usually give in to my kids' desires. In my own way I am continuing the abuse here, yet I am not strong enough to overcome it. I must forgive myself for this several times a day. I just can't take away anything or deny my kids anything when it's not a life and death situation. That is all I grew up with. Anything less is simply unimportant in my subconscious mind. So, if you have the strength in your heart to make boundaries and keep them, your children will grow up being able to function well within society's bounds.*

*from Susan's story*

Elaine reflects on her childrearing from the vantage point of grandparenting:

*I have three wonderful grandsons, and four beautiful granddaughters. I used to be quite opinionated and thought that there was only right or wrong. I felt I knew the right way; so therefore if you did not agree with what I thought was right, you were wrong. I envy those who are now enjoying their child-rearing days. I am so blessed that my children realize they have access to an abundance of child rearing information which we did not have years ago and have credited me with doing the best that I could with what I had.*

*from Elaine's story*

▼ 5.10

Overprotection is an exaggeration of the healthy desire to keep children safe. If you're afraid, especially if you're unaware of the source of your fears, it's easy to become obsessive. ...

You may try to keep your children safe by limiting their activities, but children should have the mobility and freedom appropriate for their age. You need to overcome your fears, not pass them on. ...

If you're uncertain about the limits you're setting, talk with other parents. Getting feedback from others is a useful way to gauge if you're being overprotective.

Although wanting to protect your children is a valid desire, you need to distinguish what you can protect them from and what you can't. No matter how careful you are, you cannot regulate every aspect of your child's life. Children spend time in situations and with people you cannot control. For this reason, it is essential that you teach your children to protect themselves. Children need to be educated and empowered. You must prepare them as best you can, take a deep breath and let them go.

Bass and Davis 1992

Margaret shares how she feels she expected more of her children than was "fair":

*I've never been a patient person. My children are intelligent, both with a terrific sense of humor. I feel I did a good job providing them with a moral upbringing, and they have always known they are loved. They are well-behaved, and they tell me it was because anything else wasn't an option. I'd like to think that I always allowed them to "be children." I'm not certain that is the case. I think I expected more of them than was fair, because of my impatience.*

*from Margaret's story*

We have discussed previously in this book how abusive relationships have many negative aspects, and how many women who have been sexually abused also have suffered physical abuse as well. Some of our contributors shared that the issue of corporal punishment was a very charged one for them, and they were determined not to spank or allow their children to be spanked.

*Spanking my son is one of the reasons I divorced my "ex." I try to keep to child-centered parenting and respect the core being of these little (and now not so little) people.*

*from Stacey's story*

*I probably never would have left him if he had not started correcting Lisa in a way I could not tolerate. Yelling too loud at her for something trivial, being on her about something all the time…and then one evening he hit her on her back over her right kidney and left a detailed handprint. I was in the kitchen cooking and I heard a pain-filled scream. I ran in and asked what had happened. He was sitting there drinking a beer and said, "I told her twice to not touch the TV knobs and she did it anyway, so I spanked her." I told him, "That is not how you spank a child; you are never to hit her on her skin. Do you hear me?"*

*from tedi's story*

Dealing with problems of discipline can be stressful for any mother. Like many mothers, Elizabeth struggled to unlearn the ingrained response of hitting her children:

*In my current long-term therapy I came to understand my suicidal ideation as anger directed toward myself, rather than outwardly where it belonged, but where I was afraid to have it be, because of the severe consequences. My suicidal ideation has been gone for one-and-a-half years and I have stopped hitting my children for almost as long. I would only spank them only occasionally, with one spank, but this was unacceptable to me. After noticing when I would get the most upset, I realized it was when one of the children hit me first. My spanking the children was a deep and ingrained self-defense mechanism to survive. It was as if I was the child again being hit, and I had to defend myself by lashing out. I am the adult now, not the child, so I could release the behavior as unnecessary. Now, if one of the children hurts me, I can cry or say, "Please stop, it hurts." It is no longer necessary to fight back or be scared. What a long lesson it has been to learn. I can love my children and myself so much more fully now.*

*from Elizabeth's story*

**KEEPING KIDS SAFE**
*Our baby was bright, beautiful and high-strung. I saw his life fraught with unknown, unnamed perils lurking behind every door.*

*from Lena's story*

Many survivor moms shared their feelings about the ongoing struggle to keep their kids safe from harm. They worried that they or someone else might hurt their child. As in Kim's narrative at the beginning of our chapter, the contributors resolved to create a safe environment for their children.(5.11, 5.12)

As Kim shared in her narrative at the beginning of this chapter:

*Will these structured and controlled movements be harmful to my kids as they grow and mature? As they grow, I am sure that some changes will have to be made and a certain amount of letting go will have to be done so they can retain their independence. It only takes one time, one minute, to change a person's life forever. I found the strength to survive the abuse; I know I could never survive that sort of thing happening to a child of my own if I could stop it. Who knows more about the abuse and the cries for help, than one who has suffered through it?*

Other moms echoed Kim's sentiments:

*I want to add one more thing. No one. No man will ever come between me and my children and my love for them. No one. Ever. That is truth for me and my choice.*

*from Katherine's story*

*So yes, my abuse has affected my motherhood. It has made me a better, more protective, more ferocious mother than I think I could ever have been if I hadn't been shown what happens when a mother is not.*

▼ 5.11

A Child's Bill of Personal Safety Rights
1. The right to trust one's instincts and funny feelings.
2. The right to privacy.
3. The right to say no to unwanted touch or affection.
4. The right to question adult authority and to say no to adult demands and requests.
5. The right to lie and not answer questions.
6. The right to refuse gifts.
7. The right to be rude or unhelpful.
8. The right to run, scream and make a scene.
9. The right to bite, hit or kick.
10. The right to ask for help.

When introducing these rights to children, be simple and concrete, using language they can understand. Encourage children to think for themselves by using imaginative or what-if games, role-playing, fantasies, or incidents from your own childhood. Always acknowledge the children's contribution, thus helping them to develop the ability to do spontaneous problem solving in unexpected situations.

Bass and Davis 1992

▼ 5.12

In the intergenerational caregiving system, attachment is transformed from childhood seeking protection to adulthood providing protection.

George 1996

*from Amy's story*

*I have been able to recreate myself and am now giving my children the type of life that all children deserve, a life filled with childhood joys, love and a feeling of security. No child should ever have to feel unsafe in its own home. I vowed to myself that I would not allow anyone to ever hurt my children in the way that I was hurt. Through a lot of hard work and commitment I have been able to keep that vow to myself. I have explored my inner world and decided that I am not going to discount my abilities or sell myself short because of a horrible act committed by someone else.*

*from Wendi's story*

*I do not know any words of comfort or wisdom to suggest to other survivors of childhood sexual trauma. I struggle daily with my own gut reactions, which continue to arise. For example: today, in a passing car I saw a father reach out his hand to caress the nape*

> ▼ 5.13
>
> Many abuse survivors got through childhood by NOT expressing emotions. So when it comes time to parent, they may be shaken by the intensity of their child's emotions. Some survivors do not know how much expression is okay. In her classic 1970 book *Your Child's Self-Esteem*, Dorothy Corkville Briggs provides some guidance on responding to your child's intense negative feelings:
> - Responding to negative feelings with judgment, denial, advice, or diversion teaches the child to push down the feelings.
> - Pushed-down feelings don't go away (as you may well know)
> - Expressing the feelings and being understood helps "evaporate" them.
> - Expression of negative feelings should be allowed—the limits to put in place are about to whom, when, and where these feelings get released.
>
> Perhaps the simplest way to think of this is to "handle children's feelings as we want ours handled."
>
> Briggs 1970

*of his daughter's neck and was seized with panic for her. As a child the only times that I remember ever being touched or held were either to be pinned down for my granny's belting, or held tight for my Uncle's uninvited embraces.*

*from Penny's story*

Like Penny, moms who have been subject to sexual abuse may see potential perpetrators everywhere, and they may have difficulty distinguishing what they as parents can do to keep their children safe from harm. As Kim shared in her narrative:

*My kids are more sheltered, more protected, more supervised than other kids they know. Every time they go out to play, or have a birthday invitation or play date or sleep over, or use a public restroom, I always wonder if there is a perpetrator lurking about. Anytime they leave the house without my husband or me we wonder will their caregiver be as vigilant as we are? Will they remember to hold their hands in public, or never let them walk more then two steps behind them? Not let them talk to strangers?*

We all have heard of child abuse prevention programs that stress that children "never talk to strangers." Yet these well-meaning recommendations do not reflect the reality regarding the sexual abuse of children. The truth is that most often it will not be a stranger who abuses a child, but someone the child knows. As Gavin De Becker, author of *Protecting the Gift: Keeping Children and Teenagers Safe (and Parents Sane)*, points out:

> Bottom line: *the issue isn't strangers, it is strangeness.* It is inappropriate behavior that's relevant: a stare held too long, a smile that curls too slowly, a narrowing or widening of the eyes, a rapid looking away. The muscles in the face are instruments of communication, resulting in an eloquent language that can put us at ease or give us the creeps.(p. 84)

Never talking to strangers is unrealistic: What if the child is lost, in trouble or needs assistance? De Becker also takes exception to the idea of telling children that if they are lost or in trouble to "go to a policeman." The problem with that recommendation is that no police may be anywhere near them, or they may think that anyone in uniform qualifies. Instead, he recommends we teach children that, if they are lost, to "Go to a woman." He risks being "politically incorrect" with that recommendation, yet good reasoning supports the idea. Most sexual predators are not women. Finding a woman is probably easier than finding a police officer, and a woman is likely to stay with the child until he or she is reunited with the appropriate caregiver(s).

De Becker also talks a great deal about the power of intuition and the importance of learning to understand and trust one's intuitive feelings regarding safety, and teaching children to do the same. Teaching your children to trust their intuition can involve helping them learn how to understand and honor their feelings in general.(5.13) How parents go about honoring their children's feelings is important if children are to learn to take them seriously and be able to develop a sense of boundaries and safety for themselves. Clinical social worker Melisa Schuster has the following recommendations regarding ways parents can help to keep their kids safe from abuse:

**Raising a Non-Victim Child**
Remember: You do not have to do all of these things or do them perfectly in order to keep kids safe.

**Two Keys to Keeping Kids Safe:**
- Be an approachable parent.
- Respect kids' rights, space, feelings, wishes.

What does being "approachable" mean?
- Kids can tell me anything.
- I don't overreact.
- I don't underreact.
- I respond to their concerns.
- I answer their questions honestly.
- I don't allow any topic to be undiscussable.
- I admit when I make mistakes.
- I apologize.
- I have authority without being authoritarian.

What can you do or say to become approachable?
- Provide lots of eye contact.
- Give lots of affection.
- Meet the child's physical and emotional needs.
- Work to understand what the child is trying to communicate.
- Look for benevolent motivation (ways the child is trying to be good).
- Try to see things from the child's point of view.
- Avoid encouraging the child to "stuff" feelings. (e.g., "Stop crying or I'll give you something to cry about.")
- Help the child identify feelings and express them without hurting self or others.
- Model expressing feelings appropriately.
- Don't blame and shame.
- Help the child gladly.
- Model asking for help from others.
- Give children age-appropriate choices.
- Avoid using punishment as discipline.
- Avoid spanking.
- Listen to the child's side of the story before disciplining.
- Be a good listener.
- Accept all feelings (but not all behavior).
- Don't belittle problems.
- Manage anger well.
- Be available.
- Spend uninterrupted time with the kids.

**Respect Kids' Rights, Feelings, Space and Wishes**

Rights
- Adults are not more important than children.
- Other people's rights and needs are not more important than their own.
- Children do not have to obey all adults.

Feelings
- Help children identify and express their feelings.
- Do not punish, humiliate or shame children for having "negative" feelings like fear, loneliness, sadness, uncertainty, frustration, etc.
- Connect feelings to behavior. (e.g., "We cry when we are sad.")
- Assume the child is telling the truth unless you know for a fact it is a lie.
- Feelings are as important as rules; teach them to trust their intuition.
- Call the child by name; do not use degrading nicknames or address without respect.

Space
- Allow the child to say "NO"; do not demand absolute compliance.
- Do not question the child's right to say "NO" to matters of personal preference that do not endanger the child's or others' safety or unduly disrupt family members.
- Let the child know that he/she can remove him/herself from situations that are disrespectful, abusive or harmful.
- Allow the child to have time and things all to him/herself that do not have to be shared.
- Teach your child the value of privacy by respecting the child's need for privacy.
- Allow each child to move at his or her own pace. Do not compare the child to those who are faster, smarter, calmer, nicer, prettier, more generous, more coordinated, friendlier, etc. Don't compare the child to others, even if she/he seems to be the one on top.
- Practice "The Golden Rule": Treat others (including children) the same way you would like to be treated. This models respect for the child and helps build trust between a parent and child.
- Don't allow others to give children kisses or hugs or other types of affection without their permission; don't insist children give others hugs and kisses.
- Teach the child the proper names for sexual body parts at an early age.

Wishes
- Don't let others tell you what is best for the child. Let the child tell you what he/she wants or needs.
- Acknowledge the child's wishes even if he/she can't have what is wanted.
- Take the child seriously. Many abused children try to tell what is happening, but parents ignore, minimize or do not believe first reports of abuse.

Sometimes the simplest recommendation may be the best:

*A few years ago, I heard a man say, "If someone tries to touch you in a bathing suit place, scream loudly, run away and get help. If the person you go to for help doesn't help,*

## Chapter 5—Mothering and Attachment

*keep going to other adults that you trust until someone helps you in the right way, and makes it stop." If I had been told that, my abuse would have stopped at 12, instead of 20.*
*from Nan's story*

Many mothers will feel hyper-vigilant about the task of ensuring their child's safety. For Kate, the process felt draining:

*My children came and with them a fear that somehow, something would happen to them. The underlying tension I felt was endless and draining. I was as protective as a bear, and would watch them like a hawk. If I couldn't find one of my daughters playing outside after a few minutes, the panic and terror would nearly overwhelm me.*
*from Kate's story*

Cubbi wonders whether she is being overly protective:

*My sons are now 16 and 13 years old, both teenagers, struggling for their independence. They claim that I'm too over protective and that they can take care of themselves and that I don't have to worry about them so much. I've shared with them my analogy of the transformation from a teenager to an adult. It's like a game of "tug of war"—teenagers are pulling the rope to gain their independence and parents are on the other end trying to not let go too quickly, because if you give them too much slack, they're going to fall. But how much slack is too much? I struggle with trying to decide if my own history makes me pull the rope tighter or even too tight sometimes. I remember the day my oldest son was born and that moment when I realized that he was totally reliant on me and what an awesome responsibility that was. I doubted myself; I knew nothing about babies or how to care for one, but instinct took over and today they are happy and healthy kids. I guess I'm still learning to trust my gut and eventually I'll let go of the rope and my boys will be men.*
*from Cubbi's story*

Trusting our children with others can be scary. Cubbi shared how difficult the process of finding a babysitter was for her:(5.14)

*At one point finances became an issue and I needed to get a part-time job and help out financially. That meant finding a babysitter, and that meant trusting someone else with my kids. I interviewed several women; none were good enough. After several weeks, I was interviewing a woman and as I asked the same questions that I had asked each potential babysitter over and over again I realized that eventually I would have to trust someone. With that realization, I began to sob uncontrollably. As this kind woman*

▼ 5.14
Questions for potential babysitters:
- What do you like about babysitting?
- What ages of children have you cared for before?
- Do you still babysit for any of them?
- Could I call and speak with the parents of the children you've cared for?
- What is your school life like?
- What kinds of activities do you like to do?
- What kinds of activities do you like to do with children?
- How would you handle a child who is having a temper tantrum?
- Describe a difficult situation you've been in when babysitting. How did you handle it?
- Have you had any first-aid or babysitter training?
- What do you think about the use of drugs and alcohol?
- What are your goals for the next few years?
- What do you charge?
- When are you available?

*comforted me, I began to understand and to feel that this was very natural for her. For Wendy, nurturing was second nature. Wendy cared for my children for the next three years and my children have fond memories of the time they spent with her. Looking back, it's obvious that Wendy was much more than my babysitter, she was my friend and she taught me how to trust—and trusting was the first step in my journey of healing.*

*from Cubbi's story*

Dawn says that she rarely leaves her children with sitters:

*We don't allow the children to spend the night at places alone. We're careful about what type of interaction they have with other children and adults. Very rarely do we leave them with sitters. I don't think this is bad. I believe the Bible tells us to shelter our children. We do the best we can, and then we must trust God to protect them.*

*from Dawn's story*

Keeping children away from predators is just one aspect of keeping children safe. Socioeconomic conditions can greatly affect the mother's ability to care for her children and keep them out of harm's way. Elaine shares the harsh reality of raising her children in poverty:

*So we (my children and I) lived without heat and running water that winter. I worked at the end of my street, and there was a large drop sink, which we used to wash dishes and take baths during a very cold winter with little snow. Our coal stove (too small to heat a room) did not keep us warm but it did keep the frost off our bed most nights. I knew the following year I would have to give my kids up, something I could only do because it meant their safety. I could not put them through another winter like that. It brings tears to my eyes now, just trying to write this part. This was the hardest above all else.*

*from Elaine's story*

We have discussed in general ways parents may go about keeping their children safe. Keeping them from potential abusers is one thing; but in cases where abusers are still in a survivor's life, keeping their children safe from a known source of danger can prove difficult. Cubbi shares her experience of trying to keep her perpetrator away from her children:

*After three incidents in two weeks it became apparent that these were not just chance meetings, and I realized that I needed to protect myself and my children. I went to the police, I made a report, but again was told that the statute of limitations had expired and that there was nothing I could do. They suggested that I go to the District Court and attempt to get a restraining order. I was fortunate, I was able to get a temporary restraining order against him and he was forced to stay away from me and my family. I hired an attorney to represent me and help me get a permanent order, but he told me I had little chance of success because he had never been convicted. On the day of the final hearing, after several hours in the judge's chambers, our attorneys reached a settlement and he agreed to stay away from me and my family. He asked that the settlement be reevaluated in two years. Two years will soon be up, and I assume I am going to have to go through this whole mess again.*

*from Cubbi's story*

## Chapter 5—Mothering and Attachment

Colleen also struggled with the court system in trying to keep her children safe:

*Tim has been paroled for over a year now, and at this writing, we're going through another lengthy trial to determine whether or not he'll get overnight visitation. The state law will not prevent him from seeing them or abusing them. The way the law is written, the children have a right to see their father. They don't have a right not to.*

*from Colleen's story*

Kathy shares a conversation she had with her father/abuser regarding his wish to meet her son:

*And he said, "I understand you have a son. I want to meet him." I said, "No. When he gets old enough, if he wants to meet you, and if you're still around, that will be his choice. He said, "No, it's my right to meet my grandson." And I looked at him and I said, "You have no rights when it comes to my son." This mother lioness came out in me and I continued, "No, if I have anything to say about it, you will never meet my son." Then he looked at me and said, "I'm really disappointed in you." And I said, "You'll get over it." And I walked away. And he left shortly after.*

*I probably would still have been having the same conversation with my father if he had not brought up my son. I remember thinking: "It stopped here. It's not going to continue. That genetic part of it, it's not going to go on."*

*from Kathy's story*

Tina's abuser is still "hanging around." She determines never to turn her back on him with her children:

*My stepfather is still hanging around. My mother finally divorced him, but they are still friends. He's around on the holidays and my kids know him as "grandpa." I will never turn my back on him with my children, obviously....*

*from Tina's story*

Kelly is keeping her abuser father away from her family by letting him know he is not allowed to contact her unless he is writing about his journey in recovery:

*Since then, I have read many books, been in group therapy and individual therapy, and I am also part of an online support group that is really cool, too. I have confronted my dad, but not George or Paul. I have reported my dad and am trying to get the DA to pursue a case against him in the town he abused me in. I have told my dad he cannot see his granddaughter. I have told him to get help and he has been given referrals to pursue, but I doubt he is getting any help. He admits what he has done but minimizes it. I think this is the most horrible form of denial. It's like saying, "I know what I did and it's not so bad; get over it." He is not allowed to call, e-mail, visit or write unless he is writing about his journey in recovery. Otherwise I am going to charge him with harassment or get a restraining order or something like that.*

*from Kelly's story*

Kristy's father died before she had children, yet she considers what she would have done regarding contact:

*A longtime smoker, my father died of lung cancer when I was 27 and he was 56. I truly miss him and the relationship we had developed. Despite molesting me and my sister, he had lots of admirable qualities. At the time he died, I had not yet had children, so I was spared announcing the decision I had made long ago: Dad would not be allowed access to my children unless under my direct supervision. I might not be able to alter history, but I could prevent it from repeating itself.*

*from Kristy's story*

Elaine finds herself concerned that her mother, although not her abuser, may still have a negative influence on her daughter:

*When she visits, I find myself constantly arguing with her dark and pessimistic "philosophies of life," which include "sexual abuse is part of growing up for girls." I'm scared of her infecting my daughter.*

*from Elaine's story*

### TELLING CHILDREN

Moms wondered how to go about telling their child about their history of abuse. They wondered when and why and how much to tell. Kathy decided to tell her son just what she thought he needed to know at his stage of development regarding the reason he was not allowed contact with his grandfather:(5.15)

*My son is pretty astute. He knows his grandfather is alive and that if he wants to meet him he can. He knows that he wasn't very nice to me and to grandma, and that that's why he and grandma are divorced. We have told him that his grandfather just wasn't a real nice person to be around at that time. And he knows that when he is old enough he can make his own choice about him. And when I told him about this, he looked at me and he said, "You know, if I ever met your dad, you know what I'd say? You're not my mom, and you're not my dad, you let me go!" I guess he got to this conclusion because we had been talking to him about "bad people." But I've never said that his grandfather was horrendous or villainous or whatever, because I don't think that's going to benefit anybody. When Adam asks me about specific things*

▼ 5.15

The discovery of the abuse of a child can bring changes to the mother/child relationship. A focus group of mothers whose children were abused by someone else found that the mother/child relationship was challenged by many factors, including interference of investigators, problems with the child, parental exhaustion from increased demands and parental insecurity.

Plummer and Eastin 2007

Children deserve accurate information about their families. That includes information about a child abuser in the family. It's not fair to give children a limited amount of information and then hope for the best. What kind of message does it give a child to say, "We're going over to Grandma's house. Don't let her hug you?"

Talking about abuse is a family issue. Everyone is involved, everyone needs to know. Information should be given to your children in a way that's age-appropriate. For a very young child, you could say something as simple as, "Mommy's been crying and going to a lot of meetings at night because of something that happened to her when she was a little girl. She's taking care of herself so that she can be a better mommy to you." An older child can get more specific information. With programs about abuse prevention in the curriculum of many schools, you may have a natural opening to bring up the subject. It's okay to name names. Children don't need graphic details, but Grandma should not be protected. That's how abuse gets passed from generation to generation....

You and the survivor will have to find your own way of talking to your children, but make sure you do. If you don't, your children will most likely blame themselves for the disappearance of their grandparents (or for the survivor's grumpiness, withdrawal, anger, or sadness). You're trying to break the cycle of family silence. Talking honestly with your kids is a good way to begin.

Davis 1991

*that happened, so far I have just said that his grandfather "hollered a lot." Possibly, when he's older, I'll tell him more. He's too young right now.*

*from Kathy's story*

Catherine too shared her abuse with her children in an age-appropriate manner:

*I still have days when the depression seems to get the better of me. I have explained to my boys that when I was a little girl someone hurt me very badly and sometimes it still makes me very sad. They are too young to know anything more.*

*We have made a big deal about teaching them about their "privates." And that no one has the right to touch them there. We have taught them that we don't keep secrets from each other. That no one should ever tell them not to tell Mom and Dad. We have taught them to trust their instincts. If something doesn't feel right to them, then it probably isn't right. Most of all, we are trying to love them unconditionally and develop deep relationships with each one of them. My biggest hope is that they will not be vulnerable to an abusive relationship like I was so many years ago.*

*from Catherine's story*

## MY CHILD WAS ABUSED

Sometimes, despite the best efforts of parents, their children are also abused. Colleen suspected her husband might abuse their child:(5.16, 5.17, 5.18, 5.19)

*When Jake came to see us that night, I had a terrifying vision as he held Bonnie. I focused the camera lens to take a picture, and I knew that something was going to happen to her with those hands. It made no sense, and my mind just wouldn't deal with it. I tucked the thought away because it seemed so foolish.*

*from Colleen's story*

Tedi also had to deal with uncovering the truth about her child having been abused:

*She couldn't trust me. Later when she was away from my home she told my sister some of what had happened to her. The part I can't stand is that he had touched her before we had even moved away from Florida. He had also*

▼ 5.16

Part of being a good parent is being able to confront your own behavior or the behavior of your partner. If you...are abusing your children, [you] must stop [and] seek help immediately. Call Parents Anonymous at 1-800-843-5437 or the National Child Abuse Hotline at 1-800-422-4453. If you think abuse is happening but you're not sure, call a parental stress hotline to talk about it. Don't try to deal with this alone. If you...haven't abused your children but are afraid that you might, get help now.

Once you call a public agency (or tell a therapist, doctor, teacher, or other professional), they are legally bound to investigate your situation. If they find abuse, they are mandated to file a report with child protective services. This can lead to involvement with social workers, police, and the criminal justice system, and may mean your children being temporarily removed from you home, but it can also mean getting the help you need.

Davis 1991

▼ 5.17

Some possible signs that your child may have been sexually abused include: a return to bed-wetting after having mastered this developmental task; day wetting (wetting pants during the day) after potty training has been accomplished; engaging in persistent sexual play with friends, toys or pets; initiating sexual behavior (behavior not consistent with developmental stage) with other children or adults; withdrawing abruptly from a previously enjoyed activity, club or group; exhibiting signs of genital infections; a sudden reluctance to be with a particular person; an unexplained change in personality (for example an outgoing child that becomes withdrawn); loss of appetite or other eating problems, especially gagging; excessive masturbation; nightmares, night sweats, waking up screaming; showing an unusual fear of being in a particular place like the bathtub or their own bed; or sudden reduction in school performance.

Melisa Schuster

▼ 5.18

When a childhood sexual abuse survivor's child experiences abuse, it may bring up unresolved issues for the mother about her own abuse. She may also be coping with her own posttraumatic stress symptoms and be less emotionally available to help her child recover from the trauma.

Paredes, Leifer and Kilbane 2001

▼ 5.19

Maternal support to a child after disclosure of sexual abuse has been described as including: belief in the child's account of the abuse, emotional support, choice of the child over the perpetrator and a positive attitude toward professional services.

Maternal support of the child in the aftermath of disclosure has been related to positive recovery and mental health outcomes in the child.

Everson, et al. 1989

▼ 5.20

In a South African study of college students, odds of child sexual abuse increased 60% if the student had not lived with the biological mother until at least age 16. Risk was twice as high for sexual abuse and 2.3 times as high for emotional abuse if the student had ever had a stepfather or adopted father.

Madu 2003

▼ 5.21

The Third National Incidence and Prevalence Study of Child Abuse and Neglect, published in 1996, found that 220,000 children per year were recognized by child protection services as having significant harm from child sexual abuse. Another 100,000 per year more were recognized to be endangered.

These statistics represent 87% increase from 1988 statistics in the number of confirmed child sexual abuse cases and a 125% increase in the number of children considered to be endangered.

NCCAN 1996

*been sexual with her when she was a baby. I think I thought I had protected her.*

from tedi's story

Olivia also uncovered the fact of abuse of her three-year-old:

*About eight months later, I was playing paper dolls with my three-year-old. My three-year-old had "Uncle Doll" (who represented my brother) doing some inappropriate play with the little girl doll. At one point, the uncle doll put the girl doll under a block, "Don't tell about the game or you'll go to jail!"*

*At this point in my life, I did not even recall the abuse that I had endured at my uncle's hands, but this paper doll play rang familiar. My daughter, Salina, had played similar games with my brother (who had also been abused by my uncle). Salina was reluctant to talk about what had happened with her, but she play-acted out enough for me to know there was sexual and emotional abuse going on.(5.20, 5.21)*

*I first comforted Salina and let her know that she did not do anything wrong, and that she would not go to jail.*

*I then confronted my family, my brother included. He denied everything.*

*Salina's games triggered memories that came back full-force, full of detail and just as real as if it had happened seconds before, memories of the abuse that my uncle had inflicted on me, my brother and several cousins.*

*My little sister told me of sexual abuse she had suffered at the hands of our brother. Cousins came to talk to me of their struggles with telling or not telling.*

*Salina would not speak to, or in front of, anyone else except her dad, nor would she play paper dolls for Child Protective Services. My brother took a lie detector test and failed. He was denied visitation of his five-year-old daughter, who had also been molested by him.*

*The statute of limitations was up for me to press charges against my uncle. Neither my uncle nor my brother were ever prosecuted, but their behavior was no longer a family secret.*

*Did my birth experience have an effect on how I handled my daughter's revelations?*

*Undeniably. I was strong enough to remember, strong enough to believe and trust my instincts. And I was strong enough to confront my abusers.*
from Olivia's story

Being able to recognize the signs of possible abuse may be difficult for a survivor who is in denial about her own abuse, or who is struggling with her mental health. Once you know your child has been abused, responding in an effective and appropriate manner is important. How you respond may make all the difference in your child's recovery. Therapist Melisa Schuster gives the following basic guidelines for responding to allegations of abuse:

1. Always believe your child; children rarely make up stories about abuse.
2. Don't overreact; stay calm for your child's sake; get help for your own feelings.
3. Tell the child *"It's not your fault."* "I'm so glad you told me." "I'll protect you."
4. Protect your child from the perpetrator, even if a family member.
5. Call the authorities (police, protective services, doctor).

Sometimes children do not disclose their abuse until much later. Elaine's daughter did not begin her recovery until after her mother began her own recovery:

*My oldest daughter was envious of my getting help, but kept telling herself she was okay and didn't need it. After a neighbor exposed himself to her, she has realized she did not have a healthy response to his actions and is now in counseling.*
from Elaine's story

Women have described the inability of their mothers to protect them from their perpetrators when they were children themselves. Ruth's daughter was molested by her father. After extensive therapy her husband was reconciled to her daughter and family. Ruth describes her family's experience of uncovering abuse of her daughter by her husband. This represents an ideal scenario that often is not achieved.

*It is almost impossible for me to describe the profound healing that took place between my daughter and her father. It culminated one day in the three of us sitting together, feeling better in each other's company than we had in a long time. My husband asked our daughter, "Is there anything else you need to say to me?" She replied, "I love you, Dad, but I don't love your little boy (which was who she felt was there each time she had been abused)." He responded, "It's not your place to take care of my little boy. That's my job, and I never should have put it on you." She began to cry, and then to sob, and he took her in his arms like a baby and rocked her while she cried. The tears were rolling down his face, and he was a real father at last.*
from Ruth's story

### SURVIVORS' OTHER PARENTING THOUGHTS
The narrators in this book expressed the feeling that being a survivor affected their parenting in many ways that were important to them. The following are some of the ideas about parenting in general that grew from their life experiences.

Sadie shared at the beginning of this chapter that she has tried very hard to treat her son in a manner that, publicly and privately, was consistently caring. Kristy shares what she considers to be the hallmarks of her parenting relationship:(5.22, 5.23)

*In addition to love, I plan to make trust and consistency the hallmarks of our parent-child relationships. For I know their loss is far more devastating than the physical violation of sexual abuse.*

*from Kristy's story*

▼ 5.22
There is very little research to date on child sexual abuse survivors' parenting. It is not yet clear whether a history of child sexual abuse, in and of itself, conveys risk of poor parenting or risk for the woman's children being abused. However, there are risks associated with (1) the sexually abused mother having mental health problems, and (2) her not having positive models of parenting due to the level of family dysfunction that often is the context in which abuse occurs.
DiLillo 2001

Margaret teaches her children that, "All feelings are okay, all actions are not":

*It is openly stated in our family that it is the action you take that may have a consequence, not the feeling. All feelings are okay, all actions are not. Sorting out our feelings can be learned. This is another place my husband enters the picture, because he was raised in an emotionally cold home and knew that his children had to know how to recognize and experience their emotions—all of them.*

*from Margaret's story*

▼ 5.23
Mothers who have been sexually abused may have more difficulty withstanding the emotional demands of parenting, feel more inadequate, and less able as parents.
Cole, et al. 1992

Ann strives to ensure that her children know they are in control of their bodies:

*My children are never alone with anyone who has not proved themselves worthy of my trust.*
*I am also more careful to respect the individuality and persons of my children than I might otherwise have been. They are always in control of who touches them, who kisses or caresses them, and are never required to submit to unwanted physical affection.*

*from Ann's story*

Sara has a rule in her family, "no secrets":

*My daughter is four now. She is sooo little. I have so much fear for her; I wish she could have a happy, naïve childhood. I feel the only way I have to protect her is to warn her about people who hurt children, make sure she knows she is safe telling me anything. We have a rule in our family—no secrets. It has spoiled some birthday surprises, but is worth the trade-off.*

*from Sara's story*(5.24)

Liz finds that being a survivor affects the way she mothers, both positively and negatively:

*Being a survivor has affected how I mother. In good and bad ways. On the positive side, I am determined that my sons not be cut off from their sexuality. I want them to see it as beautiful and special. For me, that means not overtly or covertly expressing things that would make them ashamed about their bodies: pooping, peeing, masturbating or being naked. Also, I want them to be comfortable with all their emotions. I don't tell them that "boys don't cry" or that feeling angry is wrong.*

*Do I mother in ways of which I am less than proud? Oh, yes. Though I encourage the expression of emotions, I overreact when my sons are aggressive towards others. My reaction can be out of proportion to a petite[sic] offense. I want them to know it is never okay to hurt people. Yet I am also afraid they will be hurt by people. Suspicious of strangers, care providers, older boys, well, really anyone male that I don't know, I can be overprotective. I only want them to have sweet, joyful play with kind, safe people. This, of course, is every mother's wish for her children and also ridiculous. It exemplifies the fine balance that mothering must accomplish; protecting one's children from the truly damaging experiences of life, while still allowing them some struggles so they develop the skills with which to cope with adversity. What doesn't kill you makes you stronger. But how is a mother to know?*

*from Liz's story*(5.25)

## GOOD ENOUGH MOMS

Claire spoke in the last chapter about being a "good enough" mom. That theme is worth revisiting here, as expressed by other moms who have come to the realization that doing your best is the best you can do:

▼ 5.24
The Centers for Disease Control and Prevention (CDC) sees at least 10 future health challenges. Three are directly or indirectly related to violence in whole or part:
Reduce the toll of violence in society: Homicide, suicide and other forms of violence can be viewed as public health issues that warrant...interventions to address them...Social norms can and do change, but only after identification of the problem, development of effective interventions and broad community support.
Recognize and address the contributions of mental health to overall health and well-being: When the burden of disease is measured in disability-adjusted life years, mental illness becomes the leading cause of disability and premature mortality in the United States.
Focus on children's emotional and intellectual development: an essential challenge is to encourage home, preschool and community environments, interactions and relationships that permit each child to achieve his or her full potential.
Koplan and Fleming 2000

▼ 5.25
In a study of 516 low income mothers, childhood sexual or physical abuse or neglect was associated with lower scores on a measure of the women's sense of competence at parenting. Conversely, higher emotional support experiences as a child was associated with higher self-reports of feeling competent as a parent.
Zuravin and Fontanella 1999

*I have lost my vision of a place of perfect mental health. I have finally realized that I will always be a work in progress. I have lost my vision of providing my son with a perfect childhood. If I can teach him to roll with life's punches in such a way that he can get back on his feet without major injuries, I will have done my job. I try to listen more than talk, praise more than reprimand, and while I don't always succeed, I improve. I try to take responsibility for my own feelings and give him responsibility for his. And overall, he's a really special little guy, with the face of an angel and a mind like a steel trap. He's four now, and I'm no longer frantic about being his mother, although I'm not entirely comfortable with it. I no longer expect that of myself, either.*

*from Tamar's story*

*I won't claim to be a perfect mom or person. But what I will say is that I'm the best mom I can be and way better than my parents were. My kids are healthy, happy and safe. I can sometimes be a little overprotective; but who wants to see something bad happen to their kids if it can be prevented?*

*from Valerie's story*

Margaret says that she felt helpless to respond to her baby's needs, and questions whether she has what it takes to be a good mother. She believes that her daughters are much more likely to be up to the task:

*I can remember being at the doctor's office with my eldest daughter when she was just a few months old, and she was crying because she had just had a shot. I felt helpless. I remember the doctor telling me that holding her was enough, that she would be okay. I didn't believe him then, and I don't believe him now. I never felt I had enough of what it took to be a good mother. I'm so glad my girls do have what it takes....*

*from Margaret's story*

### *BREAKING THE CHAIN*
One of the major messages voiced by contributors to this project is the idea that by taking control of their lives, their healing and their mothering, they can break the chain of violence that has been passed down to them as a bitter legacy. Moms are bringing a conscious awareness to their mothering, which makes all the difference for their children. Kim shared at the beginning of our chapter that she brought conscious awareness to her mothering by getting into recovery and looking at the ways in which she is affected by her abuse. She has identified the need to get help with her mothering by attending classes, and by looking to God for comfort and guidance. She is being a "good enough" mom, and moving forward in truth. The journey is not easy, and moms will need the help of others. In the next chapter we will look at how survivors sought healing and how they forged meaningful relationships to foster that healing.

Kim has the company of other survivor moms along her healing path:

*She asked me questions for a while before I broke down and decided to give her the information she wanted as simply and gently as I could. I told her that there were adults in this world who liked to have sex with children.*

*She was stunned. It took her a second or two to process this new information. She looked at me incredulously and said, "Mom, that's so gross" or some other equally sophisticated comment like that.*

*That's when I felt it. This power surge, this overwhelming feeling of success, of achievement. It's hard to find the words to express how complete I felt at that moment, how triumphant. "I did it! I won! I broke the chain of abuse, here and now. It's over." My little girl won't grow up with the shame of sexual abuse in her life. Even if someone raped her now it wouldn't be the same. She would know she could tell, she would know it's not her fault. Sexual abuse needs silence in order to thrive; it only grows in the dark. My daughter no longer has those vulnerable dark places in her soul. She is no longer ignorant about abuse; she can no longer be shamed into silence. She will never believe that it was her fault. She now knows the truth and somehow, that truth had set us both free. My years of hard work and dedication to her safety paid off big for me. I now hope to be able to help others work through*

## Chapter 5—Mothering and Attachment

*the hidden wounds of childhood sexual abuse or, even better, protect other mothers' children from ever experiencing it at all.*

*A baby is a process, not a product. With the help of my therapist, husband, friends and a support group I transformed myself from victim to survivor. I feel now I'm an adventurer. My life is not a scripted play. Every moment can bring surprises, challenges—the rediscovery of who I really am. It's not easy coaxing adventure from chaos, but at least now I get to choose to do so.*

*from Lena's story*

*Being a great Mom is my ongoing prayer.*

*Sadie*

### HEALING THROUGH MOTHERING

Sadie shared in her narrative at the beginning of our chapter that she wanted other survivor moms to know that *"we are not doomed or tainted by what happened to us. The strength we used to survive is ours. This strength is real and we bring that to our good mothering."*

Many other survivor moms shared how integral being a mother has been to their healing:

*Being a mother has healed me in more ways than I could ever count. Producing something good from my body, my self, which had been so violated was restorative to me. I am not evil, and nothing I did made me deserve to be treated as I was.*

*from Ann's story*

*Having a child didn't make my life complete. I'm a complete person without having a child. But having a child made my life so incredible. It has been a joy seeing life through a healthy child's eyes. Watching his wonder of things. I guess that in some aspects I'm experiencing my childhood again in a healthy manner with my son. And that's amazing.*

*from Kathy's story*

*Posttraumatic stress disorder—it comes and it goes. It taps my shoulder and sends shivers of fear throughout my being, making me want to run, to protect myself and my children. It comes at both expected, and unexpected times. My experiences have given me strength and a deep sense of purpose. I have faced my own death and know that I am still here for a reason; I have important work to do...a reason for living. My experiences have helped me to put things in perspective. I am quite tolerant of life's little trials and tribulations because in the bigger picture they simply are not very important.*

*from Karin's story*

*It's important for me for my child to have good memories. I get into overdecorating for the holidays. I love to hear "Remember when we did this, Mom?" It's been a riot to watch a childhood through his eyes. It really pisses me off that I don't have that. So I tend to go overboard.*

*God forbid, I could die tomorrow, and at least he knows he's loved. He'll just walk up and throw his arms around us and say I love you. I feel good that I could pass this on to him.*

*from Kathy's story*

*My son is the single best thing in my life!*

*from Nan's story*

*I think my life's experiences have made me a patient mother. I take time to really enjoy my children, my work and my garden. My children are still young—ages 10 and 12. I try to involve my children in our community in ways that make them feel empowered. We have adopted a creek and have joined other families to create a children's wet meadow. I hope that being with people who care about making the world a better place will balance the pain and violence that also exists and will help them be resilient, purposeful and joyful people.*

*from Karin's story*

*The hardest part is acting and speaking in such "unnatural" ways (for me at least). Harder still is trying to recognize all the subtle ways these issues present themselves in my world while at the same time trying not to be a control freak. Sometimes I just have to hold her when I want to push her away. I hug her when she asks for it and really try to make it a bear hug. I turn towards my husband when he wants a kiss instead of away. There's a poem I like. One of the lines is "sooner or later you realize that kisses aren't contracts" and how "if you want flowers you have to grow your own garden." That's some of what I'm realizing. I wish I had a fairy godmother, or a more loving family, or a magic wand, or even a more normal childhood but I don't and I didn't and therefore nothing is going to be easy. What I haven't been able to muster up for myself however, I'm willing to do for my family, for the people I love. Even though I think that I am incapable of love, it must be a lie because I am going to walk through this, for them if not for me, and I am not going to pass this shit on. I may not be able to protect my daughters from all the evil there is in the world but I will not create in this home the vacuum, which causes a young girl to go seeking love elsewhere. I will not judge them in ways that cause them to hate themselves to the point of self-mutilation. I will not—one day at a time, one minute at a time, sometimes one second at a time—I will not drug or drink or smoke...to squash these feelings. I will reach out and hug them; I will look them in the eyes when they speak. I will put down inanimate objects and touch living, breathing people. I will validate their feelings and acknowledge their presence. I will practice love until I get it right.*

*from Amanda's story*

*By being the best mother and wife I can be, I'm saying to my attacker that I WAS a victim but I choose not to be one anymore. I cannot change the past, but when I remember that God gave me free will, I know that I can choose how I react to it. I am free to go on with my life. I will not continue to be his victim. I prefer to think of myself as a FORMER victim, who will not let his evil continue to harm another generation of children.*

*from April's story*

*I'm at peace with myself as a woman, and as a mother. I am proud of myself, how far I have come, how tall I can stand and how much I am capable of.*

*As my children get older, I plan to share my experience on many different levels* with them, in hopes of providing education, compassion, as well as some measure of protection from becoming victims themselves from emotional or sexual abuse.

*from Otter's story*

I always thought raising children was all about giving, but already my two-month-old daughter has given me so much. She loves to be touched and cuddled, to the point where she rarely sleeps unless in my company, and by giving her unrestricted affection, I am doing the same to my "inner child" who was neglected and abused. Physical affection feels safe for the first time in my life since I was abused. It seems all the love I shower on my daughter she in turn showers on me, and while she grows, I heal.

*from Elaine's story*

I've also stopped thinking quite so much about the abuse and how it has affected me. Maybe this is because I'm busier or because my focus has moved to my children as I try to be a good mother to them. Or maybe it's because the parts of my body that were violated, that I associate with these memories, were the parts involved in producing, nurturing, birthing and nursing two beautiful children I love more than anything.

*from Melanie's story*

I went there to deliver my grandchild eight years ago. (I am a midwife.) When I saw her little head appear, I suddenly grasped a vision of myself, my daughter and my granddaughter that filled me with satisfaction and I felt like I'd done everything in life that was necessary and could die happy now.

*from Mary's story*

...being a mom helps me heal as a survivor. I will do things on my children's behalf that I would never do on my own. I hardly think about being a survivor most days. I give talks to freshman college students on safer sex and how to avoid date rape. My five-year-old knows all about birth and menstruation and genitals and has the words for them. My two-year-old knows that the words "go away" are to be heeded. We talk about personal space and how people must respect each other's space. I hope nothing bad ever happens to my kids and I think about what I would do if it did. I live a long way away from my family and I like it like that. I have learned about boundaries and being afraid and being courageous and being safe and being wise.

*from Shakta's story*

As we move into the last chapter, on healing and survivorship, we give Kelly the last word on this:

You, Reader Mom or Mom-to-be, are SO important. You are the only person who knows just what you want to keep from happening to your baby. You are strong to have made it through your life. Ask God to help you and to show you what to do when you are in doubt. Make sure you have support and resources and USE them. It is hard to go through pregnancy, childbirth and mothering even for "normal" women! Find an outlet. Read, write, paint, bang on drums or rock out with your guitar. Exercise regularly (I am still attempting this one!). Take great care of yourself. The *better shape you are in the better mom you can be. You are a gift to this child. You are so experienced in life and have so much more wisdom and love to give than many moms who don't have the emotional depth or wisdom as you. The skills you developed in surviving growing up can be so creatively and healthily used with your kiddo! What a rich upbringing you can offer. As I write this to you I realize I am speaking of myself and am thankful for the opportunity to encourage both you and me. I wish us the very best.*

*from Kelly's story*

# HEALING AND SURVIVORSHIP

**Deborah's Story**
*I was born in the early 1950s into a conservative, Christian home. I was well cared-for and felt secure. I don't believe my mother knew how to bond very well with her children, and didn't know how to relate very personally with her friends either. I did not feel close to my older brother, or even my only (older) sister, although we were only 15 months apart. I played with my two younger brothers and tried to give them the attention I felt was lacking from my mother. My dad was better at relations, and tried to spend time with us children, but was very busy with work and organizations. I was a good, compliant and reserved child. I took a very responsible view of life, including commitments to God.*

*When I was 13 and starting to mature, my older brother (by three years) started interacting more with me. He asked personal questions about the developing bodies of my girlfriend and me when she spent the night. Another time he wanted to demonstrate wrestling moves on me, and gained sexual arousal, as he had planned, I'm sure. I did not like any of this; I was shocked and unassertive. However, I never participated again. I had not had any sex education besides the fifth grade health film at school.*

*One night my sister had a friend overnight, so I slept in my brother's room. He slept in the family room, separated by sliding glass doors. He came over several times to touch my breasts and bottom, even making comments. I was scared stiff, literally, wanting to escape, yet frozen. Finally I managed to say stop, when his hands reached my vaginal area. He left. Again I waited in suspense, and he did not return. My mind and emotions were buzzing. In the morning I acted as normal as I could. I don't remember even thinking of telling my parents or sister. It was just too unbelievable and shameful.*

*A few weeks later, I told my girlfriend. I don't remember her response, other than it was short. A month or so later, my girlfriend and I spent the night with another girl. My friend threatened to tell her the story if I didn't. So I felt forced to tell it myself, to keep it short and quick. I felt I had been betrayed and that I had betrayed myself. I always felt like that betrayal affected my life more than the abuse itself. It cut me off from deeper friendships that could have allowed me to share inner thoughts and feelings, perhaps even the pain of my abuse. I decided women couldn't be trusted, and only my husband would be worthy of that trust. I don't remember thinking about it again and, in fact, treated my brother with love and respect.*

*In high school, I was more quiet and withdrawn, and sometimes sensitive to the point of tears, without knowing why. Since I could not share or even articulate my problem (I didn't connect it to my brother), I couldn't get help, and had some depression.*

*I went away to a small college, and decided it was my big chance to change. I was more outgoing and friendly, especially toward those I thought needed a friend. I had an easier time making friends with guys, and actually had some fun and happiness. I enjoyed these platonic friendships. I did date, but did not enjoy the kissing, and never allowed anything further. The dating relationships were short. I got depressed and restless, wondering what was wrong with me. I just couldn't relate closely with girls, and felt different from them, left out but not wanting to be "like them" (foolish and too talkative). I was rigid about eating only healthy foods. When I strayed I would regurgitate, although I never binged. I avoided going home by volunteering at a mental hospital for the summer. I was very depressed, thought of asking for help, but did not.*

*My second year at college, I dated a guy my intuition told me to beware of. I was so "nice" I thought I should give him a chance. Outdoors on one date, he leaned against me and made me feel his erection. I believe I spaced out after that. I remember being naked on my bed, digital penetration, and his saying I was beautiful as he walked out the door. I don't know what I did immediately afterward. I told no one. I saw him once more when he told me he was leaving campus for good. (He wasn't a student.)*

*I told God I'd quit dating until I got help, but I didn't know where to get help. Soon after, I met a guy who was different. He talked about God and didn't make a lot of physical moves toward me. He seemed to really care about me. I knew he was the one I'd marry. I told him very brief accounts about my brother and the date incident, releasing some emotion. We had a lot of fun together. We married and were part of a close-knit home church. I still did not connect with women in a deep way. I was quiet, yet nice. I still felt something was wrong with me, and sometimes felt depressed. I never thought about the abuse. Our sex life was fine. I didn't initiate, but could go along and even receive some pleasure.*

*At first I did not want children because I knew childhood as a time of pain and isolation; being in the midst of a family, yet unable to connect and share. Marriage created a desire for children, and I had no career to distract me. I thought I'd be better at parenting boys, since I didn't feel very feminine and could not connect with girls.*

*Once I was pregnant, I only wanted a healthy baby. Perhaps God has a sense of humor. We have five girls and one boy. Maybe he wanted me to learn that girls are all innately different, some more "feminine" than others, yet all normal. We had a homebirth with a midwife to help. I'd never felt so close to another human being. I was a natural at birthing and nursing. I was able to do what my mother had been unable to do for me. Mothering has been a nurturing experience for me and, therefore, a healing experience. I finally felt more connected, not only to my babies but also to a group of women called mothers.*

*Sexual abuse affected me as a mother. A side effect has been a desire to be in control or at least know what to expect of situations and people. So when I wanted children, I did a lot of reading and chose to give birth in my own home with my husband and a midwife. I like to raise my children following my own instincts. I nursed with baby-led weaning and natural family planning. I avoided the need for routine doctor visits by obtaining exemptions from immunization, which I also researched. I learned about natural remedies, nutrition, homeopathy and herbs. I also did some home schooling. I really enjoyed the children as infants and toddlers, and missed being as close as they grew older.*

*Mothering adolescent girls was especially hard for me. I read some books to them about the physical and emotional changes of puberty. I did not add personal comments. I'd often think of things to share about love and sex and how wonderful it could be, but could never say them. I knew the right words but I feared my feelings would betray my ambivalence. I relied on church youth group leaders to cover it for me. I very briefly told them of my abuse after I wrote this account.*

*In general, I was a good mother, but I know I lacked some emotional dimensions and spontaneity. I also suffered from migraines, so the older girls learned to help care for the younger ones as needed. After my fifth child, the only boy, I was really run down and began the slow descent into a major depression (three years later). I could not relax, and he was fussy for a year. Initially, he lost weight, but slowly regained it. I was homeschooling two children, we were under financial strain, the oldest girl reached puberty, and I could tolerate sex less than ever. I was just doing what I had to do, but I was dying inside.*

*I met a loving couple, and she shared about her childhood sexual abuse. I obsessed and agonized about whether to tell my story for months. When I told it, they assured me that I needed to get help. With their love and support and that of my husband, and with no more babies needing me, I let myself get help from a Christian psychotherapist. This actually made life harder, as I had to deal with emerging emotions. I didn't have much patience with my kids, or time. I was gone biking, walking, and to therapy. As therapy progressed, a lot of anger and pain came up, but I didn't know how to express it. It was very hard to pull myself together and return to my responsibilities at home. I'd often cut myself to shut down the bad emotions and anxiety. There was too much to handle all at once.*

*I signed myself into a Christian mental hospital for 22 days. This was very hard for me to do. I had rarely left my children, and it was especially hard for some of them. Although they came to see me a few times, when they left it was "out of sight, out of mind." I couldn't bear to think of the pain of separation. I was still very depressed, in therapy, and on medication for the next year.*

*All of my children were neglected, at least emotionally, during this time. My last child was born in the midst of it all, but was probably not neglected as much, because I was good at and enjoyed meeting a baby's needs. She was a ray of sunshine in the storm. At first she had considerable weight loss, probably due to my depression and stress. Mother's Milk Herbal Tea solved the problem. I took about a six-month break from therapy after the birth, and then resumed it for about two years.*

*I'm not sure why therapy took so long for me. I was distracted with so many responsibilities. I had such a block in my emotions. I took so long to trust, to accept love and acceptance. I thought too much, intellectualizing myself out of feeling emotions. It's hard for a nice, good girl to feel such bad emotions.*

*I also have a biochemical imbalance of the brain. I still take a low dose of medication. Now I feel pretty stable. My family sees a fuller range of emotions and hears more laughter. Laughter is the easiest way to gauge how I'm doing. When I get down about my failures as a mother, especially when they imitate my own childhood, I remind myself that I have improved on it. I do the best I can with what was given me, my motive is love, and I'm human. I hope my children will improve on what I've given them.*

*I have shared my story with two women who were also abused, and have formed the closest friendships I've ever had. The more I talk or journal, getting it out of my head, the more healing and proper perspective takes place. God's word and scripture songs help replace my own negative thoughts. I hope to pass on God's love and truth by co-leading a support group at my church and sharing one-on-one. Only by sharing the story with a loving and accepting person can the shame be lifted and love be felt.*

*God can bring good out of evil, as we accept His healing love and extend it to other hurting people.*

When I was two-and-one-half, my mother noticed vaginal bleeding and took me to our doctor. He wrote on my chart, "vaginal bleeding secondary to trauma." I found this on my chart when my mom gave it to me as part of my health records. I asked her if she knew what had happened. She has a bad memory, and could offer no plausible explanation. I was in therapy at this time, and I shared this with my therapist, whose immediate gut reaction was that this was probably sexual trauma and explained what he had seen as "developmental problems originating at age 2–3, especially the issue of trust."

I also asked my medical doctor what these words would mean to a doctor. He said quite definitely something was pushed with some force against the vagina, and today would have been reported as possible abuse.

This incident is frustrating to me. If it were sexual abuse, it certainly would explain my difficulty in therapy, especially with trust and sexual issues. I could say, "See, this is why I have such a hard time." It would explain why I froze with my brother and spaced out with the date in college. I wasn't weak and stupid, but previously traumatized, and "split off" for safety. Thankfully, I don't have to know. I can still deal with symptoms, poor ways of relating, negative thoughts and automatic reactions to certain stimuli.

Abuse affects how I relate to others with trust and vulnerability, and how I see myself. I can always look to Christ and loving friends, and risk relating in a new way. Healing comes through relationships, not new intellectual knowledge alone.

## Chapter 6—Healing and Survivorship

> "One or two things I know for sure; and one of them is what it means to have no loved version of your life but the one you make."
> 
> Dorothy Allison

> The day I read the above quote was the day I decided that being a victim no longer had to be my primary identity. I was a survivor and I could embrace that. I may not be able to change my history, but I could write my future.
> 
> from Kate's story

> Ring the bells that still can ring.
> Forget your perfect offering.
> There is a crack in everything.
> That's how the light gets in.
> from the song "Anthem" by Leonard Cohen

### RELATIONSHIPS

As Deborah points out, "Healing comes through relationships, not through intellectual knowledge alone." This is the key to healing: being able to risk making connections with others and forming trusting relationships. As Judith Herman explained, in *Trauma and Recovery:*

> The core experiences of psychological trauma are disempowerment and disconnection from others. Recovery, therefore, is based upon the empowerment of the survivor and the creation of new connections. Recovery can take place only within the context of relationships; it cannot occur in isolation. In her renewed connections with other people, the survivor re-creates the psychological faculties that were damaged or deformed by the traumatic experience. These faculties include the basic capacities for trust, autonomy, initiative, competence, identity and intimacy. Just as these capabilities are originally formed in relationships with other people, they must be reformed in such relationships.(p. 133)

We have been looking at the life experiences of survivor women across the childbearing year. Being pregnant and giving birth has provided many survivor moms with opportunities to make connections with a variety of people, including childbirth educators, doctors, midwives, doulas, nurses, La Leche League leaders, lactation consultants and parent educators. These relationships have been significant and important. Deborah shares that the relationship she formed with her midwife was a very important connection. She says that she had *"never felt so close to another human being."* Prior to this relationship Deborah reports feeling unable to relate closely with other women. Deborah's relationship with her midwife was the first in which Deborah was able to connect with another woman, and she went on to make connections with other women later. Like many other survivor moms, Deborah also reports finding healing through the process of becoming a mother, in general. She says, *"I was able to do what my mother had been unable to do for me. Mothering has been a nurturing experience for me and, therefore, a healing experience. I finally felt more connected, not only to my babies but also to a group of women called mothers."*

Deborah's story goes on to describe her journey of recovery and the many ways she sought healing through other therapeutic and spiritual relationships and a lot of personal hard work.

The childbearing years are special and transformative. But life goes on, and survivor moms must continue to deal with their personal recovery, even in the midst of wiping noses, car-pooling to soccer games, punching time clocks and writing dissertations. No matter how important the relationships with caregivers like doctors or midwives or childbirth educators have been, these relationships have a natural ending point and moms must shift their attention toward other connections. Survivor moms go on to form other important connections, which strengthen them in their journey. This chapter highlights the many ways in which survivor moms sought healing in the context of relationships with intimate partners, therapists of many varieties, faith-based communities, God and self.

## *FAMILY*

For many survivors, relationships with families of origin are complicated. Often, they have needed to be greatly limited or severed in the service of protecting the survivor or her children. But survivors often do continue to have relationships with non-abusive parents or siblings or other extended family members. Determining whether or not such relationships are good to maintain is an individual decision.

Bass and Davis, in *The Courage to Heal,* offer the following considerations regarding ongoing relationships with family of origin members:

> It is up to you to decide how you want to relate to your family. It is not a requirement of healing that you work toward reconciliation. Nor is it always necessary to stop seeing your family altogether. One course of action is not more courageous than the other. You can choose either end of the spectrum or anywhere in the middle, as long as your choice is based on what is genuinely in your best interests.

Look realistically at your relationship with each member of your family. Ask yourself:
- Do we have any contact now? Why? When? Is it because I want to, or is it out of obligation? Who initiates the contact?
- Have I told this person what happened to me? Does he or she acknowledge it? Is he or she supportive of my healing?
- How do I feel when we talk?
- Do I take more drugs, drink more alcohol, or eat too much or too little when we're together?
- Does this person criticize me, insult me, hurt my feelings, or show a lack of interest in my life?
- How do I feel after a visit? Depressed? Angry? Like I'm crazy? Nurtured and supported? Relaxed? Basically okay, but not great?
- What do I get from this relationship?(p. 233)

# Chapter 6—Healing and Survivorship

Otter shares the intricacies of being in relationship with her mother:

*I had never told my mother, my best friend in the whole world, what had happened to me. My mother knew more about me than anyone else; I shared all my problems with her and cherished her support and love, but this time I didn't have it.*

*I simply couldn't bring myself to tell her, to let her blame herself one bit for what Don had done to me. I had to spare her the pain that I was sure would haunt and trouble her seemingly more than it had me. Even though my mom's support gave me courage and strength, I loved her too much to tell her what had happened, for what seemed like selfish reasons, on my part. But somehow I felt guilty for keeping it a secret.*

*The doctor asked me why I felt guilty for not telling. My only reason was, I had always been honest with my mom and had never kept anything really serious from her, and for that reason I felt a need to have to tell her. The doctor just told me "No, you don't."*

*WOW! I didn't? The doctor continued, "What purpose will it serve?" None really, and that means it is okay not to tell her. I didn't really want to tell her and the doctor made me realize that the obligation I was feeling to tell her was unfounded. I don't always have to tell her everything.*

*from Otter's story*

Cindy did disclose to her mother, with whom she felt close, and was therefore shocked when her mother spoke in defense of the abuser many years later:

*Speaking of my mother...about 10 years ago, before my mother died, she came to my house. We had a wonderful relationship; I turned to her for help all the time. Somehow the subject of my stepfather came up—which had never come up with her before, EVER, and I said, "He was an evil man." After all these years—about 30, I guess, I thought that we could finally talk about him. My mother just said, "Nobody understood him." I was shocked, devastated—sent right back to being a little girl. She obviously chose his side, and after all these years and all we'd shared, she still chose him. I dropped it right there. I realized that this was going nowhere, that she probably wouldn't admit to it, that she still loved him, and that she felt that she had made this ultimate sacrifice by giving him up for us. That was hard to hear. She was such a good grandmother by then, and a good friend. I felt that a wall was put up then, that my sister and I were separate in her mind, which is why we spent a year with my dad, my grandparents, foster care, camp. We were always second in our mother's life.*

*from Cindy's story*

For Paulette, the death of her mother propelled her into recovery:

*When I was starting the prerequisites for the program, my mother had her second open-heart surgery. She never survived. My last son never knew his grandmother. And that's when the dam broke.*

*I felt so depressed and didn't know what to do. My eldest was emotionally disturbed and led us to have to get counseling. During that time, I was asked privately if I was sexually abused. The tears came. I couldn't stop crying and shaking. The counseling and healing began at that time. I went through books and support groups. I realized a lot of reasons why I did things. I grew stronger and was able to handle the children better. My eldest still pushes my buttons. But, I am changing. I am able to do things differently. I realize when he or the others are trying to bait me, most of the time.*

*from Paulette's story*

Denise realized she needed to sever the relationship with her family of origin altogether:

*That was a turning point for me. It just epitomized how it had been for all the years. I knew then that I had to get myself away from these people because nothing was ever going to change with them. No matter how much I fought not to be a victim I was just totally a victim in the family pattern and I would just have to break out completely to change anything. I gave up on the hope of normality for my family.*
*from Denise's story*

### FRIENDS

Survivor moms shared the importance of having good friends as supports on their healing journey:

*I have been fortunate to have many strong women in my life, young and older, who have assisted me along the way with support and wisdom of their own experiences. This group of women, that seems to expand and has grown to include caring and great men, has been a blessing for me. In so many ways.*
*from Gina Renee's story*

*Other things that have been helpful are prayer, both praying and having people pray over me, and having women friends. Good friends who can listen without saying a word to interrupt are essential to every woman, I think.*
*from Ann's story*

Amy felt particularly grateful to be in relationship with a friend who was also a survivor:

*I finally made a good friend, Maxine, a year after we moved to New York, whose husband worked with Ray. We quickly became inseparable and we began to tell each other everything. She was also abused as a child and teen. She became my angel. I again started to see a psychologist, and even though it didn't last very long, it was a big step. Maxine has been my counselor for many years as she has given me her love and support. She showed me that everything I was going through was okay, it would pass.*
*from Amy's story*

Kristy shares that forming relationships was not easy, even though she wanted to do so. She felt unable to trust either men or women:

*To say I developed "control issues" would be an understatement. I had learned at 13 that I could trust neither men nor women. It was a disturbing revelation that led me to be highly independent. Most of the men I met and seemed intent on hurting (before they could hurt me, of course) were actually nice guys whom I had attracted via my good qualities. Even though that registered intellectually with me, I never allowed the knowledge to penetrate the tight hold I had on my emotions. I wanted to be close to people, but feared if I let them get close they would betray me as my parents had.*
*from Kristy's story*

Another survivor, tedi, shares how she has always tried to have people in her life while not being part of the relationship personally:

*With all my relationships I've always known that my love was contaminated. I have always tried to have people in my life while not being part of the relationship personally because I was so contaminated. I have always been an object, even to myself.*
*from tedi's story*

**INTIMATE PARTNER RELATIONSHIPS**
Relationships with intimate partners can be particularly challenging because they involve sexuality and strong feelings of love and attachment—two adult relationship components that can be reminders of abuse-related experiences and problematic early life relationships.
Kathy shares that she sometimes feels triggered by her husband:

*I have not been in therapy since the breakup of my first marriage. Sometimes Phil will do stuff that triggers the past for me, but I can identify that that's coming from behind, from the past. I ask myself, "What do you need right now?" It allows me that time to back up.*
*from Kathy's story*

Not all "triggers" are aversive. Sometimes memories surface of strongly positive moments, but these too can be bittersweet or stimulate grief or sad reactions because they throw into relief what was more often missing. Kathy shared how witnessing a simple intimate interaction between her husband and son triggered a memory from her own childhood related to intimacy with her mother:

*I find that I don't remember a time when I ever felt loved—except for once—and actually my mom remembered this too when we were talking about it. She had sewed me an Easter dress and it was made of yellow dotted Swiss; I remember my mother looking at me and there was love and affection in her eyes; she told me, "You look good in yellow" and that became a trigger phrase for me. That same trigger phrase came up once recently when my son Adam had a yellow teeshirt on and my husband Phil turned to him and said, "Gosh Adam, you really look good in yellow" and I started crying... And I told my husband I was struck by the fact that our son has love all the time and he doesn't have to deal with all that other crap. To this day though I don't wear yellow. I make excuses, like I don't look good in it or...I don't like it...I think I don't feel deserving of it.*
*from Kathy's story*

That intimate partner relationships are difficult for trauma survivors, especially those with posttraumatic mental health problems, seems evident at the population level. People with PTSD are more likely to be single, separated or divorced (Kessler, et al. 1995). Nina realized she was unhappy in her relationship and asked her husband for a divorce:

*My son now is almost six years old, my daughter two and I am 27. I feel like I am just beginning to get to know myself and my power. I love my children and am so thankful for them. They have helped me to grow and experience love. I still fight depression and have moved to a sunnier climate to cope with the winters better. I recently asked my husband for a divorce. I had been very unhappy with our relationship. He was terribly upset. We sought counseling, and I have seen that he is trying to be more supportive and helpful. So, I am trying to make it work. But I feel strong enough now that I know I can go on without him if I need to.*

*from Nina's story*

Many survivors shared having difficulties being in an intimate relationship and being at ease with sex. Bass and Davis share their recommendations in *The Courage to Heal* on how a survivor can go about dealing with sexual fear. They point out that such fears are a natural result of being abused, and offer the following considerations:

- Go slow. Back off to whatever is more comfortable.
- Find a place in the middle. Many survivors fluctuate between extremes—shutting down totally or trying for complete sexual abandon.
- Stay in the present. Pay attention to the sensation of touch.
- Listen to your fear. What is it trying to tell you? Is something unsafe in your current environment? Or is it the kind of buried fear you want to push through?
- Find ways other than sex to connect deeply to yourself. If you start to confront painful feelings and memories in other settings (like therapy), sex will no longer be the only access point for connecting deeply with yourself, and you will gradually break the connection between passion, letting go, intensity and abuse.
- Check in with your lover. If you're afraid you're being abusive when you have strong sexual feelings, ask your lover if he or she feels abused. (Your lover probably likes your passion.)
- Push yourself a little. If you want to make love and you're afraid, push yourself a little. Stay in touch with yourself and your partner. Communicate like crazy. Be prepared for a lot of feelings. Don't expect simple sex.
- Stop if you need to. Sometimes the gap between what you want to experience and what you are experiencing gets too wide. If your terror is too great, take a break. Find another way to be close.(p. 255–56)

Survivor moms shared their feelings about the intricate dance of sexual intimacy:

*My husband and I haven't had sex for weeks. Now that's not really that odd for a young couple with an almost three-year-old and a five-month-old, despite what all the magazines and columnists like to tell you. But the truth is, I prefer it that way. I have absolutely no desire to have sex, and the feeling has gotten progressively worse with time. I dream of the days when men went to other women so as not to burden their wives with those sordid desires. Do not get me wrong: I love my husband. I can't imagine being with anyone else despite the days he drives me nuts. It's sex I don't like, at all.*

*from Amanda's story*

*What have I learned so far? I may have been the immediate victim of my perpetrator but it affects everyone that loves me closely. It affects my husband. He has been hurt by my denials and refusals. He has had to live with a picture in his own mind. He has had to learn extra patience and tenderness, and to sometimes just let me have the space. I have needed to deal with how and what I was feeling. It has affected him as a father; he knows how closely there can be predators out there and has become as protective as I, or even more at times.*

*from Kim's story*

## Chapter 6—Healing and Survivorship

*I have sex at this point in my marriage because I love my husband and I don't have the heart to tell him no. I do, however, feel relief when the babies stay up late, preventing any extracurricular activity. In fact, I'm grateful for anything that prevents sex. And that breaks my heart because I do love him and I don't know how to love him and I don't know how to exorcise the demons that prevent me from having a normal sex life. Most of all, I hate the acting "as if." I wish I enjoyed sex but at this point that is still a far distant goal.*

*from Amanda's story*

*The first year, my husband and I almost never had sex. I began to relive things and even holding hands made me want to throw up. Anything that even whispered of sex repulsed me. It was a slow climb up. I was advised by a therapist who "specializes" in sexual abuse to not have sex for as long as it took. But how do you tell a 23-year-old newly married man that sex is off limits?*

*from Tara's story*

*We had moved into a better house by now with three bedrooms. One day while Joe was at work I moved him into the spare bedroom. At first he resented me for it, and then he started liking it, and we have been that way ever since. It's like we now have the "rooms of our own" that we never had. Joe and I have always needed our own space. I truly believe that is why we have managed to stay together all these years. He has really been there for me as I have been writing this down and seeing what I have really done in my life. I was afraid he might leave me after he read it. We had some adjustments to make and through the grace of God we are better than ever. He was willing to see his role in the mess of my life also. He, too, has been sexually abused and didn't even realize that truth until later as I started coming to grips with my own abuse. We have always had trouble sharing feelings with one another, but we were so much alike we didn't know we were not okay. We miss each other very much if we are not there but we don't actually try to get our needs met through one another. We simply enjoy being with each other. This has taken years to happen. I realize now our way of being together is not for everyone. He has been committed to being there and taking care of me in the way a man's role used to be. Since this has never happened before in my life it had taken me years to realize how important and valuable he is to me. At this writing we have been together over 25 years. If you have had trouble trying to have and maintain relationships like I have, then maybe you can appreciate this fact for the miracle it is.*

*from tedi's story*

*I'm now married and have two beautiful little girls, and I believe that has really sped up the healing process. An intimate relationship with my husband has not always been easy. Fortunately, I'm married to a wonderful man who has always held me and let me talk about the abuse when I've needed comfort and support. He has tried to understand when my past interferes in our sex life and has been completely supportive of my doing anything I need to do to heal.*

*from Melanie's story*

A good book to recommend for partners of survivors is *Allies in Healing* by Laura Davis. Heather's husband read books to help him understand what his wife was going through:

*My husband has been a rock for me, learning alongside me, encouraging and supporting my growth. He relies on the results to measure the success, rather than*

▼ 6.1

It's a good idea to create a safe spot in your house, a place you can go when you're scared. Make an agreement with yourself that as long as you're in that spot, you won't hurt yourself or anyone else—you'll be safe. And make an agreement that if you start to feel out of control and afraid of what you might do, you'll go to that spot and stay there, breathing one breath at a time until the feeling passes.

Your safe spot might be a window seat on the stairway, your bed or a favorite reading chair. Or it might be a hiding place where no one can find you. One woman spent the night sleeping in her closet on top of her shoes, something she'd done as a small child to comfort herself in a house where no place was safe.

Take your own nurturing seriously, no matter how odd it may look. When all else fails, Laura's been known to head for bed with her teddy bear and a baby bottle full of warm milk.

Bass and Davis 1992

▼ 6.2

Is My Relationship Abusive?

Determining whether or not you are in an abusive relationship can be difficult if you grew up in an abusive environment. In her book, *Getting Free: You Can End Abuse and Take Back Your Life* (2004), Ginny NiCarthy offers some guidelines for helping to determine whether or not there are aspects of abuse in your intimate relationship. Some of these acts are more severe than others, but even the ones that seem not so severe have the potential to escalate into a more severe form of abuse, and are troubling in and of themselves. Understanding and recognizing what is happening to you is the first step in ending your exposure to and tolerance for such things:

Physical Abuse
- pushed or shoved you
- held you to keep you from leaving, or locked you out of the house
- slapped, bit, kicked, or choked you
- hit or punched you
- thrown objects at you
- abandoned you in dangerous places
- refused to help when you were sick, injured, or pregnant

**continues...**

*dismissing any peculiar method as unscientific. He read books like* Ghosts in the Bedroom *to help him deal with living with a woman who had been molested before she could even talk, who had been lied to in destructive ways, and who was just starting to learn some fundamental things about life. This man has broken all the rules of what I was told by my abusers, even just by marrying me at all. I had been told that nobody would want to marry me if they knew. But here I was, married to a guy who knew all about my history. The fact of my marriage made the abuser's words into a lie, and that released another part of me.*

*from Heather's story*

Stephanie was married to a man but came to the understanding that she is a lesbian:

*In 1998 I also made a dramatic discovery about myself, and my marriage. Matt and I had been together for 10 years, and the basis of happiness for that marriage was not the man I was with, but our children. After many months of therapy, I realized I could not stay in the marriage. After several more months of thought on my part, I also realized that I am a woman-associated woman…I am a lesbian.*

*from Stephanie's story*

People sometimes ask women whether they are lesbian because they were abused. Certainly if that were true then there would be a far greater number of lesbian women than there are today, considering how very many women have been abused. No studies have been done that suggest that more women become lesbians or more men become gay because they have been abused. Davis, speaking in *Allies in Healing* (p. 206), says that she has noticed in her experience in working with survivors that a higher proportion of lesbians and gay men have stepped forward to say they were abused:

I think this is indicative of: (a) the fact that lesbians have less need to protect men, and a majority of abusers are men; (b) there's more support in the gay community for exploring these issues; and (c) gay men and lesbians have actively looked at their sexuality in order to come out in the first place; because of this increased awareness, there's more of

# Chapter 6—Healing and Survivorship

an opportunity for them to stumble upon the information that they were sexually abused.

## *THERAPY*

Deborah, in her narrative at the beginning of our chapter, shares that she has had extensive therapy as part of her recovery process. The majority of the participants in our project (nearly 76%) sought therapy at some point along their healing journey. The form of therapy most often used was individual counseling sessions (over 85%). The majority of women found their therapy to be helpful, although some of their therapy experiences were problematic. We will look at the issues survivor moms related regarding the therapy relationship: finding the right match between survivor and therapist, the intensity of being in therapy, troubles within the therapeutic relationship and the positive results. (6.1, 6.2, 6.3)

Finding a therapist with whom you can relate is critically important. Anita Rubin-Meiller, MSW, is a therapist in private practice who sees survivor women in both individual and group settings. She refers us to the following questions survivors can consider when looking for a therapist:

In *The Body Remembers,* Babette Rothschild identifies 10 foundations for safe trauma therapy. While oriented towards the clinician's choices and behavior, these ideas (p. 98–99) can be re-worded as questions a survivor might want to consider when seeking out a therapist:

1. Will this therapist work with me to establish safety, both inside and outside of the therapy session?
2. Does the therapist give me time to feel connected before addressing traumatic material? Can I feel safe and trusting with [her]?
3. Will this therapist help me establish skills for "applying the brakes," tools for containing reactions to the therapy and to triggers, before we begin to work with the traumatic memories?
4. Can this therapist help me to identify and build on my resources and strengths?
5. How will we approach coping strategies and defenses? Can this therapist respect the ones I have felt necessary to use, as well

**...continued**
- subjected you to reckless driving or kept you from driving
- raped you
- threatened or hurt you with a weapon

Sexual Abuse
- made demeaning remarks about women
- treated women as sex objects
- been jealously angry
- insisted you dress in a more sexual way than you wanted
- minimized the importance of your feelings about sex
- criticized you sexually
- insisted on unwanted touching
- withheld sex and affection
- called you names like "whore" or "frigid"
- forced you to strip when you didn't want to
- publicly shown interest in other women
- had affairs with other women after agreeing to monogamy
- forced sex
- forced particular unwanted sex acts
- forced sex after beating
- committed sadistic sexual acts

Emotional Abuse
- ignored your feelings
- ridiculed or insulted women as a group
- insulted your valued beliefs, religion, race, heritage, or class
- withheld approval or affection as a punishment
- criticized you, called you names, shouted at you
- insulted your family or friends
- humiliated you
- refused to socialize with you
- kept you from working, controlled your money, made all decisions
- refused to work or share money
- taken car keys or money away
- regularly threatened to leave or told you to leave
- threatened to hurt you or your family
- punished the children when he (or she) was angry at you
- threatened to kidnap the children if you left him
- abused pets to hurt you
- manipulated you with lies and contradictions

as help me create new choices?
6. Can this therapist explain how my brain works as related to the trauma and how we can reduce the pressure from a hyperaroused system?
7. Does this therapist offer a variety of ways of working with trauma, or is she wedded to a specific technique?
8. Is this therapist comfortable with the idea of working as partners, and allowing me to set the pace of the therapy?
9. Is she available in between sessions and in case of emergency?
10. Do I feel listened to and understood?

I believe the most important principle to follow in choosing a therapist is to follow your gut. No matter what someone's credentials are, [she] will not be an effective partner for you in your healing journey unless you feel like it is a right match.

Anita Rubin-Meiller

### GETTING INTO THERAPY

Making the decision to begin therapy takes a lot of courage. You are saying you are ready to enter into a relationship in which you will be facing yourself in a deep way and sharing yourself with another person.

Wendi was depressed, but didn't think anyone could help her:

*I was having all the symptoms of clinical depression but didn't seek help because of a lack of trust. I didn't think anyone could help me.(6.4, 6.5) I bought a book for a friend about alcoholic parents and read it before giving it to her. I was surprised to find that my stepdad fit much of this description, yet I rarely saw him drink. I have since found out that he was a closet drinker and cocaine addict. This book helped me to see that many of my problems were a result of his treatment of me. This was a major realization for me. This allowed me to start to think about my life in different terms. If children who were abused have many different problems as adults maybe there was hope for me. Enduring his treatment had given me the belief that something was very wrong with me. I felt that if I were a different person he wouldn't have treated me that way. That was the first belief that I had to change to begin to reclaim myself. I learned that as a child I was vulnerable and in need of care and love. I needed to feel safe in my environment to develop a healthy belief system. Since I never really felt safe I developed a belief system that was flawed at its core. Rebuilding a belief system is not an easy task, especially when you don't trust anyone.*

*from Wendi's story*

▼ 6.3

Treatment for PTSD that is effective, resulting in long-term reduced symptoms, often involves a period of focusing on memories of the trauma. It is appropriate to discuss with the therapist readiness to do this phase of therapy.

Things to consider:
1. Do you have the support you need to bear strong emotions and to rest if you need to?
2. Do you have resources for as many sessions as it will take plus some follow-up?
3. Are you at risk for turning to alcohol or drugs if feelings get too intense?
4. Might taking an antidepressant during this therapy help make any heightened PTSD or depression more manageable?
5. Is the therapist available for between-session contact if needed?

Pitman, et al. 1991

Melanie has been working intensively on healing but has not yet found the courage to get counseling:

## Chapter 6—Healing and Survivorship

*It's a painful process that I've been working on for probably 15 years now, and I'm still far from done. I've read a couple of books for survivors of sexual abuse, talked to a few close friends about what happened to me and spent a lot of time thinking about how to move beyond this experience and grow from it. I think that counseling would probably help me deal with it more quickly and fully, but have not found the courage to go that far yet. I'm still afraid of digging too deeply. I've spent a lot of time trying not to blame myself and not be ashamed of what happened. I do think that talking to others about it and admitting that it happened has helped a lot. Somehow, just letting it out and telling others what happened takes away some of the power it has over me.*

*from Melanie's story*

Sarah got into therapy after disclosing to her boyfriend and telling him she wanted to die:

*One night I just broke down with my boyfriend and told him I wanted to die. I knew I needed to get help. I started seeing a counselor, talking about the abuse, and reading everything I could about sexual abuse. Just talking to someone about it helped a lot. I didn't feel like I was hiding such a shameful secret anymore. I started to accept myself, and forgive myself.*

*from Sarah's story*

Mary began therapy as a result of seeing how counseling was helping her son. She says that she was amazed that she had gotten so far without counseling:

*I saw how counseling was helping him and asked him to ask his counselor if he knew of anyone who could help me. So it was this compassionate, guilty, angry son of mine who helped me get into counseling.*

*from Mary's story*

▼ 6.4

In the National Comorbidity Survey, the average time it took for PTSD symptoms to subside was 36 months among those who sought professional treatment and 64 months among those who did not. However, PTSD became chronic in approximately 40% of people, whether or not they received treatment.

Kessler, et al. 1995

▼ 6.5

In a study of 801 mothers, 13.8% had had PTSD in their lifetime. Those with PTSD were 2–3 times as likely to also have had an alcohol or drug problem. 43.2% of the mothers with PTSD also had major depression.

Breslau, et al. 1997

Mary read about other abuse survivors at the suggestion of her husband:

*He said to me, "I think that incest with your brother had more of an effect on you than you may have realized." He bought me a book and I read other women's stories, and cried and cried, knowing my husband was right. I was amazed that I had gotten so old with no counseling. The ladies in the book were all a lot younger than I and were getting help. Part of me didn't think I was like them. Maybe I'd made a lot of the abuse up? Maybe it was my fault, like my mom said, "I'd asked for it," so I wasn't really abused, etc. So I asked my son for help getting a counselor.*

*from Mary's story*

Amanda's midwife referred her to a therapist:

*My midwife suggested counseling. She knew a therapist who used to be a midwife. Was I interested? Yes. I went. It was good for me. We stayed in the moment and dealt with the immediate issues. We talked a lot about my parenting because once I got more comfortable with the pregnancy, I developed new fears. But I had no idea that my biggest problem would be the relationship with my daughters.*

*from Amanda's story*

Joanna's doctor referred her for counseling:

*It was when my son was three weeks old that the memories started coming back. They began slowly, but cascaded faster and faster into my life. My wonderful doctor handed me a card at one of our numerous visits, telling me that he thought these people could help me. Apparently, he realized that something was going on that I couldn't talk about with him.... He saw the symptoms, yet I'd never told him a thing about my history or what I was going through. I had no idea what he meant, but decided he might be right. It turned out that "these people" ran an organization for survivors of abuse. With their help, I joined a support group, and used the book,* The Courage to Heal *(Bass and Davis).*

*from Joanna's story*

### TROUBLES WITH THERAPY

Not all therapists will be familiar with treating survivors of sexual abuse. They may make inappropriate suggestions, as a result, or practice in an insensitive manner. Obviously finding an experienced therapist who is sensitive to their client and abides by a code of ethics is critically important to a survivor. Many therapists who work with survivors use peer consultation groups or seek supervision from a more senior therapist in order to get input about challenges in working with women with complicated needs, and/or to learn new and useful therapeutic methods. Inquire as to whether or not your therapist is engaged in supervision. The contributors had some negative experiences with therapists:

Joanna chose a counselor who was also a minister, who minimized her pain by suggesting that she had to just "move on":

*I tried therapy, but chose the wrong person. I had always believed in God, and I wanted a therapist who would include those beliefs in my "treatment." I found a counselor who was also a minister. I remember the day I tried to tell him what had happened to me. He asked me, "Is it in the past?" I answered that it was, and he told me, "Then it's over. You have to move on." That was it...the entire amount of help I would receive from him. I don't blame God for this man's refusal to help me—I think it's just that some people can't believe that our past affects us in such strong ways. I wrote to him a few years ago, telling him how hard it was for me to tell him my secret, and what damage his response did to me. He denied saying what he did.*

*from Joanna's story*

Joanna was able to find a therapist with whom she could work. Unfortunately this therapist moved away without giving her the opportunity to terminate her care in a healthier way:

## Chapter 6—Healing and Survivorship

*My therapist worked with me for almost a year and I dealt with my memories as best I could. I started having flashbacks regularly, and that was the worst part. At one of my support group meetings, however, I was told that my therapist had moved out of state. She hadn't told me goodbye; she hadn't even told me that there were plans to move. She just left without a word. I was devastated, and didn't think I could trust anyone again.*

*from Joanna's story*

Cindy found her therapists' insistence on discussing sex and their inept approaches off-putting, but she persisted until she found someone with an approach and level of skill more suited to her needs:

*I tried to see a psychiatrist when my kids were young. The first session the first or second question was "How is your sex life?" And I was very put off by that. I thought, "Am I exuding this thing that everyone thinks that's all there is to me?" I went three or four more times, but that was it. I did go to group meetings, and finally got the courage to say something, but it was the end of session and it was like, "Whoops, time's up." I never went back. The second person I went to see was years later, a psychologist. When I told her I thought that my sexual abuse was a problem for me she said, "It made you feel dirty didn't it?" But I thought, "Why? I didn't do it, they did! Why should I feel dirty?" Now why would that be the question she would ask me? So I saw a correlation there and I didn't want to go back to a psychologist. It was more damaging than helpful. But I finally did see another woman after that, and she said that that was a very inappropriate thing for her to say to me. She must have been new, and going by the book or something.*

*from Cindy's story*

Jennie's therapists basically ignored her disclosure of sexual abuse:

*Several years later a scandal erupted in a day care center in our neighborhood. It was alleged that several of the workers had sexually abused many of the children there. I remember being filled with anxiety, I couldn't sleep. When my husband made love to me I felt as if he was raping me. I didn't know where the feelings were coming from. I mentioned to two of my therapists that I "thought" I might have been raped when I was 11. They looked at me and changed the subject. Naturally, based on their reaction, I figured that the abuse was not the cause of my depression and that perhaps it was due to the fact that I was raised in an alcoholic home. For years afterwards I continued in therapy and read a lot of material on adult children of alcoholics.*

*from Jennie's story*

Kristy came to feel that she knew more about the dynamics of sexual abuse than did her therapists:

*I've spent money on therapy and time in support groups to deal with the effects of growing up in a sexually dysfunctional family. I stopped this guided exploration of my past in my late 20s because I found the process to be more recovery-sabotaging than empowering. I found I'd researched more into sexual abuse dynamics than had most therapists and I tired of educating them at my expense.*

*from Kristy's story*

Susan stresses the importance of choosing the right therapist:

*Whenever one has a therapist who goes on and on about themselves or tells you they believe you but are lying, even if they think it's in your best interest to do so, it's very damaging. Trust is more important than anything. Anyone who truly cares can help you. Truth will set you free.*

*from Susan's story*

**BEING IN THERAPY**
For the most part our contributors, like Deborah, shared that while therapy was very hard, it was very important, nonetheless, to their recovery. Kate uses the language of midwifery to describe her relationship with her therapist:

*She was experienced in dealing with abuse survivors and we worked together for two full years on a weekly basis. There is no way that I can ever repay the gift that she gave to me of her time, her energy, her love. She mothered me toward health and healing and was the midwife to my most difficult birth. My husband was a rock, staunchly loyal, protective and patient. He even sought counseling himself as he tried to deal with my depression. He held me or didn't as I needed, coached me, comforted me, cooked for me and prayed for me. And I had a doula too, a brave survivor herself, further along her healing path, who held my hand, raged with me, wept with me and believed in me.*

*from Kate's story*

Kate goes on to say that eventually she came to embrace life, rather than fear it:

*Within the next two years, my marriage ended. I joined the work force after staying home for eight years caring for my daughters, and I began therapy. Between my therapist and my survivor's support group, I retrieved some memories, but most importantly I created a life for myself. I stopped thinking that I was a victim who had to fear life, and found that I could make the choice to embrace the life I would make for myself.*

*from Kate's story*

Elizabeth gained awareness during therapy regarding the pace of her life:

*I just assumed that everyone was like me, being busy all the time. Just recently, through my therapy, I realized that most people are not as busy as I am. They sleep eight hours each night. They watch television and movies. They sometimes don't do anything at all and just "be." I still always seem to be on a mission about something, even writing this story. My trick is to slow down even in the midst of three children and a full-time career. I now realize that part of my busy-ness was running away all the time. I was very good at school. It was a way of feeling good about myself, because I had so few other ways of feeling good because of the physical and sexual abuse in my past. It legitimized my not dealing with a lot of ugly stuff with my parents and others. Now I spend as much time as possible with my children and try to focus on them. I am trying to be less busy at work, at home and inside. I have stopped needing to run incessantly and am trying to make each day more meaningful, slower and complete, with God's help.*

*from Elizabeth's story*

Lynelle learned patience and forgiveness in her intensive therapy:

*All in all I spent about two years in intensive therapy. A lot of it was to resolve and let go of the c-section, the rape and the molestation. But I also learned patience and forgiveness. I became my own best advocate. I became my children's best defender and biggest fan. I became a mother. Now don't get me wrong, those were the hardest, most painful years of my life. I would NOT want to do that over again. I cried so many tears.*

*from Lynelle's story*

Nan was able to notice how she is "outside" of herself, looking in:

*It wouldn't be until I was in my late 20s, with a child of my own, that I finally discussed these experiences with a female therapist. It was after more than one year of therapy when, quite by accident, she asked me a question. I don't remember what. I told her that I was sexually abused for over seven years while growing up. I remember that she was so startled that she almost fell off her chair. I said it so matter of factly, so coldly, without any emotion or change in expression, as if I was giving a weather report. I often hear and do things as if someone else is saying them or doing them. It's like I'm outside myself, watching someone else. It makes me feel strange, but I've gotten used to it. I've been like that so long.*

*from Nan's story*

Lena also gained insight:

*When I remembered my self betrayed at a gut-wrenching level, I understood why I married a man who is emotionally unavailable. When I remembered the child sexual abuse, I knew exactly what my therapist meant by "Your life sounds so exhausting." Yes, it's tough running the marathon with a hole in your heart.*

*from Lena's story*

Heather began her healing journey by working through the book *The Courage to Heal* and the accompanying workbook:

*The Courage to Heal set (book and workbook) was a big help in my healing journey. I also relied heavily on* An Adult Child's Guide to What's Normal, *and began to solidify my spiritual practices within a group of women. In the space of a year or two I had made huge leaps in growth and healing. I "came out" to others I considered safe and found that many of my friends had also been abused, and those who were not survivors were no less supportive. It wasn't long before I became a resource for others discovering their own abuse history. Still, I didn't tell anyone in my family for years after that.*

*from Heather's story*

## GROUP WORK

Oftentimes survivors benefit from the therapeutic power of counseling in a group setting. Anita Rubin-Meiller, MSW, leads a therapy group specifically for women survivors of sexual trauma:

Participating in a group can be a powerful healing tool for a survivor. A group experience helps to challenge and dissipate the shame and distrust that for many survivors hinders their relationships and fosters a sense of loneliness and isolation.

In the context of a group, each woman has the opportunity to realize they are not alone in their pain, confusion, anger and despair. She can witness the way others take risks and share their courage to walk a path of healing. She can begin to experience the power of helping herself while being available to help others and to receive help and support from them. For many survivors, group participation is the beginning of being able to connect to themselves and others, with compassion and understanding.

> ▼ 6.6
>
> Among 89 treatment seeking women with a history of child sexual abuse, those who dissociated during the abuse experienced more severe mental health symptoms as adults (PTSD, depression, and dissociation).
>
> Johnson, Pike and Chard 2001

While integration and resolution of traumatic experiences is the overarching goal of any trauma therapy, my experience co-leading groups for survivors has shown how important it is to proceed with caution and respect. As Dusty Miller and Laurie Guidry point out in their description of their ATRIUM model:

> The most important reason to block the rehashing of early traumatic material in the initial stages of treatment is based on our understanding of how the biological impact of early trauma is re-stimulated by recalling trauma memories.
>
> Rather than stir up the physiological distress recreated by the retelling of distressing memories, the focus is instead on the ways the survivors have been doing their best currently to deal with the legacy of trauma.(Miller and Guidry 2001)

Some of the women who have participated in our group have had previous experience with models of group therapy where survivors were encouraged to share their story of abuse. Without the skills in place to minimize hyper-arousal and dissociation (6.6) and to stay present to their feelings, the telling of their trauma and the exposure to hearing others' stories is more overwhelming than healing.

The group model that I have offered, and found to be successful, is strength-based and oriented towards skill building. It provides education and information that allows survivors to make sense of their experiences, evaluate their coping skills and try new ones. It gives an opportunity for synthesis of the information through experiential techniques such as guided imagery, crafts and the learning of several relaxation methods. It also provides time for checking in and sharing.

The way that I approach group reflects my belief that survivors hold the key to their own recovery and need to pay attention to the internal signals that allow them to know what they need. In this regard, we have found it helpful to have interviews with at least two perspective group members at a time. This allows the women to get a sense of each of the group leaders and of at least one other possible participant. It has been useful in enhancing an environment of safety for the first session, as each member will already have a familiarity with one other member. We also take much of that first session to have a discussion of group guidelines, allowing each woman to have input as to what she needs included in the structure of our time together to feel safe.

Women may experience many challenges and changes through the 15 weeks of our structured group. Sally was one such woman. A 28-year-old, married, graduate student, she had only started having memories of her abuse two years before we met her. Overwhelmed by flashbacks, nightmares, impulses to hurt herself and suicidal thoughts, she began individual psychotherapy. Her therapist referred her to the group to have more support and increased coping skills. At her interview, Sally barely spoke nor met our eyes. She wondered if she was "making things up" and did she have to believe that the abuse happened for sure in order to participate. In the early group sessions, she struggled to stay present and not dissociate when the information, discussion or exercise felt triggering. But almost immediately, she felt relief to be sitting with other women who shared similar symptoms and struggles and to learn that there was a scientific, biochemical explanation for some of what she was experiencing. Sally held onto group like a lifeline. Despite a period of increased depression, a hospitalization and more dissociative episodes, she embraced the group and the group embraced her. When the 15-week group ended, she continued on in the support group. Over time, she began to share pieces of what she remembered about her trauma. Over time she began to recognize feelings of hurt and anger and find validation for them in the group. Through growing friendships and supportive connections with the other women survivors, Sally found a confident voice, a connection to her truth, a beginning of a less pain-filled life.

I have felt moved and honored to be a witness to the process of transformation that happens in group. Women, who were deprived of the earliest opportunities for trust and nurturing, take risks and learn to trust and nurture each other. The journey is not smooth or easy, but it seems to be

▼ 6.7

The basic steps to making changes are:
- Become aware of the behavior you want to change.
- Examine the reasons you developed that behavior to begin with. When do you first remember feeling or acting that way? What was going on then? Try to understand why you needed that behavior.
- Have compassion for what you've done in the past. Even if you didn't make the wisest, healthiest choices, you took the options you saw at the time. And now you're making better choices. Focus on that.
- Find new ways to meet your needs. Although every change doesn't expose an unmet need, many do. By taking such needs seriously and finding new ways to meet them, you make it possible to maintain the change.
- Get support. The environment in which you live—the people you see—affects your ability to make changes. People who are working to grow and change in their own lives will support you with encouragement and by example. People who are living out the patterns you're trying to break will continually suck you back in. Respect the power of influence.
- Make several tries. Although sometimes you can soar, usually making changes is a plodding process that doesn't look very heroic or exciting. Yet those everyday steps lead to real changes and a more rewarding life.
- Be persistent. Most of the changes we make in our lives require repetition. If not smoking one cigarette were sufficient, if wouldn't be so hard to quit smoking.

Bass and Davis 1992

▼ 6.8

Web sites for "twelve-step" programs:

Alcoholics Anonymous:
    www.alcoholics-anonymous.org
Al-Anon (for families and friends of problem drinkers:
    www.al-anon.alateen.org
Narcotics Anonymous:
    www.na.org

worth every step.

Here is what my client would like to add…

"For me, being in group meant that I knew I was never alone in my pain and confusion. I knew that one evening a week, I could open up and allow all the feelings that had accumulated over the past seven days to come out. More importantly, I knew that I could trust my group to listen and stand by me when I had difficult things to admit, such as cutting or taking too much of my medication. I knew they cared about me and wanted to help me keep myself safe."(6.7)

In addition to group therapy, contributors also reported being involved with various "step" programs, such as Alcoholics Anonymous and Al-Anon.(6.8) Many people find that forging relationships in these programs is helpful to their healing process.

*Suddenly I realized that I'd been eating like this for years, dieting, losing weight, always gaining more back, eating, binging, trying to exert great will power and losing it. Realizing that I'm a food addict has made me cry so much. The same feelings about being sexually abused come up for me. I get what I deserve. I eat too much; of course I'm fat. I asked for weird sex, of course I'm screwy. I'm on the First Step of my 12-step program. It's like I'm starting over again; will I ever be normal?*

*from Mary's story*

### CONFRONTING THE ABUSER
Some survivors felt the need to confront their abuser as a part of their healing journey. This brought mixed results for the contributors. Penny confronted her grandmother about her childhood abuse:

*I confronted my Granny on one occasion after the birth of my first son. Her response was to tell me that I was a BAD girl and that I had always had a "cheap and saucy attitude" to the men in our house. I reminded her that the first full penetration had taken place in my third year of age. She shrugged, saying that Jezebels start early!*

*from Penny's story*

Sarah also got a disappointing response from her father when she confronted him:

*I even confronted my dad and asked him why he did that, and asked him if that happened to him when he was younger. He said not, that he was sorry, but that it was in the past. I didn't feel any better after talking to him.*

*from Sarah's story*

Cindy's father was too infirm to understand the confrontation, still, she felt good about saying what she had to say:

*He didn't comprehend what I was saying, but his wife was having fits. She slammed her fist on the table and said, "That's a lie! Your mother put you up to this." I said, "My mother's dead" and repeated what I said to him: "You did some horrible things to my sister and [me] and I want you to know that we are aware of it, and that you didn't get away*

## Chapter 6—Healing and Survivorship

*with it…and we know about it." "Oh, it's so nice to see you," he says.…*
*But at least I got to say what I had to say, you know? It was disappointing that he didn't understand me. I was glad my friend was in the car after, because I did break down. I wish she had been inside with me because I would have loved to have a witness. I was glad that I did it, but I was sad.*

*from Cindy's story*

Kate felt relief at the death of her father:

*As my brother told me the details over the church phone, I felt a weird calmness come over me. I hung up the phone and sat down next to my husband. He asked me what was the matter. The first words I said were, "I don't have to be afraid any longer."*

*from Kate's story*

Kristy was finally able to tell her father about the impact of his abuse:

*My words completely took the wind out of his sails. His reply was, "Whew, I can't believe you still think about that." I turned and began the litany I had unconsciously been formulating for 10 years. "I think about it every day. I think about it every time I meet a nice man and can't let myself trust him. I think about it every time I'm afraid to think about having children because someone like you might molest them. I think about it every time when I wish I'd gone away to college instead of commuting from home so I could protect my younger sisters from you. I think about it every time I can't let myself relax and enjoy life like other people seem to be able to."*

*from Kristy's story*

Kristy's father did apologize to her:

▼ 6.9

*Over the next four years, I was able to rebuild my relationship with my father. I learned he had grown up in a highly dysfunctional environment and that his alcoholic father and one of his brothers had also been sexually inappropriate toward other family members. I would love to be able to say we established the kind of love and trust that usually develops between characters toward the end of Disney films, but that was not the case. I was able to care about and enjoy Dad from the perspective of a competent adult who is no longer vulnerable because she knows her strengths, weaknesses and options. And unlike many women, I did get to hear from him the most highly coveted phrase: "I'm sorry."*

Guidelines for medication treatment are published periodically by the International Society for Traumatic Stress Studies.

Foa, Keane and Friedman 2000

*from Kristy's story*

Kathy came to the conclusion that wanting to hear "I'm sorry" from her father was a way of allowing him to have power over her:

*I have learned how important it is to visualize. Deciding what you want to be, how you want to be, working through it, allowing yourself to accept that you could be that. I've found that it's also important to be realistic. When I started, the biggest thing I wanted was my father to say, "I'm sorry." Well, that's not going to happen.*

*Then I thought I could get him to just acknowledge what he had done. Well, that's not going to happen either. Finally I started realizing that by still wanting those things I let him have the power.*

*He doesn't have the power anymore. There are still little things that trigger me. But the power is mine.*

*from Kathy's story*

## RECOVERY AS A LIFELONG PROCESS

*I wish I could say life is wonderful now. I wish I could say I am fully recovered, and never struggle. I can't. Recovery is a lifelong process. I will always be in the recovery mode. I will always live in a fallen world where there is illness, sin, death and sadness. I still have control issues and try to deaden my negative feelings with over eating and over spending. I am still taking medication.(6.9)*

*from Ann's story*

We have spoken of recovery as a lifelong process. This is underscored in the narratives.

Jennifer shares that she has progressed, and yet, she also does not feel that she has "healed."

*I know that I have progressed in healing from my experiences; but I do not believe that I am healed. There is a residue in every part of my being that I continue to scrub at. At first when I started to deal with the pain of my experience I would often find myself curled up in a ball, heaving with sobs, or else beating my pillow uncontrollably almost every other day. Now I can go a year, sometimes a little longer, between these episodes.*

*from Jennifer's story*

Sara uses the metaphor of childbirth to describe her healing journey:

*Healing for me really has been like childbirth. I had no conscious control over when the contractions came. They came when I was in a space that felt safe. I coped with the feelings and memories when they came, then they went away and I got back to living. Over the years, it seemed like the resting between became shorter, the episodes became more intense until it became time to "push." I was in the safest, healthiest relationship of my life, with the man I later married. I was unemployed, living with him and being supported by him. The book* Courage to Heal *(Bass and Davis) leapt off the display at my favorite bookstore. My parents left the country for a year, and we moved into their house. I found out about a survivor group in town. I spent about a month sobbing in the bath and shower, writing in a journal, and talking to my partner. I went to the weekly group meetings, and met normal, functioning women with similar stories. My partner cooked, paid bills and lost sleep with me, while feelings and memories washed over me, preventing me from working on anything else. I don't think there was a precipitating event this time, only that the external environment was finally ready.*

*from Sara's story*

Margaret read a lot of books to aid her recovery, as well as getting counseling and joining a support group. She shares her experience:

*My early experiences have made me who I am. To deny the experiences is to deny the source of what makes me a strong woman now. Through my recovery I sought out books to read on alcoholism, psychology, family dynamics and self-help books of many kinds. For a while I attended a women's support group. I went to a counselor for about two years right after my memories began to surface. But always, somewhere inside of me, I knew I had the answer—that no one else had my answer. I would also become impatient with the other women I met who seemed to use their memories and experiences as excuses for being who they are. Sometimes there was just too much whining and making excuses for not getting on with getting stronger. During my recovery I wrote a lot. I wrote in journals, and I wrote poetry of sorts—most of which is filled with anger and sadness.*

*from Margaret's story*

### FAITH-BASED HEALING

Deborah shared with us in her narrative at the beginning of this chapter how important her relationship to God was to her healing. She had many years of therapy with a Christian therapist and spent some time at a Christian hospital. She also related how important her personal faith in God was to her healing.

Many of the narrators found their spiritual beliefs to be an integral part of the healing process for them, and shared the importance of addressing the healing of the spirit as well as the mind.

Sarah shared her perspective that she saw God as a protector:

*Looking back, I see how God protected me and helped me. He really loved me when I was a confused and troubled teenager and I would cry out to Him for His help. It wasn't always easy. We would sing a song at church that went, "Something beautiful, something good, all my confusion, He understood. All I had to offer Him was brokenness and strife, but He made something beautiful of my life." I would cry singing, because He did make something beautiful of my life. To God be the Glory!*

*from Sarah's story*

Elaine shared how her spiritual beliefs were an important part of working through shame:

*The first book I read,* The Wounded Heart *by Dr. Dan B. Allender, helped me to understand that my soul had been damaged, and why that happened. He knew! He understood! Dr. Allender held a sexual abuse seminar a few hours away and I was happy to be able to attend. Here I learned how shame attacks us. I have been blessed in that when I make a connection to a reason why I feel the way I do, and understand it, then I'm okay with it. Jesus loves me, the Bible tells me so and I believe everything that the Lord tells me. I have learned a lot about myself and the abuse through reading books....*

*Today, after accepting the Lord, counseling, a 10-step program, support program, reading many books and going to two seminars, I finally feel good about who I am becoming.*

*from Elaine's story*

Kelly found reassurance in a religious experience and unconditional love through her relationship with Jesus:

*One time I was at a church and the pastor in the middle of praying opened his eyes right at me and started prophesying about me and my hard life and God healing the relationship with my dad. It was as though God was reassuring me of His plan and his love for me....*

*Through my relationship with Jesus I have been shown unconditional love and how a true father ought to be.*

*from Kelly's story*

Tara, Cathleen and Ann share their understanding about God and the exercise of free will:

*There is no way on earth that I could have survived by myself the things that I went through as a child, and the things that I am going through now as an adult as a result. Only God could have given me the strength to endure. Many would ask, "Where was God when you were going through all of that?" I reply to that, "He was right next to me crying because someone that He created was being hurt by someone else that He created." God did not create the human race as robots. He gave each of us a free will. We have the right to choose what we do and do not do.*

*from Tara's story*

*How then can we help ourselves? First, admit that the damage done in our hearts by whatever abuse or evil that has impacted our lives and understand that we cannot heal without help. We have a choice: Remain in the prison we have built around our hearts (which robs us of joy, love and relationships, and finally our health and our very life), or break out of our denial and seek diligently for help and healing. Go to God, however you understand Him. See your doctor, a counselor, get involved in group therapy, all the while remain teachable (if you are prideful you will not be teachable) and seek God for direction. Above all seek a relationship with God, ask Him to purify your heart and be honest with yourself about the damage done in your heart and how it is currently affecting your life, health and relationships.*

*from Cathleen's story*

*I think I get along okay with what I have. Knowing that ultimately I am the person who controls me has been a great discovery. I believe it was Victor Frankl who said, "Everything can be taken from a person but one thing, the last of human freedoms, and that is to choose one's response in any given set of circumstances, to choose one's own way." I believe this to be true. No matter what else may happen to me in my life, I can still choose my response to it; I can still choose my own way. My healing is within my reach if I will have the courage to open my heart to my God and allow Him to heal me. "For nothing can separate us from the love of God, no height, nor depth, nor creature that thrives..."(Romans 8:35–39)*

*from Ann's story*

Dawn shares the freedom from shame she experiences through prayer:

*Caring people in my church prayed for deliverance for me, getting rid of all the demonic oppression that came in through the abuse and replacing it with the love*

# Chapter 6—Healing and Survivorship

*of God. I was finally set free of a constant state of feeling rejected, abandoned and unloved. Hallelujah! I'm captive no longer. The mantle of shame that covered me was finally lifted.*

*from Dawn's story*

Laura feels peace and a sense of calm through prayer and meditation:

*But most importantly, I believe it has been a strong faith that has carried me through these difficult years. Prayer and meditation give me calm and a sense of peace that I can find nowhere else. My belief in God has helped me see that in spite of what has happened, I can love and I can forgive and I can grow from my past experiences. As difficult as the journey has been, I am thankful that the pain has not been buried but has been freed, for it allows me to open myself up and be free as well.*

*from Laura's story*

Otter takes comfort is the sense of connectedness she feels in her faith:

*I found these spiritual studies empowering, because it conceptualizes the understanding that we are all connected to one another and also all possess a tiny piece of the divine, the All. An All that is neither male nor female, a divine that could be all things to me and all other people, simultaneously, a multifaceted god.*

*Taking my faith's teachings, I created a Ritual of Release for the rape, which I could use to help me come to terms with and let go of some of what had happened, at least the part it was time to let go of. It was a very personal, moving and profound experience, that any woman can create using her own religious system, and a little imagination.*

*from Otter's story*

Wendi finds wholeness and love of self through her belief in the Goddess:

*To be a woman in charge of my own reality was the most important task for me. I started by looking around my life and deciding what was my creating and what was a result of my flawed beliefs. I started to wade through my world tossing out things along the way that didn't work for me. I read as many books as I could, looking in the bibliography of each book for more recommendations. I kept a journal to document my thoughts and feelings. This allowed me to go back and see the changes I had made, giving me strength to keep going during the dark times. During this time I realized that a key piece to my health was missing. I had heard over and over about integrating body, mind and spirit. I knew my body, I knew my mind, but my spirit: Where was that? I began to look for spirit in my life. I wanted to find my spirit and feed it and nurture it. I felt this must be the way to regain my wholeness. While seeking for spirit in my life it began to manifest more and more. I began to uncover my own beliefs and values. I realized that I needed balance in my life and that I needed to honor both sexes. This led me to a belief in a creative Goddess and her consort and lover God. I had finally found a structure of belief that allowed me to be all woman and be responsible for my own destiny....*

*The Goddess I found myself believing in loved me. She wanted me to be my best. As I looked around I saw new things, exciting things. The world looked more beautiful. When looking around at the creations of the Goddess I felt that I was one of those beautiful creations and I loved myself for the first time since I was a very young child. It was a freeing feeling, although it only lasted a moment. The feeling has returned and each time it does, it stays a little longer.*

*from Wendi's story*

Stephanie feels filled with peace and love through her connection to her pagan family:

*I am also very blessed to have a pagan family here in West Virginia. We get together quite often to celebrate Sabbats, and many other times just because we love to be together. I teach Sarah to love and respect her body, and being around this group helps to solidify what I have told her. I teach Casey also to love his body and to be respectful to women. Our group is very relaxed, but fills me with peace and love. I get surrounded by woman love each time I see my friends, and it helps me heal.*

*from Stephanie's story*

Lisa learns love and compassion for self through teachings she receives that focus on Divine Sexuality:

*Doing my healing through a spiritual path has broadened my perspective about everything and shaken up my perspective about everything. I have learned about spiritual law (self-responsibility, brotherhood/sisterhood, cause and effect), when in my life I am aligned with spiritual law, when I am disconnected and what manifests. Some of the most intense work I have done is with a woman in Toronto, named Sagewalker.*

*She has offered a transformative process called, "Stages of Initiation, Divine Sexuality," which focuses on one's expression of sexuality, to see where one is connected and disconnected from God. My personal work with Sage has been so helpful. I actually feel that I am reclaiming who I am. I actually feel that I am disconnecting more and more from those places in me that were drawn to, attached to and connected to abuse. She has helped me to see the gifts in the challenges and helped me to honor and hold sacred the lessons that life brings to me. She has helped me to have compassion and love for myself.*

*from Lisa's story*

Nan says Buddism has saved her life:

*Namu—Amida—Butsu. Nam—Myoko—Renge—Kyo. Buddhism has saved my life since 1972. Without this light to guide me, I would have been forever lost in darkness, pain and suffering.*

*from Nan's story*

## *ABUSE BY CLERGY*
We need to mention that not all spiritual relationships have been helpful to survivors. Often, as we've seen in the narratives throughout this book, some clergy's responses to disclosure have included denial of the impact of abuse and suggestions to maintain the family order. Instances of sexual abuse at the hands of clergy have come to light in recent years, and the narrators also faced this:

## Chapter 6—Healing and Survivorship

*I thought, geez, even preachers do that sort of thing; is nothing sacred? ... It was awful; I have almost no words for it.*

*from tedi's story*

Ruth was shocked at her religious leader's response to when she revealed to him that her husband had been molesting her child:

*The days that followed were like a nightmare to me. I felt out of control and on the edge of insanity. I went to the preacher of the religion into which I had been born and told him. He was very kindly, but he said to me, "Go home and stand by your husband. Children soon forget these things." I was in a state of deep shock as I drove home. I only knew she could not forget.*

*from Ruth's story*

Communities of faith have a critical obligation to meet the challenge of speaking out about the issues of sexual abuse in a healthy and non-shaming way. Monica A. Coleman, PhD, is an ordained elder in the African Methodist Episcopal Church, and is the founder and former director of The Dinah Project. In her book *The Dinah Project* (p. 4), Coleman writes about the importance of the church response to sexual violence:

> We need the church. There is a need for an explicitly religious response to this crisis of sexual violence. First, there is a large amount of biblical ambiguity about sexual violence. The story of Sodom and Gomorrah does not condemn the attempted gang rape of Lot's visitors. The story of Dinah's rape involves vengeance, but it does not mention Dinah outside the fact of her rape. The story of Tamar's incestuous rape encourages Tamar's silence. Some Levitical rules condemn rape; others do not. The story of Potiphar's wife and Joseph leads many people to believe that women often lie about being raped. The second chapter of Revelation justifies the rape of Jezebel as punishment for her false prophecy. Some biblical passages seem to support the unconditional submission of children to parents regardless of abuse. The list continues. If one looks for a single unified biblical response to sexual violence, it cannot be found. These passages need attention and interpretation in the context of the pervasive extent of sexual violence.
>
> Second, sexual violence has numerous religious and spiritual effects. Many victims of sexual violence question God's presence and agency as they deal with extreme suffering in the context of their faith. For the Christian victim of sexual violence, concepts of forgiveness and evil arise in new ways and must be addressed. Although there are legal, medical and psychological personnel to respond to many aspects of sexual violence, only the religious institutions are trained, equipped and permitted to address issues from a spiritual perspective. Only the church can speak to the presence of God in the midst of the experience of sexual violence. Only the church can bring words of hope, promise and healing in a society torn by the evil of sexual violence. Only the church can speak of God's unconditional love, unfailing grace and power to restore the fallen and heal the broken.
>
> Third, there is a need for a compassionate response to sexual violence in our midst. For every incident of sexual violence, there are the victims, the victimizers, and the people who love both or either of them. They all go into some state of crisis. They are all traumatized. We may find that these parties exist within the

same family and within the same church. Do we embrace? Do we ignore? Do we judge and condemn? The church is called to give the kind of response that legal, psychological and medical personnel do not and cannot give. The church is called to name and condemn sin where it is found, but also to extend God's love and grace to all human beings. To be able to find righteous indignation, justice, grace and love in a situation of horror and violence is nothing but the work of God.

## ON FORGIVENESS

The idea of "forgiveness" or "letting go" came up in many narratives, though the form it took, the reasons for forgiving and *who* needed to be forgiven varied.

*Finally, after many unsuccessful attempts to have a normal life, and many hundreds of therapy sessions later, I realized, I had to just let it go. I came to the conclusion that the abuse was never my fault, that I had no control and was not a bad person, and I had not been a bad child and I deserved none of it. I made the decision not to let my past rule the life I now had with my husband and my son. It was a difficult choice to make, to keep the abuse close to me or to let it go, and even now sometimes it comes creeping back to cloud my judgment. I see abusers everywhere I go. In the mall I wonder if that man walking by is a pedophile.*

*from Judy's story*

*It's funny how even though cognitively I know that it wasn't my fault, guilt still follows me around. I find myself on the freeway wondering whether or not the person behind me is happy with my driving, or if I was nice enough to the cashier at the grocery store. If something is bothering my husband my first thought is, "What did I do?" It really makes no sense. Luckily, after years of doing this I have a second following thought, "Stop that, Jennifer."*

*from Jennifer's story*

*When I finally settled down at 18, I began reading many inspiring and empowering books on women's issues, herbs and healing. Among these wonderful books was* Hygeia *by Jeannine Parvati-Baker. There is a section in the back of the book, of letters written by other women to the author about their own personal life experiences, including abortion. I read these and I felt a door open, a door that contained all that I repressed. I knew that I wanted to grow, to release this pain and to move forward in my life. Before I went to sleep that night, I talked and prayed to the Universe, to allow me to release this hurt, and to release the anger I felt toward the men who had hurt me, and also the guilt I felt relating to the abortion I had. I no longer had room for this pain, even though repressed. That night I had a dream; it was a beautiful dream, and I wish to keep it to myself, but it was very insightful and healing for me. I awoke feeling different, lighter somehow. I knew I was healing.*

*from Gina Renee's story*

We have read how many survivors struggle with guilt and shame. These emotions can prove to be as toxic to us as the sexual abuse that triggered them. Bass and Davis, in *The Courage to Heal,* consider forgiving yourself to be very important:

## Chapter 6—Healing and Survivorship

The only forgiveness that is essential is for yourself. You must forgive yourself for having needed, for having been small. You must forgive yourself for coping the best you could. As one woman said, "I've had to forgive my genitals for responding. I've had to forgive myself for not being able to second-guess my father and avoid the abuse."

You must forgive yourself for the limitations you've lived with as an adult. You must forgive yourself for repeating your victimization, for not knowing how to protect your own children or for abusing others. You must forgive yourself for needing time to heal now, and you must give yourself, as generously as you can, all your compassion and understanding, so you can direct your attention and energy toward your own healing. This forgiveness is what's essential.(p. 154)

Kathy's shares her thoughts on forgiveness for her father and for herself:

*Forgiveness is a hard concept. I'm not sure it's the right word. By moving on, that's a "forgiveness" in some aspect. I'm not sure I'm the person to judge if I should forgive my father. I think in some ways I have forgiven. The divine has an answer for it. I don't think about him, except those little trigger times. Don't spend any energy on him. I don't hate, dislike, like.... It took me a long time to get there. I hated him for a long time. But that just gave him more power. I did need to forgive myself for the things I did later because of the situation, the first marriage, the tubal and those kinds of things.*

*from Kathy's story*

Sarah was able to forgive her parents:

*I'm so happy now. I never thought life could be so wonderful. I have a great relationship with both my parents. I love them deeply, and have forgiven them. My husband has been very supportive of me.*

*from Sarah's story*

Amy feels that only God can absolve:

*Forgiveness is for the perpetrator, it doesn't benefit the survivor. Think about it. What am I telling you if I forgive you? I'm telling you that I am forgiving you of your sins upon me, I am giving you absolution. I can't do that. Only God can do that.*

*from Amy's story*

Tara thinks of forgiving as an ongoing process:

*I know God wants me to forgive, and with his help I have. Some days I have to forgive all over again. It is an ongoing process.*

*from Tara's story*

Kala feels she may forgive, but not forget:

*My stepfather is dying from untreated cancer. I know I should feel some type of pity or remorse for his suffering, but those feelings just won't manifest. I look at it as Karma. I hope that I have forgiven him in some measure for what he's done not only* to me, but also to his grandchildren in the long run. I have forgiven my mother for turning a blind eye and using me as a pawn in a lot of her bribery tactics with my grandparents. I just won't forget.

*from Kala's story*

Ann shares that while she has forgiven her perpetrator, that doesn't mean that she will ever be associated with him again:

*The most helpful therapies were one-on-one and Al-Anon. Finally learning to be in control of the things I should control and to leave alone what I cannot or should not control has been very good for me. I love Al-Anon—it has been a lifesaver for me. Through that group and the exercise of my faith I have forgiven Mark. I hated him for a long time, wished him in Hell or at least dead. I wish these things no longer.... Having said this, I can assure you I have no desire to see, talk to, or be associated with him ever again.*

*from Ann's story*

Gina does not blame, and recognizes change, however slow:

*I feel sorry for him; he is not the abusive man he once was. I believe that we are taught how to love, and he was not taught properly. So I do not blame him, for I know he knows his wrongs, and tries in his own way to change. And he is. Slowly.*

*from Gina Renee's story*

Margaret's mother tells her to "forgive and forget." She has forgiven much in her life, but does not feel compelled to forgive her abuser:

*I never told my parents about the abuse when it was happening. I thought it was my fault somehow, and my uncle threatened me with harm if I "squealed." My father went to his grave without knowing. I finally told my mother because she was adamant I go to a family reunion, to be held at my uncle's home. She wouldn't accept my excuses, so I told her the truth. She cannot understand why I can't just "forgive and forget. After all, it happened a long time ago...."*

*I have forgiven ex-husbands, co-workers, supervisors, etc., but I cannot forgive my uncle. For this I feel no guilt. He doesn't deserve forgiveness. Unfortunately, I have missed out on family gatherings, and have pretty much distanced myself from most of the relatives from that side of the family. I cannot chance running into him. I remember when my grandmother died, and he attempted to hug me at the funeral. I nearly vomited when he touched me. I have made certain I have not seen him since.*

*from Margaret's story*

Kristy feels that adopting a polarized view of sex offenders as evil is not helpful:

*I worked six years as a probation officer and in that time handled several cases involving sexual abuse. A lot of criminal justice and corrections employees have trouble dealing rationally with this population. But I believe I was able to proceed relatively objectively and comfortably with the perpetrators on account of my experiences with my father. I also did a counseling internship with an agency that treated sex offenders and other sex addicts. That further reinforced to me that they are more than just the sum of their deviant behavior. While I don't believe sexual addiction can be cured, I do believe it can be managed. And although my view is not popular among those who believe sex offenders should be taken out and shot, it nevertheless is informed by both personal and professional experience. How many people can say that? I fail to see where a polarized view of sex offenders as "evil" serves anyone.*

*from Kristy's story*

The topic of forgiveness and reconciliation is a broad one that is core to many spiritual traditions and informs many therapeutic processes. The narrators informed themselves from many sources, secular and religious. Discussion of the issues related specifically to reconciliation between abuse survivors and perpetrators can be found in a workbook written by Laura Davis, co-author of *The Courage to Heal,* which is available free on her Web site: www.lauradavis.net.

## ALTERNATIVE HEALING MODALITIES

*When one learns hatred as a child it is excruciatingly painful to unlearn that the love you knew was actually pain. It is very hard to retrain the mind, heart, muscles, emotions; the whole nervous system of a human being is geared to accept that which it experienced as a child. It takes tremendous effort for me to accept peace as love, when silence and "peace" meant I didn't know what was coming next.*

*from Susan's story*

▼ 6.10

Belly Breathing
  Belly breathing is a great thing to do when you panic—when you're scared that you may stop breathing altogether, or close to it. Your breath becomes shallow, uneven, and catches high up in your chest. To belly breathe, lie on your back and place one hand on your stomach, one hand on your chest. If the hand on your chest is the one moving up and down, you're breathing from your chest. Practice sending your breath deeper into your belly, until the hand on your stomach begins to rise and fall. Consciously blow the air out of your mouth, and let your belly refill with air.

Bass and Davis 1992

▼ 6.11

Most of the well-researched therapies for survivors of trauma focus on healing the psychological after-effects. But physical conditions are also associated with traumatic stress, ranging from fibromyalgia to irritable bowel syndrome to chronic pelvic pain. Some scholars conceptualize these pain conditions as residual effects of our instinctual "freeze" reaction that did not get discharged in the moment of overwhelm. They are developing body-focused, or somatic, therapies to "unfreeze" or discharge the energy that got blocked when fight or flight was not possible.

Levine 1997
Scaer 2001
Rothschild 2000

We have spoken at various times in this book of the "bodily" experience of feelings triggered by aspects of childbearing. How do survivors go about healing their bodies as well as their minds and spirits? (6.10, 6.11) Many of the narrators found that talking therapy alone was not enough to effect a deep healing that includes the body with the mind. Many used a variety of body-focused or "somatic" healing modalities, among them various types of massage and other "bodywork" techniques, music therapy, art therapy and EMDR (eye movement desensitization and reprocessing). For a deeper look at a range of healing modalities, look at *The PTSD Sourcebook* by Glenn R. Schiraldi.

Providing a thorough presentation of all of these methods is beyond the scope of this book. However, we will share a few perspectives from clinicians who practice in some of the healing methods mentioned as being useful to the contributors: massage therapy, EMDR, music therapy and art therapy.

## *MASSAGE THERAPY*
Tiffany L. Mazurek, MSW, CSW, NCTMB, is a psychotherapist who has also become a massage therapist. She shares the following about the work she does:

> I have worked for over 10 years with the issue of sexual assault and child abuse. I have provided psychotherapy for six years and although my clients have made wonderful progress in their treatment, there always seemed to be something missing. They would begin to integrate the concepts that we talked about week after week into their healing, ideas such as self-forgiveness and self-care, but they never seemed to be able to get over that invisible wall that separated them from the people in their lives who loved and cared for them. Many of my clients would describe their relationships with their family, children and others as "distant" or "lacking a connection." They would lament their inability to "feel love" for another person. As I searched for answers as to how to help them get past this point, I realized that most of them have never truly been inside their own bodies since the time of their abuse. They have spent years dissociating and depersonalizing in order to survive and so they are not able to access those deep emotions that are required in order to engage in a relationship with another human being.
>
> It was during a time in my life when I was experiencing some emotional ups and downs that I sought out some alternative therapies for my own healing process. As soon as I began to experience the effects of receiving bodywork (energy work and massage) I knew that this was the missing piece. Traditional psychotherapy allows the mind to begin to process the emotions that can keep us stuck. However, it can fail to address the physical and energetic blocks that accompany trauma and emotional distress. By utilizing massage and in turn working with the whole self, the individual is able to begin to experience healing of the Body, Mind and Soul.

Preliminary evidence shows that body therapy approaches, such as massage, reduce dissociative experiences among survivors of childhood sexual abuse, and that the reduction of dissociation may be an important mediator for improving overall health among survivors in recovery (Price 2004). Body-oriented therapist and researcher Cynthia Price, who has worked with women survivors of sexual trauma for 17 years, had the following to say about the potential benefits of massage therapy for survivors:

> Survivors of sexual trauma who receive bodywork, and who pay attention to their body in the process, tend to become connected to their inner body experience. Increased awareness and connection to one's body facilitates the reduction of dissociation, leading to greater psychological and physical well-being, and fewer traumatic symptoms. Women survivors typically seek bodywork after many years of psychotherapy. They tend to feel uncomfortable in their bodies, have difficulties with intimacy with their sexual partner, or live with an overall feeling of disconnection—feeling "cut off from the head down." They seek a sense of inner connection, a necessary core element in the healing process from childhood physical and sexual abuse.
>
> In order for connection to inner bodily self to occur, the client must feel safe with her bodywork practitioner. There are things a bodyworker can do to promote trust and a sense of safety. The massage therapist must let

the client feel in control of where and how she is touched. Being in control and feeling safe are two sides of the same coin. The client may choose to not take her clothes off, for example; or ask to not be touched in a certain area of her body. There needs to be constant communication between client and therapist about what feels comfortable. People who dissociate are often unaware, at first, of what is and is not comfortable, so the pace of the bodywork must be slow enough that it provides every opportunity for awareness and communication.

Working with sexual abuse survivors involves an educational emphasis within the bodywork session. The process involves gently prodding the client to ask herself, "How am I feeling? What amount of pressure feels right? What area of my body needs attention?" Because so many survivors dissociate, bodywork practitioners need to be able to identify when a client is dissociating. Likewise, they need to help the client to develop awareness of her dissociative patterns and triggers, enabling the client to understand her reactions to touch and to bring this awareness into the session. For example, "When you touched me there, it made me feel scared." When a client is dissociating, nothing therapeutic can happen; there is no awareness gained. Many bodyworkers are not familiar with dissociation or do not know how to work with it therapeutically; this is an area that survivors may want to ask about when seeking a practitioner to work with.

### EMDR

Peggy Holtzman, MSW, is a therapist who sees many clients who are survivors. She is also trained as an EMDR therapist and shares her perspective on the usefulness of that technique for survivors:

> I find EMDR to be a tremendous tool to help people heal from traumatic experiences. In working with survivors of sexual abuse for the past 18 years, I have a perspective of the work both before and after being trained as an EMDR therapist. Before I was trained in EMDR, I found that healing would take place but over a much longer period of time (i.e. months or years with a particular event vs. days or weeks using EMDR to process the

▼ 6.12

One clinical trial of EMDR conducted with women sexual abuse survivors found the EMDR group had fewer symptoms of pain, PTSD, and depression at the end of six treatment sessions than control group members who had six sessions of routine treatment. In the three months following treatment they experienced continued symptom improvement and sought treatment less often.

Edmond, Rubin and Wambach 1999

In an 18-month follow-up assessment they maintained their improvement.

Edmond and Rubin 2004

In a companion qualitative study, women in the EMDR group expressed a greater sense of trauma resolution.

Edmond, Sloan and McCandy 2004

▼ 6.13

EMDR is included as a recommended treatment for PTSD by many professional organizations. In the US these include the American Psychiatric Association, the Department of Veterans Affairs & Department of Defense, the International Society for Traumatic Stress Studies, and the National Institute of Mental Health. Similar organizations in Israel, Ireland, the Netherlands, France, Sweden, and England also list this approach as one they recommend.

www.emdr.com

▼ 6.14

For more information about EMDR and to contact an EMDR trained therapist in your area, contact the EMDR Web site at:

www.emdria.org

▼ 6.15

Recent research has shown that music therapy can:

- potentiate exercise benefits for patients undergoing cardiac rehabilitation
- lower anxiety, stress and beta-endorphin levels in patients with coronary heart disease
- raise self-esteem scores for women participating in jazz dance classes
- reduce irritability, improve language skills, improve the ability to relax and sleep and reduce state anxiety in Alzheimer patients
- reduce depression and anxiety symptoms
- improve motor function in stroke patients
- relieve pain in postoperative patients
- temporarily increase spatial-temporal intelligence scores of college students on IQ tests (The Mozart effect). The Mozart effect is being used to treat premature infants and children with neurodevelopmental challenges such as autism and attention deficit disorder.
- reduce anxiety and pain during childbirth
- relieve anxiety preoperatively and during surgery

Horowitz 2004

▼ 6.16

A comparative analysis of the cost-effectiveness of music therapy as a procedural support in the pediatric healthcare setting found that music therapy-assisted procedures led to successful elimination of patient sedation, reduction in length of procedures, and decrease in the number of staff members present for procedures.

DeLoach Walworth 2005

same type of event). When strong memories came up and continued to come up for a client, seemingly without much resolution, I began to feel the client's helplessness and felt my own methods of working through the memory with the client to be very slow and at times ineffectual. This led me to search out other types of treatment for survivors.

Much research was being conducted in the late 80s and early 90s with Vietnam War veterans who were diagnosed with PTSD to find out what were the most effective psychological treatments. Several large studies pointed to EMDR as an effective new treatment (first discovered in 1987). EMDR is now considered to be among the most researched and recommended forms of treatment for PTSD by the American Psychological Association.(6.12, 6.13)

EMDR therapy is both simple and very elegant in its design. It involves integrating thoughts, emotions and memories about a traumatic event by speaking them aloud while moving the eyes side to side following the rhythmically moving hand of the therapist. It is to be used within the context of a therapeutic relationship by a licensed mental health practitioner who has undergone EMDR training.(6.14)

The use of EMDR in processing memories involves having the client bring up a disturbing memory, the negative thought (belief) that goes with that memory and a corresponding positive thought (belief). The positive cognition serves as a "map" ...of where the client wants to go with his/her belief about self. EMDR processing involves attending to the thoughts, emotions and body sensations that are elicited with a disturbing memory. The therapist checks in while the client is processing and gets a reading on the level of disturbance of the target memory and the validity of the positive belief after the disturbing memory has been processed and no longer carries a negative charge.

With EMDR, a person has to suspend one's belief about how quickly traumatic material can be processed and symptoms relieved. By the time a disturbing memory has been processed, sometimes in a single session, a person with an abuse memory can go from being highly sensitive to triggers (and therefore flashbacks) in the present to feeling and believing that the abuse is over and in the past. It no longer holds the same negative power over the client. It has become a part of the client's history but is no longer the focus and drain on the client's life energies.

Like Peggy's clients, Joanna found EMDR to be helpful:

*This technique was so effective for me; I really was dealing with things for the first time. EMDR was the trick, for me, in bringing those memories out and letting me take the emphasis off of them.*
*from Joanna's story*

## MUSIC THERAPY

*Through visualization exercises in therapy, I became aware of a coarse rope around my neck, inhibiting access to my voice. This made it difficult for me to cry, to become angry, to voice any scary feelings, to make sounds. I had to regain my voice. I began group therapy in a women's "circle of sound" for survivors. A combination of music and voice therapy, I grew more in this setting than anywhere else.*
*from Liz's story* (6.15, 6.16, 6.17, 6.18)

Kathleen Moore, voice teacher and board certified music therapist, has the following to say about working with survivors:

As a music therapist, I focus on the particular elements of the human voice in music. Because the voice is an integral part of a person's body, breathing, personal expression, identity and hour-to-hour life experience, working with the voice in healing produces many layers of effect.

Music therapy is the use of music as a primary modality in helping people with a wide range of physical, emotional, intellectual, social and psychological challenges. To be effective, it does not require any particular level of musical competency from the clients whom it serves.

Breath and healthy projection of voice often become compromised even in a normal set of life experiences. The amount of impact when a person is traumatized is far more dramatic. Someone who is abused gives up their voice. Someone who lives in an alcoholic family keeps the family secret by keeping their mouth shut. Someone who is sexually violated is often threatened never, never to tell. Someone who experiences posttraumatic stress often feels there are no words to express how they feel about what is remembered, if it's remembered. In fact, the very process of recovering a healthy functioning voice can help to rediscover lost or denied memory.

In my Circles of Sound, I bring together small groups of women or of men to share in the healing process of finding voice and using the body instrument

▼ 6.17
The American Music Therapy Association has this to say about music therapy:
Music Therapy is an established healthcare profession that uses music to address physical, emotional, cognitive, and social needs of individuals of all ages. Music therapy improves the quality of life for persons who are well and meets the needs of children and adults with disabilities or illnesses. Music therapy interventions can be designed to:
- promote wellness
- manage stress
- alleviate pain
- express feelings
- enhance memory
- improve communication
- promote physical rehabilitation.

American Music Therapy Association
www.musictherapy.org

▼ 6.18
Noted neurologist Oliver Sacks has this to say about music therapy:
"I regard music therapy as a tool of great power in many neurological disorders (…) because of its unique capacity to organize or reorganize cerebral function when it has been damaged."

American Music Therapy Association
www.musictherapy.org/quotes.html

not just to speak, but to cry and laugh and sing. Music is a language of melody, harmony, rhythm and form. It can provide a safe container and a very deeply meaningful process in which to explore, discover and communicate. Music can give expression to the otherwise inexpressible. When this powerful combination of voice and music is shared in the context of a small community of people who are linked in a common life story of trauma and loss, the end results can be life altering.

There are many other situations in which music therapy has demonstrated its efficacy. Music therapy is in the hospitals helping patients of all ages, and their families, to reduce pain, manage anxiety and recover healthy physical functioning. Repeated hospital studies have shown that the therapeutic administration of music significantly reduces the amount of pain medication required. Music therapy is in the schools helping young people with autism and a spectrum of learning and behavior disorders. Music therapy is in retirement residences helping with memory loss, loneliness and fear.

## ART THERAPY

▼ 6.19

Materials: Paper appropriate to the medium (newsprint, heavier white drawing paper for pastels and paint, plain unlined paper); crayons; charcoal; craypas; pastels; paint; magazines for collage; clay; masking tape, aluminum foil.

Resources:
Allen, Pat. *Art is a Way of Knowing*. Boston/London: Shambala, 1995.
Cameron, Julia. *The Artist's Way*. New York: G.P. Putnam's Sons, 1992.
Cohen, Barnes and Rankin. *Managing Traumatic Stress through Art*. Baltimore: Sidran Press, 1995.

*As I healed, my creative expression emerged as a fine artist. I have always loved fine art, but never developed my talent because of the creative block that was there.*

*from Cathleen's story*

*I went to counseling for five years, once a week. I got acupuncture, went to a Feldenkreis (a form of bodywork focusing on posture) trainer, went to an incest survivors group, did art therapy. I continue to do art, which lets me feel something so beautiful; especially, the quickness of relief that comes with the colors that can tell everything about my feelings so fast. I paint; I make clay sculptures; and I have tremendous peace from these. I love to have them around me and just look at them. I can hear myself speak through them, and I feel like my voice is returning.*

*from Mary's story*

*The most graphic thing that I have done is to tell my own and the stories of ALL of the Voiceless Ones in my Art. For it is in telling and re-telling our Oral History that we render it harmless, that we milk the poison from its fangs, that we become the carriers of the Light into Incest's unspeakable darkness.*

*from Penny's story*

Sue McDonald, MA, ACSW, shares her experience using art in a therapeutic context:

Let's talk for a moment about what the use of art and art materials in the therapeutic context is and is not. Above all, this adjunct to personal work, with or without a therapist, is easy. The materials used are meant to be "ready-at-hand." Ordinary paper, crayons, and charcoal work just as well, and sometimes better than more sophisticated mediums. A flat surface helps, but people can and do work with a notebook held on their laps. Music sometimes provides a nice background but that is very much a matter of individual taste.

Making art in this context is not the same as art therapy. There is no interpretation by a professional, or anybody else, unless requested. Self-understanding and self-healing are the standards.

The work produced in these settings is not considered "art" (although it is!). Pieces are never judged on their artistic merit, or lack of it.

The premise upon which the art making activities used in this context are based has been best stated by author/artist Pat Allen.(6.19) That premise is that: "Art is a way of Knowing" that process by which intuitive and emotional realities can be accurately expressed and fully understood through art making, and without the use of words. This is "knowing" at its most basic level and it is the art that permits an ever-deepening awareness, understanding and integration of the self. The creative spark that is ignited also helps in the healing of losses of the past, by providing the experience of "making something out of nothing again and again and again."

There are many other benefits to be gained from the use of art activities in the context of personal work. A few are listed below:

First, for those who warm to the idea, these periods spent with the materials of art are just plain fun. The time flies and people don't want to stop because they are enjoying themselves so much. A great deal can be said for the pure joy of making marks on paper, scribbling, painting in great swaths of color or finding just the right image to express an inner truth.

Second, there can be times during the recovery and healing periods when feelings are very intense, confusing and hard to manage. Moving unruly and uncomfortable sensations out of the self and on to the paper can provide great relief, and often gets rid of the trapped energy that is blocking further progress. Openings are created for new feelings, and different ideas.

Third, it sometimes happens that a serious talent is discovered or recovered as a result of participation in the art making process. When this happens, an unexpected treasure unfolds, and a life trajectory changes.

On a more personal note: As a clinician, I have never ceased to be amazed by the total focus and concentration that occurs when people have become fully engaged in an artistic project. There is absorption and a complete connection with the self that I seldom see in any other context. I never fail to be impressed by the strong evidence of pride and ownership as each individual gathers up his or her piece and heads for home. At that moment, the hope and the confidence in a new future are almost tangible.

How To: The only real difference between doing personal work with art materials alone and being with a group or with a therapist, is that the latter settings are more structured and have the added advantages of support and connection. In any setting, however, the process is essentially the same. Again, Pat Allen is the best reference for this work.

Step 1: The materials to be used for the art making are gathered. Then the "artists" take a moment or two to leave the cares of the day behind and to get grounded in the present.

Step 2: An intention is made and written down. (It is often helpful to have an ongoing notebook for this, and other written parts of the process. Also, all work should be dated, and the most important pieces kept.) This intention is designed to make a connection with inner resources. It is kept very simple and is expressed in the present tense. Either statements or questions work for intentions. Some examples might be: "I am having fun with making art today," "I am making marks to fit my present mood," "I wonder what my anger looks like?" "I am finding my key to inner peace," etc.

Step 3: Once the intention is written, the individual simply waits for whatever comes up next. That may be a desire to begin working with a specific color; an urge to simply scribble; an image that asks to be made or drawn or a story that needs its own picture. The idea here is to trust the first inclination that comes up. A period of between 20 minutes and two hours is then spent working with the art materials to get this original idea on paper or into structural form.

Step 4: When the piece is finished, several minutes are spent looking at it with some of the following kinds of questions in mind:
What do I see here?
To what do I respond most strongly in the work?
Could this piece be telling me anything?
What was this experience like for me?

Step 5: After the period of observation, a 10-minute witness is written that contains some of the responses to the questions asked and/or any other thoughts or impressions that seem important.

The work may or may not be shared as circumstances permit. Again, it is not to be judged, either by the individual or those present, for its artistic merit.

## *ABOUT BEING A SURVIVOR: TERMINOLOGY*

Survivors had a lot to say about what being a survivor means. They weighed in on the terminology of survivorship and their understanding of the power of words to describe the effects on them and what they have in common:

*From hearing and reading other women's sexual abuse stories, I know mine is not at the severe end of the spectrum. Many women had it much worse over a much longer period of time, frequently at the hands of multiple perpetrators. But I think we are bound together by the universal feelings of fear, distrust and betrayal that have continued to affect our outlooks and relationships long after the sexual abuse stopped. As when a nuclear bomb is detonated, the fallout/exposure is worse than the initial explosion.*

*from Kristy's story*

*I can tell you that I have been on a healing journey for a long time. Some of my healing has been specific to recovering from sexual abuse. Most of my healing has been about discovering me. My journey has been about seeking, and so it has been a necessary and an important part of my process to move beyond the labeling of "survivor." Sure, I have had to admit and face the fact that I have been violated sexually. And in doing so I have learned that violation has many forms and presents in the subtlest of ways. Violation is self-hate, self-abuse, criticism, betrayal, deception, manipulation, judgment, cruelty, hostility and all the places in my soul that I have separated from. I have learned that it doesn't really matter, in the long run, what form violation takes, whether it is blatant or subtle, violation impacts the spirit regardless. It is the spirit, along with the wounded child, that needs attention and healing. It is through connection to my spirit that I have found healing.*

*from Lisa's story*

I prefer the term "object of sexual abuse" because I think it more accurately reflects the objectification that must occur in order for the sexual abuser and his/her secrecy collaborators (i.e., my mother) to carry through with their selfish behaviors. I have come to view sexual abuse as an unhealthy way the abuser uses the abusee to get his/her needs met. A true victim is someone who was helpless in a situation. In my case, I did what I could to the best of my abilities to cope with what was going on. I didn't shut up and put up like my father requested and I used what options I had available. I always wonder what a dramatic difference would be made if the first responder professionals in sexual abuse cases made it clear to the abusees that they were "objects" versus "victims." They could actually tell someone, "It looks like you just happened to be at the wrong place at the wrong time when someone tried to use you for their own sexual gratification." Such a reframing would arouse a natural, healthy anger at being used, rather than induce shame. Surely it's more recovery-enhancing to recognize you were more pawn than prey.

I also resist describing myself as a "survivor" of sexual abuse, for that implies a nobility of behavior that simply wasn't there. I only did what I could to get my needs met under less than desirable circumstances. Such is life.

*from Kristy's story*

▼ 6.20

One way that individuals cope with negative experiences, including victimization, is by finding some meaning or purpose in their suffering.

Frankl 1963

An analysis of 44 interviews showed commonalities in this process of making meaning among adult survivors of sexual abuse and assault. They described this meaning-making process as "learning the harsh realities of life" and responded by "taking it upon themselves" to accomplish three tasks:

1. Pursuing one's own safety, which involved (a) learning you are on your own, (b) looking over your shoulder, (c) looking out for dangerous men, and (d) seeking a safe spot.
2. Taking justice into one's own hands, which involved (a) realizing it's up to you, (b) gaining token justice, (c) getting even by getting better, and (d) deciding enough is enough.
3. Creating something good out of something bad, which involved (a) becoming stronger through adversity, (b) passing the lessons on, and (c) truly understanding the pain of others.

Draucker 2001

## *ABOUT BEING A SURVIVOR: ACTIVISM*
Several of the contributors went on to become activists for the cause of healing from sexual abuse. They became politically active, formed advocacy groups, became clinic workers, midwives, doctors and teachers.(6.20) They found the courage to share their stories and minister to others. Here are some of their stories:

*Recently, because of my experiences, I took a lead role in our state in working to extend the statute of limitations on incest. I testified before the state legislature and told the same story I'm telling you now. The statute of limitations was extended from age 24 to age 40 and incest was made a Class A felony. I will continue to work to protect survivors of sexual violence and make the world a safer place for all of our children.*

*from Cubbi's story*

*I can offer hope to those who feel they will never smile again, never trust again, never love again, never see the sun shine again. I can tell people, "God IS good, He was right there crying for you!" I cannot make sense of what I went through as a child, BUT I am using my past to minister to others.*

*from Ann's story*

*Because I have found my voice, I can help others do the same. I am currently working on starting a support group for mothers of survivors called M.O.S.A.C. (Mothers of Sexually Abused Children) and working on a newsletter, which I will call "Find Your Voice."...*

*I've learned that everyone's recovery must come in his or her own time.*

*from Jennie's story*

*Six more months passed and I began coming to terms with what happened. I had even joined a peer education group, called "Sex, Drugs and Improv." We were run through the drama and health services departments of the university. We did improvisational skits about relationships, STDs, rape, and drug and alcohol use. By joining this group, I was heavily educated on all these issues.*

*Understanding rape was something that had a second use for me. I could look at the cases we studied and I could see myself and Don. I read about and became familiar with many cases just like mine. I learned the law, and found out exactly what constitutes rape. I learned the statistics on rape.*

*Suddenly I wasn't alone. I hadn't made some mistake, I had been raped, and I knew now for sure. I had ingrained the legal meaning of rape and not society's impressions of what a rape should be, in my head. I embraced it, and made it mine....*

*I continued with "Sex, Drugs and Improv" for a total of three years and loved it. It was a super outlet for me, and a great release of stress from my schoolwork and studies. "Sex, Drugs and Improv" gave me a voice. And there was always the chance that I would reach some other woman the way the health educator had reached me at orientation. Maybe I was able to stop a rape from ever happening or begin the healing cycle for some other woman.*

*from Otter's story*

*Because I have been able to come so far along my road to healing, I now want to help other survivors and provide a place and forum for them to find support and community to help them on their journey to healing. Now that I have come so far, I have started a foundation for survivors of childhood sexual abuse called "Thriving Souls." The purpose of "Thriving Souls" is to encourage communication, awareness, and prevention of childhood sexual abuse, to help in the healing of survivors and to educate parents, so that we may end the silence, and break the chain of abuse that continues to lock innocent children in a world of confusion and pain. "Thriving Souls" is a warm, positive, uplifting name that denotes where survivors have come from and celebrates where they are going. Because of where I am today, I want to give back to others, so that they can heal, too, and hopefully live a less traumatizing future.*

*from Kim's story*

*My calling in life, my Vocation if you will, was to deliver babies safely into their parents' home. To ensure gentle beginnings for all of the children whose lives I touched. My second desire was to find a way to heal myself...a journey, which is still not completed after 58 years of trying....*

*In all, I have aided at over 2500 births.... I have also helped their mothers to bring all but two of our 15 grandchildren into this world. As I write we await the imminent arrival of number 16!*

*from Penny's story*

*I now work for a highly respected woman's clinic, helping to provide services and care for the women of my community. This too, is part of the healing for me.*

*from Gina Renee's story*

*My experience as a survivor has also helped to shape my professional life. I worked for years at Planned Parenthood to support women in their choices about their bodies and sexual lives. In public health graduate school, I studied women, social power and support, culture and birth. I worked with inner-city, community-based organizations to increase the choices that women had in birth. Through these experiences I was reminded of what I knew well in my own heart: the best way to help women is to listen to women.*

*from Liz's story*

*Now I'm a new person. People who knew me years ago are astounded at the person I've become. I work in maternal child health as a birth doula and lactation consultant. I regularly pick fights with the medical establishment to test my resolve. I don't let people push me around and I speak my mind regularly, much to the dismay of a few of my more timid family members and friends. I'm a bit of a bitch!*

*from Lynelle's story*

*I write, teach and conduct research on violence, especially against women. It is at once therapeutic to be a bridge for my patients and colleagues and is exhausting always being focused on violence in some way.*

*from Elizabeth's story*

▼ 6.21

Infants whose mothers are erratic in providing positive emotional interaction and adequate soothing, or whose mothers are frightening or abusive, develop hyperarousal and dissociation. They have insecure attachment. Early abuse negatively impacts the development of the right brain, affecting attachment, emotion regulation and stress modulation, setting the stage for mind and body coping deficits that characterize PTSD.

Review of data from numerous studies suggests that early intervention to help mothers who have been abused and have PTSD can significantly decrease the intergenerational transmission of posttraumatic stress disorders.

Schore 2002

## *CONCLUSION*
We have spoken of many types of relationships in this chapter, with family of origin, partners, friends, therapists, groups and body workers. Survivors who are mothers also have a primordial relationship with their children. All of these connections matter, but so does our relationship with our self.(6.21) When we travel on an airplane, and the attendants give us the safety instructions, they remind us that when the oxygen mask pops out due to a loss of pressure, we need to secure our own mask before securing our child's mask. The same is true for healing; we must secure our own mental health and well-being so we can ensure the safety and well-being of our children.

The narrators' stories indicate that the journey can be long and hard. They describe it as a deep personal exploration, a task that takes a toll, but a process worth the effort. And we don't make the journey alone; like Deborah shared at the beginning of this chapter, **"Healing comes through relationships, not through intellectual knowledge alone."**

*It helps me to see my abuse as a building block that created the strong woman I am today.*

*from Amy's story*

*I have learned to love myself. In learning to love myself, I give myself the nurturing and support that was not available when I was little. The version I've made of this life continues to evolve, and I feel certain that it's going to unfold in a way where inner peace is a primary focus. I've earned it.*

*from Kate's story*

*Posttraumatic stress disorder… it comes and it goes. It taps my shoulder and sends shivers of fear throughout my being, making me want to run, to protect myself and my children. It comes at both expected, and unexpected times. My experiences have given me strength and a deep sense of purpose. I have faced my own death and know that I am still here for a reason; I have important work to do…a reason for living. My experiences have helped me to put things in perspective. I am quite tolerant of life's little trials and tribulations because in the bigger picture they simply are not very important.*

*from Karin's story*

*It is like having an arm and a leg, on opposite sides of the body, amputated. You can have therapy, have prosthetics, to replace the missing limbs, but it is never the same as never having the real ones removed. The scarring is permanent and the handicap is forever! There is no going back to what you were before the experience. There is only trying to heal and going on with whatever you have become. Some days are good; some years are bad. If I could prevent these things from happening to everyone else, I would spend my life doing it. That's why I'm part of this book. Knowledge is the only protection!*

*from Nan's story*

*Sometimes a wide plain, sometimes barely a trail, the path is ever changing and long. In places it has deep ruts that fill with water from the rains, elsewhere there is only twisting sand, under the intense beating sun. It can be almost impassable with thorny overgrowth or so steep and exposed that nothing can grow. But as I travel it, I learn to weather its challenges and recognize its patterns. And I try to always remember it is my path. It does lead somewhere. It goes on.*

*from Liz's story*

*I learned to trust myself. I learned that there is truth in me buried deep down under the garbage of my childhood, and that if I listen to that truth, I will be able to hear other things, too. It's like being pregnant and listening for the beat of that tiny heart through a stethoscope. You have to look for it, but once you know where to find it, it comes through solid and strong. If you buy a stethoscope, you can listen to it any time you want to. And when you're quiet enough to hear it, you hear a lot of other life noises, too.*

*from Tamar's story*

## Chapter 6—Healing and Survivorship

*Since I have moved again, I have not found a counselor nor am I looking. I know my journey has not ended. It is a never-ending spiral. When the time comes for me to go find someone I will. Until then, I will continue to grow and heal, building on my last therapy. The abuse is a part of me and it shapes who I am today, and I am very proud of who I am. I am not only an incest survivor: I am a mother, a friend, a wife, a certified nurse-midwife and a strong, beautiful woman.* **I hope my story helps women to see that they are not alone and regardless of what is happening in their lives that they too are strong, beautiful, and survivors.**

*from Gwen's story*

*Is there a higher power for someone like me? As a kid I imagined my guardian angel was nailed to the wall and couldn't help me. This is still a vivid image for me. I didn't deserve the love of God, of the Universe, still don't. Yet I have been the recipient of love beyond belief. My husbands, my children, my family of origin, my friends, my clients, my community, people all over have heaped love on me, called me an angel. I have prayed for angels to help at the births I attend and have felt their presence as they filled the room with unconditional love and peace. Yet, I have not believed it could be true for me. Surely all this love and affection is a mistake? If they all really knew the truth about me, would they still love me so very much? I have achieved amazing things in my life. I remember being born, nursing, feeling so loved as a tiny baby; I discovered very young that nature was my ally; I'm bilingual; I am a mom, a wife, have a great home, have learned how to really communicate about and enjoy sex with my husband; I have a beautiful career, am in a Masters program, the president of a college, the founder of an accrediting agency, the founder and director of an amazing birth center, a clinical and academic midwifery educator, an artist, I'm recognized and beloved by my community and my family, adored by my dog! My youngest wants to become a pediatrician and come to work for me!*

*I'm in the dark and in the light; I am cursed and blessed; I imagine only black and white, but the doors to the in-between, where life just is what it is, are cracking open, and I'm still alive to see it.*

*from Mary's story*

# Afterword

The experiences you have read about in this book have been difficult. They also are not novel—women and children are the objects of such abuses of power around the world, to an alarming degree. We still have much to learn about how trauma changes people, in physical, psychological and spiritual ways, and how these changes impact our culture as a whole. Although this book breaks the silence on childbearing experiences and healing journeys for women, talking about sexual abuse appears to be even more difficult for men, and as yet no public discussion has occurred regarding how being a survivor affects men on their journey to fatherhood. We also have much to learn about how trauma inflicted on parents affects their babies and children. Perhaps by looking at sexual abuse and its effects on mothers, we can open some doors to looking at the effects on fathers and subsequent generations of children, as well.

Healing from abuse is not easy. Being a good mother is not easy. Both are possible. The women contributors to this volume have shared many messages of hope for others on the healing and mothering journeys. They stress the importance of finding someone with whom you can share your history and all its challenges, and how forming positive, trusting relationships is the key to healing and having the support needed to parent. They reach out to form primary relationships with trusted partners and friends. They do powerful and deep work with therapists and clergy. They seek assistance with their needs from midwives, doctors, nurses, childbirth educators, doulas, massage therapists and other alternative health practitioners. They show us how pregnancy, birth and motherhood, despite many challenges, can be real opportunities to re-frame relationships with body and self. They help us to see that being a good mother is not about perfection, but rather about being "good enough"—raising children with healthy boundaries, keeping them safe from known perpetrators, and providing them with more love and compassion than you may have had. They encourage us with their resolve to break the chains of violence that have bound them, and to not repeat the cycle with the next generation. They inspire us with their resolve to learn and grow and heal, to speak out, and to act on behalf of others who have shared their struggles.

I am deeply grateful to all the women who contributed their voices to this effort. Because it was not possible to include all 81 voices of the women who contributed narrative material for this book project in their entirety, we have set up a space on the www.survivormoms.com Web site to include more complete narratives by authors who opt to have their story posted in its entirety, and we encourage you to read more there.

From these women's stories we learn that strength may be gained in the struggle, and that learning to love, appreciate and trust in yourself is worthwhile and essential. We learn that the baby steps we take can lead to adult strides in our understanding, growth and healing, that we—and our children—deserve to live in safety, and that we are worthy of giving and receiving love. Every step you make toward realizing your own healing will help build your capacity to be a "good enough" mother. Whatever your past, and whatever your current situation, you are not alone. Many, many others share your struggle. Reach out for help, and don't stop until you find it. In healing yourself, you heal the generations to come.

If you are wondering what to do next, check out the resource section on our Web site at www.survivormoms.com.

~Mickey Sperlich, Ann Arbor, 2008

The key to realizing a dream is to focus not on success but significance—and then even the small steps and little victories along your path will take on greater meaning.

~Oprah Winfrey

> For a current list of resources check our Web site at www.survivormoms.com

## Hotlines and Web sites

Adult Survivors of Child Abuse: www.ascasupport.org

Centers for Disease Control and Prevention: www.cdc.gov

Childhelp USA, National Child Abuse Hotline: 1-800-4-A-Child. This telephone number can be used 24 hours a day and also serves Canada, Guam, Puerto Rico and the US Virgin Islands.

Childhelp Web site: www.childhelpusa.org. Individual states have toll-free reporting lines too, and these are listed on this site, along with the main instructions, "TRUST YOUR INSTINCTS."

National Child Abuse Hotline: 1-800-422-4453. Resource for help to stop abusing.

National Domestic Violence Hotline: 1-800-799-SAFE (7233) 1-800-787-3224 (TDD)

National Hopeline Network: 1-800-SUICIDE (784-2433)

Parents Anonymous: 1-800-843-5437. www.parentsanonymous.org. Resource for help to stop abusing.

Rape, Abuse & Incest National Network Hotline: 1-800-656-HOPE. This line routes instantly to the rape crisis center nearest the caller.

Sidran Institute: www.sidran.org. The International Society for Traumatic Stress Studies and the Sidran Foundation together offer this online information and referral resource.

Veterans with PTSD can also learn about resources available to them via links at the Web site of the National Center for PTSD: www.ncptsd.va.gov

## "Twelve-step" programs

Alcoholics Anonymous: www.alcoholics-anonymous.org

Al-Anon: www.al-anon.alateen.org. Resource for families and friends of problem drinkers.

Narcotics Anonymous: www.na.org

## For pregnancy and birth preparation

Coalition for Improving Maternity Services (CIMS): www.motherfriendly.org. Using a questionnaire like the one available on this site may be helpful in preparing for birth and deciding on a care provider.

### To find childbirth classes:

ALACE (The Association of Labor Assistants and Childbirth Educators): www.alace.org

Birthing from Within: www.birthingfromwithin.com

Birthworks: www.birthworks.org

Bradley Method: www.bradleybirth.com

International Childbirth Education Association, Inc. (ICEA): www.icea.org

Lamaze International: www.lamaze.org

### To find a practitioner:

American College of Nurse Midwives (ACNM): www.acnm.org

American College of Obstetricians & Gynecologists (ACOG): www.acog.org

DONA International: www.DONA.org. Resource to find a doula certified by DONA International

Midwives Alliance of North America (MANA): www.mana.org

## Resources for the postpartum period, breastfeeding and parenting

Depression After Delivery, Inc. (DAD): www.depressionafterdelivery.com

International Board of Lactation Consultant Examiners (IBLCE): www.iblce.org; IBLCE consultant registry: www.iblce.org/US%20registry.htm

International Cesarean Awareness Network (ICAN): http://ican-online.net

La Leche League: www.llli.org or www.lalecheleaguecanada.ca for the Canadian Web site. If you can't find a La Leche League group near you in our Group Web listings and you can't find the information locally, dial 1-800-LALECHE (US). In Canada, telephone 1-800-665-4324.

Postpartum Depression Screening Scale: The scale can be purchased by qualified professionals through Western Psychological Services, at www.wpspublish.com, or by calling toll-free: 800-648-8857.

Postpartum Support International (PSI): Web site: www.postpartum.net; 1-800-944-4PPD

Trauma and Birth Stress: www.tabs.org.nz. Resource for help with the postpartum period and breastfeeding.

### Some books on the postpartum period, including mental health and adjustment struggles:

*The Hidden Feelings of Motherhood,* by Kathleen Kendall-Tackett

*Rebounding from Childhood,* by Lynn Madsen

*Postpartum Survival Guide,* by Ann Dunnewold and Diane G. Sanford

### Some helpful books on parenting:

*Your Child's Self-Esteem,* by Dorothy Corkille Briggs

*Your Baby and Child,* by Penelope Leach

*The Happiest Baby on the Block,* by Harvey Karp, MD

*Touchpoints,* by T. Berry Brazelton

*You Are Your Child's First Teacher,* by Rahima Baldwin

*Growing Together,* by William Sears, MD

*Raising Your Spirited Child,* by Mary Sheedy Kurcinka

## Resources to aid in healing

*Allies in Healing,* by Laura Davis. A good book to recommend for partners of survivors.

The "Am I Ready to Reconcile" Workbook, by Laura Davis, co-author of *The Courage to Heal,* which is available free on her Web site: www.lauradavis.net. Discussion of the issues related specifically to reconciliation between abuse survivors and perpetrators.

*The PTSD Sourcebook,* by Glenn R. Schiraldi. A deeper look at a range of healing modalities.

*Getting Free: You Can End Abuse and Take Back Your Life* (2004), by Ginny NiCarthy. This book offers some guidelines for helping to determine whether or not there are aspects of abuse in your intimate relationship.

### To find out more about art and art therapy:

*Art is a Way of Knowing,* by Pat Allen

*Managing Traumatic Stress through Art,* by Cohen, Barnes and Rankin

*The Artist's Way,* by Julia Cameron

*She Who Was Lost is Remembered: Healing from Incest through Creativity,* by Louise Wisechild

### To find out more about EMDR:

For more information about EMDR and to contact an EMDR trained therapist in your area, contact the EMDRIA Web site at: www.emdria.org

### To find out more about music therapy:

American Music Therapy Association Web site: www.musictherapy.org

## Additional literature

*Addictions and Trauma Recovery: Healing the Body, Mind & Spirit,* by D. Miller and L Guidry

*Allies in Healing: When the Person You Love Was Sexually Abused as a Child,* by L. Davis

*Betrayal Trauma: The Logic of Forgetting Childhood Abuse,* by J.J. Freyd

*Birthing from Within: An Extra-Ordinary Guide to Childbirth Preparation,* by P. England and R. Horowitz

*EMDR in the Treatment of Adults Abused as Children,* by L. Parnell

*Incest and Sexuality: A Guide to Understanding and Healing,* by W. Maltz and B. Holman

*Lovers and Survivors: A Partner's Guide to Living with and Loving a Sexual Abuse Survivor,* by S.Y. de Beixedon

*Protecting the Gift: Keeping Children and Teenagers Safe (And Parents Sane),* by G. DeBecker

*Rebounding from Childbirth: Toward Emotional Recovery,* by L. Madsen

*The Body Bears the Burden: Trauma, Dissociation, and Disease,* by R.C. Scaer

*The Body Remembers: The Psychophysiology of Trauma and Trauma Treatment,* by B. Rothschild

*The Courage to Heal: A Guide for Women Survivors of Child Sexual Abuse,* E. Bass and L. Davis

*The Happiest Baby on the Block,* by H. Karp

*The Hidden Feelings of Motherhood: Coping with Stress, Depression, and Burnout,* by K. Kendall-Tackett

*The Posttraumatic Stress Disorder Sourcebook,* by G.R. Schiraldi

*The Secret Trauma: Incest in the Lives of Girls and Women,* by D.E.H. Russell

*Trauma and Recovery: The aftermath of violence—from domestic abuse to political terror,* by J.L. Herman

*When Survivors Give Birth: Understanding and Healing the Effects of Early Sexual Abuse on Childbearing Women,* by P. Simkin and P. Klaus

# References

Acierno, R., et al. 2000. Assault, PTSD, family substance use and depression as risk factors for cigarette use in youth: Findings from the National Survey of Adolescents. *J Trauma Stress* 13: 381–96.

ACOG (American College of Obstetricians & Gynecologists). 2001. ACOG Educational Bulletin #259: Adult manifestation of childhood sexual abuse. Jul 2000. Clinical management guidelines for obstetrician-gynecologists. *Int J Gynaecol Obstet* 74(3): 311–20.

ACOG (American College of Obstetricians & Gynecologists). 1995. ACOG Technical Bulletin #209: Domestic violence. Aug 1995. *Int J Gynaecol Obstet* 51(2): 161–70.

American Music Therapy Association Web site: www.musictherapy.org. Accessed 11 Jul 2007.

American Psychiatric Association. 1994. *Diagnostic and Statistical Manual of Mental Disorders, 4th Ed.* Washington, DC: American Psychiatric Association.

American Psychiatric Association. 2000. *Diagnostic and Statistical Manual of Mental Disorders: DSM-IV-TR.* Washington, DC: American Psychiatric Association.

Andreski, P., H. Chilcoat and N. Breslau. 1998. Post-traumatic stress disorder and somatization symptoms: a prospective study. *Psychiatry Res* 79(2): 131–38.

Ayers, S., and A.D. Pickering. 2001. Do women get posttraumatic stress disorder as a result of childbirth? A prospective study of incidence. *Birth* 28: 111–18.

Ballard, C.G., A.K. Stanley and I.F. Brockington. 1995. Posttraumatic stress disorder (PTSD) after childbirth. *Brit J Psychiatry* 166(4): 525–28.

Bass, E., and L. Davis. 1992. *The Courage to Heal: A Guide for Women Survivors of Child Sexual Abuse.* New York: Harper Perennial.

Bassuk, E.L., et al. 2001. Posttraumatic stress disorder in extremely poor women: Implications for health care clinicians. *J Am Med Women's Assoc* 56(2): 79–85.

Bayatpour, M., R.D. Wells and S. Holford. 1992. Physical and sexual abuse as predictors of substance use and suicide among pregnant teenagers. *J Adolesc Health* 13(2): 128–32.

Beck, C.T. 1992. The lived experience of postpartum depression: A phenomenological study. *Nurs Res* 41(3): 166–70.

Beck, C.T., and R.K. Gable. 2002. *Postpartum Depression Screening Scale: PDSS Manual.* Los Angeles: Western Psychological Services.

Becker, et al. 1982. The incidence and types of sexual dysfunction in rape and incest victims. *J Sex Marital Ther* 8(1): 65–74.

Benedict, M.I., et al. 1999. The association of childhood sexual abuse with depressive symptoms during pregnancy, and selected pregnancy outcomes. *Child Abuse Negl* 23(7): 659–70.

Bennett, H.A., et al. 2004. Prevalence of depression during pregnancy: systematic review. *Obstet Gynecol* 103(4): 698–709.

Bowlby, J. 1977. The making and breaking of affectional bonds. I. Aetiology and psychopathology in the light of attachment theory. An expanded version of the Fiftieth Maudsley Lecture, delivered before the Royal College of Psychiatrists, 19 November 1976. *Br J Psychiatry* 130: 201–10.

Brady, K.T. 1997. Posttraumatic stress disorder and comorbidity: Recognizing the many faces of PTSD. *J Clin Psychiatry* 58: 12–15.

Breslau, N. 2001. Outcomes of posttraumatic stress disorder. *J Clin Psychiatry* 62(Suppl 17): 55–59.

Breslau, N., and G.C. Davis. 1992. Posttraumatic stress disorder in an urban population of young adults: Risk factors for chronicity. *Am J Psychiatry* 149(5): 671–75.

Breslau, N., et al. 1997. Psychiatric sequelae of posttraumatic stress disorder in women. *Arch Gen Psych* 54(1): 81–87.

Breuer, J., and S. Freud. 1895/1955. "Studies on hysteria." In *The Standard Edition of the Complete Psychological Works of Sigmund Freud: Vol. 2*, ed. and trans J. Strachey. New York: W.W. Norton & Co.

Briere, J., and M. Runtz. 1987. Post-sexual abuse trauma: Data and implications for clinical practice. *J Interpersonal Violence* 2: 367–79.

Briggs, D.C. 1975. *Your Child's Self-Esteem.* Garden City, New York: Doubleday and Company, Inc.

Brown, D.P., A.W. Scheflin and D.C. Hammond. 1998. *Memory, Trauma Treatment, and the Law.* New York: W.W. Norton & Co.

Campbell, J.C., ed. 1995. *Assessing Dangerousness.* Newbury Park, California: Sage.

Carter, S.C., M. Altemus and G.P. Chrousos. 2001. Neuroendocrine and emotional changes in the post-partum period. *Prog Brain Res* 133: 241–49.

Chilcoat, H., and N. Breslau. 1998. Posttraumatic stress disorder and drug disorders: Testing causal pathways. *Arch Gen Psychiatry* 55(10): 913–17.

Clum, G.A., P. Nishith and P.A. Resick. 2001. Trauma-related sleep disturbance and self-reported physical health symptoms in treatment-seeking female rape victims. *J Nerv Ment Dis* 189: 618–22.

Cohen, L., et al. 2006. Relapse of major depression during pregnancy in women who maintain or discontinue antidepressant treatment. *JAMA* 295(5): 499–507.

Cohen, M.M., et al. 2004. Posttraumatic stress disorder after pregnancy, labor, and delivery. *J Women's Health* 13(3): 315–24.

Cole B., M. Scoville and L.T. Flynn. 1996. Psychiatric advance practice nurses collaborate with certified nurse midwives in providing health care for pregnant women with histories of abuse. *Arch Psychiatr Nurs* 10(4): 229–39.

Cole, P.M., et al. 1992. Parenting difficulties among adult survivors of father-daughter incest. *Child Abuse Negl* 16(2): 239–49.

Coleman, M.A. 2004. *The Dinah Project: A Handbook for Congregational Response to Sexual Violence.* Cleveland, Ohio: The Pilgrim Press.

Colley Gilbert, B.J.C., et al. 1999. Prevalence of selected maternal and infant characteristics, Pregnancy Risk Assessment Monitoring (PRAMS), 1997. *MMWR* 48(SS-5): 1–37.

Courtois, C.A., and C.C. Riley. 1992. Pregnancy and childbirth as triggers for abuse memories: Implications for care. *Birth* 19(4): 222–23.

Creedy, D.K., I.M. Shochet and J. Horsfall. 2000. Childbirth and the development of acute trauma symptoms: Incidence and contributing factors. *Birth*. 27(2): 104–11.

Dansky, B.S., et al. 1997. The National Women's Study: Relationship of victimization and post-traumatic stress disorder to bulimia nervosa. *Int J Eat Disord* 21(3): 213–28.

Davis, L. 1991. *Allies in Healing: When the Person You Love Was Sexually Abused as a Child.* New York: Harper Perennial.

Davis-Floyd, R. 1992. *Birth as an American Rite of Passage.* Berkeley: University of California Press.

DeBecker, G. 1999. *Protecting the Gift: Keeping Children and Teenagers Safe (And Parents Sane).* New York: Dell Publishing.

de Beixedon, S.Y. 1995. *Lovers and Survivors: A Partner's Guide to Living With and Loving a Sexual Abuse Survivor.* San Francisco: Robert D. Reed Publishers.

DiLillo, D. 2001. Interpersonal functioning among women reporting a history of childhood sexual abuse: Empirical findings and methodological issues. *Clin Psychol Rev* 21(4): 553–76.

DiLillo, D., and P.J. Long. 1999. Perceptions of couple functioning among female survivors of child sexual abuse. *J Child Sex Abus* 7(4): 59–76.

Dong, M., et al. 2003. The relationship of exposure to childhood sexual abuse to other forms of abuse, neglect, and household dysfunction during childhood. *Child Abuse Negl* 27(6): 625–39.

Douglas, A.R. 2000. Reported anxieties concerning intimate parenting in women sexually abused as children. *Child Abuse Negl* 24(3): 425–34.

Draucker, C.B. 2001. Learning the harsh realities of life: Sexual violence, disillusionment, and meaning. *Health Care Women Int* 22(1-2): 67–84.

Edmond, T., and A. Rubin. 2004. Assessing the long-term effects of EMDR: results from an 18-month follow-up study with adult female survivors. *J Child Sex Abus* 13(1): 69–86.

Edmond, T., A. Rubin and K.G. Wambauch. 1999. The effectiveness of EMDR with adult female survivors of childhood sexual abuse. *Social Work Research* 23(2): 103–16.

Edmond, T., L. Sloan, and D. McCarty. 2004. Sexual abuse survivors' perceptions of the effectiveness of EMDR and eclectic therapy. *Research on Social Work Practice* 14(4): 259–72.

Edwards, V.J., et al. 2003. Relationship between multiple forms of childhood maltreatment and adult mental health in community respondents: Results from the Adverse Childhood Experiences Study. *Am J Psychiatry* 160(8): 1453–60.

Einarson, T.R., and A. Finarson. 2005. Newer antidepressants in pregnancy and rates of major malformations: a meta-analysis of prospective comparative studies *Pharmacoepidemiol Drug Safety* 14(12): 823–27.

EMDR Institute Web site. www.emdr.com. Accessed 23 Feb 2006.

Engel, S.M., et al. 2005. Psychological trauma associated with the World Trade Center attacks and its effect on pregnancy outcome. *Paediatr Perinat Epidemiol* 19(5): 334–41.

Engelhard, I.M. 2004. Miscarriage as a traumatic event. *Clin Obstet Gynecol* 47(3): 547–51.

Engelhard, I.M., M.A. van den Hout and A. Arntz. 2001. Posttraumatic stress disorder after pregnancy loss. *Gen Hosp Psychiatry.* 23(2): 62–66.

Engelhard, I.M., et al. 2003. Peritraumatic dissociation and posttraumatic stress after pregnancy loss: A prospective study. *Behav Res Ther* 41(1): 67–78.

England, P., and R. Horowitz. 1998. *Birthing from Within: An Extra-Ordinary Guide to Childbirth Preparation.* Albuquerque, New Mexico: Partera Press.

Everson, M.D., et al. 1989. Maternal support following disclosure of incest. *Am J Orthopsychiatry* 59(2): 197–207.

Farber, E.W., S.E. Herbert and S.L. Reviere. 1996. Childhood abuse and suicidality in obstetric patients in a hospital-based urban prenatal clinic. *Gen Hosp Psychiatry* 18(1): 56–60.

Finkelhor, D. 1994. The international epidemiology of child abuse. *Child Abuse Negl* 18(5): 409–17.

Finkelhor, D., and A. Browne. 1985. The traumatic impact of child sexual abuse: a conceptualization. *Am J Orthopsychiatry* 55(4): 530–41.

Fishwick, N.J. 1998. Assessment of women for partner abuse. *J Obstet Gynecol Neonat Nurs* 27(6). 661–70.

Foa, E.B., T.M. Keane and M.J. Friedman, eds. 2000. *Effective Treatments for PTSD: Practice Guidelines from the International Society for Traumatic Stress Studies.* New York: The Guilford Press.

Frankl, V.E. 1963. *Man's Search for Meaning: An Introduction to Logotherapy.* New York: Washington Square Books.

Freyd, J.J. 1996. *Betrayal Trauma: The Logic of Forgetting Childhood Abuse.* Cambridge: Harvard University Press.

Friedman, M., and P.P. Schnurr. 1995. The relationship between trauma, posttraumatic stress disorder, and physical health. In *Neurobiological and Clinical Consequences of Stress: From Normal Adaptation to Posttraumatic Stress Disorder*, Friedman, M., D. Charney and A. Deutch, eds. Philadelphia: Lippincott-Raven; 507–24.

Frost, M., and J.T. Condon. 1996. The psychological sequelae of miscarriage: a critical review of the literature. *Aust N Z J Psychiatry* 30(1): 54–62.

Gamble, J., et al. 2005. The effectiveness of a counseling intervention after a traumatic childbirth: a randomized controlled trial. *Birth* 32(1): 11–19.

Gaskin, I.M. 1978. *Spiritual Midwifery (Revised)*. Summertown, Tennessee: The Book Publishing Company.

Gentile, S. 2005. The safety of newer antidepressants in pregnancy and breastfeeding. *Drug Safety* 28(2): 137–52.

George, C. 1996. A representational perspective of child abuse and prevention: Internal working models of attachment and caregiving. *Child Abuse Negl* 20(5): 411–24.

Gjerdingen, D. 2003. The effectiveness of various postpartum depression treatments and the impact of antidepressant drugs on nursing infants. *J Am Board Fam Pract* 16(5): 372–82.

Golding, J.M. 1994. Sexual assault history and physical health in randomly selected Los Angeles women. *Health Psychol* 13(2): 130–38.

Gottvall, K., and U. Waldenstrom. 2002. Does a traumatic birth experience have an impact on future reproduction? *BJOG* 109(3): 254–60.

Grimstad, H., et al. 1998. Abuse history and health risk behaviors in pregnancy. *Acta Obstet Gynecol Scand* 77(9): 893–97.

Grimstad, H., and B. Schei. 1999. Pregnancy and delivery for women with a history of child sexual abuse. *Child Abuse Negl* 23(1): 81–90.

Hall, J.M. 1996. Geography of childhood sexual abuse: Women's narratives of their childhood environments. *Adv Nurs Sci* 18(4): 29–47.

Hanson, R.F., et al. 2001. Impact of childhood rape and aggravated assault on adult mental health. *Am J Orthopsychiatry* 71(1): 108–19.

Haugen, W.A., E.N. Jackson, and J.R. Brendle. 2005. Anxiety symptoms and disorders at eight weeks postpartum. *J Anxiety Disord* 19(3): 295–311.

Herman, J.L. 1997. *Trauma and Recovery: The aftermath of violence—from domestic abuse to political terror.* New York: Basic Books.

Holmes, M.M., et al. 1996. Rape-related pregnancy: estimates and descriptive characteristics from a national sample of women. *Am J Obstet Gynecol* 175(2): 320–24.

Hoffman, S., and M.C. Hatch. 2000. Depressive symptomatology during pregnancy: Evidence for an association with decreased fetal growth in pregnancies of lower social class women. *Health Psychol* 19(6): 535–43.

Horan, D.L., L.D. Hill and J. Schulkin. 2000. Childhood sexual abuse and preterm labor in adulthood: An endocrinological hypothesis. *Women's Health Issues* 10(1): 27–33.

Horon, I.L., and D. Cheng. 2001. Enhanced surveillance for pregnancy-associated mortality. Maryland, 1993–1998. *JAMA* 285(11): 1455–59.

Horowitz, S. 2004. Music therapy: Notes from research and clinical practice. *Alternative and Complementary Therapies* 10(5): 251–56.

Huth-Bocks, A.C., A.A. Levendosky and G.A. Bogat. 2002. The effects of domestic violence during pregnancy on maternal and infant health. *Violence Vict* 17(2): 169–85.

Jankowski, M.K., et al. 2002. Parental caring as a possible buffer against sexual revictimization in young adult survivors of child sexual abuse. *J Trauma Stress* 15(3): 235–44.

Johnson, D.M., J.L. Pike and K.M. Chard. 2001. Factors predicting PTSD, depression, and dissociative severity in female treatment-seeking childhood sexual abuse survivors. *Child Abuse Negl* 25(1):179–98.

Johnson, P.J., and W.L. Hellerstedt. 2002. Current or past physical or sexual abuse as a risk marker for sexually transmitted disease in pregnant women. *Perspect Sexual Reprod Health*

34(2): 62–67.

Josephs, L. 1996. Women and trauma: A contemporary psychodynamic approach to traumatization for patients in the OB/GYN psychological consultation clinic. *Bull Menninger Clin* 60(1): 22–38.

Karp, H. 2002. *The Happiest Baby on the Block: The New Way to Calm Crying and Help Your Baby Sleep Longer.* New York: Bantam Books.

Kelly, R.H., et al. 1999. Chart-recorded psychiatric diagnoses in women giving birth in California in 1992. *Am J Psychiatry* 156(6): 955–57.

Kelly, R.H., et al. 2002. Psychiatric and substance use disorders as risk factors for low birth weight and preterm delivery. *Obstet Gynecol* 100(2): 297–304.

Kendall-Tackett, K. 2001. *The Hidden Feelings of Motherhood: Coping with Stress, Depression, and Burnout.* Oakland, California: New Harbinger Publications, Inc.

Kendall-Tackett, K. 2004. Breastfeeding and the Sexual Abuse Survivor. *La Leche League International Independent Study Module.*

Kennell, J., et al. 1991. Continuous emotional support during labor in a US hospital. A randomized controlled trial. *JAMA* 265(17): 2197–201.

Kennedy, H.P., and E.L. MacDonald. 2002. "Altered consciousness" during childbirth: potential clues to posttraumatic stress disorder? *J Midwifery and Womens Health.* 47(5): 380–82.

Kessler, R.C., et al. 1995. Posttraumatic stress disorder in the National Comorbidity Survey. *Arch Gen Psychiatry* 52(12): 1048–60.

Kimerling, R., and K.S. Calhoun. 1994. Somatic symptoms, social support, and treatment seeking among sexual assault victims. *J Consult Clin Psychol* 62(2): 333–40.

Kimerling, R., et al. 1999. Traumatic stress in HIV-infected women. *AIDS Educ Prev* 11(4): 321–30.

Kimerling, R, et al. 2002. PTSD and medical comorbidity. In *Gender and PTSD,* Kimerling, R., P. Ouimette, and J. Wolfe, eds. New York: Guildford Press, 271–304.

Kindlon, D., and M. Thompson. 2000. *Raising Cain: Protecting the Emotional Life of Boys.* New York: Ballantine Books.

King, W.J., M. MacKay and A. Sirnick. 2003. Shaken baby syndrome in Canada: clinical characteristics and outcomes of hospital cases. *CMAJ* 168(2): 155–59.

King, S., et al. 2005. Project Ice Storm: Effect of prenatal cortisol levels on obstetric complications. Presented at International Society for Psychoneuroendocrinology Annual Meeting, Montreal, Quebec, Canada.

Krulewitch, C.J., et al. 2001. Hidden from view: Violent deaths among pregnant women in the District of Columbia, 1988–1996. *J Midwifery Womens Health* 46(1): 4–10.

Koniak-Griffin, D., and J. Lesser. 1996. Impact of childhood maltreatment on young mothers' violent behavior towards themselves and others. *J Pediatr Nurs* 11(5): 300–08.

Koplan, J.P., and D.W. Fleming. 2000. Current and future public health challenges (Commentary). *JAMA* 284(13): 1696–98.

Langer, A., et al. 1998. Effects of psychosocial support during labour and childbirth on breastfeeding, medical interventions, and mothers' well-being in a Mexican public hospital: a randomized clinical trial. *Br J Obstet Gynaecol* 105(10): 1056–63.

Leeners, B., et al. 2006. Childhood sexual abuse (CSA) experiences: an underestimated factor in perinatal care. *Acta Obstet Gynecol Scand* 85(8): 971–76.

Leeners, B., et al. 2006. Influence of childhood sexual abuse on pregnancy, delivery, and the early postpartum period in adult women. *J Psychosom Res* 61: 139–51.

Leeners, B., et al. 2007. Effect of childhood sexual abuse on gynecologic care as an adult. *Psychosomatics.* 48: 385–93.

Lesser, J., and D. Koniak-Griffin. 2000. The impact of physical or sexual abuse on chronic depression in adolescent mothers. *J Pediatr Nurs* 15(6): 378–87.

Leserman, J., et al. 1996. Sexual and physical abuse history in gastroenterology practice: How types of abuse impact health status. *Psychosom Med* 58(1): 4–15.

Letourneau, E.J., et al. 1996. Comorbidity of sexual problems and posttraumatic stress disorder in female crime victims. *Behav Ther* 27(3): 321–36.

Levine, P. 1997. *Waking the Tiger: Healing Trauma.* Berkeley: North Atlantic Press.

Liberzon, I., et al. 1999. Neuroendocrine and psychophysiologic responses in PTSD: A symptom provocation study. *Neuropsychopharmacology* 21(1): 40–50.

Light, K.C., et al. 2000. Oxytocin responsivity in mothers of infants: A preliminary study of relationships with blood pressure during laboratory stress and normal ambulatory activity. *Health Psychol* 19(6): 560–67.

Lobel, M., et al. 2000. The impact of prenatal maternal stress and optimistic disposition on birth outcomes in medically high-risk women. *Health Psychol* 19(6): 544–53.

Loeb, T.B., et al. 2002. Child sexual abuse: Associations with the sexual functioning of adolescents and adults. *Annu Rev Sex Res* 13: 307–45.

Loveland Cook, C.A., et al. 2004. Posttraumatic stress disorder in pregnancy: prevalence, risk factors, and treatment. *Obstet Gynecol* 103(4): 710–17.

Low, L.K., et al. 2003. Adolescents' experiences of childbirth: Contrasts with adults. *J Midwifery Womens Health* 48(3): 192–98.

Lubell, A.K.N., and C. Peterson. 1998. Female incest survivors: Relationships with mothers and female friends. *J Interpers Violence* 13(2): 193–205.

Madsen, L. 1994. *Rebounding from Childbirth: Toward Emotional Recovery.* Westport, Connecticut: Bergin & Garvey.

Madu, S.N. 2003. The relationship between parental physical availability and child sexual, physical, and emotional abuse: A study among a sample of university students in South Africa. *Scand J Psychol* 44(4): 311–18.

Major, B., et al. 2000. Psychological responses of women after first-trimester abortion. *Arch Gen Psychiatry* 57(8): 777–84.

Maltz, W., and B. Holman. 1987. *Incest and Sexuality: A Guide to Understanding and Healing.* Lexington, Massachusetts: Lexington Books.

Manning-Orenstein, G. 1998. A birth intervention: The therapeutic effects of Doula support versus Lamaze preparation on first-time mothers' working models of caregiving. *Altern Ther Health Med* 4(4): 73–81.

Marmar, C.R., D.S. Weiss and T.J. Metzler. 1997. The Peritraumatic Dissociative Experiences Questionnaire. In *Assessing Psychological Trauma and PTSD: A Practitioner's Handbook,* J.P. Wilson and T.M. Keane, eds. New York: Guilford Press, 412–28.

Mauger, B. 2000. *Reclaiming the Spirituality of Birth: Healing for Mothers and Babies.* Rochester, Vermont: Healing Arts Press.

McGrath, S., et al. 1999. Doula support vs epidural anesthesia: impact on cesarean rates. *Pediatric Research* 45(4): 16A.

McNally, R.J. 2003. *Remembering Trauma.* Cambridge, Massachusetts: Belknap Press of Harvard University Press.

Miller, A. 1983. *For Your Own Good: Hidden Cruelty in Child-rearing and the Roots of Violence.* New York: The Noonday Press.

Miller, D., and L. Guidry. 2001. *Addictions and Trauma Recovery: Healing the Body, Mind & Spirit.* New York: W.W. Norton & Co.

Moberg, K.U., et al. 2003. *The Oxytocin Factor: Tapping the Hormone of Calm, Love, and Healing.* Cambridge, Massachusetts: Da Capo Press.

# References

Molnar, B.E., S.L. Buka and R.C. Kessler. 2001. Child sexual abuse and subsequent psychopathology: Results from the National Comorbidity Survey. *Am J Public Health* 91(5): 753–60.

Morland, L., et al. 2007. Posttraumatic stress disorder and pregnancy health: preliminary update and implications. *Psychosomatics* 48(4): 304–08.

National Center on Child Abuse and Neglect (NCCAN). 1981. *Study Findings: National Study of the Incidence and Severity of Child Abuse and Neglect.* Washington, DC: US Department of Health and Human Services.

National Center on Child Abuse and Neglect. 1996. Third National Incidence and Prevalence Study. Publication No. N15-3, CD-23595. Washington, DC: US Dept. of Health and Human Services.

National Institute of Child Health and Human Development. 1999. Chronicity of Maternal Depressive Symptoms, Maternal Sensitivity, and Child Functioning at 36 Months. *Dev Psychol* 35(5): 1297–310.

Noll, J.G., P.K. Trickett and F.W. Putnam. 2003. A prospective investigation of the impact of childhood sexual abuse on the development of sexuality. *J Consult Clin Psychol* 71(3): 575–86.

O'Hara, M.W., et al. 1991. Controlled prospective study of postpartum mood disorders: psychological, environmental, and hormonal variables. *J Abnorm Psychol* 100(1): 63–73.

O'Hara, M.W., and A.M. Swain. 1996. Rates and risk of postpartum depression—a meta-analysis. *Int Rev Psychiatry* 8: 37–54.

Paluzzi, P.A., and C. Houde-Quimby. 1996. Domestic Violence: Implications for the American College of Nurse-Midwives and its members. *J Nurse Midwifery* 41(6): 430–35.

Paarlberg, K.M., et al. 1995. Psychosocial factors and pregnancy outcome: A review with emphasis on methodological issues. *J Psychosom Res* 39(5): 563–95.

Paredes, M., M. Leifer and T. Kilbane. 2001. Maternal variables related to sexually abused children's functioning. *Child Abuse Negl* 25(9): 1159–76.

Parker, B., et al. 1999. Testing an intervention to prevent further abuse to pregnant women. *Res Nurs Health* 22(1): 59–66.

Parnell, L. 1999. *EMDR in the Treatment of Adults Abused as Children.* New York: W.W. Norton & Co.

Pitman, R.K., et al. 1991. Psychiatric complications during flooding therapy for posttraumatic stress disorder. *J Clin Psychiatry* 52(1): 17–20.

Plummer, C.A., and J. Eastin. 2007. The effect of sexual abuse allegations/investigations on the mother/child relationship. *Violence Against Women* 13(10): 1053–71.

Prentice, J.C., et al. 2002. The association between reported childhood sexual abuse and breastfeeding initiation. *J Hum Lact* 18(3): 219–26.

Price, C. 2004. Body-oriented therapy in recovery from child sexual abuse: an efficacy study. *Altern Ther Health Med* 11(5): 46–57.

Resnick, H.S., et al. 1993. Prevalence of civilian trauma and posttraumatic stress disorder in a representative national sample of women. *J Consult Clin Psychol* 61(6): 984–91.

Reynolds, J.L. 1997. Post-traumatic stress disorder after childbirth: the phenomenon of traumatic birth. *CMAJ* 156(6): 831–35.

Rhodes, N., and S. Hutchinson. 1994. Labor experiences of childhood sexual abuse survivors. *Birth* 21(4): 213–20.

Rogal, S.S., et al. 2007. Effects of posttraumatic stress disorder on pregnancy outcomes. *J Affect Disord* 102(1-3): 137–43.

Rosen, D., et al. 2007. Intimate partner violence, depression, and posttraumatic stress disorder as additional predictors of low birth weight infants among low-income mothers. *J Interpersonal Violence* 22(10): 1305–14.

Roth, S., et al. 1997. Complex PTSD in victims exposed to sexual and physical abuse: Results from the DSM-IV Field Trial for Posttraumatic Stress Disorder. *J Trauma Stress* 10(4): 539–55.

Rothschild, B. 2000. *The Body Remembers: The Psychophysiology of Trauma and Trauma Treatment.* New York: W.W. Norton & Co.

Rubin, R. 1984. *Maternal Identity and the Maternal Experience.* New York: Springer Publishing.

Rue, V.M., et al. 2004. Induced abortion and traumatic stress: a preliminary comparison of American and Russian women. *Med Sci Monit* 10(10): SR 5–16.

Ruscio, A.M., et al. 2002. Male war-zone veterans' perceived relationships with their children: The importance of emotional numbing. *J Trauma Stress* 15(5): 351–57.

Russell, D.E.H. 1986/1999. *The Secret Trauma: Incest in the Lives of Girls and Women.* New York: Basic Books.

Ryding, E.L., et al. 2003. An evaluation of midwives' counseling of pregnant women in fear of childbirth. *Acta Obstet Gynecol Scand* 82(1): 10–17.

Sampselle, C.M., et al. 1992. Prevalence of abuse among pregnant women choosing certified nurse-midwife or physician providers. *J Nurse Midwifery* 37(4): 269–73.

Scaer, R.C. 2001. *The Body Bears the Burden: Trauma, Dissociation, and Disease.* New York: Haworth Medical Press.

Schiraldi, G.R. 2000. *The Posttraumatic Stress Disorder Sourcebook.* Los Angeles: Lowell House.

Schore, A.N. 2002. Dysregulation of the right brain: a fundamental mechanism of traumatic attachment and the psychogenesis of posttraumatic stress disorder. *Aust N Z J Psychiatry* 36(1): 9–30.

Seng, J.S., et al. 2006. PTSD and physical comorbidity among women receiving Medicaid: Results from service-use data. *Journal of Traumatic Stress* 19(1): 45–56.

Seng, J.S., et al. 2004. Abuse-related post-traumatic stress during the childbearing year. *J Adv Nurs* 46(6): 604–13.

Seng, J.S., L.P. Kohn-Wood and L.A. Odera. 2005. Exploring disparity in post-traumatic stress disorder diagnosis: Implications for care of African American women. *J Obstet Gynecol Neonat Nurs* 34(4): 521–30.

Seng, J.S., et al. 2001. Posttraumatic stress disorder and pregnancy complications. *Obstet Gynecol* 97(1): 17–22.

Seng, J.S., et al. 2002. Abuse-related posttraumatic stress and desired maternity care practices: Women's perspectives. *J Midwifery Womens Health* 47(5): 360–70.

Seng, J.S., et al. 2007. Service use data analysis of pre-pregnancy psychiatric and somatic diagnoses in women with hyperemesis gravidarum. *J Psychosom Obstet Gynecol* 28(4): 209–17.

Sichel, D., and J.W. Driscoll. 1999. *Women's moods. What every woman should know about hormones, the brain, and emotional health.* New York: William Morrow & Company, Inc.

Silva, C., et al. 1997. Symptoms of post-traumatic stress disorder in abused women in a primary care setting. *J Womens Health* 6(5): 543–52.

Simkin, P. 1992. Overcoming the legacy of childhood sexual abuse: The role of caregivers and childbirth educators. *Birth* 19(4): 224–25.

Simkin, P., and P. Klaus. 2004. *When Survivors Give Birth: Understanding and Healing the Effects of Early Sexual Abuse on Childbearing Women.* Seattle, Washington: Classic Day Publishing.

Simkin, P., and K. Way (for DONA). 1998. *Position Paper: The Doula's Contribution to Modern Maternity Care.* www.DONA.org. Accessed 2 May 2004.

Söderquist, J., K. Wijma and B. Wijma. 2004. Traumatic stress in late pregnancy. *J Anxiety Disord* 8(2): 127–42.

Söderquist, J., K. Wijma and B. Wijma. 2002. Traumatic stress after childbirth: The role of obstetric variables. *J Psychosom Obstet Gynecol* 23(1): 31–39.

Soet, J.E., G.A. Brack and C. DiIorio. 2003. Prevalence and predictors of women's experience of psychological trauma during childbirth. *Birth* 30(1): 36–46.

Sperlich, M. Unpublished data.

Spinelli, M.G., and J. Endicott. 2003. Controlled clinical trial of interpersonal psychotherapy versus parenting education program for depressed pregnant women. *Am J Psychiatry* 160(3): 555–62.

Stein, M.B., et al. 1997. Full and partial posttraumatic stress disorder: Findings from a community survey. *Am J Psychiatry* 154(8): 1114–19.

Steiner, M. 1998. Perinatal mood disorders: Position paper. *Psychopharmacol Bull* 34(3): 301–06.

Stevens-Simon, C., and E.R. McAnarney. 1994. Childhood victimization and adolescent pregnancy outcome. *Child Abuse Negl* 18(7): 569–75.

Stewart, S.H., et al. 1998. Functional association among trauma, PTSD, and substance-related disorders. *Addict Behav* 23(6): 797–812.

Tallman, N., and C. Hering. 1998. Child abuse and its effects on birth. *Midwifery Today* 45: 19–21, 67.

Trotter, C., et al. 1992. The effect of social support during labour on postpartum depression. *S Afr J Psychol* 22(3): 134–39.

Turell, S.C., and M.W. Armsworth. 2000. Differentiating incest survivors who self-mutilate. *Child Abuse Negl* 24(2): 237–49.

Turton, P., et al. 2001. Incidence, correlates and predictors of post-traumatic stress disorder in the pregnancy after stillbirth. *Br J Psychiatry* 178: 556–60.

Walsh, B., and P. Rosen. 1988. *Self-mutilation: Theory, research and treatment.* New York: Guilford Press.

Warshaw, C. 1996. Domestic violence: changing theory, changing practice. *J Am Med Womens Assoc* 51(3): 87–91.

Wenzel, A., et al. 2005. Anxiety symptoms and disorders at eight weeks postpartum. *J Anxiety Disord* 19(3): 295–311.

World Health Organization. 2002. *World Report on Violence and Health.* Geneva: WHO.

Zimmerman, M., and J.I. Mattia. 1999. Is posttraumatic stress disorder underdiagnosed in routine clinical settings? *J NervMent Dis* 187(7): 420–28.

Zlotnick, C., et al. 1996. Differences in dissociative experiences between survivors of childhood incest and survivors of assault in adulthood. *J Nerv Ment Dis* 184(1): 52–54.

Zoellner, L.A., M.L. Goodwin and E.B. Foa. 2000. PTSD severity and health perceptions in female victims of sexual assault. *J Trauma Stress* 13(4): 635–49.

Zuravin, S.J., and C. Fontanella. 1999. Parenting behaviors and perceived parenting competence of child sexual abuse survivors. *Child Abuse Negl* 23(7): 623–32.

**Mickey Sperlich** is a certified professional midwife with nearly 20 years experience helping women on the journey of pregnancy and birth. She currently coordinates a study on the effects of posttraumatic stress on childbearing at the University of Michigan's Institute for Research on Women and Gender.

**Julia Seng** is a certified nurse-midwife and Research Associate Professor at the University of Michigan Institute for Research on Women and Gender. She studies the effects of posttraumatic stress on childbearing.

Photograph of the authors by Harriette Hartigan

For more information or resources, please check our Web site, whether you are a survivor yourself or are helping survivors. **www.survivormoms.com**